Electrified Democracy

The story of how the UK Parliament came to use the Internet from the 1960s onwards has never been told. *Electrified Democracy* places the impact of technology on parliamentary workings in its longer-term historical context. The author identifies repeating patterns of perception and analysis, and cultural tendencies in the perception of inventions dating back over centuries that have reasserted themselves in connection with the parliamentary response to networked computers. He uncovers evidence and makes new connections while situating all this within the wider global debates on connections between communication and democracy in the age of the Internet, constitutional law and history, and 'law and technology'. This book will be of interest to a wide readership including policymakers, researchers and all those interested in contemporary controversies about the role of the Internet in modern societies.

Andrew Blick is Reader in Politics and Contemporary History and Head of the Department of Political Economy at King's College London. He has extensive experience of working inside political institutions, including the United Kingdom Parliament, and has written widely on constitutional matters.

Law in Context

Since 1970, the Law in Context series has been at the forefront of a movement to broaden the study of law. The series is a vehicle for the publication of innovative monographs and texts that treat law and legal phenomena critically in their cultural, social, political, technological, environmental and economic contexts. A contextual approach involves treating legal subjects broadly, using materials from other humanities and social sciences, and from any other discipline that helps to explain the operation in practice of the particular legal field or legal phenomena under investigation. It is intended that this orientation is at once more stimulating and more revealing than the bare exposition of legal rules. The series includes original research monographs, coursebooks and textbooks that foreground contextual approaches and methods. The series includes and welcomes books on the study of law in all its contexts, including domestic legal systems, European and international law, transnational and global legal processes, and comparative law.

Books in the Series

Acosta: *The National versus the Foreigner in South America: 200 Years of Migration and Citizenship Law*
Ali: *Modern Challenges to Islamic Law*
Alyagon Darr: *Plausible Crime Stories: The Legal History of Sexual Offences in Mandate Palestine*
Anderson, Schum & Twining: *Analysis of Evidence, 2nd Edition*
Ashworth: *Sentencing and Criminal Justice, 6th Edition*
Barton & Douglas: *Law and Parenthood*
Baxi, McCrudden & Paliwala: *Law's Ethical, Global and Theoretical Contexts: Essays in Honour of William Twining*
Beecher-Monas: *Evaluating Scientific Evidence: An Interdisciplinary Framework for Intellectual Due Process*
Bell: *French Legal Cultures*
Bercusson: *European Labour Law, 2nd Edition*
Birkinshaw: *European Public Law*
Birkinshaw: *Freedom of Information: The Law, the Practice and the Ideal, 4th Edition*
Blick: *Electrified Democracy: The Internet and the United Kingdom Parliament in History*
Broderick & Ferri: *International and European Disability Law and Policy: Text, Cases and Materials*

Brownsword & Goodwin: *Law and the Technologies of the Twenty-First Century: Text and Materials*
Cane & Goudkamp: *Atiyah's Accidents, Compensation and the Law, 9th Edition*
Clarke: *Principles of Property Law*
Clarke & Kohler: *Property Law: Commentary and Materials*
Collins: *The Law of Contract, 4th Edition*
Collins, Ewing & McColgan: *Labour Law, 2nd Edition*
Cowan: *Housing Law and Policy*
Cranston: *Commercial Law from the Nineteenth Century: Law as Backcloth*
Cranston: *Legal Foundations of the Welfare State*
Darian-Smith: *Laws and Societies in Global Contexts: Contemporary Approaches*
Dauvergne: *Making People Illegal: What Globalisation Means for Immigration and Law*
David: *Kinship, Law and Politics: An Anatomy of Belonging*
Davies: *Perspectives on Labour Law, 2nd Edition*
Dembour: *Who Believes in Human Rights?: Reflections on the European Convention*
de Sousa Santos: *Toward a New Legal Common Sense: Law, Globalization, and Emancipation*
Diduck: *Law's Families*
Dupret: *Positive Law from the Muslim World*
Estella: *Legal Foundations of EU Economic Governance*
Fortin: *Children's Rights and the Developing Law, 3rd Edition*
Garnsey: *The Justice of Visual Art: Creative State-Building in Times of Political Transition*
Garton, Probert & Bean: *Moffat's Trusts Law: Text and Materials, 7th Edition*
Ghai & Woodman: *Practising Self-Government: A Comparative Study of Autonomous Regions*
Glover-Thomas: *Reconstructing Mental Health Law and Policy*
Gobert & Punch: *Rethinking Corporate Crime*
Goldman: *Globalisation and the Western Legal Tradition: Recurring Patterns of Law and Authority*
Haack: *Evidence Matters: Science, Proof, and Truth in the Law*
Harlow & Rawlings: *Law and Administration, 4th Edition*
Harris: *An Introduction to Law, 8th Edition*
Harris, Campbell & Halson: *Remedies in Contract and Tort, 2nd Edition*
Harvey: *Seeking Asylum in the UK: Problems and Prospects*
Herring: *Law and the Relational Self*
Hervey & McHale: *European Union Health Law: Themes and Implications*
Hervey & McHale: *Health Law and the European Union*
Holder & Lee: *Environmental Protection, Law and Policy: Text and Materials, 2nd Edition*
Jackson & Summers: *The Internationalisation of Criminal Evidence: Beyond the Common Law and Civil Law Traditions*
Kostakopoulou: *The Future Governance of Citizenship*
Kreiczer-Levy *Destabilized Property: Property Law in the Sharing Economy*
Kubal: *Immigration and Refugee Law in Russia: Socio-Legal Perspectives*
Lewis: *Choice and the Legal Order: Rising above Politics*
Likosky: *Law, Infrastructure and Human Rights*

(Continued after the Index)

Electrified Democracy

The Internet and the United Kingdom Parliament in History

ANDREW BLICK

CAMBRIDGE
UNIVERSITY PRESS

CAMBRIDGE
UNIVERSITY PRESS

University Printing House, Cambridge CB2 8BS, United Kingdom

One Liberty Plaza, 20th Floor, New York, NY 10006, USA

477 Williamstown Road, Port Melbourne, VIC 3207, Australia

314–321, 3rd Floor, Plot 3, Splendor Forum, Jasola District Centre, New Delhi – 110025, India

79 Anson Road, #06–04/06, Singapore 079906

Cambridge University Press is part of the University of Cambridge.

It furthers the University's mission by disseminating knowledge in the pursuit of education, learning, and research at the highest international levels of excellence.

www.cambridge.org
Information on this title: www.cambridge.org/9781108473057
DOI: 10.1017/9781108602006

First published 2021

A catalogue record for this publication is available from the British Library.

Library of Congress Cataloging-in-Publication Data
Names: Blick, Andrew, author.
Title: Electrified democracy : the internet and the United Kingdom Parliament in history / Andrew Blick.
Description: Cambridge, United Kingdom ; New York, NY : Cambridge University Press, 2021. | Series: Law in context | Includes bibliographical references and index.
Identifiers: LCCN 2021005364 (print) | LCCN 2021005365 (ebook) | ISBN 9781108473057 (hardback) | ISBN 9781108460927 (paperback) | ISBN 9781108602006 (epub)
Subjects: LCSH: Great Britain Parliament–History–20th century. | Great Britain Parliament–History–21st century. | Internet–Political aspects–Great Britain. | Democracy–Great Britain–History–20th century. | Democracy–Great Britain–History–21st century. | Great Britain–Politics and government–1945–. | BISAC: LAW / Constitutional | LAW / Constitutional
Classification: LCC JN550 .B55 2021 (print) | LCC JN550 (ebook) | DDC 325.4100285/4678–dc23
LC record available at https://lccn.loc.gov/2021005364
LC ebook record available at https://lccn.loc.gov/2021005365

ISBN 978-1-108-47305-7 Hardback

Contents

Acknowledgements

As usual, I have accumulated various debts in the writing of this book. The first is to Finola O'Sullivan, Marianne Nield, and the team at Cambridge University Press for their support, including during the difficult completion period in a time of global pandemic. The second is to my colleagues at the Department of Political Economy and elsewhere in King's College London. The third is to the international network of historians linked to the History & Policy initiative. It was under this banner that I worked with Dr Jennifer Doyle on a literature review on the subject of printing and Parliament. The fourth is to the group of constitutionally fascinated people surrounding the Constitution Society, at which Emily Barrett worked with me on research into the contemporary Internet. The fifth is to the assorted parliamentarians, parliamentary clerks, and other internet users with whom I have discussed and worked on the issues covered in this book over the years. The sixth – and as ever – is my family: my parents, Karen Blick and Robin Blick, and my sister, Katharine Blick. The three people who have to bear the most are of course my two sons, Frederick Blick and George Blick, and my wife Nicola Blick.

Introduction

Approach, Literature Review, and Methodology

The Internet is the most remarked-upon technology of our time. The Westminster Parliament lies at the centre of the United Kingdom (UK) political and legal system. This book explores, in historical context, the relationship between the two. The subject is important, first, in its own right. Change in the way in which the UK legislature operates is significant. Parliament is the primary institution of representative democracy in the UK, and one of the longest operating and most influential such entities in the world. It has encountered numerous prior transformations in modes of communication, and its responses to them have generated much comment as they occurred and subsequently. In the context of an 'uncodified' or 'unwritten' constitution, Parliament possesses supreme legal authority or 'sovereignty'. A key focus for public debate, governments are formed out of this body, and ministers are in turn accountable to it. Parliament – the primary chamber of which, the House of Commons, is elected – carries out its tasks on behalf of the public. The Internet has impacted upon the way in which it functions and the legislature has taken an interest in shaping the environment within which this technology operates.

Secondly, the issues with which this work engages form part of a wider international debate about the consequences of the Internet for society as a whole.[1] At one extreme, this device can appear as a vehicle for malign ends, such as social manipulation and exploitation. At the other, it is a saviour, as during the coronavirus pandemic, when it provided a means for the swift dissemination of vital information, and of overcoming enforced social isolation (yet at the same time being a conduit for the so-called 'infodemic' of misleading assertions[2]). There are many points in between. A prominent sub-discussion, that dates back over decades but seems to have grown in intensity over time, centres on the extent to which the Internet is a force supportive of democracy and meaningful individual empowerment, or is inimical to these ends.

[1] See Ch. 1 of this volume.

[2] Julia Carie Wong, 'Tech Giants Struggle to Stem "Infodemic" of False Coronavirus Claims', *The Guardian*, 10 April 2020, available at: www.theguardian.com/world/2020/apr/10/tech-giants-struggle-stem-infodemic-false-coronavirus-claims, last accessed 17 September 2020.

The present work seeks both to explore the particular instance of the UK Parliament in relation to these concerns, and contribute to this broader discourse. It considers both the way in which technology is perceived, and put into practice, and the connection between the two themes. The book performs this task through introducing the subject, placing it in a wide and long context, and then returning to it in detail. Alongside the Internet itself, it assesses inventions that predated this digital network, or developed contemporaneously with it. It considers the overall development of Parliament as an institution and branch of the constitution. Ultimately it asks: what use has Parliament made of the Internet? How and with what consequences has Parliament sought to influence the development of the Internet? What overall difference has the Internet made to Parliament, including its position within the UK constitution? What more general conclusions can we draw?

To define certain terms, by 'Internet' I refer – using a proper noun – to a digital network the historic function of which was the joining together of multiple computer networks, to which mass connections became possible. But as a technology it has many complex implications and discerned meanings, that I explore further in Chapter 1 and beyond. The 'UK Parliament' is the legislature of the United Kingdom, including within it two Houses: an elected Commons and mainly appointed (though hereditary in its origins) Lords. It is the repository of legal supremacy or 'sovereignty' and not limited by a 'written' or 'codified' constitution (itself defined in the following paragraph). The UK Parliament is in some respects descended from the English Parliament, an institution with origins lying at least as far back as the thirteenth century. Formally it ceased to operate with the Union of Scotland and England, implemented in 1707, succeeded at this time by the Parliament of Great Britain and then (following Union between Ireland and Great Britain, that came into force in 1801) of the United Kingdom.

'Constitution' is used to refer to the structures, rules, and principles of the political system; and the relationship that different governmental institutions have with each other and with the people. In many countries, core features of this type are included in a single text with special legal status – a 'written' or 'codified' constitution. In the UK, they are spread more diffusely across a variety of documents or more amorphous understandings or 'conventions'. Hence the UK is often described as having an 'unwritten' or 'uncodified' constitution. By 'democracy', I mean a system of government which is subject to popular control of some kind and within which there is a basic principle that all people are politically equal to one another. I refer to two different subvarieties of democracy. The first – 'representative democracy' – entails decision-making power being vested in a set of institutions that govern on behalf of the public, and are accountable to them, including via elections. The second – 'direct democracy' – involves voters as a whole, rather than intermediary entities, making choices, for instance through referendums. There can be a degree of tension between these two types of democracy, though they often to some extent co-exist.

The book makes particular use of long-term analysis. In trying to appreciate the value of this approach, it is instructive to consider some of the written output of an Elizabethan and Jacobian politician, lawyer, philosopher – and member of the English predecessor to the UK Parliament (both in the House of Commons and House of Lords). Francis Bacon saw great potential in technology. Writing in *Novum Organum* in 1620, he referred to a need to 'note the force, effect, and consequences of inventions'. The most significant among them, he judged, 'have changed the appearance and state of the whole world'.[3] He both discerned importance in existing devices and sought to anticipate the nature and consequences of advances yet to come. Many examples falling in the latter category appeared in his unfinished work *A New Atlantis*. Published after his death in 1626, it depicted an imaginary, isolated, and scientifically advanced island society. This essay is noted for the prescience it displayed.[4] Bacon described, for instance, flying machines, submarine vessels,[5] 'towers' up to 'half a mile in height', the creation of new breeds of plants and animal life, and means of modifying the temperature.[6] He suggested the use of technology to overcome distance, writing that the society had 'means to convey sounds in trunks and pipes, in strange lines and distances'.[7] It had developed telescopes and microscopes to a high level of sophistication.[8] There were 'perspective-houses' for the display of various simulated images.[9] Bacon also described 'houses of deceits of the senses'. Within them it was possible to 'represent all manner of feats of juggling, false apparitions, imposture, and illusions; and their fallacie'.[10]

Given the ingenuity on display, the science of the island could easily have gone far in creating means to 'deceive the senses'. However, an organisation that had responsibility for inventions, called Salomon's House, was firmly opposed to 'all impostures and lies'. It had 'severely forbidden it to all our fellows, under pain of ignominy and fines, that they do not shew any natural work or thing, adorned or swelling but only pure as it is, and without all affection or strangeness'.[11] Bacon described how members of Salomon's House held discussions as to 'which of the inventions and experiences which we have discovered shall be published, and which not: and take all an oath of secrecy,

[3] Cited e.g. in Elizabeth L. Eisenstein, *The Printing Revolution in Early Modern Europe*, 2nd edn (Cambridge University Press, 2005), p. 13.
[4] e.g. Lewis Mumford, *The Myth of the Machine: The Pentagon of Power* (Harcourt Brace Jovanovich, New York, 1970), p. 117.
[5] Francis Bacon, *The Major Works* (Oxford University Press, 2002), p. 486.
[6] Ibid., pp. 481–4.
[7] Ibid., p. 485.
[8] Ibid., p. 484.
[9] Ibid., pp. 484–5.
[10] Ibid., p. 486.
[11] Ibid.

for the concealing of those which we think fit to keep secret'. Salomon's House might in some instances even withhold such knowledge from the 'state'.[12]

With these passages, Bacon suggested that technology could be negative in its implications. It should, in the model he set out, be subject to social regulation based on assessments of impact upon public welfare. The 'state' itself could not necessarily be trusted with some devices. Such concerns are perennial, and have surfaced in debates about the Internet. The contemporary piquancy of Bacon magnifies because of a particular prospective problem he identified. He anticipated potential for the use of visual communications technology to mislead the viewer. It has in some respects found a manifestation in reality in the form of online disinformation and misinformation, commonly known as 'fake news'. Those who discern problems in the nature of online political discourse frequently argue that it exploits a tendency for people to prefer exposure to material that fits with their pre-existing outlooks. In the process, they hold, rather than fostering open debate between people of differing positions, and the consideration of evidence-based propositions, it magnifies social divisions, and confines those who participate online to groups of like-minded individuals, entrenching their mutual prejudices.[13] Bacon, writing elsewhere, anticipated this possibility also, suggesting that, once someone forms a view, they tend only to recognise information that serves to support it. As he put it in *Novum Organum*, '[o]nce a human intellect has adopted an opinion . . . it draws everything else in to confirm and support it'. A preconception, he held, was psychologically entrenched '[e]ven if there are more and stronger instances against it than there are in its favour, the intellect either overlooks these or treats them as negligible or does some line-drawing that lets it shift them out of the way and reject them'. It is common nowadays to present Bacon, with this theory, as anticipating the tendency known as 'confirmation bias'. He saw the phenomenon he discerned as a problem to be overcome by those who sought to expand the range of human knowledge.[14]

Bacon, therefore, had a nuanced view of science, the way in which people and society might employ it, what the consequences could be, and the disposition of the human mind. There was both caution and optimism in his work. He was enthusiastic about an actual rather than anticipated communications technology first introduced to Europe in the mid-fifteenth century. In *A New Atlantis*, Bacon describes how Salomon's House makes use of 'two very long and fair galleries', one of which housed 'the statues of all principal inventors' including 'the inventor of printing', who was unnamed.[15] In his discussion in *Novum Organum* of 'the force, effect, and consequences of inventions' that

[12] Ibid., p. 487.

[13] See e.g. Dominic Spohr, 'Fake News and Ideological Polarization: Filter Bubbles and Selective Exposure on Social Media', *Business Information Review* 34(3) (2017): 150–60.

[14] See e.g. 'Confirmation Bias', available at: https://rintintin.colorado.edu/~vancecd/phil3600/Bacon.pdf, last accessed 4 August 2020.

[15] Bacon, *The Major Works*, p. 487.

'have changed the appearance and state of the whole world', he emphasised the importance of 'three which were unknown to the ancients'. The first in his list, followed by 'gunpowder, and the compass' was 'printing'.[16] The particular value he attached to this technology was the possibilities it created for the dissemination of learning. It was in this account an advance that in itself might facilitate more such development.

By considering the different strands of his thought discussed here, it is possible to construct a dilemma that Bacon did not extrapolate or directly address. If a communications technology seemed to offer benefits similar to those he ascribed to printing, but also created the potential to 'deceive the senses' and promote 'impostures and lies', playing upon the capacity for self-deception inherent in human psychology, what would be the proper response? Restrictions, imposed by an equivalent to Salomon's House, might protect us from abuses – including those perpetrated by 'state' authorities. But how extensive would they need to be if they were to prove effective? Might the benefits that the system produced as a disseminator of information be lost in the process? Such questions would arise in the context of various devices in the centuries that followed, including – in the decades that followed the death of Bacon – with respect to the technology he venerated. A discussion of printing in Western Europe (though it appeared elsewhere earlier[17]), its supposed impact, and relationship with the English Parliament, is apt at this point.

Printing in History

In their classic history of printing, Lucien Febvre and Henri-Jean Martin describe how, around 1450, 'some rather unusual "manuscripts" made their appearance in the northern regions of Western Europe'. Their production took place 'with the mechanical aid of a printing press which used moveable type'. Their means of production became 'the object of considerable curiosity and fascination'. These 'new books', Febvre and Martin argue, would 'cause profound changes not only in the habits of thought but also in the working conditions of' the intellectual community. Furthermore, they 'made considerable impact on the world outside'.[18] In popular conception, the advent of printing is often treated as associated with immense transformative change, particularly in Europe (and North America) during the sixteenth through to the eighteenth centuries.[19] For instance, a connection is often drawn between

[16] Eisenstein, *The Printing Revolution in Early Modern Europe*, p. 13.

[17] Lucien Febvre and Henri-Jean Martin, *The Coming of the Book: The Impact of Printing, 1450–1800* (Verso, London, 2010), p. 7.

[18] Ibid., pp. 71–6.

[19] For a critical account of such views, see Michael Warner, *The Letters of the Republic: Publication and the Public Sphere in Eighteenth-Century America* (Harvard University Press, Cambridge, 1990), esp. ch. 1.

it and the Reformation.[20] The technology helped disseminate the ideas of Luther. His precursors, in particular John Wycliffe and Jan Hus, did not have this particular advantage and in, this sense, it may have made an important difference. Luther himself remarked, in discussion with Pope Leo X, that '[i]t is a mystery to me how my theses, more so than my other writings, indeed, those of other professors were spread to so many places. They were meant exclusively for our academic circle here ... They were written in such a language that the common people could hardly understand them.'[21] Printing may have done more at this time than simply spread specific arguments, generating general reputational momentum around the Luther cause. Leo X could have followed the same approach taken to Hus and had Luther put to death, regardless of previous assurances given. That he did not, and that Luther survived, Andrew Pettegree attributes to 'publicity'. Luther, whose 'defiance became a public event' generated a 'torrent of publicity' without precedent, achieved through print. Pettegree concludes: 'the Reformation was Europe's first mass-media news event' and Luther a 'celebrity', drawing large gatherings on his journey to the Diet of Worms of 1521.[22]

Given its immense (though as we will see, contested) historic reputation, assessments of developments in communications technology often use printing as a reference point.[23] To invoke printing in an act of description is often to imply immense significance for a subject.[24] Those making reference to this invention might do so to create heightened expectations about changes yet to come. For instance, in an article first published in 1964, Gerald Barry, a journalist who was Director General of the Festival of Britain of 1951, described the possible development in coming decades of 'resources of total visual communication' that could 'occasion social changes in the areas of knowledge and understanding as radical as those brought about by the invention of printing itself'.[25] In a 1972 work considering the prospects for communications technology, another journalist, Brenda Maddox, held it was 'possible that the worldwide sharing of information at enormous speeds will actually raise the collective intellectual potential of the human race, just as the printing press and the computer have done'.[26] Depiction of the Internet and related

[20] John Naughton, *From Gutenberg to Zuckerberg: What You Really Need to Know about the Internet* (Quercus, London, 2012), p. 11.

[21] Eisenstein, *The Printing Revolution in Early Modern Europe*, p. 168.

[22] Andrew Pettegree, *The Invention of News: How the World Came to Know about Itself* (Yale University Press, New Haven, 2014), pp. 67–70.

[23] e.g. Luciano Floridi, *The 4th Revolution: How the Infosphere Is Shaping Human Affairs* (Oxford University Press, 2014), p. 4.

[24] e.g. Joseph Weizenbaum, *Computer Power and Human Reason: From Judgement to Calculation* (W. H. Freeman and Company, New York, 1976), p. 19.

[25] Sir Gerald Barry, 'Mass Communication in 1984' in Nigel Calder (ed.), *The World in 1984: The Complete New Scientist Series* (Penguin, Harmondsworth, 1965), vol. I, pp. 157–60, 160.

[26] Brenda Maddox, *Beyond Babel: New Directions in Communications* (Andre Deutsch, London, 1972), pp. 254–5.

devices through reference to this earlier invention has long been commonplace.[27] For instance, Howard Rheingold, an influential exponent of the use of networked computers during its initial period of mass expansion, held in 1994 that, appropriately deployed, this practice had 'democratizing potential in the way that alphabets and printing presses had democratizing potential'.[28] If we are to understand the Internet and its relationship with the UK Parliament in an historical sense, then, it is worth reflecting upon the perceived and actual nature of this earlier medium. Such consideration might lead us to qualify some more widely accepted assessments of the role of printing and to question how appropriate is the comparison between it and the Internet. Yet even through these acts of questioning (though not outright dismissal) we can develop more sophisticated tools for the analysis of the Internet.

A consideration of literature relating to the historical role of printing suggests a series of ambiguities and areas of disagreement. It is important to recognise the technology from the perspective of a series of connected inventions and innovations that took place over a prolonged period of time, rather than being a fixed development that took place at a specific point. The arrival of paper into 'Europe via Moorish Spain in the twelfth century' helped make it viable.[29] The technology itself had precursors and the specific invention attributed to Johannes Gutenberg was a compound of parallel achievements.[30] Some of the subsequent impact on European affairs associated with it came about because of its intersection with a particular administrative mechanism: the European postal system. As Paul Arblaster writes, '[t]he appearance of the newspaper followed upon the conjunction of two technical preconditions: cheap print and regular posts', a combination achieved by 1600, around a century-and-a-half after Gutenberg.[31]

This linking to a network is of particular importance to an assessment of parallels with the Internet. While – like the Internet – the printing press could facilitate the transmission of information, it is a means of producing hard copies of content for dissemination, but not the actual conduit through which this distribution takes place. In the same way, standalone computers had many uses; but their incorporation into networks (gaining momentum during the 1960s and among which the Internet eventually became the all-embracing system) provided a new context within which they functioned. It is important,

[27] e.g. Bill Gates, *The Road Ahead* (Viking, New York, 1995), pp. 8–9, 120–1; Esther Dyson, George Gilder, George Keyworth, and Alvin Toffler, 'Cyberspace and the American Dream: A Magna Carta for the Knowledge Age', *Future Insight*, Release 1(2) (August 1994); Naughton, *From Gutenberg to Zuckerberg*.

[28] Howard Rheingold, *The Virtual Community: Finding Connection in a Computerised World* (Martin Secker & Warburg, London, 1994), p. 279.

[29] Pettegree, *The Invention of News*, p. 41.

[30] Febvre and Martin, *The Coming of the Book*, chs. 1 and 2.

[31] Paul Arblaster, 'Posts, Newsletters, Newspapers: England in a European System of Communications' in Joad Raymond (ed.), *News Networks in Seventeenth-Century Britain and Europe* (Routledge, Abingdon, 2006), p. 19.

therefore, to consider not only physical devices (whether presses or computers) but also the network (whether postal or digital) into which they integrated as distinct but related matters. To this end, in this work, I consider approaches specifically to the computer – particularly from within Parliament – and the extent to which they took into account the potential of this invention as a communications mechanism (and to which they failed to do so), as well as the Internet as a subject for itself.

The print network was a technological and social system comprising a portamento of inventions and distribution mechanisms appearing at staggered intervals (though there was a key coming together in the mid-fifteenth century[32]). Ongoing development continued over time. Techniques became more sophisticated, efficient, and reliable.[33] Furthermore, different applications appeared. An initial impulse was to employ printing for the more efficient and reliable production of familiar texts such as worship materials, indulgences or royal edicts.[34] But, over time, other forms – such as pamphlets and newspapers – developed.[35] Internet history has seen similar patterns of changing technology and usage. Mobile devices, for instance, have become increasingly significant. There has, moreover, been a shift away from online versions of the static text found in hardcopy publications and towards more interactive functions, such as those provided by social media. The way in which people perceived printing altered over time: for instance, Adrian Johns argues that only over a prolonged period did a wide trust in the reliability (or 'fixity') of books develop.[36] Perhaps the Internet today faces similar challenges.

Though printing became important and widespread in Europe (and elsewhere), it never supplanted earlier communications techniques; and in many cases was – and continues to be – used in complex combination with them. For instance, a text written in longhand could then be reproduced by a press, the output of which a reader might choose to annotate personally. Speech can be delivered given from a printed text, perhaps marked in pen, then recorded in shorthand before being transferred into printed form. Though they utilised printed material and postal systems, the European information networks developing by the early seventeenth century were fed by gossip, personal contacts, and intelligence supplied perhaps orally or on

[32] Febvre and Martin, *The Coming of the Book*, pp. 49–56.

[33] For discussion of debate on this point in the context of the Internet, see Thomas Streeter, 'The Internet as a Structure of Feeling: 1992–1996', *Internet Histories* 1(1–2) (2017): 79–89, 86.

[34] Pettegree, *The Invention of News*, p. 60; Jason Peacey, 'The Print Culture of Parliament, 1600–1800' in Jason Peacey (ed.), *The Print Culture of Parliament, 1600–1800* (Edinburgh University Press, 2007), pp. 3–4.

[35] See e.g. Joad Raymond, *Pamphlets and Pamphleteering in Early Modern Britain* (Cambridge University Press, 2003), pp. 301–2; Andrew Thrush, *The House of Commons 1604–1629*, vol. I: *Introductory Survey, Appendices* (Cambridge University Press, 2010), pp. 331–2.

[36] Adrian Johns, *The Nature of the Book: Print and Knowledge in the Making* (University of Chicago Press, 1998), pp. 622–38.

handwritten notes.[37] The Internet, similarly, has intersections with other media. To regard it crudely as rendering them obsolete or replacing them would be a mistake. Offline and online activities overlap – for instance, with the employment of social media as a means of arranging physical political events; or for arranging in-person dating. In some ways, the Internet has been employed to imitate or subsume other forms of communication, including mail, radio, television, telephone, and even (via such packages as Zoom, Teams, and Skype) traditional conversations or group meetings. The digital network carries copies of signatures and has incorporated printing – both through carrying digital versions of documents that reproduce written texts and because people (still) print out hardcopies of content accessed via the Internet. (When envisaging what is now regarded as a prototype for the computer in the mid-nineteenth century, Charles Babbage anticipated that it would include typesetting as a function.[38]) As the House of Lords Select Committee on Democracy and Digital Technologies put it in 2020: '[p]eople now have a printing press, a broadcast station and a place of assembly in their pockets'.[39]

Based on the aspects of printing discussed so far, provisional conclusions are possible regarding how we might approach the history of the Internet (and by extension its specific application to Parliament). Any such study must take into account certain observations. This system of networked computers did not appear immediately in fixed form. The closest to a moment of origin comes in 1969 with the launch of ARPANET (see p. 27 below).[40] But this event was preceded by much scientific significant development; more of which has followed continued thereafter. In a related phenomenon, the uses to which the Internet has been put have changed substantially over time. It has never been a fixed, stable entity. This changeability – or perhaps volatility – has meant that, despite sometimes confident predictions, paths followed were not fully knowable in advance. Furthermore, study should not be confined to the Internet and directly supporting technologies. Earlier and parallel devices have helped open a path for and worked in conjunction with its operation. Finally, notwithstanding the difficulties of precise dating, consideration of printing reminds us that the Internet is relatively new. Changes in the nature and use of this prior technology – and the dramatic developments with which it was associated – occurred over centuries. Enough has transpired for us to begin

[37] Joad Raymond and Noah Moxham (eds.), *News Networks in Early Modern Europe* (Brill, Leiden, 2016). This point is clear in the introduction by the editors, and in the subsequent individual chapters.

[38] Martin Campbell-Kelly, William Aspray, Nathan Ensmenger, and Jeffrey R. Yost, *Computer: A History of the Information Machine*, 3rd edn (Westview Press, Boulder, 2014), p. 6.

[39] House of Lords Select Committee on Democracy and Digital Technologies, Report of Session 2019–21, HL 77 (House of Lords, London, 2020), p. 9.

[40] See e.g. Camille Paloque-Bergès and Valérie Schafer, 'ARPANET (1969–2019)', *Internet Histories* 3(1) (2019): 1–14.

considering a history of the Internet – but there might (or might not) be much to more come. Eventually, one day, newer inventions – of which we cannot yet fully conceive – could come to challenge its primacy as a device for remote communication. But in keeping with its relationship with printing, they might come to interact with or absorb – rather than completely replace – the Internet. To take into account the various technological indeterminacies identified, it is necessary to begin studies at an earlier period, and to give them a broader scope, than might initially appear necessary.

Beyond the nature and uses of inventions, what does assessment of the role of the printing press reveal about their impact? As we have seen, there has been a tendency to link it to major historic developments. The remarks of Bacon show that some who were closer to events involved perceived the invention as of great significance. Jason Peacey conveys the idea of contemporaries in positions of authority regarding printing as undermining of the existing order. He recounts how, in England during the first half of the seventeenth century, significant concerns were felt and expressed, from the monarchy downwards, about the supposedly distorting, vulgarising, and ultimately destabilising consequences of the wider permeation of printed material. Those expressing such views feared that it had the effect of encouraging participation in political discussion by people who could not properly understand it.[41] Complaints about changes in communications technology having negative consequences for public discourse, and the idea that the response they elicit from the wider population might not be of an appropriate equality, have recurred since, including in analysis of the Internet.[42]

Later in the seventeenth century the poet, Andrew Marvell made great claims on its behalf. A renowned author and politician, he was an ally of John Milton, Oliver Cromwell, and Thomas Fairfax, and Member of the House of Commons for Hull from 1659 until the end of his life in 1678.[43] In his *Rehearsal Transpros'd*, he made a case for the printing press as a politically disruptive force.[44] It first appeared in 1672, initially without his name attached, owing to the controversial nature of the text in its treatment of religious matters (a second part appeared the following year). In this work Marvell presented a parody of the outlook of those to whom printing was a malign generator of upheaval. In doing so, he made a connection between this process and turmoil of his time.

[41] Jason Peacey, *Print and Public Politics in the English Revolution* (Cambridge University Press, 2013), Introduction, section i.

[42] See e.g. Committee on Standards in Public Life, *Intimidation in Public Life: A Review by the Committee on Standards in Public Life*, Cm. 9543 (Stationery Office, London, 2017), pp. 33, 27, 34.

[43] Annabel Patterson, 'Introduction' in Martin Dzelzainis and Annabel Patterson (eds.), *The Prose Works of Andrew Marvell*, vol. I: *1672–1673* (Yale University Press, New Haven, 2003), pp. xiv–xv.

[44] Martin Dzelzainis and Annabel Patterson, 'Introduction' to Martin Dzelzainis (ed.), 'Rehearsal Transpros'd' in Martin Dzelzainis and Annabel Patterson (eds.), *The Prose Works of Andrew Marvell*, vol. I: *1672–1673* (Yale University Press, New Haven, 2003), p. 4.

Marvell referred to 'The Press (that *villainous* Engine) invented much about the same time with the Reformation, that hath done more mischief to the Discipline of our Church, than all the Doctrine can make amends for.'[45] He went on, still in ironic mode, to describe the 'happy time when all Learning was in Manuscript, and some little Officer, like our Author, did keep the Keys of the Library'. In this earlier era, neither clergy nor laity had much need for reading. Marvell had associated two key concepts. A development in communications technology had led to authorities losing control and it had enabled the dissemination of information beyond the usual exclusive circles – a dangerous tendency from the perspective of established groups. Marvell also seemed to make a specific point about the nature of the invention to which he referred. It had effect partly through enabling the rapid production of work and responses to the interventions of others. As he put it: 'since Printing came into the World, such is the mischief, that a Man cannot write a Book but presently he is answered'. The implication was that technology had increased the pace of discourse, leading to wider material changes.

Marvell described hapless attempts to restore conformity. There were difficulties in ensuring that 'the Press but once be conjured to obey only an *Imprimatur*', by which he meant submission to the system of official pre-publication censorship, signified by an official mark of approval. Suppression of dissent was possible in other areas. There had 'been wayes found out to banish Ministers, to fine not only the People, but even the Grounds and Fields where they assembled in Conventicles'. However, printing was resistant to such measures and 'no Art yet could prevent these seditious meetings of Letters'. Describing how small operations could achieve impact on a scale previously unknown, Marvell presented the image of 'Two or three brawny Fellows in a Corner' working 'with mere Ink and Elbow-grease' who could 'do more harm than a *hundred Systematical Divines* with their *sweaty Preaching*'. Technology already in use before printing was deployed in conjunction with the newer invention to opposite ends. 'Spunges', once used to 'deface and blot out' literature, were now used 'to make things legible'. Official censors might extract 'Their ugly Printing-Letters, that look but like so many rotten-Teeth'. But 'these rascally Operators of the Press have got a trick to fasten them again in a few minutes, that they grow as firm a Set, and as biting and talkative as ever'. Concluding his account of the technology, Marvell issued his frequently quoted exclamation: 'O Printing! How hast thou disturb'd the Peace of Mankind! that Lead, when moulded into Bullets, is not so mortal as when founded into Letters!'[46] The device appeared as an armament that could bring about (perhaps literally) violent upheaval.

The idea that a technology might have close association with socially and politically turbulent episodes has recurred, including in relation to the

45 'Rehearsal Transpros'd', pp. 44–5.
46 Ibid., pp. 45–6.

Internet. For instance, some commentators at the time of the so-called Arab Spring of 2011 emphasised the importance of social media to this episode of regional unrest.[47] To help develop a framework by which we might assess propositions about the impact of the Internet, applicable in particular to the UK Parliament, it is useful to consider debates about the role of printing following its introduction to Europe in the early modern era. Some historians have treated it as having had a deep social impact. Pre-eminent among them was Elizabeth Eisenstein. She argues, for instance, that '[p]rinting encouraged forms of combinatory activity which were social as well as intellectual. It changed relationships between men of learning as well as between systems of ideas.'[48] Eisenstein holds that it created openings for people not previously suited to the wielding of political influence, who we might liken to the online influencers of today. In the scenario she posits, '[n]ew forms of political influence were exerted by would-be-tribunes who lacked oratorical skills but knew how to attract attention when harnessing their pens to presses'.[49]

But, when we consider the possible association of printing with disruption to existing social structures and practices, we should remain aware that it had many other purposes. As Eisenstein (who displays more balance than some criticism of her work has allowed for) reminds us, subversion of existing authority was only one of number of uses for printing, that soon came to be employed for a range of content that extended to material such as pornography.[50] Furthermore, rather than being used to challenge established institutions such as Church or monarchy, these very bodies might use it to promote their own purposes.[51] Moreover, causality is always hard to establish definitively. That certain events followed the introduction of printing (sometimes after a long delay) does not in itself determine that the technology fully brought them about, or even made a contribution to such an outcome. A further important observation is that printing interacted with existing social and political environments rather than replacing them. Some societies adopted the technology without major disruption occurring.[52] Moreover, the inability of authorities in Europe wholly to supress or control

[47] For a depiction of social media as 'fostering' the Arab Spring, linking it to past technological developments with a supposedly similar impact, see Francis Fukuyama, *Political Order and Political Decay: From the Industrial Revolution to the Globalization of Democracy* (Profile, London, 2014), p. 25. For a critical assessment of such claims, see Evgeny Morozov, *To Save Everything, Click Here: Technology, Solutionism and the Urge to Fix Problems that Don't Exist* (Penguin, London, 2014), p. 127.

[48] Eisenstein, *The Printing Revolution in Early Modern Europe*, p. 49.

[49] Ibid., p. 331.

[50] Elizabeth L. Eisenstein, *Divine Art, Infernal Machine: The Reception of Printing in the West from First Impressions to the Sense of an Ending* (University of Pennsylvania Press, Philadelphia, 2011), pp. 27–8.

[51] Pettegree, *The Invention of News*, p. 60.

[52] As remarked in a discussion of internet comparative history by Marc Weber, 'A Common Language', *Internet Histories* 1(1–2) (2017): 26–38, 30. For some examples, see Febvre and Martin, *The Coming of the Book*, pp. 71–6.

printing[53] is perhaps suggestive of a system already susceptible to subsequent political developments.

Some analysis of printing suggests that it helped generate a new arena of intellectual discourse and interaction that was separate from governmental authority. In his study of news circulation taking place in Europe by the early seventeenth century, Paul Arblaster states that '[t]he transmission of regular newsletters by the public posts so tightly interwove communication networks across Western Christendom that it is difficult not to speak of a single information community'.[54] Some accounts of the intellectual history of the following century refer to printing as helping to facilitate the emergence of a 'public sphere'.[55] (Analysis of the Internet has considered the idea that it has had a similar impact, sometimes expressly adopting the 'public sphere' term.[56]) However, some literature also suggests that forms of engagement that printing facilitated were not always wholly inclusive. It could create the possibility among more marginalised groups for entry into the political process. In the 1640s, for instance, 'groups of women were quick to exploit the potential of the petition as a medium for public protestation and campaigning'. The texts might be printed and distributed 'regardless of whether they had been welcomed by Parliament' in 'an attempt to manipulate public opinion'. They might also appear in newsbooks. But journals of the same type could also contain vicious written attacks on the women who produced them[57] – another phenomenon familiar to the observer of contemporary online discourse.[58] Furthermore, in a consideration of developments of the following century, James Van Horn Melton writes that 'The legacy of the public sphere … was ambiguous. It was neither inexorably emancipatory, and if it was not irredeemably masculinist, neither was it unqualifiedly feminist.'[59] A prerequisite for full participation in the 'public sphere' was literacy. Analysing data from Britain, France, and Germany, Van Horn Melton shows that, while there was an overall rise in this skill through the eighteenth century, men and people living in urban areas were more likely to have acquired the necessary ability, and higher levels of personal prosperity

53 For the limitation upon censorship in seventeenth-century England, see Jason McElligott, '"A Couple of Hundred Squabbling Small Tradesmen"? Censorship, the Stationers' Company, and the State in Early Modern England' in Joad Raymond (ed.), *News Networks in Seventeenth-Century Britain and Europe* (Routledge, Abingdon, 2006), p. 96.

54 Arblaster, 'Posts, Newsletters, Newspapers', p. 19.

55 For the classic text in this field, translated from German, see Jürgen Habermas, *The Structural Transformation of the Public Sphere* (Polity, Cambridge, 1992).

56 Zizi Papacharissi, 'The Virtual Sphere: The Internet as a Public Sphere', *New Media & Society* 4 (1) (2002): 9–27.

57 Raymond, *Pamphlets and Pamphleteering in Early Modern Britain*, pp. 301–2.

58 For a parliamentary perspective on this tendency, see Digital Democracy Commission, *Open Up! Report of the Speaker's Commission on Digital Democracy* (Speaker's Commission on Digital Democracy, London, 2015), p. 38.

59 James Van Horn Melton, *The Rise of the Public in Enlightenment Europe* (Cambridge University Press, 2001), e-book location 244.

were the most significant determining factor of all.[60] Addressing the subject of the present work, Van Horn Melton notes: 'In our day, the computer and the internet have wrought a revolution in communications riven with the same contradiction that marked the Enlightened public sphere – expanded networks of information on the one hand, but also a growing gap between those who enjoy access to it and those who do not.'[61] Melton wrote in 2001. Since this time, access to the Internet has expanded (though it is not universal in the UK or elsewhere). However, there remain disparities of usage of the technology across social groupings,[62] and its effectiveness as a means of bringing about political participation other than by those who are already engaged is questionable.[63]

Printing and the English Parliament in the Mid-Seventeenth Century

The relationship between the English Parliament and printing, especially in the middle decades of the seventeenth century, has generated much scholarly interest. It was a period of sustained constitutional disruption. The wider background was one of military conflict on the continental mainland and general religious division. In England, tension built between Parliament and a monarchy with absolutist leanings, leading to civil war. The conflict was complex, with a variety of different interests and outlooks involved. Parliament, for instance, was not a single unified entity – an important point to bear in mind whenever we assess it as an institution. Eventually, King Charles I was removed from power and put to death in 1649. An experiment in government without monarchy commenced under Oliver Cromwell, followed by the Restoration under Charles II in 1660.[64] In the long run, it is common to regard this turbulent episode as helping to shape the English and then UK constitution, and in particular the principle of parliamentary government. Print played a prominent role throughout. It was a means for the promotion of various causes and dissemination of ideas. As the Marvell work cited above demonstrates, contemporaries recognised its presence. But what did it mean from point of view of Parliament?

It is possible to identify three themes of particular interest. Their significance from the point of view of a successor institution – the UK Parliament – and the Internet, will become apparent over the course of this book. The first area of consideration involves the idea that printing changed the way in which the public interacted with and perceived Parliament. The second is the use that

[60] Ibid., 1152.

[61] Ibid., 247.

[62] Ofcom, *Online Nation: 2019 Report* (Ofcom, London, 2019), p. 3.

[63] Hansard Society, *Audit of Political Engagement 15: The 2018 Report* (Hansard Society, London, 2018), pp. 28, 30.

[64] See Mark Kishlansky, *A Monarchy Transformed: Britain 1603–1714* (Penguin, London, 1996), chs. 6–8.

Parliament made of printing for its own purposes, in particular in asserting its authority relative to that of the monarchy. The third is the efforts of Parliament to regulate use made of the technology within wider society. Taken together, developments across each of these categories – whatever the precise interpretation placed upon them – had implications for the constitutional role of Parliament; that is to say, its place within the system of governance of England.

To turn to the first category, the impact of printing upon relations between Parliament and the public in the mid-seventeenth century, the use of this technology subjected Parliament to considerable pressure. England was not a democracy at this time; only a tiny minority could vote in elections. Parliament was nonetheless regarded in some sense as representative of the country. During this period, various publications appeared calling upon the institution to assist numerous different causes.[65] It could not possibly deliver on all of these demands and was therefore liable to become a target itself. Printing both served to emphasise the constitutional centrality of Parliament, but also made it vulnerable. It became exposed in another, more literal, sense. A basic principle on which Parliament operated was that, while it might make the conclusions it reached public, its proceedings were confidential. This rule was frequently broken. Versions of parliamentary speeches, for instance, might be disseminated – sometimes at the instigation of the individual members who made them, for publicity purposes. This practice was possible even in handwritten form. But the particular uses made of printing from the 1640s intensified the officially unsanctioned coverage of what went on in Parliament. As well as facilitating the wide distribution of particular speeches, Jason Peacey notes that it enhanced public awareness of procedures and their results. Crucially, it could reveal how individual parliamentarians voted on specific issues. It consequently became possible to discern the existence of particular factions sharing broad attitudes on particular important issues: precursors to parties. The exposure of the voting record of MPs might in turn affect their prospects for being returned to Parliament at a future election. Scrutiny of MPs could also take in questioning of their personal integrity and probity. The concept of representation began to shift away from Parliament as a single entity, and towards the individual people who composed it.[66]

A protracted struggle followed between those publishing accounts of debates and those within Parliament who wanted to supress them. Reasons for wanting to produce reports included possible commercial gain and the pursuit of political goals, including the widening of participation in the system. Opposition among parliamentarians could be motivated by a desire to avoid public scrutiny or persecution by the government for what they said, and that the content of supposed reproductions of speeches could be to a large extent

[65] Thrush, *The House of Commons 1604–1629*, vol. I, pp. 331–2.

[66] For this thesis, see Peacey, *Print and Public Politics in the English Revolution.*

fabricated. Tension built in the second half of the eighteenth century, especially with the campaign by John Wilkes, the radical MP, for press freedom. During the 1770s, the bar on coverage became increasingly less effective.[67]

Consideration of external reporting of Parliament takes us to the second analytical category proposed here: that of Parliament making direct use of printing for its own purposes. Publication of details of proceedings in contradiction of the prohibition of such coverage often took place with the collusion or on the initiative of individual parliamentarians. The members involved clearly saw the technology as potentially beneficial, and their activities are indicative of a significant tendency: for certain people within Parliament to embrace a communications device for practices towards which the institution as a whole was more resistant. Beyond the actions of particular MPs, a wider parliamentary usage can be found in the case of the *Grand Remonstrance*, a text Parliament presented to King Charles I on 1 December 1641. It took the form of a long list of complaints about his behaviour, though adopting the customary approach of blaming them on sinister forces within the court rather than the monarch himself. The text referred to '[t]he multiplied evils and corruption of fifteen years ... and the concurrent interest of many powerful delinquents' (paragraph 106), and to 'evil counselors' (paragraph 121). It also set out a positive programme, including principles about the prominent, fixed constitutional role it felt Parliament should have. It asserted, for instance, that royal appointments to ministerial, diplomatic, and advisory posts should be individuals in which Parliament could trust, and that if it did not it could withhold financial support from the monarch.[68]

As well as presenting it to the King, the Commons chose to mass-produce the *Grand Remonstrance*, 'thus transforming a document which began as a petition to the king into an appeal to the people'.[69] It proved to be a critical text in constitutional history, and the manner of its promulgation was significant. Raymond describes how the decision to issue the remonstrance as a manuscript and subsequently to print it was groundbreaking. 'Never had a king been exposed before so many of his subjects as a jury.'[70] In his response to the *Grand Remonstrance* dated 23 December 1641, Charles I suggested that the printing of the text was a break with proper practice; he may, furthermore, have resented the effectiveness of the tactic that the Commons had deployed. In *The King's Answer to the Petition Accompanying the Grand Remonstrance*, he explained that he 'had taken some time to consider' the document because of its 'great moment' and 'unusual nature'. Charles had been 'confident' that,

[67] John Vice and Stephen Farrell, *The History of Hansard* (House of Lords, London, undated), pp. 7–10.

[68] 'The Grand Remonstrance, with the Petition accompanying it', Reproduced in Samuel Rawson Gardiner (ed.), *Constitutional Documents of the Puritan Revolution, 1625–1660* (Oxford University Press, 1936), pp. 202–32.

[69] Peacey, 'The Print Culture of Parliament, 1600–1800, pp. 3–4.

[70] Raymond, *Pamphlets and Pamphleteering in Early Modern Britain*, p. 151.

out of its 'own reason and regard' to him, and in accordance with an 'express intimation' made on his behalf, the Commons 'would have restrained . . . from the publishing of it till such time as you should have received our answer to it'. Yet, on the contrary, 'the said declaration [was] already abroad in print, by directions from your House as appears by the printed copy'. Charles was, as he put it, 'very sensible of the disrespect'.[71]

The nature of the communications technology itself, as well as the particular content of the messages it disseminated, was a factor in relations between the legislature and the executive. Printing had provided a means by which Parliament (or forces within it) could seek to shape and deploy public sentiment in support of its goals and against those of the monarch: a dangerous proposition (though, of course, it was possible to employ the technology for the opposite cause). Parliament had, in strained circumstances, displayed a collective ability to harness such opportunities to radical effect. But alongside this ability to change, there was also institutional inertia.

It was not until 1804 that publication of what later became *Hansard* – an official printed public record of the previous day's proceedings – commenced. Around three-and-a-half centuries had elapsed since the advance attributed to Gutenberg. A fully official record took even longer to appear, finally coming into being in 1909.[72] The lag is a reminder of how prolonged the process of dissemination of an invention can be, and how – once adopted – different uses of it can be adopted over time. (As we will see, though parliamentary take-up of the Internet was swifter, it was not instantaneous, and the use made of it developed.) Barriers to take-up and innovation can be more than technical – though limitations of this kind can be significant – and might be of a social, cultural, and political character. Nonetheless, change eventually came, and provided a basis for future development. One of the early purposes of the parliamentary website was to make Hansard available in electronic form.

The third aspect to parliamentary engagement with printing was the role it took upon itself in seeking to control the use others made of it. Up to 1641, a regime of pre-publication censorship operated under royal authority, via a Star Chamber Decree. In July of this year, this system ceased to function with the collapse of the Star Chamber itself. There followed the so-called 'pamphlet explosion' – a surge in the production and circulation of published materials dealing with controversial matters. Parliament then moved to establish its own system of licensing subject to prior vetting of content, initially through an Ordinance of 1643. The following year, John Milton criticised the measure in his pamphlet, *Areopagitica*. The work would come to be regarded as a historic assertion of the principle of freedom of expression. That he supported the continuation of significant controls, and

[71] 'The King's Answer to the Petition Accompanying the Grand Remonstrance', Reproduced in Gardiner (ed.), *Constitutional Documents of the Puritan Revolution, 1625–1660*, pp. 233–6.

[72] It began as *Cobbett's Parliamentary Debates*. Vice and Farrell, *The History of Hansard*, pp. 5, 18.

that the motivations for his intervention have been a subject of discussion, cannot be a basis for dismissing the importance of this text.[73] Parliamentary efforts to bring about oversight of printing helped trigger major developments in political thought. The system amounted to more than the mere regulation of the use of a type of machinery. In fact, as Milton identified, the measure entailed a central institution of governance imposing itself upon the intellectual discourse and development of a polity.

In his text Milton likened the parliamentary licensing order to the efforts of the Inquisition ('as if St Peter had bequeathed them the keys of the press ... out of paradise'[74]) to suppress heresy. He therefore condemned '[t]his Spanish policy of licensing books'.[75] Milton questioned the practicality of censorship, including the potential for identifying and retaining suitable operators of the system. Moreover, he held, even if it were possible only to allow the publication of works containing correct beliefs, the reading public would not then have come to the truth by themselves. It was preferable for individuals to have access to a range of opinions from which, using their own judgement, they could discern what to believe. As Milton put it, 'what wisdom can there be to choose, what continence to forbear without the knowledge of evil?'[76] Milton contended that 'all opinions, yea, errors, known, read and collated, are of main service and assistance toward the speedy attainment of what is truest'.[77] Exposure to a span of diverse literature, including within it the bad as well as the good, was therefore a positive advantage. Hence 'the benefit which may be had of books promiscuously read'.[78] Milton had confidence in 'the ingenuity of truth, who when she gets a free and willing hand, opens herself faster than the pace of method and discourse can overtake her'.[79] Yet there were limits to the freedom he envisaged. Milton felt that those who advocated outlooks such as 'popery' and 'superstition'[80] should be denied the ability to print their work. He also advocated possible legal action after publication, allowing for 'the church and commonwealth, to have a vigilant eye how books demean themselves as well as men'. It should be possible 'to confine, imprison and do the sharpest justice' to any 'malefactors'.[81]

Critically, from the point of view of this study, Milton presented his pamphlet as an imaginary address given by himself to Parliament (the 'High Court of Parliament'). The subheading is 'A Speech of Mr John Milton for the Liberty of

[73] John Milton, *Areopagitica and Other Writings*, ed. William Poole (Penguin, London, 2014), p. xl.
[74] Ibid., p. 105.
[75] Ibid., p. 141.
[76] Ibid., p. 111.
[77] Ibid., p. 110.
[78] Ibid., p. 111.
[79] Ibid., p. 114.
[80] Ibid., p. 138.
[81] Ibid., p. 101.

Unlicensed Printing. To the Parliament of England'.[82] Joad Raymond notes that, in presenting it as a speech, Milton aimed his work both at Parliament and 'a wider audience, the reading public'. It followed the format used for petitions presented to Parliament and pamphlets containing accounts of speeches genuinely delivered in the legislature. On occasions, collections of this type actually included *Areopagitica* within them and it 'was thereby treated as an authentic parliamentary interjection'. It 'thus imagined that pamphlets created a virtual parliament, broadening the franchise of representation to include non-MPs'. Through this means, Raymond contends, 'the arena of print is figured as a massive parliament-without-doors, in which the citizen can represent him or herself'.[83] In this scenario, a communications technology had made possible the coming into being of an inclusive arena for political interaction. Official interference, in the supposed public good, was a threat to it.

Parliament reissued the Ordinance (in modified form) in 1647, and then – from 1649 – began using Acts of Parliament for the same purpose. Only in 1695 did pre-publication censorship end, when Parliament allowed the Licensing Act to lapse.[84] But withdrawal of this legal control did not mark an end to the possibility of public authorities exerting influence on the press. Legal action after publication remained an option (as Milton, indeed, had thought it should), and it was possible to shape the content of work that appeared, for instance through financial inducements to those producing it. Other levers were available. In the period after the end of the Napoleonic Wars, the UK Parliament passed the notorious 'Six Acts' of 1819. Two of these laws had (intended) negative consequences for the autonomy of the press, with the effect of making political periodicals more expensive, creating new costs for anyone involved in producing or circulating such literature, and expanding the enforcement powers of local magistrates.[85]

These various measures, the struggles against them, and their eventual defeat, created a powerful historical narrative linked to a strong cultural antipathy to legal interference, via Parliament, in journalism and its printed expression. But a view would also develop that for public authorities simply to refrain from action was not sufficient to facilitate a public environment of genuinely free and socially beneficial discourse. Some supposed problems could involve the workings of the market. During the twentieth century, criticism developed that a concentration of newspaper ownership had the effect of restricting the range of views presented to the public. Proprietors could become influential in their own rights. Politicians were likely to court and ingratiate themselves with these figures, in the hope of obtaining

[82] Ibid., p. 98.

[83] Raymond, *Pamphlets and Pamphleteering in Early Modern Britain*, pp. 267–8.

[84] For reference, see the table in Johns, *The Nature of the Book*, pp. 232–3.

[85] William H. Wickwar, *The Struggle for the Freedom of the Press: 1819–1832* (George Allen & Unwin, London, 1928), pp. 136–40.

favourable coverage, rather than seek to coerce them. A further perceived problem, connected to commercial pressures, was that the press was prone to abusing its position, with journalists allegedly using inappropriate information-gathering methods and producing misleading stories. Individuals who were adversely impinged upon by such activities, it was held, lacked meaningful forms of redress. Yet for Parliament to take legal measures aimed at correcting these claimed problems would run counter to the powerful aversion that had developed against intervention in the field of the published word. Even during the twenty-first century (by which time newspapers existed in online as well as in physical formats), this tension continued to manifest itself, as demonstrated by arguments about the establishment of a legal regulator following the 'phone hacking' scandal of the early 2010s. Nearly four centuries after regular political media coverage – supported by the printing press – began, the relationship between its purveyors and Parliament remained uneasy.[86]

The terms of the debate about freedom of expression, the quality of discourse, and the role of public authorities could also change as new inventions came into use. From the 1920s onwards, broadcasting – first radio and then television – did not allow for the same degree of diversity of content as printing, partly because of bandwidth restrictions.[87] For these media, the model developed in the UK was broadly one of active regulation to ensure channels (both public and private) were editorially impartial while providing space for contrasting viewpoints.[88] Inevitably, this approach became subject to complaints that it operated in a way that was biased towards or away from particular viewpoints, or that it excluded certain outlooks, especially those that decision-makers deemed beyond the mainstream.[89] Some disliked the passivity broadcasting media supposedly instilled in their audience, and saw them as a potential tool of authoritarianism.[90]

Policymakers considering approaches to these newer devices might well have been aware of the historical context in which they operated. An official inquiry into the financing of the British Broadcasting Corporation (BBC) published in 1986, for example, drew attention to 'the analogy between broadcasting and publishing'. Noting that both had met with resistance from established groups in society which perceived them as 'dangerous', the text

[86] For an account of these issues produced by the most recent of a series of public inquiries into the press, see Lord Justice Leveson, *An Inquiry into the Culture, Practices and Ethics of the Press: Report*, vol. 1, HC 780–I (London, Stationery Office, 2012), esp. pp. 53–68.

[87] For recognition of this distinction, see *Report of the Committee on Financing the BBC*, Cmnd 9824 (1986), pp. 4–5.

[88] For a discussion of the 'public service broadcasting' principles and how they developed, see Colin Seymour-Ure, *The British Press and Broadcasting since 1945*, 2nd edn (Blackwell, Oxford, 1996), pp. 59–73.

[89] See Ch. 5 of this volume.

[90] See Ch. 4 of this volume.

went on to provide a truncated account of the development and decline of press censorship, from the mid-fifteenth century onwards. It included a reference to the reintroduction of censorship (by Parliament) 'in 1643 which prompted Milton to write the *Areopagitica* in favour of freedom of the press'.[91] An awareness and particular interpretation of past developments could also influence views within the UK Parliament of the specific approach it might take towards radio and television. In a debate on the possibility of sound and picture broadcasting of the House of Commons in November 1972, for instance, the Liberal MP David Steel explained that the Commons had long 'shown a strong resistance to allowing the public to have access to what goes on here'. In 1641 it had 'passed the Resolution making it a breach of privilege to report our proceedings'. As late as 1771 Parliament was 'still despatching printers and publishers of the proceedings of this House to the Tower'. Steel concluded that '[w]e ought not to be afraid . . . to allow the public direct access to what happens here. We should no longer accept the secondhand interpretations . . . [T]his House belongs not to us as some kind of exclusive club, but to the nation. If we believe that, we cannot deny the most effective medium of communication today between the politician and the public.'[92]

A further technology, the Internet, reframed the issues once more. As we will see later in this book, generally it potentially allowed for the widest imaginable range of contributors to express the most diverse span of views (as well as make contact with one another and organise politically). It could be a two-way medium with audience members potentially also being active producers. Parliament, as we will see, came to utilise the Internet, considerably more swiftly than it had printing. A motivation for this approach was the belief that the technology was potentially a positive force for political inclusion and could strengthen the relationship with the public. Computer-based communications became a central means of interaction between Parliament and the people it represented. But the Internet came increasingly to be regarded as a means of distortion, simplification, and dissemination of false information. Some complained that it was a mechanism for the promotion of manipulative propaganda, potentially from forces hostile to the interests of the UK and its political system. Rather than promoting moderate views, critics claimed, it favoured extremism. The issue of monopoly reasserted itself, with corporations such as Facebook and Google achieving predominance in their respective fields, and being judged to have attained immense power. By the beginning of the 2020s, increasing interest had developed within Parliament in bringing about regulation of the Internet to correct these perceived defects. Yet, were it to be implemented, it would have to manage dilemmas of the type Milton had helped identify long before.

[91] *Report of the Committee on Financing the BBC*, pp. 4–5.
[92] Hansard, HC Debates, 19 October 1972, cols. 483–4.

Literature, Scope, and Research Questions

A central tenet of this work, aspects of which are already addressed above, is that to understand the Internet and Parliament we must take a dynamic and broad approach. It is important to understand patterns of development prior to the introduction of this technology, and the way in which it, and uses made of it, changed thereafter. Also necessary is consideration of the wider context in which all these processes unfolded. In carrying out this task I engage with a variety of existing literature across a number of fields. To begin with my specific subject, there has been little direct consideration from a historic perspective of the relationship between the Internet and the UK Parliament, and nothing of book length, with the potential for detailed consideration such a format provides. A wide variety of works have taken a contemporary perspective on the implications of the Internet for democracy.[93] A recurring theme, particularly in the latter half of the 2000s, was the extent to which this network might help reverse a supposed decline in public engagement with the political system.[94] Often such contributions focused on the work of legislatures[95], sometimes specifically the UK Parliament.[96]

Some studies of the relationship between the Internet and democracy have recognised the importance of cumulative patterns of development over time. Matthew Hindman, for instance, has placed perceptions of the technology in the context of increasing interest in deliberative public engagement mechanisms in recent decades.[97] But the literature – including that which deals specifically with the UK Parliament – has tended not to emphasise the historical aspects of the subject. A notable contribution that did take this perspective came in an article by Stephen Coleman, a pre-eminent analyst of, and influence upon, the UK legislature in its employment of the Internet. Entitled 'Westminster in the Information Age', it appeared in a 1999 volume of which he was co-editor.[98] He placed parliamentary interaction with the Internet in the context of 'at least two previous "information revolutions"' in the preceding six centuries. Coleman identified the first as the introduction of

93 e.g. Jan A. G. M. Van Dijk and Kenneth L. Hacker, Internet and Democracy in the Network *Society* (Routledge, London, 2018).

94 See e.g. numerous contributions in Andrew Chadwick and Philip N. Howard (eds.), *The Routledge Handbook of Internet Politics* (Routledge, London, 2009).

95 Oxford Internet Institute, *Parliaments in the Digital Age* (Oxford Internet Institute, Oxford, 2008).

96 Richard Allan, 'Parliament, Elected Representatives and Technology 1997–2005 – Good in Parts?, *Parliamentary Affairs* 59(2) (2006): 360–5; Warner Lusoli, Stephen Ward, and Rachel Gibson, '(Re)connecting Politics? Parliament, the Public and the Internet', *Parliamentary Affairs* 59(1) (2006): 24–42.

97 Matthew Hindman, *The Myth of Digital Democracy* (Princeton University Press, 2009), ch. 1, esp. p. 7.

98 Stephen Coleman, 'Westminster in the Information Age' in Stephen Coleman, John Taylor, and Wim van de Donk (eds.), *Parliament in the Age of the Internet* (Oxford University Press, 1999), pp. 9–25.

printing, leading eventually to the appearance of Hansard. Second came 'the rise of telegraphy, followed by radio and then television'. He described how broadcasters gained, by 1958, the ability to cover matters addressed in Parliament as they arose. In doing so, they dispensed with the 'Fourteen Day' rule that had previously prevented them from dealing with issues likely to be addressed in the legislature in the following two weeks. Subsequently, regular radio broadcasts of proceedings began in 1978, and television followed for the House of Lords in 1985 and the House of Commons in 1989.[99]

Coleman took 1983 as the starting point for consideration specifically of computers and their uses. He uncovered a valuable source in an inquiry that the Computers Sub-Committee of the House of Commons Select Committee on Services instigated in this year into the information technology needs of MPs. It included a survey-based report from the Economist Intelligence Unit. Coleman considered subsequent contributions from the House of Commons Services Committee, from the House of Commons Information Committee and events leading to the establishment of the parliamentary website, parliament.uk. He identified individual parliamentarians who drove forward the use of computers and the Internet within the institution, and the influence derived both from UK civil society and from the observation of foreign practices.[100]

Based on this analysis, Coleman detected 'a pattern' that was generally discernible in the 'parliamentary response to new technologies of information and communication'. Initially, 'the new technology is distrusted and regarded as an intrusion into parliamentary business'. Subsequently, 'with some reluctance, the new technology is accepted and regulated rigidly'. Ultimately, it 'becomes an inherent part of parliamentary activity and MPs realise that they cannot operate without it'. At the time he wrote, Coleman perceived that 'the latest new technologies of electronic mail, the Internet and web-based discussion hover somewhere between the first and second stage of this process'. A 'distrust of the unknown' had lessened significantly 'as more MPs and their staff have become not only IT-literate, but PC-dependent'. As Coleman put it, 'Parliament has come to accept the regulated use of ICTs.'[101] This work will explore the thesis Coleman advanced in 1999. As I have already begun to do, I will consider how far common patterns can be identified in parliamentary responses to different technologies that have appeared over time. I broadly accept the interpretation he proposed as accurate at the time, but use a longer timeframe. As we will see, close parliamentary encounters with computing (and with the embryonic Internet) had already begun more than a decade before 1983. I commence in the early 1960s (while also reviewing other tendencies extending over centuries).

[99] Ibid., pp. 9–10.
[100] Ibid., pp. 10–16.
[101] Ibid., p. 10.

My research also antedates the starting point used by another historical overview, included in a 2007 report for the Hansard Society (to which Coleman was also attached at the time of his earlier work), *Parliament for the Future: Forecasting the Form of a Digitally-Enabled Parliament*. The authors, Ross Ferguson and Laura Miller, present a chronology of events that commences in 1980, followed by a narrative account, totalling seven pages.[102] As well as beginning my consideration at an earlier point, I have been able to expand on both works by considering the years subsequent to their respective dates of publication, considering events up to 2020. This extended timeframe provides a broader perspective on the theses these (relatively short) works present. It enables me to assess their veracity and to consider the relationship between developments in the periods they assess and those that come before and after.

Ferguson and Miller, like Coleman, suggest that we should perceive parliamentary usage of the Internet as a continuation of its approach to earlier technologies ('the printing press, telephone, radio, and television, for example'[103]). They also propose that we consider this development in a wider context, comparing Parliament to other private and public sector bodies, to discern similarities and differences of approach. The authors draw attention to Parliament's taking an interest in the use made of computers and the Internet in wider society.[104] They suggest an irregular process of development in parliamentary employment of computer technology from the early 1980s, to which an effort to provide library research support was important, and remark upon the activities of individuals and groups within the institution who promoted interest in this field. Ferguson and Miller note the rapid increase in public internet use from the late 1990s and the development of concerns about the existence of a 'digital divide', as well as supposed dangers connected to 'harm, offence and online security'. They see parliamentary committees and All-Party Parliamentary Groups (APPGs) as encouraging attention to such matters. The authors note that 'Parliament's own website was launched in autumn 1996' (though as we will see, there seems to have been an experimental service operational before this point). But they are critical of a perceived failure to develop online provision in the years that followed: 'it was based on static webpages and not upgraded until six years later in 2002'.[105] The authors remark that from 2001 there were improvements in the general availability of equipment through central provision. But MPs, they observe, displayed a reluctance – though gradually overcome – to engage fully with the potential of the Internet. The report encourages us to perceive parliamentary online activity from a number of perspectives: its website, its use of electronic

[102] Ross Ferguson and Laura Miller, *Parliament for the Future: Forecasting the Form of a Digitally-Enabled Parliament* (Hansard Society, London, 2007), pp. 2–9.

[103] Ibid., p. 4.

[104] Ibid., pp. 4–5.

[105] Ibid., p. 5.

forums and consultations, MPs' individual blogs and sites, the use of email, and participation in social media by MPs and by Parliament institutionally. It also takes into account the activities of Peers.[106]

The following work will engage with these various aspects, adding to them through the lengthened timeframe already set out. It will also expand upon Ferguson and Miller (and Coleman) by exploring in greater depth what were the main factors, from within and without the institution, driving and inhibiting employment of the Internet by Parliament; and what were the political and constitutional implications. I will consider the range of perceived options in the use of the technology on offer at given times and why some developments rather than others took place. My work seeks to apply a nuanced view of Parliament. When we consider it as an entity responding to and acting upon technological developments, it is important to understand what precisely it is. Rather than being a monolithic body, it is made up of diverse components. They include two chambers – the House of Commons and the House of Lords; multifarious committees; individual MPs in the Commons; and Peers in the Lords; officials; and entities such as the House of Commons and House of Lords libraries. They do not come under a single unified leadership as such. All played a distinct part in the history examined here. Attempts to assess how Parliament reacted to the Internet need to recognise this internal differentiation, and accordingly avoid generalisation.

The complexity of Parliament intensifies because the nature of these various elements, and the way in which they operate and interact with one another, was subject to significant change over the period of assessment.[107] In this respect, I intersect with, add to, and provide a new perspective on a variety of literature in this field, dealing with, for instance, developments in the Lords[108] and select committees in the Commons,[109] and in the behaviour of MPs.[110] It is useful to ask: how did the Internet fit into these patterns of change; what difference did they make to it, and it to them? One particular issue addressed is that of the concept of Parliament (and possibly democracy as a whole) as in some way being in decline, and what its interactions with the Internet reveal about this supposed tendency. As other scholars have suggested, claims about a deterioration in the status of the legislature are perennial. They may arise from observations of what are in fact set structural characteristics of the

[106] Ibid., pp. 6–10.

[107] See e.g. Alexandra Kelso, *Parliamentary Reform at Westminster* (Manchester University Press, 2009).

[108] e.g. Chris Ballinger, *The House of Lords 1911–2011: A Century of Non-Reform* (Oxford, Hart/Bloomsbury, 2009).

[109] e.g. Philip Aylett, 'Reform and Consolidation: A New Perspective on Commons Select Committees 1960–1980', *Parliamentary Affairs* 72(4) (2019): 742–60.

[110] e.g. Phil Cowley, *The Rebels: How Blair Mislaid His Majority* (Politico's/Methuen, London, 2005).

constitutional system, more than actual changes within it.[111] This point is significant because – as we will see – the Internet was for some a means of dealing with supposed difficulties of this nature.

This book also contributes to literature on the history of Parliament by considering the categories of consideration identified above with respect to previous studies of printing. In this context a series of further questions arise. First, what external social influences and pressures, connected to the Internet, were there upon Parliament? What implications did it have upon the constitutional status of Parliament? What implications were there for representative democracy? How were such developments perceived from within Parliament, and why did the institution respond to it in the ways it did? Secondly, what use did Parliament make of the Internet for its own purposes, applied both to its internal, day-to-day functions and its relations with the outside? What impact did its use of the Internet have upon its interactions with governmental institutions such as the UK executive, and with the public? How far were such activities new, or a continuation in online form of existing functions? Thirdly, what efforts has Parliament made to shape the application and social consequences of the Internet? Themes can recur across different categories, such as the idea that there was some kind of decline in the democratic system taking place that this communication system might help resolve. As we will see, given a historical perspective, this particular perception requires at the least careful qualification.

Beyond the specific focus on Parliament, the subject matter of this book makes it possible to contribute to the constitutional history of the UK. In part it hopes to complement the work of Jon Agar, who in *The Government Machine: A Revolutionary History of the Computer*, discusses the historic development of this device from the perspective of the UK executive. Agar includes discussion of the development and take-up of networked devices from the 1960s onwards, leading to 'the galloping enthusiasm for all things Internet' by the early twenty-first century.[112] I engage with these themes from the perspective of a different constitutional branch, the legislature. Accounts of the development of the UK system of government depict the period during which the Internet came into being and was eventually adopted by Parliament as one of significant constitutional change. Areas of development included participation (and eventually withdrawal from) the European Union; the rise of the referendum as a method of political decision-making; the introduction of devolution to Wales and Scotland (and its suspension and re-establishment in Northern Ireland).[113] Since Parliament is a principal organ of the UK

[111] Matthew Flinders and Alexandra Kelso, 'Mind the Gap: Political Analysis, Public Expectations and the Parliamentary Decline Thesis', *The British Journal of Politics and International Relations* 13(2) (2011): 249–68.

[112] Jon Agar, *The Government Machine: A Revolutionary History of the Computer* (MIT Press, Cambridge, 2003), p. 384.

[113] For my overview, see Andrew Blick, *Beyond Magna Carta: A Constitution for the United Kingdom* (Bloomsbury/Hart, Oxford, 2015), esp. Pt 2.

constitution, to consider its response to and employment of a given communications technology can provide a new aspect to this particular area of study. It is also possible to make some contributions to political history. I discuss how perceptions and uses of the Internet and associated technology have interacted with various outlooks, groupings, and movements. In exploring such associations, I seek to add to the work of scholars discussing the political orientation of particular groups interested in this communications technology.[114] This work seeks to add to media history in the UK, in particular developing concepts found in the study of printing and broadcasting and their political implications, including for Parliament.[115]

This book also seeks to make an addition in the field of Internet history. This sub-discipline has only begun properly to develop relatively recently, for the obvious reason that it deals with a relatively new technology. Probably the nearest equivalent to a beginning came on 29 October 1969, at about 10.30 p.m. Pacific Standard Time. At this moment, a computer housed in the University of California Los Angeles successfully connected with and then sent a message to another at the Stanford Research Institute (though initially there was a crash after the first two letters of the phrase 'LOGIN' had been sent and the operative at the Los Angeles end typed 'G'). [116] The link took place over the Advanced Research Projects Agency Network (ARPANET), an initiative of the US Department of Defense. The form of data transfer ARPANET used – 'packet switching', involving the division of a message into smaller units that are transmitted separately, each by the most efficient possible route, and then reassembled at point of destination – became a basis for the Internet technology. So too did the protocol it came to employ to determine all the particulars of how communication should take place – often known as TCP/IP (Transmission Control Protocol/Internet Protocol). By the time of the closure of ARPANET in 1990 the Internet, which it had made possible, was on the brink of a rise to intensive global penetration. Accepting the former system as progenitor of the latter provides us with half a century, and rising, of history to consider.[117]

Internet history is a growing field with its own dedicated journal.[118] I respond to and engage with a number of aspects of it that have emerged. One facet of the work of scholars in this area is that of its prehistory – ideas and technology antedating the Internet and providing a revealing perspective

[114] Z. Isadora Hellegren, 'A History of Crypto-Discourse: Encryption as a Site of Struggles to Define Internet Freedom', *Internet Histories* 1(4) (2017): 285–311, 289.

[115] See e.g. Seymour-Ure, *The British Press and Broadcasting since 1945*; Bob Franklin, 'Televising the British House of Commons: Issues and Developments' in Bob Franklin (ed.), *Televising Democracies* (Routledge, London, 1992), pp. 3–26.

[116] Katie Hafner and Matthew Lyon, *Where Wizards Stay Up Late: The Origins of the Internet* (Simon and Schuster, New York, 2006), p. 153.

[117] For ARPANET as the beginning of the Internet, see Paloque-Bergès and Schafer, 'ARPANET (1969–2019)'.

[118] *Internet Histories.*

upon it.[119] A productive activity in this regard has been tracing the impact of 'countercultural' social movements that became prominent in the 1960s upon later perceptions and uses of the Internet. Its significance to the subject of the Internet and the UK Parliament might not be immediately evident. But my work will demonstrate it is in fact of high salience from this point of view. It involves the development of the idea of employing the technology for purposes of democratic engagement, in ways that could be both challenging and beneficial to Parliament. Indeed, efforts to explain how the Internet came to be seen and then employed as a means of enhanced involvement of the public in political processes (for good or otherwise) have concentrated on the countercultural contribution perhaps more than any other. A purpose of this book is to ask how far can we can detect the influence of this movement specifically in parliamentary engagement with the Internet, and what such a consideration in turn reveals about the counterculture and its significance for this technology.

A brief elaboration of this school is appropriate at this point. A reading of this particular literature conveys that the upheaval of the 1960s should not be considered as constituting a single, homogenous force. Fred Tuner, for instance, makes distinctions between the 'New Left', focused on political action, and the more inward-facing 'counterculture'.[120] Others present the 'New Left' as itself a part of the counterculture.[121] In this work, I employ the term counterculture generally to apply to a movement and set of sub-movements, with a strong youth aspect to them, the participants in which were self-consciously challenging what they saw as established authorities and behaviours, to varying extents in political or cultural senses. While applying this label I recognise that it is far from precise and open to a variety of challenges. As the historian Theodore Roszak, in a 1969 work that popularised the term 'counter culture' (he used two separate words at this point), put it: 'As a subject of study, the counter culture with which this book deals possesses all the liabilities which a decent sense of intellectual caution would persuade one to avoid like the plague.'[122] I proceed – with the reticence this passage inspires – on the grounds that there is much potential analytical benefit to be obtained from consideration of the counterculture concept.

Notwithstanding definitional challenges, observers have identified a set of intersections between such tendencies originating in the 1960s and internet culture. Stewart Brand was an entrepreneur in the realm of ideas whose personal career trajectory – as we will see – embodied this link. In a 1995 article

[119] Weber, 'A Common Language', pp. 28–9.

[120] A differentiation used in Fred Turner, *From Counterculture to Cyberculture: Stewart Brand, the Whole Earth Network, and the Rise of Digital Utopianism* (University of Chicago Press, 2008).

[121] Richard Barbrook and Andy Cameron, 'The Californian Ideology' *Science as Culture* 6(1) (1996): 44–72.

[122] Theodore Roszak, *The Making of a Counter Culture: Reflections on the Technocratic Society and Its Youthful Opposition* (Anchor Books, Garden City, 1969), p. xi.

for *Time* that drew on three decades of experience, he wrote: '[f]orget antiwar protests, Woodstock, even long hair. The real legacy of the sixties generation is the computer revolution.' The Internet, rather than being 'some soulless colony of technocrats' struck those first encountering it as 'a flowering remnant of the '60s, when hippie communalism and libertarian politics formed the roots of the modern cyberrevolution'. Brand held that 'the counterculture's scorn for centralized authority provided the philosophical foundations of not only the leaderless Internet but also the entire personal-computer revolution'.[123] He noted the influences on this cohort of promoters of technology included the cultural theorist Marshall McLuhan and the designer and philosopher Buckminster Fuller, describing how 'we bought enthusiastically into the exotic technologies of the day, such as Fuller's geodesic domes and psychoactive drugs like LSD'. While '[m]ost of our generation scorned computers as the embodiment of centralized control . . . a tiny contingent – later called "hackers" – embraced computers and set about transforming them into tools of liberation'. They were the ancestors of those who, in the 1990s, 'transformed the Defense Department-sponsored ARPAnet into what has become the global digital epidemic known as the Internet.'[124]

Considering the same general theme, in his 2008 work, *From Counterculture to Cyberculture*,[125] Turner discerns within the counterculture a subcategory he labels 'new communalism'. In his account, the concept of the Internet as an environment suited to the better realisation of humanity was a transposition of earlier – failed – attempts, that began in the 1960s, to leave behind the urban environment and establish new communities. Though based in rural settings and in some senses rejecting modernity, Turner shows, participants in this movement saw value in technological inventions, including computers, as a means of assisting their cause. I give particular attention in this work to the nature and genesis of the idea of the Internet as more than just a device and as composing a landscape or world: a concept that eventually appeared in parliamentary considerations of the technology. The New Left also figures in the literature as an influence on perceptions of the Internet. In a 1996 article, entitled 'The Californian Ideology', Barbrook and Cameron detected in the ideas of the former a source for interpretations of the latter as a vehicle for radical democracy.[126] As we will see, ideas with a New Left flavour figured in early advocacy of computer-based democracy by a leading UK politician. For Barbrook and Cameron, the values of the earlier movement became distorted in translation. They presented mid-1990s ideas about the transformative impact of the Internet as derived in part from West Coast radical activism of the 1960s. But, they concluded, while this school had

[123] Stewart Brand, 'We Owe It All to the Hippies', *Time Magazine* 145(12), 1 March 1995.
[124] Ibid.
[125] Turner, *From Counterculture to Cyberculture*, esp. ch. 1.
[126] Barbrook and Cameron, 'The Californian Ideology', p. 46.

promoted democratic political participation, an economic variant of libertarianism, emphasising freedom of market transactions, had now gained force. This transition, in their view, entailed a neglect of causes that had once been central to the movement that commenced in the 1960s, such as social and racial equality and protection of the environment.[127]

A central purpose of this work is to investigate and expand upon such ideas through the specific prism I employ. In particular, I challenge aspects of a particular thesis advanced in this field. Writing decades after his earlier work on the counterculture, Roszak observed a link between this phenomenon and digital technology. In 1994 he described the role played by computer enthusiasts who appeared from the late 1960s, 'emerging mainly on the West Coast from the ranks of the antiwar movement ... who were destined to give the computer a dramatically new image and a political orientation ... At their hands, information technology would make its closest approach to becoming an instrument of democratic politics.'[128] In discussing their orientation, Roszak makes an important claim. He holds that '[u]topian visions of the future have generally been divided between two philosophical camps'. He described the first as 'the *reversionary* scenario'. It involved 'wishing the world away'. An archetypal exponent of this perspective was '[t]he nineteenth century socialist leader and artist William Morris'. The second category comprised 'other utopians – the *technophiles*' who 'enthusiastically embraced the urban-industrial system'. They anticipated that it would 'mature into a wholly new order of life in which science and technology have permanently mastered the forces of nature and have undertaken to redesign the planet'. In this group Roszak placed Francis Bacon and H. G. Wells.

He then claimed that the movement centring on the West Coast of the 1960s with which he was concerned represented a departure from these dichotomous categories and was in this sense 'unique'. What made participants in this tendency different was their 'determination to synthesize these two seemingly contradictory images. They wanted to have it both ways.' People of this type were attracted by their disposition and abilities 'to the expansion of high tech'. They therefore 'had no hesitation in seeking to play through the full repertory of computer electronics and global telecommunications'. Yet at the same time, 'the new technology would be contained within an organic and communitarian political context'.[129] The present book partially accepts the important observation Roszak made. Social movements of the 1960s certainly had implications for the development and for perceptions of the possible applications of networked computers. The technology and

[127] Ibid.

[128] Theodore Roszak, *The Cult of Information: A Neo-Luddite Treatise on High-Tech, Artificial Intelligence, and the True Art of Thinking* (University of California Press, Berkeley, 1994), p. 138.

[129] Ibid., p. 146.

approaches that came into being, partly as a consequence of this pattern of influence, provided the context in which Parliament adopted the Internet. But the particular outlook Roszak identified, rather than being an entirely new combination, was the extension of a tradition. Within it, a series of exponents have argued that a better society is obtainable through the harnessing of technology, but in accordance with specifically defined human values.

The following chapters will demonstrate this point and its significance, including through the reassessment of thinkers such as Morris, Bacon (already discussed), and Wells. While Roszak places them on one side or the other of a divide, in some respects they transcended it, just as some participants in the counterculture he describes would do subsequently. Nonetheless, like Roszak, I recognise that for there to be a school of thought that seeks to 'have it both ways', it is necessary to have contrasting narratives around the social role of technology. In identifying such competing views, I will engage with the output of scholars in this field including W. Russell Neuman. In his 1991 work *The Future of the Mass Audience*, Neuman sought to analyse more and less optimistic schools of thought regarding digital communications and democracy. In doing so, he noted that this discussion had antecedence, including in the immediate post-Second World War period. Neuman showed how, during this period, one theoretical approach identified a 'mass society' in which communications technology could facilitate governmental manipulation of the population. A contrasting frame of interpretation at the time came from 'development theory', according to which media mechanisms could stimulate democratic development.[130] The themes Neuman identified came to be taken up by many others over the subsequent two decades, whether or not they were aware of the extent to which they were retreading old ground. They clearly emerge in a study of the Internet and Parliament. One point I make here is that there are two central means through which such ideas attain persistence. One is via particular expressions of concepts achieving specific influence on others who take them on in some form (or react against them). Another is that they can occur and reoccur spontaneously, without those adopting them necessarily being aware of their provenance. The reasons they do so might be their explanatory or motivational strength, or that they fulfil particular needs.

An important part of the historical approach to the Internet employed here is emphasising that technological development can be a protracted process and that patterns of usage are difficult to predict in advance. I take into account the work of, for instance, the Internet historian Z. Isadora Hellegren in this respect. Hellegren notes the lag that can occur between an invention taking place and its coming more widely into use, and the possible distinction between the purpose for which it was designed and the

[130] W. Russell Neuman, *The Future of the Mass Audience* (Cambridge University Press, 1991), pp. 22–47.

actual application to which it was put.[131] Hellegren also describes how technological advances – such as mass usage audio-visual communications devices – can come into being in a workable sense only after long periods of anticipation and experimentation.[132] Historians have proposed, moreover, that consideration be given to the significance of technological paths not taken – ideas that, for whatever reason, were not implemented or proved not to be viable. Agar describes frustrated efforts in the 1960s to introduce 'a national packet-switching network' in the UK.[133] Marc Weber notes that during the early years of the Internet technology in the 1970s, other, commercial, computer-based telecommunication systems that later fell into disuse were more significant.[134] In this work, rather than focusing solely on the emergence of a precise technology, I consider wider conceptions at various points before and after the ascendancy of the Internet (including in the 1970s) of electronic or digital networks and their possible uses. It is important to adopt a nuanced version of causality. As three authors concerned with internet history have conveyed, there is scope for varied interpretations about whether developments are the work of groups or of individual people; how far they are the outcome of prior intent or chance; and the extent to which technical imperatives, or the needs of consumers, brought them about.[135] We need, as Andrew L. Russell puts it, to avoid a 'whiggish approach that is common throughout histories of science, technology and medicine', that treats 'the Internet's creation and development' as a story of 'success and triumph'. An approach that avoids these faults needs, in the process, to recognise 'that the Internet is flawed, dangerous and ephemeral'.[136]

A group of authors have recommended that, given 'the essential plurality of the Internet', the historians of this entity shift to a 'historiography rooted in the experience of users'.[137] The UK Parliament might be regarded as a user rather than a creator, as can the members of the public with whom it has sought to engage using this medium. Leopoldina Fortunati makes a similar point, arguing that 'we need to explore more concerning how the Internet is used, when, where, how and by whom for communication, information, knowledge, teaching and learning, sociability, political organisation and business'.[138] A study of parliamentary engagement with the technology offers to

[131] Hellegren, 'A History of Crypto-Discourse'.

[132] Benjamin Burroughs, 'A Cultural Lineage of Streaming', *Internet Histories* 3(2) (2019): 147–61, 8.

[133] Agar, *The Government Machine*, p. 381.

[134] Weber, 'A Common Language', p. 27.

[135] Valérie Schafer, Sarah Cooper, and Camille Paloque-Bergès, 'Back to the Roots of ARPANET and Internet History with Alexandre Serres', *Internet Histories* 3(1) (2019): 51–67, 54–5.

[136] Andrew L. Russell, 'Hagiography, Revisionism and Blasphemy in Internet Histories', *Internet Histories* 1(1–2) (2017): 15–25, 22.

[137] Kevin Driscoll and Camille Paloque-Berges, 'Searching for Missing "Net Histories"', *Internet Histories* 1(1–2) (2017): 47–59, 56.

[138] Leopoldina Fortunat, 'For a Dynamic and Post-Digital History of the Internet: A Research Agenda', *Internet Histories* 1(1–2) (2017): 180–7, 180.

contribute to such a project. The Fortunati remark comes from an important 2017 article in which the author notes the difficulties in 'making Internet history' owing to 'the breadth and complexity of such a technological artefact and of social relations it entails'. Fortunati proposes various means of managing this challenge, in the form of 'urgent research directions'. Those of particular significance to this work include the issue of 'regulation' – something in which Parliament came to take an interest; the consideration of the Internet in the context of other technologies and media – an objective of this book; and, finally, the taking into account of the idea of 'sociability', meaning that 'especially ... after the advent of social networks' that the Internet has become 'the place in which the self of the humankind has had the possibility to network for the first time on a very large scale'.[139] This aspect of the technology was a pre-eminent concern within Parliament as it considered how it might use and impact upon the Internet.

The United States – and in particular parts of California – has been a centre of the computer industry and philosophising about its implications (and the West Coast was previously a hub for the counterculture). Understandably, it has been the subject for much attention in Internet history,[140] the 'US-centric'[141] nature of which has been remarked upon. The extent to which we should regard the technology as American is a subject of interest for historians.[142] In this work I shift the focus to developments in the British Isles (and to some extent elsewhere in Europe), and their interaction with the United States. In pursuing this approach, I follow the lead of those Internet historians who have lately sought to extend such research beyond the United States[143] – for instance, to the Global South – emphasising the plurality of their subject.[144] However, I do so by shifting attention to a territory that is now a developed economy, and which has been historically, culturally, and linguistically intertwined with the United States, an association that necessarily receives consideration. In particular, I challenge the claim advanced by James W. Carey and John J. Quirk that there is 'a unique American idea of a new dimension in social existence through which people might return to an Edenic estate through a

[139] Ibid.

[140] See e.g. the remark in Burroughs, 'A Cultural Lineage of Streaming', p. 13.

[141] Driscoll and Paloque-Berges, 'Searching for Missing "Net Histories"', p. 56.

[142] Camille Paloque-Bergès and Valérie Schafer, 'French Memories about the ARPANET: A Conversation with Michel Élie and Gérard Le Lann', *Internet Histories* 3 (1) (2019): 81–97; Schafer, Cooper, and Paloque-Bergès, 'Back to the Roots of ARPANET and Internet History with Alexandre Serres', pp. 61–2.

[143] Mark McLelland, 'Early Challenges to Multilingualism on the Internet: The Case of Han Character-Based Scripts', *Internet Histories* 1(1–2) (2017): 119–28; Patrick Pétin and Félix Tréguer, 'Building and Defending the Alternative Internet: The Birth of the Digital Rights Movement in France', *Internet Histories* 2(3–4) (2018): 281–98.

[144] Herman Wasserman, 'African Histories of the Internet', *Internet Histories* 1(1–2) (2017): 129–37,

harmonious blending of nature and manufactures'.[145] While Roszak was wrong to claim that such an outlook was the creation of the counterculture in the 1960s, their error was in attaching it to one country. This book demonstrates that such perceptions of the incorporation of the technological and the natural have a strong basis in thought originating in the UK and its precursors.

I extend upon the work of historians who have assessed earlier technological developments,[146] and in particular those pertaining to communications, such as the printing press,[147] radio, and television,[148] and their significance, including from the perspective of the UK Parliament (or its English forerunner).[149] Analysis of the Internet, by historians[150] and others, often seeks to place it in the context of such earlier technologies.[151] Some accounts make passing references to such possible comparators,[152] while others are more systematic.[153] I pursue the latter approach and relate it to the specific subject of the UK Parliament, in its wider context, considering a long historical span of events. Analysis of these past occurrences suggests a series of questions it is important to bear in mind when addressing my subject: how should we define a particular communications technology? At what point or over what period did it come into being? How did it change over time? What resistance to and support for its implementation existed? To what extent, when, how quickly, how, and why did it come to be utilised in practice? What uses was it put to and did they change? How did contemporaries perceive it, and what discussions did they have about it? To what form of regulation was it subject?[154] What impact did it have, and how far

145 James W. Carey with John J. Quirk, 'The Mythos of the Electronic Revolution' in James W. Carey, *Communication as Culture: Essays on Media and Society* (Routledge, London, 1992), pp. 113–41, 118.

146 David E. Nye, *Electrifying America: Social Meanings of a New Technology* (MIT Press, Cambridge, 1992).

147 For contrasting views, see Eisenstein, *The Printing Revolution in Early Modern Europe*; Johns, *The Nature of the Book*.

148 e.g. Richard Barbrook, *Media Freedom: The Contradictions of Communication in the Age of Modernity* (Pluto, London, 1995); Seymour-Ure, *The British Press and Broadcasting since 1945*.

149 For printing and English/British Isles politics, including Parliament, see Raymond, *Pamphlets and Pamphleteering in Early Modern Britain*; Peacey, *Print and Public Politics in the English Revolution*. For a multi-author collection on the televising of Parliament, including historical material, see Bob Franklin (ed.), *Televising Democracies* (Routledge, London, 1992), e.g. Franklin, 'Televising the Commons', pp. 17–26.

150 Weber, 'A Common Language', pp. 28–30.

151 Floridi, *The 4th Revolution*, p. 5.

152 e.g. Amnesty International, *Surveillance Giants: How the Business Model of Google and Facebook Threatens Human Rights* (Amnesty International, London, 2019), p. 5. Rheingold, *The Virtual Community*, p. 279.

153 e.g. Naughton, *From Gutenberg to Zuckerberg*; Tom Standage, *Writing on the Wall: The Intriguing History of Social Media, from Ancient Rome to the Present Day* (Bloomsbury, London, 2014).

154 e.g. Patrice Flichy, *The Internet Imaginaire* (MIT Press, Cambridge, 2007), pp. 158–9.

was that impact inherent within the invention itself, or the product of the social environment in which it functioned?

A rich body of work considers historical perceptions of technology, including its political implications. Some of it has extended analysis to encompass the Internet and related fields. Sadie Plant, for instance, takes this approach in her discussion of the relationship between feminism and computers – including the Internet – over a period from the early nineteenth century onwards.[155] I follow some of this work in accepting the view it advances that the mythology surrounding inventions (actual or anticipated) amounts to something more than falsification. As Vincent Mosco puts it in his 2004 work, *The Digital Sublime: Myths, Power, and Cyberspace*: '[u]seful as it is to recognize the lie in the myth, it is important to state at the outset that myths mean more than falsehoods or cons: indeed they matter greatly'. For him '[m]yths are stories that animate individuals and societies by providing paths to transcendence that lift people out of the banality of everyday life. They offer an entrance to another reality.' They 'are not true or false, but living or dead. "Disproving" a myth by pointing to its failure to conform to an accepted truth or to evidence usually does little to dispel it.' Mosco holds that proper appreciation of 'a myth' necessitated 'figuring out why the myth exists, why it is so important to people, what it means, and what it tells us about people's hopes and dreams'.[156]

As this passage suggests, by shaping perception, myth helps determine the way in which technology develops, the environment into which it appears, and the use made of it. Patrice Flichy, whose book *The Internet Imaginaire* appeared in an English translation in 2007 (following its publication in French in 2001), presents a similar approach. He proposes a framework for the analysis of the Internet from the point of view of perception surrounding it, of which myth forms a part. Flichy explores the motives of 'actors as different as computer scientists who design software, managers and employees who have to produce and coordinate within their firms, individuals who interact and entertain themselves at home, or politicians who dialogue with citizens' in universally consenting to become Internet users. He enquires further: '[w]hy did computer scientists, sometimes voluntarily, design this technique rather than another one in the first place?' Moreover, Flichy asks why 'ordinary people agreed to' acquire knowledge about this technology and then 'use the Internet for activities as commonplace as communicating with their family or friends, conducting information searches, or listening to music, as well as for design, administrative, or managerial work?' He concludes it is necessary to consider what 'are the social actors' frame of representation of the new technique'.[157]

155 Sadie Plant, *zeros + ones* (Fourth Estate, London, 1997), pp. 5–9.
156 Vincent Mosco, *The Digital Sublime: Myths, Power, and Cyberspace* (MIT Press, Cambridge, 2004), pp. 1–3, 29.
157 Ibid., p. 2.

Flichy consequently contends that a proper means of analysis of the Internet (as for other technologies) involves placing it in a framework wider than that of inventors and their work. Within his thesis, perceptions of the potential, the appropriate application, and the possible effects of a given mechanism are central to the actual outcome. Flichy refers to a 'corpus of discourses' that motivates choices made during scientific development and has an impact upon the public in the extent of its take-up and the way in which it employs a particular device.[158] His analytical technique divides them into three types: 'myth' – that is, tales or images that depict a wider concept; utopias, that make it possible to appreciate 'the full range of possibilities'; and ideologies, functioning as a mechanism for introducing new systems.[159]

I apply this general approach, assessing the ideas shaping parliamentary approaches to the Internet, and where they originated from. This perspective follows the views of David Streeter, who calls for an approach to internet history that 'would emphasise that cultural expectations of the Internet shaped the development of and thus are part of the artefact itself'. As Streeter writes, '[c]ultural expectations and technological artefacts exist in an inextricably intertwined way. Technologies are perhaps best understood, not so much as agents in their own right, but as thought-objects for the collective enactment and exploration of hopes, desires and political visions.'[160]

Some of the literature suggests that, when identifying perceptions or myths surrounding technology, it is possible to discern a cyclical pattern. Particular inventions – including electrical communications devices – have gained support as a potential means of achieving sweeping social improvement, and perhaps of overcoming problems caused by earlier inventions. Yet the new advances came to disappoint, themselves figuring in accounts of perceived shortcomings, possibly promoted by those who were previously enthusiastic about them. Another invention could then appear as a potential source of redemption.[161] This work explores perceptions of this kind from the particular standpoint of communications technology and its political implications. It holds that in some senses this pattern of high expectation and despondency has played out with respect to the Internet and the UK Parliament.

The book discusses the implications of its findings for policymakers. It treats this category broadly as including all those involved in influencing and making decisions that have a general social impact, extending to, for instance, government officials, journalists, academics, think tanks, charities,

[158] Ibid., p. 7.

[159] Ibid., pp. 7–12.

[160] Streeter, 'The Internet as a Structure of Feeling: 1992–1996', p. 86.

[161] See e.g. Carey with Quirk, 'The Mythos of the Electronic Revolution', p. 129; James W. Carey with John J. Quirk, 'The History of the Future' in James W. Carey, *Communication as Culture: Essays on Media and Society* (Routledge, London, 1992), pp. 173–200, 178; Mosco, *The Digital Sublime*, pp. 117–40, and for disillusion among those who previously advocated radio, see in particular p. 132.

and private corporations. History does not provide precise prescriptions (indeed, no one discipline can do so). But it can supply a contextual background. It helps, for example, to distinguish that which is genuinely new from that which is pre-existing, or part of an established cycle. Such insight can, in turn, guide policymakers, helping them to identify and respond appropriately to risk and opportunities, avoiding both overreaction and failure to act or to do so with sufficient force, when required. History can also furnish examples of past approaches to analogous circumstances, including their successes and shortcomings, to take into account. In his historical analysis Weber identifies how choices made in the formative stages of the implementation of a technology can have lasting and major consequences. As Weber remarks, the contemporary Internet is in a comparable stage of development. It is important that those making regulatory decisions in this field are aware, on past evidence, of the scale of the impact they might have.[162]

Policymakers often conceive of the challenges they face in historical terms. In a speech given as US Secretary of State in 2010, for instance, Hillary Clinton presented the Internet in the context of previous developments. She likened it to the telegraph as an earlier device the introduction of which had impacted upon patterns of communication and the functioning of US foreign policy. She also recalled 'the courageous men and women' of the Eastern Bloc during the Cold War era who had 'made the case against oppression by circulating small pamphlets called samizdat ... their words helped pierce the concrete and concertina wire of the Iron Curtain'. In the contemporary world, Clinton noted, authoritarian regimes were creating 'electronic barriers that prevent their people from accessing portions of the world's networks'. Tactics included removing 'words, names, and phrases from search engine results' and intruding into 'the privacy of citizens who engage in non-violent political speech'. Clinton concluded that 'a new information curtain is descending across much of the world.' Behind it, 'viral videos and blog posts are becoming the samizdat of our day'.[163]

Regardless of the extent to which one accepts such analogies, they can form part of the narratives that policymakers deploy when presenting their actions. It is reasonable to assume that they also help provide the conceptual basis for decisions themselves. Writers such as Evgeny Morozov, a critic of the Clinton narrative, have therefore called for a more sophisticated consideration of history in contemporary analysis of the Internet, especially in its relationship with the promotion of democracy. Morozov has questioned, for instance, the degree of importance attached to *samizdat* publishing in undermining

[162] Weber, 'A Common Language', pp. 28–9.

[163] Hillary Rodham Clinton, United States Secretary of State, 'Remarks', The Newseum, Washington DC, 21 January 2010, available at: https://ia800706.us.archive.org/20/items/Index_20180423/Index.html https://2009-2017.state.gov/secretary/20092013clinton/rm/2010/01/135519.htm, last accessed 4 February 2020.

Communism, insisting that '[t]o argue that it was the photocopies that triggered change in Russia and then the rest of the region is to engage in such a grotesque simplification of history that one may as well abandon practising history altogether'. He did not seek 'to deny that they played a role, but only to deny the monocausal relationship that many want to establish'.[164]

Taking into account these reservations, using the perspective that the past provides, this work considers the present debate about the Internet and politics. What are the consequences of this technology for democracy? Are they detrimental or supportive? Do they drive it to change in some way? How far is it appropriate to regard the Internet as having revolutionary implications? Is it appropriate to perceive it as associated with the emergence of a world of its own? What are the specific implications for the UK Parliament? Overall, what conclusions should we draw regarding the importance of the Internet – in absolute terms, and relative to other comparable inventions? What can we learn about the relationship between technology and politics?

Structure, Methods, and Sources

The structure of the book is as follows. Chapter 1 sets out the scope of the debate about the Internet, including its implications for democracy, in the period since 1990. It considers definitions of the Internet and concepts such as technological determinism, and identifies key themes considered in the remainder of the book, as well as the policy dilemmas at stake. Chapter 2 gives an overview of the use Parliament has made of this technology in the period since the autumn of 1996, when – after an experimental phase – the parliamentary website launched in full form. It focuses on what happened, with discussion of why and how taking place subsequently. Chapter 3 considers the development of ideas about the transformative potential of technology up to 1945. It centres upon thought in the UK, also taking into account contributions in the United States and in mainland Europe, on the grounds that while it is possible to concentrate on one geographical location, such categorisation has limitations and no one territory exists in isolation. Chapter 4 continues the discussion of scientific invention in political thought from 1945 up to 1990. While any cut-off point has an arbitrary aspect, selecting 1945 – a commonly chosen end or start date in historical studies – has value. As Neuman records, the Second World War produced 'some spectacular technological breakthroughs in rocketry, atomic energy, high-frequency radio, and electronic computing'. In the period that followed, television sets disseminated swiftly and 'rockets lifted communications satellites to connect the world with instantaneous electronic communications'. Moreover, 'the computer moved from a room-size, multi-million-dollar

[164] Evgeny Morozov, *The Net Delusion: How Not to Liberate the World* (Penguin, London, 2011), p. 53.

prototype to a desktop model for the home, priced in the same range as a color television set'.[165] During this era the computer became increasingly prominent, and the Internet came into being. The chapter takes a particular focus on these developments and the response to them, alongside other communications technology.

Chapter 5 discusses the political and constitutional context in the UK within which the Internet came into use. It discusses the ideas one senior UK politician, Tony Benn, promoted in the field of technology and communication. The chapter considers the constitutional framework and the ways in which it was changing, including a discussion of the introduction of radio and television broadcasting of Parliament. The chapter then presents two case studies of connection between activism and the Internet. The first considers a subset of the environmental movement during the 1970s and early 1980s, associates of which promoted the use of 'Alternative Technologies'. The second assesses a cluster of groups in the UK in the mid-to-late 1990s employing the Internet as a device for promoting community activism and wider participation in policy formation. The overall purpose of Chapter 5 is to convey the structural, political, and ideological framework through which the Internet became a factor and to understand dynamics that were at work, revealing and shaping the environment in which the meeting of Parliament and this technology took place.

In Chapter 6, the book considers developments within Parliament from the 1960s up to 1996. During this period the Internet came into being as a technology, eventually achieving international dissemination and usage. The chapter discusses attitudes within Parliament towards computers in general, and the idea of their being employed as networked communications devices – though not necessarily as part of the Internet – during this period. It assesses steps taken towards adoption of associated technologies, and the eventual focus that developed on the Internet. Chapter 7 returns to the subject of parliamentary use of this technology during 1996–2020 first discussed in Chapter 2, taking into account the observations made in the intervening portions of the book. It considers specifically what motivated parliamentary use of the Internet, what were the objectives of its employment, and what barriers existed to the take-up and use of it. Chapter 8 covers the same period, but focuses on the ways in which Parliament perceived wider social application of the Internet, the policy options it promoted, and the impact it had. The conclusion offers a general account of the perception of technology and politics, and considers patterns of practical development, focused on Parliament. It considers the implications for policymakers.

I use two methodological techniques of particular relevance from the perspective of the subject matter of this book. I propose here a tripartite

[165] Neuman, *The Future of the Mass Audience*, p. 22.

distinction, that builds partly on work by Richard Rogers.[166] The first is digital history – that is, research conducted using technologies such as online search facilities. The second is that of Internet history – the study of developments over time connected to the Internet. As I have noted, this branch of the discipline is passing through a process of enrichment and refinement, to which I hope to contribute. I take a lead from others already working in the field in favouring a broad approach to the subject. The third is web history – the study of online content, such as comparisons between different websites at a given point, or of successive changes to a particular site. In Chapter 2, I carry out an exercise of the latter type with respect to the parliamentary website during the period 1996–2020. I have utilised the Wayback Machine, provided by the Internet Archive to enable searches for historic snapshots of online material, as well as electronic parliamentary depositories of social media content.[167] A technique I apply is to frame discussion through analysis of the earliest available version of the homepage of parliament.uk, from 1996, and a version from April 2020. The chapter treats these sources as both revealing and limited, extracting meaning from them in their own right, while providing contextual material and analysis. Like all methods of historical research, web history has limitations. There will always be barriers to the full reconstruction of the actual past experience of use.[168] Furthermore, the availability of material has an arbitrary aspect, and is constrained and shaped by earlier retention policies.

The book also relies on more traditional techniques (though often conducted partly through the use of digital technology – in this sense, the subject I research, parliamentary engagement with the Internet, has made the research itself possible). I make extensive use of materials produced by the UK Parliament, including the Hansard record of debates and questions in both Houses. The work attaches particular significance to the activities of parliamentary committees of various types. They are significant in that they express a collective view, if not on behalf of the whole of Parliament, at least of the cross-party membership of the body concerned (to which other parliamentarians also might choose to defer). They seek to provide reasoning for the conclusions they reach and act as a focus for public discourse on the subjects they address in that they receive, publish, and engage with evidence from outside groups and individuals. Clearly, the final content they produce is the outcome of various preconceptions and internal trade-offs, rather than a pure

[166] Richard Rogers 'Doing Web History with the Internet Archive: Screencast Documentaries', *Internet Histories* 1(1–2) (2017): 160–72, 161.

[167] For a discussion of archives of online material see e.g. Jane Winters 'Breaking in to the Mainstream: Demonstrating the Value of Internet (and Web) Histories', *Internet Histories* 1 (1–2) (2017): 173–9, 173.

[168] For a discussion of some of the challenges in this area, see Gerard Alberts, Marc Went, and Robert Jansma, 'Archaeology of the Amsterdam Digital City; Why Digital Data Are Dynamic and Should Be Treated Accordingly', *Internet Histories* 1(1–2) (2017): 146–59.

consideration of the material they receive, which might itself have its own distortions. Nonetheless, committee publications can represent substantial outputs that provide insight into attitudes prevailing at the time they were published, and which themselves have in some instances influenced outcomes. I focus less on the activities of individual parliamentarians in their own right or on political and electoral campaigning, though these areas could clearly merit analysis in a different work. A source not utilised (though, again, one certainly of immense potential for other studies), which is technically a parliamentary product, is that of legislation. While Parliament makes law, generally it emerges in the first instance from the executive, albeit subject to various external influences including the legislature. I do take into account those occasions on which parliamentarians have called for particular forms of legislation, though I do not focus on the texts that might ultimately emerge.

In seeking to understand perceptions and myths surrounding technology – including but extending beyond the Internet – I consult a variety of primary texts including pamphlets, books, periodical articles, and diaries. I expand into the consideration of works of fiction. Such literature can illuminate general patterns of thought, and can influence the perceptions of others, often powerfully and for long periods of time. Examples from fiction can feature prominently in political rhetoric, deployed in support of particular cases. Studying this type of material and its impact can reveal the form that myths can assume, how they can take hold, and the uses made of them. One example that helps illustrate the potential influence of speculative or science fiction is a Fabian Society pamphlet from 1978. Entitled *The Computer and Society*, it was the work of two computer scientists based at Thames Polytechnic, Tom Crowe and John Hywel-Jones. They considered subjects including the embryonic Internet.[169] Though their principal focus was on contemporary matters and the implications of scientific developments, Crowe and Hywel-Jones overtly demonstrated how historical assessment and awareness of creative writing shaped their perspective. They opened by noting that George Bernard Shaw, an early Fabian and playwright, had in 1918, writing in *New Left Review*, predicted that medical facilities would one day use 'machines' that would be able, by processing 'symptoms', to diagnose illnesses and prescribe 'treatment ... according to rule', issuing them on 'a card'. The authors, in illustrating the connection between technological and social change, then went on to cite the 1872 satirical fantasy novel by Samuel Butler, *Erehwon*, and the E. M. Forster 1909 short story, 'The Machine Stops'.[170]

Such allusions occur continuously in the literature. The most heavily cited work of all in this context is the 1949 George Orwell novel, *Nineteen Eighty-*

[169] Tom Crowe and John Hywel-Jones, *The Computer and Society*, Fabian Tract 457 (Fabian Society, London, 1978), p. 5.

[170] Ibid., p. 1.

Four. In this work, as we will see, the author presented a pessimistic view of an authoritarian government – with its 'Big Brother' figurehead – making heavy use of electronic communications technology to monitor, intimidate, and control the perceptions of the public. Orwell did not write about computers, which were at this point only at an early stage of development. But it has been possible to overlay this technology on the concepts presented in *Nineteen Eighty-Four*. For instance, the 1985 Terry Gilliam film, *Brazil*, clearly referenced Orwell in its depiction of a near-future society in which an authoritarian administration focused on the manipulation of information employs computers to this end. In an advertisement for the Macintosh, directed by Ridley Scott, broadcast during the 1984 Superbowl in the United States, again deliberately invoking Orwell, Apple appeared as an individualistic insurgent challenging an oppressive regime, envisaged by some[171] (but perhaps not the filmmakers) as representing IBM, then the long-established leader in the computer market.[172] Commentators on the Internet and its social implications have had a powerful urge to refer, or position themselves relative, to the Orwell scenario.[173] Kevin Kelly, executive editor of *Wired* magazine, was a key promoter of the potential of digital technologies from the 1990s onwards. Misattributing the literal representation of computers to the 1949 novel, Kelly wrote in 1994 that '[n]o one has been more wrong about computerization than George Orwell in *1984*. So far, nearly everything about the actual possibility-space which computers have created indicates they are the end of authority and not its beginning.'[174] Shoshanna Zuboff, whose concept of 'surveillance capitalism' using the Internet is discussed in Chapter 1, took a contrasting approach. Referring expressly to Orwell and *Nineteen Eighty-Four*,[175] Zuboff adapted the term 'Big Brother', applying the label 'Big Other' to the 'digital apparatus' employed by the intrusive, manipulative, and exploitative system she judged to be undermining democracy, and that she sought to reveal.[176]

A recent study by Dorian Lynskey, *Ministry of Truth: A Biography of George Orwell's 1984*, considers at length the sources on which Orwell drew and the impact he had.[177] It provides an account of the development of literary views of possible societies, to which novel technology is often central. As Lynskey recounts, there is a tendency to divide them into two types: optimistic utopias and horrific dystopias. *Nineteen Eighty-Four* is generally received as within the

171 e.g. Manuel Castells, *The Information Age: Economy, Society and Culture, vol. I: The Rise of the Network Society* (Wiley-Blackwell, London, 2010), p. 6, fn. 6.
172 See Dorian Lynskey, *Ministry of Truth: A Biography of George Orwell's 1984* (Picador, London, 2019).
173 e.g. Neuman, *The Future of the Mass Audience*, p. 23.
174 Kevin Kelly, *Out of Control: The New Biology of Machines, Social Systems, and the Economic World* (Perseus, Cambridge, 1994), p. 466.
175 Shoshana Zuboff, *The Age of Surveillance Capitalism* (Profile, London, 2019), p. 352.
176 Ibid., p. 376.
177 Lynskey, *Ministry of Truth.*

latter category, with individuals such as Kelly and Zuboff responding to it in terms of whether they judge it prescient or otherwise. But, as Lynskey shows, we should be cautious about applying this binary distinction. Even in *Nineteen Eighty-Four* it is possible to find some scraps of optimism. Furthermore, when we consider the entire career of certain writers, simple categorisation can become even more difficult. Wells, for instance, has a reputation for buoyancy regarding the anticipated scientific future. In fact, he raised numerous concerns about the possible uses and impact of inventions. The balance between these contrasting perspectives could differ between one of his works and another. But the totality of his output is more mixed than perceptions of him might suggest. The overall impression is that technology has immense potential for achieving a better – even ideal – society, but that it can also be a source of instability, and be employed for oppressive and destructive purposes. On this analysis, if the benefits are to be realised and negatives avoided, careful handling is required. This book considers how Parliament came to take on such a responsibility with regard to the Internet.

1

The Internet Debate since 1990

The central premise of this book is that the relationship between the Internet and one of the most well-established and prominent institutions of representative democracy in the world merits close consideration. Recognition of the importance of this connection can be found in a report entitled *Open Up!*, published on 26 January 2015, by the Speaker's Commission on Digital Democracy.[1] The Commission described how it had worked for a year 'to consider, report and make recommendations on how parliamentary democracy in the United Kingdom can embrace the opportunities afforded by the digital world'.[2] While this wording did not explicitly refer to it, much of the focus of the Commission was, in practice, on the entity known as the Internet (the definition of which is discussed below). The Commission had eight members. Two were MPs (one each from the Conservative and Labour parties). Among the remainder were representatives of the creative community, academia, and the third sector. The core support staff numbered four.[3] Seeking evidence widely, between them this group undertook a task substantial in scope.[4] Its terms of reference focused specifically on how Parliament could 'become more effective in' law-making, in 'scrutinising the work and performance of government', in 'representing citizens', in 'encouraging citizens to engage with democracy', and in 'facilitating dialogue amongst citizens'. A further task was to assess means by which Parliament might 'become more relevant to the increasingly diverse population it serves'.[5] In this sense, from a parliamentary perspective, the Commission looked inward, at the work of the institution itself, and outward, considering ways of promoting more beneficial uses of technology in society beyond.

In his Foreword to the report, the initiator of the inquiry, John Bercow MP, Speaker of the House of Commons, asserted that '[o]ver the past 25 years we have lived through a revolution – created by the birth of the world wide web and

[1] Digital Democracy Commission, *Open Up! Report of the Speaker's Commission on Digital Democracy* (Speaker's Commission on Digital Democracy, London, 2015).
[2] Ibid., p. 77.
[3] Ibid., p. 76.
[4] Ibid., p. 5.
[5] Ibid., p. 77.

the rapid development of digital technology. This digital revolution has disrupted old certainties and challenged representative democracy at its very heart.' Bercow went on: '[w]ith social media sources such as Twitter, blogs and 24/7 media, the citizen has more sources of information than ever before, yet citizens appear to operate at a considerable distance from their representatives and appear "disengaged" from democratic processes'. Bercow identified a particular problem from the point of view of Parliament: 'The jargon and practices of the House can be alienating.' Moreover, 'the sheer weight of information about politics, now available, can act as a wall, keeping the citizen out of the mysterious world of Westminster'. Bercow perceived his role as Speaker as partly entailing being 'a champion of democracy, an advocate for the House of Commons and a public catalyst for participation in politics'. With this responsibility in mind, he set up the Commission 'to consider the challenges and opportunities for our democracy that digital technology presents'.[6]

The Commission made five core recommendations. They were, first, that the House of Commons should, by 2020, 'ensure that everyone can understand what it does'. Secondly, Parliament would become 'fully interactive and digital' by 2020. Thirdly, the Commons returned at the General Election due in May 2015 would 'create immediately a new forum for public participation in the debating function of the House of Commons'. Fourthly, 'secure online voting' would be universally available by 2020. Fifthly, 'all published information and broadcast footage' emanating from Parliament would, by 2016, be 'freely available online in formats suitable for re-use'; and Hansard was to be 'available as open data by the end of 2015'.[7]

Between them, the Commission itself, the Foreword by the Speaker, and the recommendations it made, provoke a series of interlinked questions. They are as follows. What precisely did the Commission mean when using terms such as 'digital technology'? How was it possible (for Bercow writing in the Foreword) to refer to the advent of a technology-inspired 'revolution' as though axiomatic, and not needing detailed explanation or justification? Why did the authors of the report-proper refer to a 'digital world' with a similar casual confidence that readers would know what was meant by such an entity and accept that it existed? How well-founded were these assumptions about revolutions and worlds? To what extent did qualities inherent in technology itself determine the changes that would occur, or were they shaped by a wider social environment? What were the opportunities that the Internet and related mechanisms created for democracy, and why might they also entail difficulties, including for the representative version of this system of government? What were the political connotations of the Internet? What, more specifically, were the implications for Parliament, the principal instrument of representative democracy in the UK? How has it responded to this

[6] Ibid., p. 5.
[7] Ibid., p. 7.

development in methods of communication, both in the way it operates and in the actions it takes as an organ of governance?

This book engages with these questions from a historical perspective. As with the other aspects of the work, to do so is in keeping with the premises on which the Speaker's Commission rested. To advance ideas of revolution, of timeframes of a quarter of a century, and of challenges to existing arrangements, is to invite consideration of earlier periods against which it is possible to assess such ideas. Issues addressed in the Commission report have recurred frequently during the time period that Bercow, in his reference to twenty-five years, proposed. Tracing back a quarter of a century from the publication of *Open Up!* leads to 1990. At this point, the rise of the Internet as a mass-usage technology was about to commence, owing to the introduction of the World Wide Web. The person credited as the inventor of this system, Tim Berners-Lee, depicts it as 'riding on top of the Internet'.[8] It made, as two authors put it, 'the Internet easier to navigate with point-and-click programs'.[9] In the period since 1990, the potential and actual significance of this technology has been the subject of intense scrutiny and debate. Many commentators have presented the Internet as of immense importance; for instance, by referring to it alongside other inventions of perceived enormous historical significance, such as the printing press,[10] the telegraph, the telephone, and satellite communications.[11] To begin with definition of terms, when referring to 'the Internet' and related concepts, participants in this discussion can have one or more of a variety of different concepts in mind.[12] They might mean simply a combination of hardware.[13] They might regard the Internet as a tool,[14] as a communications network,[15] as a road,[16] as a business opportunity,[17]

[8] Tim Berners-Lee, *Weaving the Web: The Past, Present and Future of the World Wide Web by Its Inventor* (Orion, London, 1999), p. 21.

[9] Katie Hafner and Matthew Lyon, *Where Wizards Stay Up Late: The Origins of the Internet* (Simon and Schuster, New York, 2006), p. 258.

[10] Bill Gates, *The Road Ahead* (Viking, New York, 1995), pp. 8–9, 120–1.

[11] e.g. Geoff Mulgan, *Connexity* (Chatto & Windus, London, 1997), p. 21.

[12] For the complexities of defining the internet for regulatory purposes, see e.g. Robin Mansell, *Imagining the Internet: Communication, Innovation and Governance* (Oxford University Press, 2012), p. 153.

[13] Fred Turner, 'Can We Write a Cultural History of the Internet? If So, How?', *Internet Histories* 1(2017): 39–46, 40.

[14] e.g. Martin Thomas, *The Financial Times Guide to Social Media Strategy: Boost Your Business, Manage Risk and Develop Your Personal Brand* (The FT Guides, London, 2018).

[15] e.g. Helen Donelan (ed.), *Online Communication and Collaboration: A Reader* (Routledge, Abingdon, 2009).

[16] In the early years of the period under examination in this chapter, there was something of an overlap between the concepts of the Internet and of an 'information highway' (see below), e.g. Gates, *The Road Ahead*, p. xii. To underline the point, the author appears on the cover standing in front of an open road stretching into a rural distance. On the reverse cover, Gates has vanished and there is only the highway.

[17] For an emphasis on the business aspects, see e.g. Chris Skinner, *Digital Human: The Fourth Revolution of Humanity Includes Everyone* (John Wiley & Sons, Chichester, 2018).

as a weapon,[18] as a persuasive device[19] or – as we will discuss – a place or even world.[20] Further interpretations still are possible.

Divergence exists also about whether to use 'the Internet' as a proper or common noun. I have opted for the former, on the grounds that it is a specific piece of technology. In this regard I follow the Internet historian, Morton Bay. In a 2017 article Bay writes that '"internet" is in fact a unique entity' that 'should be considered a proper noun and therefore should be capitalised'. Bay holds that '"internet" was not used as a proper noun from the outset . . . nor was it originally used as a common noun, as other sources suggest'. In the early period, 1973–6, '"internet" was not even used to describe a thing or a place, but a class or a category, and was used as a classifying adjective'. When initial use 'as a noun' came in 1976, 'it was in the proper noun form'. This application came 'to name an actual infrastructure that was emerging from attempts at connecting several separate networks'.[21]

Generally, this book eschews rigid definitions. It allows the authors of the accounts of the Internet to delineate their subject matter for themselves. Such perspectives are revealing in themselves. It is also important to allow for the use of terms such as 'cyberspace',[22] 'information superhighway',[23] and 'web'[24] (an abbreviation of World Wide Web) that might not precisely refer to the Internet, but are employed in ways that are closely associated with it. I recognise that there are connections to other important discussions such as those about machine learning, algorithms, and 'artificial intelligence', but as far as possible in the present work I confine myself to the central topic, substantial enough in itself.

Revolutions and New Worlds

The Internet and related technology have certainly attracted much attention in the period from 1990. Commentary began as speculation about a prospect, and then came to relate to an increasingly large-scale, global form of

[18] e.g. Christopher Whyte and Brian Mazanec, *Understanding Cyber Warfare* (Routledge, Abingdon, 2018).

[19] e.g. Samuel C. Woolley, *Computational Propaganda: Political Parties, Politicians, and Political Manipulation on Social Media* (Oxford University Press, 2018).

[20] e.g. the journalist John Seabrook uses the phrase 'on-line world' in Deeper: A Two-Year Odyssey in Cyberspace (Faber and Faber, London, 1997), p. 107. See also Marc Weber, 'A Common Language', *Internet Histories* 1(1–2) (2017): 26–38, 32.

[21] Morten Bay, 'What Is "Internet"? The Case for the Proper Noun and Why It Is Important', *Internet Histories* 1(3) (2017): 203–18, 204–5.

[22] e.g. Lawrence Lessig, *Code: And Other Laws of Cyberspace* (Basic Books, New York, 2006). For the 1984 science-fiction novel often credited as bringing this term into use in the context of computer networks, see William Gibson, *Neuromancer* (Gollancz, London, 1984).

[23] e.g. John Bray, *The Communications Miracle: Telecommunications Pioneers from Morse to the Information Superhighway* (Springer, Berlin, 1995).

[24] For a work by the inventor of the World Wide Web technology, see Berners-Lee, *Weaving the Web.*

communication. In 1995, discussing the 'so-called information highway', the Microsoft co-founder Bill Gates referred to 'endless newspaper and magazine articles, television and radio broadcasts, conferences and rampant speculation. There has been an unbelievable amount of interest in this subject during the last few years, both inside and outside the computer industry.'[25] This fascination manifested itself in the UK. As Sadie Plant remarked in an article for *New Statesman and Society* entitled 'Babes in the net', also in 1995, '[s]uddenly, cyberspace is everywhere'.[26] Often the Internet appeared not only as of pronounced importance, but in a transformative or disruptive way. The word 'revolution' and associated imagery has frequently occurred in discussion of this technology.[27] Gates wrote of two such transitions. The first 'revolution' had already taken place, involving the reduction in 'size' and expansion 'in power' of computers, that had in parallel become substantially less costly. Following the permeation of technology this development had facilitated, 'we stand at the brink of another revolution. This one will involve unprecedentedly inexpensive communication; all the computers will join together to communicate with us and for us. Interconnected globally, they will form a network, which is being called the information highway.'[28] The idea that such impacts would be of an international, unifying character would recur.

Portrayals have presented the Internet not only as a technological transformation, but as in turn bringing about other – rapid and extensive – forms of change. They might be, for instance, sexual, economic, social, or political in character.[29] Analysts might discern consequences for the physical environment in which people lived, holding that the Internet would perhaps trigger a dispersal of population away from urban centres, raising a variety of planning issues.[30] A 1994 multi-authored text, entitled 'Cyberspace and the American Dream: A Magna Carta for the Knowledge Age'[31] opened with the grand assertion that '[t]he central event of the 20th century is the overthrow of matter'. It depicted 'cyberspace' as an entity that included within it the

[25] Gates, *The Road Ahead*, p. xii.

[26] Sadie Plant, 'Babes in the Net', *New Statesman and Society*, 27 January 1995, p. 28.

[27] For the use of the word in a limited sense, see Landy Chase and Kevin Knebi, *The Social Media Sales Revolution: The New Rules for Finding Customers, Building Relationships and Closing More Sales through Online Networking* (McGraw Hill Education, New York, 2011).

[28] Gates, *The Road Ahead*, p. 3.

[29] See e.g. Manuel Castells, *Networks of Outrage and Hope: Social Movements in the Internet Age* (Polity, Cambridge, 2015); Aleks Krotoski, *Untangling the Web* (Faber & Faber, London, 2013).

[30] Gates, *The Road Ahead*, pp. 155–6; Karen F. Evans, *Maintaining Community in the Information Age: The Importance of Trust, Place and Situated Knowledge* (Palgrave, Basingstoke, 2004), pp. 32–4.

[31] Esther Dyson, George Gilder, George Keyworth, and Alvin Toffler, 'Cyberspace and the American Dream: A Magna Carta for the Knowledge Age', *Future Insight*, Release 1(2) (August 1994). For an account of the genesis and significance of the text, see e.g. Fred Turner, *From Counterculture to Cyberulture: Stewart Brand, the Whole Earth Network, and the Rise of Digital Utopianism* (University of Chicago Press, 2006), e-book edition, locations 3383–431.

Internet as well as encompassing all means of electronic data storage and transmission. This system would, the authors claimed, bring about a new historical era with 'profound implications for the nature and meaning of property, of the marketplace, of community and of individual freedom'. They discerned this entity as prompting 'new codes of behaviour that move each organism and institution – family, neighbourhood, church group, company, government, nation – inexorably beyond standardization and centralization, as well as beyond the materialist's obsession with energy, money and control'. Furthermore, cyberspace 'also spells the death of the central institutional paradigm of modern life, the bureaucratic organization'.[32]

Plant in 1995 referred to a 'digital revolution', one of the consequences of which was that 'everything in the vicinity of sex, gender, and sexuality is being transformed', among other dramatic ruptures fundamental to the nature of humanity. She judged that 'by a suitably bottom-up and piecemeal process distributed far beyond the social world, the digital revolution is reengineering the very conditions of patriarchy'.[33] John Perry Barlow issued in 1996 what would become a celebrated manifesto, the title of which – 'A Declaration of the Independence of Cyberspace'[34] – deliberately invoked the 1776 text marking the commencement of the American Revolution.[35] In another 1996 article entitled 'The Californian Ideology' – a title presumably intended to recall 'The German Ideology', the 1846 work by Karl Marx and Frederick Engels – Richard Barbrook and Andy Cameron wrote that '[a]t the end of the twentieth century, the long predicted convergence of the media, computing and telecommunications into hypermedia is finally happening'. The development of 'the ability to produce and receive unlimited amounts of information in any form' was 'combined with the reach of the global telephone networks', meaning that 'existing forms of work and leisure can be fundamentally transformed. New industries will be born and current stock market favourites will be swept away.'[36] Manuel Castells, a highly influential scholar in this field, wrote in a 2010 edition of a work first published in 1996 that '[t]he prophetic hype and ideological manipulation characterizing most discourses on the information

[32] Dyson, et al., 'Cyberspace and the American Dream'.

[33] Plant, 'Babes in the Net', p. 28.

[34] John Perry Barlow, 'A Declaration of the Independence of Cyberspace', *Electronic Frontier Foundation*, 8 February 1996, available at: www.eff.org/cyberspace-independence, last accessed 20 January 2021.

[35] For critical assessments of the text, see Amiée Hope Morrison, 'An Impossible Future: John Perry Barlow's "Declaration of the Independence of Cyberspace"', *New Media and Society* 11 (1–2) (2009): 53–72; Reilly Jones, 'A Critique of Barlow's "A Declaration of the Independence of Cyberspace"', *Extropy #17* 8(2) (1996); Alex Kosinski and Josh Goldfoot, 'A Declaration of the Independence of Cyberspace', *Columbia Journal of Law and the Arts* 32 (2008–9): 365. For the views of Barlow on his own statement twenty years on, see 'A Declaration of the Independence of Cyberspace: How John Perry Barlow Views His Internet Manifesto on Its 20th Anniversary. Online Idealism versus the World's Realism', *The Economist*, 8 February 2016.

[36] R. Barbrook and A. Cameron, 'The Californian Ideology', *Science as Culture* 6(1) (1996): 44–72, 44.

technology revolution should not mislead us into underestimating its truly fundamental significance'. Castells observed 'an historical event' underway of equal or greater importance to 'the eighteenth-century industrial revolution, inducing a pattern of discontinuity in the material basis of economy, society, and culture'.[37] Among the impacts he detected, Castells noted that the Internet and connected systems were facilitating co-ordination between members of the public from local to international level, and interaction between them and governors.[38]

The idea of a dramatic historic juncture persisted. Luciano Floridi published in 2014 a book entitled *The 4th Revolution: How the Infosphere Is Reshaping Human Reality*. He discerned the onset of a transition for humanity, from an era of 'history' to one of 'hyperhistory'.[39] The defining characteristic of countries that had reached this new epoch was that 'ICTs [information and communication technologies] and their data-processing capabilities are not just important but essential conditions for the maintenance and any further development of societal welfare, personal well-being, and overall flourishing.'[40] The revolution Floridi envisaged, then, involved societies becoming 'ICT-dependent'.[41] This notion recurred across a variety of literature dealing with the Internet.[42] Some who discerned such a collective need found it worrisome, even suggesting that humanity had become ensnared in a system of digital exploitation.[43] Others could see reliance on the Internet as demonstrating the exceptional worth of this system – in particular, during the coronavirus emergency.[44]

Observers who saw the Internet as bringing about or contributing to major social change saw the technology itself as – rather than a fixed device – itself passing through transformation, the precise nature of which was difficult to predict, that would lead to more disruption still in future.[45] In a 1997 book, Geoff Mulgan, a UK political thinker who was influential upon and within the Labour governments that commenced under Tony Blair in that year, discussed the global ascendancy of a phenomenon he termed 'connexity', involving

[37] Manuel Castells, *The Information Age: Economy, Society and* Culture, vol. I: *The Rise of the Network Society* (Wiley-Blackwell, London, 2010), p. 29.
[38] Ibid., pp. 391–2.
[39] Luciano Floridi, *The 4th Revolution: How the Infosphere Is Reshaping Human Reality* (Oxford University Press, 2014), p. 5.
[40] Ibid., p. 4.
[41] Ibid., p. 6.
[42] Amnesty International, *Surveillance Giants: How the Business Model of Google and Facebook Threatens Human Rights* (Amnesty International, London, 2019), p. 5.
[43] This scenario is central to the thesis of Shoshana Zuboff, *The Age of Surveillance Capitalism* (Profile, London, 2019), e.g. p. 468.
[44] David Omand, 'Hackers Will Try to Exploit Covid-19. How to Stop Them?', *Prospect*, 19 March 2020, available at: www.prospectmagazine.co.uk/science-and-technology/gchq-hackers-will-try-to-exploit-covid-19–how-to-stop-them-coronavirus-internet-cyber-intelligence-security, last accessed 21 March 2020.
[45] Gates, *The Road Ahead*, p. xii.

mass, instantaneous communication between people. He considered that the Internet had already contributed to this tendency, partly as a consequence of 'the invention in 1974 of the TCP/IP interconnection protocol that allowed networks to be connected and enabled the Internet to get off the ground'. Mulgan anticipated that future 'great inventions may include the full integration of television into the Internet, so that is ceases to be a one-way medium, and, further ahead, the implant of a serial port for plugging a computer or network into the human brain itself'.[46] The idea that much more was to come proved enduring. In a 2013 book entitled *The New Digital Age: Reshaping the Future of People, Nations and Business*, the authors of which were Erich Schmidt and Jared Cohen, then respectively executive chairman of Google and director of Google Ideas, it was held that '[m]ass adoption of the Internet is driving one of the most exciting social, cultural and political transformations in history, and unlike earlier periods of change, this time the effects are fully global ... And we're barely in the starting blocks.'[47] As well as conveying a sense of ongoing change, accounts of internet-related technology might present this process as accelerating, possibly rapidly.[48]

According to many observers, an actual change came in the nature of the Internet during the first decade of the twenty-first century, with the appearance of 'Web 2.0'. This development saw the introduction of applications such as Facebook, Wikipedia, and YouTube, making the online creation and dissemination of content far easier. It had implications for a range of social activities, including the those of a political nature.[49] Attempts to convey the significance of Web 2.0 and the 'social media' that characterised it came, once again, to employ the term 'revolution'.[50] Such uses of the technology in themselves might be presented as constituting an uprising, or could be linked to actual insurrections in the real world. Following revolts across the Middle East and North Africa in 2011 – comprising the so-called 'Arab Spring' – interest focused on the role that such applications had played in the movement.[51] Around this time, terms such as 'Twitter' and 'Facebook revolutions' came into use to describe various disturbances internationally.[52]

[46] Mulgan, *Connexity*, p. 21.

[47] Eric Schmidt and Jared Cohen, *The New Digital Age: Reshaping the Future of People, Nations and Business* (John Murray, London, 2013), p. 3.

[48] Ray Kurzweil, *The Singularity Is Near: When Humans Transcend Biology* (Duckworth, London, 2010), ch. 1.

[49] Yana Breindl and Pascal Francq, 'Can Web 2.0 Applications Save e-Democracy? A Study of How New Internet Applications May Enhance Citizen Participation in the Political Process Online', *International Journal of Electronic Democracy* 1(1) (2008): 14–31, 19–22.

[50] e.g. Jason Gainous and Kevin M. Wagner, *Tweeting to Power: The Social Media Revolution in American Politics* (Oxford University Press, 2013).

[51] e.g. Badreya Al-Jenaibi, 'The Nature of Arab Public Discourse: Social Media and the "Arab Spring"', *Journal of Applied Journalism & Media Studies* 3(2) (2014): 241–60.

[52] Stefano Passini, 'The Facebook and Twitter Revolutions: Active Participation in the 21st Century', *Human Affairs* 22(3) (2012): 301–12.

The idea of the Internet as comprising a place or universe (or at least helping to facilitate the existence of such an environment) has recurred over the twenty-five-year period that Bercow posited. The proposition of a digitally generated space occurred frequently in artistic representations; for instance, in films such as *The Lawnmower Man* (1992), *Dark City* (1988), *eXistenZ* (1999), *The Matrix* (1999), and *Source Code* (2011); episodes of the television series *Black Mirror* (2011–); and novels including *Ready Player One* by Ernest Cline (2011)[53] and *Bleeding Edge* by Thomas Pynchon (2013).[54] As the manner of usage by the Speaker's Commission on Digital Democracy in 2015 suggested, the authors of commentaries have felt able to advance this concept as though self-evident.[55] Another parliamentary entity, the House of Lords Select Committee on Communications, published a report entitled *Regulating in a Digital World* in 2019. It described the 'digital world' that was the subject of its consideration as 'an environment composed of digital services facilitated by the internet'.[56]

The places envisaged could take a variety of forms. In her 1995 article, Plant depicted a 'virtual world' and described how 'women . . . are . . . increasingly, discovering new possibilities for work, play, and communication of all kinds in the spaces emergent from the telecoms revolution'. This environment had transformative qualities: '[y]ou can go online and be anyone. You can go online and be no one at all.' These 'deregulated possibilities have star appeal for women – and for all those who've struggled within the straightjacket of identity'. Plant regarded the way in which the 'Net' functioned, as being suited to women. It replaced 'centralised, top-down structures' with a system that had 'no organising core, but pulls itself together from the bottom-up, replicating networks and making connections, just as women have organised themselves'.[57]

Some political analysis considered the Internet as potentially making up a realm of discourse or – alluding to Jurgen Habermas – a 'public sphere'.[58] In 2015, the Intelligence and Security Committee of Parliament conceptualised the perennial dilemma of the balance between liberty and security through considering the Internet as a place. It asked: 'to what extent should the internet be a private space for individuals to communicate?'[59] The Committee went on:

[53] Filmed by Steven Spielberg in 2018. See Ch. 9 of this volume.

[54] Thomas Pynchon, *Bleeding Edge* (Penguin, London, 2013), e.g. ch. 7.

[55] For a more recent parliamentary body employing the terms, see e.g. House of Lords Select Committee on Democracy and Digital Technologies, Report of Session 2019–21, HL 77 (House of Lords, London, 2020), p. 4.

[56] House of Lords Select Committee on Communications, *Regulating in a Digital World*, Second Report of Session 2017–19, HL Paper 299 (House of Lords, London, 2019), p. 3.

[57] Plant, 'Babes in the Net', p. 28.

[58] e.g. Zizi Papacharissi, 'The Virtual Sphere: The Internet as a Public Sphere', *New Media & Society* 4(1) (2002): 9–27. See also: Anthony G. Wilhelm, *Democracy in the Digital Age* (Routledge, London, 2000), p. 9.

[59] Intelligence and Security Committee of Parliament, *Privacy and Security: A Modern and Transparent Legal Framework*, HC 1075 (House of Commons, London, 2015), p. 9.

'if the internet is an ungoverned space it can also be a dangerous space, threatening the liberty of all'.[60] Accounts of the communication techniques of Donald Trump, who became US President following his election success of 2016, described him as generating 'his own reality', partly through the employment of social media.[61] The Internet could even be perceived as a potential theatre of military combat. In 2018, the House of Lords described how 'NATO had been working closely on cyber issues since 2014.' This supranational military organisation had 'defined cyberspace as an operational domain: that is, a likely battlefield' at a summit at Warsaw in 2016, and it now intended 'to implement cyberspace as a domain of operations'.[62]

One way of analysing and differentiating such theses is through considering the relationship they suggest exists between the new world or place and the old.[63] In some accounts, the purpose of an internet-enabled parallel environment has been to help us interact with our own universe and to improve it in the process.[64] Plant, for instance, regarded 'cyberspace' as a realm that created possibilities for the supplanting of 'patriarchal power'.[65] In January 2010, while serving as US Secretary of State, Hillary Clinton gave a speech emphasising the importance of global internet use being free from intervention by governments. Clinton conveyed the idea of an electronically generated place, asserting that '[t]he freedom to connect is like the freedom of assembly, only in cyberspace. It allows individuals to get online, come together, and hopefully cooperate.' For Clinton, the purpose of this activity was – in combination with other forms of campaigning – to achieve wider objectives such as the advancement of human rights.[66] Other accounts of digital realms might suggest their real-world impact was deleterious – discussion of Trump from this perspective, for instance, was often negative in its depiction of the outcomes. From the perspective of intelligence, security, and defence, the Internet was perceived partly as a place from which threat might appear, an irony given the part that US military programmes played in its genesis. If the Internet was a world necessarily in communion with the pre-existing universe, important questions, noted in the literature, arose. On the one hand, how far could and should the online environment be subject to the norms of the offline? Or – on the other hand – how far could and should the supposed digital realm modify and

60 Ibid., p. 10.

61 Dorian Lynskey, *Ministry of Truth: A Biography of George Orwell's 1984* (Picador, London, 2019), ch. 13.

62 House of Lords Select Committee on International Relations, *UK Foreign Policy in a Shifting World Order*, Fifth Report of Session 2017–19, HL Paper 250 (House of Lords, London, 2018), p. 58.

63 A question posed in e.g. Schmidt and Cohen, *The New Digital Age*, p. 80.

64 David Gelernter, *Mirror Worlds: Or the Day Software Puts the Universe in a Shoebox . . . How It Will Happen and What It Will Mean* (Oxford University Press, 1993).

65 Plant, 'Babes in the Net', p. 28.

66 Hillary Rodham Clinton, United States Secretary of State, 'Remarks'.

transform the physical world in its own image?[67] This discussion relates to matters addressed elsewhere in this work: the extent to which the Internet – though it might be important – has been only a factor within existing social interactions, or has fundamentally altered them, imposing a logic of its own.

In other interpretations, internet-related technologies appeared as generating a separate, perhaps superior environment. In his 1996 'Declaration of the Independence of Cyberspace', Barlow presented himself as an emissary 'from Cyberspace, the new home of Mind'.[68] The physical world and its power structures, he held, lacked authority in this environment. Barlow referred to 'the global social space we are building' that 'grows itself through our collective actions'. The participants were 'creating a world that all may enter without privilege or prejudice accorded by race, economic power, military force, or station of birth'. Within this environment 'anyone, anywhere may express his or her beliefs, no matter how singular, without fear of being coerced into silence or conformity'. Such 'legal concepts' as 'property, expression, identity, movement and context' were not relevant. 'They are all based on matter, and there is no matter here.' The ultimate goal was to 'create a civilization of the Mind in Cyberspace'.

A more radical proposition still has been that humanity will eventually leave behind physical existence and be absorbed into the digital environment, at an approaching point of transcendence labelled 'the singularity'.[69] Though arising from scientific speculation, the religious parallels to this concept are plain. The idea of the Internet as a world in itself – and the particular properties it possesses when considered in this light – has been of interest to Christian observers. In 1996, the Science, Medicine and Technology Committee of the Church of England Board for Social Responsibility proposed the formation of 'a working party to set out some of the ethical and spiritual implications of' recent 'extraordinary developments' in information technology.[70] The outcome was a 1999 report entitled *Cybernauts Awake! Ethical and Spiritual Implications of Computers, Information Technology and the Internet.* In its imagery (and its use of the term 'cyberspace') the authors clearly asserted the idea of an online environment, with qualities that were striking from a theological standpoint. They described how 'changing from analogue to digital form gives cyberspace an extraordinary, even unique, characteristic: *it transcends familiar physical limits* [emphasis in original], and this lack of familiar physical limits lies at the heart of the perplexing opportunities of cyberspace'. The report noted that '[m]uch of the world we are used to is governed, in one

[67] Patrice Flichy, *The Internet Imaginaire* (Cambridge, The MIT Press, 2007), pp. 158–9. See also endorsement from General Michael Hayden, previously the Director of the US Central Intelligence Agency (CIA) in Schmidt and Cohen, *The New Digital Age*, p. 3.

[68] Barlow, 'A Declaration of the Independence of Cyberspace'.

[69] Kurzweil, *The Singularity Is Near.*

[70] Cybernauts Awake! Ethical and Spiritual Implications of Computers, Information Technology and the Internet (Church House Publishing, London, 1999), p. ix.

way or another, by physical limits'. Vehicles could not exceed certain speeds; while humans could not work for more time than was available in a day. Conversely, '[c]omputers and digital communications do away with many such limits; in particular, they make it possible to copy, manipulate and transmit digital information essentially for nothing'.[71]

Alongside the excitement about breaches in continuity and the creation of a new universe, others have expressed scepticism. While tending to acknowledge that it has made a difference, they question the extent of change connected to the Internet. Some cast doubt, for instance, on the extent to which the potential it possessed had come to be realised. Jaron Lanier – a technical pioneer in the field for a number of decades, associated in particular with 'virtual reality'[72] – complained in 2010 that 'I long to be shocked and made obsolete by new generations of digital culture, but instead I am being tortured by repetition and boredom.' One supposed achievement the extent of which Lanier questioned was 'the creation of Wikipedia, which is a copy of something that already existed: an encyclopedia [sic]'.[73] In 2018, the House of Lords Select Committee on International Relations reported being told by Gareth Evans, a former Australian Foreign Minister, that '[t]he digital revolution has been used as an excuse for everything, with 24/7 media cycles and people's passion for Twitter and 140-symbol communication being seen as a dumbing down – an inability to cope with complexity'. While Evans heard 'this all the time', he thought 'it is an excuse rather than an explanation'.[74]

Others have questioned the idea of a parallel digital space. Analysis of the technology and its development has stressed the importance of the geography of the physical world. [75] It has noted, for instance, the links to a particular country, the United States, and within that, the West Coast and California, the location of 'Silicon Valley', the name attached to the concentration of digital commerce and expertise based in this area.[76] The historian Fred Turner advances a firm counterview to the idea of the Internet as comprising an environment. He does so with his suggestion of some 'guiding principles' to facilitate an appreciation of the importance of the Internet, and goes on to propose a rebuttal of the idea that it is a whole entity at all. Turner holds that 'first, the Internet is not a place, nor is it merely a new platform for creative expression'. On the contrary, 'it is an infrastructure: a complex assemblage of

[71] Ibid., p. 21.

[72] For his memoir containing extensive discussion of Virtual Reality, see Jaron Lanier, *Dawn of the New Everything: A Journey through Virtual Reality* (Bodley Head, London, 2017).

[73] Jaron Lanier, *You Are Not a Gadget: A Manifesto* (Penguin, London, 2010), p. 121. While disappointed by outcomes, he nonetheless believes that something momentous had transpired, dedicating this book to 'my friends and colleagues in the digital revolution'.

[74] House of Lords Select Committee on International Relations, *UK Foreign Policy in a Shifting World Order*, p. 39.

[75] Tung-Hui Hu, *A Prehistory of the Cloud* (MIT Press, Cambridge, 2015).

[76] Barbrook and Cameron, 'The Californian Ideology'.

wires and switches, institutions and individuals, through which financial data and love notes travel intermingled'. Secondly, 'it has no inhabitants. Instead, its streams of bits and bytes run through the lives of people who live, as they always have, in bodies, locations and societies.' Thirdly, 'it has no culture apart from the communities who have built, used and sought to regulate its electronic networks. In other words, there is no such thing as a single universal Internet culture.'[77]

A connected debate about the Internet turns on the extent to which – on the one hand – it has a preordained impact derived from qualities inherent to it, or – on the other hand – external factors, such as cultural, legal, political, and constitutional tendencies, shape the use to which it is (or is not) put, and the difference it makes. In this context, the label 'determinism' can occur as descriptive of interpretations that maximise the impact that technology might have in this way. Those who use this word often do so disparagingly, as a means of suggesting a flawed conception of causality.[78] In this work, I suggest that technological determinism can have one or more of a number of different facets. First is the idea that the Internet or associated inventions had unavoidable and immense consequences for the destiny of humanity. The 1994 text, 'Cyberspace and the American Dream' had this flavour to it, positing a technologically induced historical transition or 'Third Wave' that 'will affect virtually everything government does'.[79] Secondly, some – including those commenting on the development of the Internet – take this philosophy a stage further, holding the view that inventions are foreordained, and awaiting discovery.[80] Thirdly, they might also present the wide adoption of certain devices, and their use in particular ways, in a light that suggests they are predetermined.[81] Fourthly, they might even depict the whole history of humanity as an unfolding process following a set pattern, for which technological development is the central motivating force.[82] Fifthly, often, those who see technology as driving outcomes appear to regard them as inherently desirable.[83] Others have disputed such approaches. Critics have argued, for instance, that particular courses followed in the history of what is now the Internet need not (and perhaps should not) have been taken.[84] They have, furthermore, questioned the degree to which the nature of a system determines

[77] Turner, 'Can We Write a Cultural History of the Internet?', p. 40.

[78] For reference to this debate, see e.g. Stephen Coleman, *Can the Internet Strengthen Democracy?* (Polity, Cambridge, 2017), pp. 3–4.

[79] Dyson et al., 'Cyberspace and the American Dream'.

[80] Morten Bay, 'Conversation with a Pioneer: Larry Roberts on How He Led the Design and Construction of the ARPANET, *Internet Histories* 3(1) (2019): 68–80, 77.

[81] Kurzweil, *The Singularity Is Near*, ch. 1.

[82] Floridi, *The 4th Revolution*, pp. 1–6.

[83] For a tone of this type, see 'Free our Bills!', available at: www.theyworkforyou.com/freeourbills/, last accessed 3 July 2020.

[84] Jaron Lanier, *Who Owns the Future?* (Penguin, London, 2014), pp. 221–2.

the outcome.[85] As Benjamin Barber put it in 1998, 'technology is often less a determinant than a mirror of the larger society. Who owns it, how it is used and by whom, and to which ends: these are the critical questions whose answers will shape technology's actual role in the coming century.'[86]

Democratic and Political Implications

Throughout the period since 1990, discussion of the transformative or world-building potential of the Internet has included within it a focus on its implications for democracy.[87] Berners-Lee, for instance, held in 1999 that '[i]f we end up producing a structure in hyperspace that allows us to work together harmoniously, that would be a metamorphosis'. He hoped the process he envisaged would take place by stages, but nonetheless held 'it would result in a huge restructuring of society'. It would be possible to 'find a whole new set of financial, ethical, cultural and governing structures to which we can choose to belong, rather than having to pick the ones we happen to physically live in'. Eventually, 'those structures that work best would become more important in the world'. Berners-Lee concluded that 'democratic systems might take on different shapes'.[88]

For the purposes of this book, democracy rests on the principle that government should draw its authority from and be subject to some form of control by the people, who should be equal in their enjoyment of basic rights.[89] If the Internet can alter the speed, nature, and scale of interactions between individuals and institutions or people who represent them,[90] what impact might it have upon the realisation of this ideal?[91] Discussion of this question often rested on an assumption that democracy was in some way under threat or in decline.[92] Such debate from 1990 onwards was to some extent the continuation of a pre-existing discourse regarding the potential of various forms of electronic and communications technology to enhance

85 For opposition to determinism in the context of internet history, see Weber, 'A Common Language', p. 30.

86 Benjamin R. Barber, 'The New Telecommunications Technology: Endless Frontier or the End of Democracy?' in *A Passion for Democracy: American Essays* (Princeton University Press, 1998), pp. 258–82, 261.

87 For a useful overview of works in the field, see Coleman, *Can the Internet Strengthen Democracy?*, pp. 120–5. For an earlier review, see Matthew Hindman, *The Myth of Digital Democracy* (Princeton University Press, 2009), ch. 1.

88 Berners-Lee, *Weaving the Web*, p. 224.

89 See e.g. Beetham, David, Edzia Carvalho, Todd Landman, and Stuart Weir, *Assessing the Quality of Democracy: A Practical Guide* (International IDEA, Stockolm, 2008), pp. 20–1; Robert A. Dahl, *Democracy and Its Critics* (Yale University Press, New Haven, 1989).

90 e.g. Committee on Standards in Public Life, *Intimidation in Public Life: A Review by the Committee on Standards in Public Life*, Cm. 9543 (Stationery Office, London, 2017), pp. 32–3.

91 Wilhelm, Democracy in the Digital Age, p. 4.

92 e.g. Stephen Coleman and Jay G. Blumler, *The Internet and Democratic Citizenship: Theory, Practice and Policy* (Cambridge University Press, 2009), p. 166.

public engagement in politics.[93] One of the co-authors of 'Cyberspace and the American Dream', Alvin Toffler, had made contributions in the field for more than two decades prior to its publication in 1994.[94] Writing in 1991, Mulgan described how 'proponents of electronic democracy' had already placed their confidence in '[a] range of technologies'. They included '[t]he opinion poll, or television and radio call in . . . interactive cable, videoconferencing, computer conferencing and electronic mail'. Mulgan described various 'small-scale experiments in the USA', such as 'the Televote Project in Hawaii' and 'the "QUBE" cable system in Columbus, Ohio'. Mulgan was a relative sceptic, holding that '[i]n the absence of a serious discussion of the structural foundations of democracy, the claims for an electronic agora are deceptive'.[95] We will explore these precursors to online political engagement projects in subsequent chapters.

The optimistic view of the Internet and democracy has had various components.[96] They include the idea that the technology supported a more healthy and open public debate of options and issues.[97] According to one strand of positive interpretation, it enabled individuals to obtain more information to help them to make decisions.[98] A related sense in which the Internet might be held to support democracy was in leading to greater transparency and less secrecy on the part of official authorities,[99] with the public better placed to hold them to account.[100] Contact between governors and public was supposedly rendered more sophisticated and easier to achieve, leading – in optimistic accounts – to more responsive and therefore more democratically satisfactory administration.[101] In theory, the Internet made it easier for people to combine for political purposes, so that they could exert influence in ways

[93] Benjamin R. Barber, *Strong Democracy: Participatory Politics for a New Age* (University of California Press, Berkeley, 1984/2003), pp. 273–8.

[94] See Ch. 4 of this volume.

[95] G. J. Mulgan, *Communication and Control: Networks and the New Economies of Communication* (Polity Press, Cambridge, 1991), pp. 66–8.

[96] For a succinct overview, see Jan A. G. M. Van Dijk and Kenneth L. Hacker, *Internet and Democracy in the Network* Society (Routledge, London, 2018), pp. 3–6.

[97] e.g. Breindl and Francq, 'Can Web 2.0 Applications Save e-Democracy?', p. 18; Coleman, *Can the Internet Strengthen Democracy?*, p. 99; Antje Gimmler, 'Deliberative Democracy, the Public Sphere and the Internet', *Philosophy & Social Criticism* 27(4) (2001): 21–39.

[98] Kevin Kelly, *Out of Control: The New Biology of Machines, Social Systems, and the Economic World* (Perseus, Cambridge, 1994), p. 466; Schmidt and Cohen, *The New Digital Age*, p. 56.

[99] Douglas C. Walton, 'Is Modern Information Technology Enabling the Evolution of a More Direct Democracy?', *World Futures* 63(5–6) (2007): 365–85, 378–80.

[100] Hindman, *The Myth of Digital Democracy*, p. 7.

[101] Breindl and Francq, 'Can Web 2.0 Applications Save e-Democracy?', pp. 18–19; Stephen Coleman and John Gotze, *Bowling Together: Online Public Engagement in Policy Deliberation* (Hansard Society, London, 2001), p. 5; Prime Minister and Minister for the Civil Service, *Modernising Government*, Cm. 4310 (Cabinet Office, London 1999), ch. 5, 'Information Age Government', available at: https://webarchive.nationalarchives.gov.uk/20131205122601/http://www.archive.official-documents.co.uk/document/cm43/4310/4310-05.htm, last accessed 9 February 2020; Van Dijk and Hacker, *Internet and Democracy in the Network* Society, pp. 174–88.

they might not otherwise have been able to do.[102] In these various interpretations, the Internet was a force for individual empowerment.[103]

The Internet, its advocates held, provided for freedom of expression, a vital component of democracy.[104] As a technology it was, according to the positive strand of thought, more egalitarian in nature than previous mass media such as newspapers, radio, and the television. In contrast to these predecessors (or at least the form they came to take in practice) it was argued that the Internet dissolved the old boundaries between a small group of producers and a mass audience of consumers. It was easier to become a disseminator of messages and potentially achieve wide exposure for them.[105] Users of the Internet could both receive and send communications and were therefore less passive than they would be when engaging with other media.[106] The Internet in theory provided for greater diversity of content and allowed for the expression of a wider range of opinions, arguably fostering the plurality that is essential to democracy.[107] It was, perhaps, harder than it was in the case of other media for powerful forces, such as governments or large corporations, to subordinate to their own agendas or to censor.[108] Some interpretations attached particular democratic potential to devices associated with Web 2.0. As the UK Committee on Standards in Public Life (which also discerned problems with their use for intimidation) put it in 2017: '[s]ocial media can be a democratising force, enabling citizens to communicate with those standing for office and their elected representatives more directly than ever before'. The Committee noted that '[d]uring elections, Parliamentary candidates can engage more easily and directly with those they are seeking to represent. Through social media, candidates can mobilise support, engage with opponents, and promote their political platforms.'[109]

Powerful support for the view that the Internet could enhance democracy came from Hillary Clinton in the January 2010 speech cited above. She saw it as promoting this objective on a global scale, asserting that '[t]he spread of information networks is forming a new nervous system for our planet', and that 'in many respects, information has never been so free. There are more ways to spread more ideas to more people than at any moment in history. And even in authoritarian countries, information networks are helping people discover new facts and making governments more accountable.' Clinton acknowledged that internet censorship took place in some parts of the world

102 Gates, *The Road Ahead*, p. 271; Schmidt and Cohen, *The New Digital Age*, pp. 3–4.

103 Mansell, *Imagining the Internet*, pp. 19–20; Schmidt and Cohen, *The New Digital Age*, p. 3.

104 Evans, *Maintaining Community in the Information Age*, pp. 51–2.

105 Breindl and Francq, 'Can Web 2.0 Applications Save e-Democracy?', p. 18; W. Russell Neuman, *The Future of the Mass Audience* (Cambridge University Press, 1991), p. ix.

106 e.g. Coleman and Blumler, *The Internet and Democratic Citizenship*, p. 168.

107 Walton, 'Is Modern Information Technology Enabling the Evolution of a More Direct Democracy?', pp. 377–8; Wilhelm, Democracy in the Digital Age, p. 147.

108 Breindl and Francq, 'Can Web 2.0 Applications Save e-Democracy?', p. 18; Walton, 'Is Modern Information Technology Enabling the Evolution of a More Direct Democracy?', pp. 377–80.

109 Committee on Standards in Public Life, *Intimidation in Public Life*, p. 31.

and that non-democratic regimes and terrorist groups might utilise the technology. But US foreign policy – her brief at the time as Secretary of State – was to promote 'a single internet where all of humanity has equal access to knowledge and ideas', advancing the values encapsulated in the US Bill of Rights, the 'Four Freedoms' that Franklin D. Roosevelt had articulated 1941, and the subsequent Universal Declaration of Human Rights in which Eleanor Roosevelt had played a central role. She saw the Internet and associated technologies as a force for religious freedom, for greater understanding between people of different faiths, and a means of achieving greater socio-economic equality of opportunity across the world. As Clinton put it: '[a] connection to global information networks is like an on-ramp to modernity'.

She referred approvingly to the fact that '[d]uring his visit to China in November ... President Obama held a town hall meeting with an online component to highlight the importance of the internet'. Clinton noted that, as well as being a means by which members of the public could promote causes such as fair elections in states including Iran and Moldova, 'even in established democracies like the United States, we've seen the power of these tools to change history. Some of you may still remember the 2008 presidential election here.' Yet Clinton had a complaint. She noted that '[a]s it stands, Americans can consider information presented by foreign governments'. The US did not 'block ... attempts to communicate with the people in the United States'. However, 'citizens in societies that practice censorship lack exposure to outside views. In North Korea, for example, the government has tried to completely isolate its citizens from outside opinions.'[110]

In hindsight, this speech contains many ironies. Clinton praised the use Obama made of digital technologies, and the US openness to external communications. But she was subsequently cast as the victim of online activities in her defeat by the Republican candidate, Donald Trump, in the 2016 presidential election. The part that the Internet played in this outcome became the subject of close scrutiny and controversy.[111] A number of observers were critical of the use the Trump team made of digital technology. They complained about supposedly aggressive, simplistic, misleading, contradictory online messages and problematic use of personal data. There were also allegations about online Russian interference in support of Trump, including via social media.[112] The term 'fake

[110] Hillary Rodham Clinton, United States Secretary of State, 'Remarks'.

[111] For analysis of social media in the 2016 presidential campaign, see Gunn Enli, 'Twitter as Arena for the Authentic Outsider: Exploring the Social Media Campaigns of Trump and Clinton in the 2016 US Presidential Election', *European Journal of Communication* 32(1) (2017): 50–61.

[112] See e.g. Scott Shane, 'The Fake Americans Russia Created to Influence the Election', *New York Times*, 7 September 2017, available at: www.nytimes.com/2017/09/07/us/politics/russia-facebook-twitter-election.html, last accessed 17 February 2020; Brian L. Ott, 'The Age of Twitter: Donald J. Trump and the Politics of Debasement', *Critical Studies in Media Communication* 34(1)(2017): 59–68.

news' – often applied to internet-based deceitful messaging – came into wider use in this year.[113] It was employed to describe the dissemination of dubious information serving to support the Trump campaign, though he himself came to use the same label in describing communications to which he objected.[114] The 'fake news' idea connected to other emergent concepts involving a tension between digital communications and reality, such as 'post truth'.[115] Similar doubts to those raised about the 2016 US contest would emerge in relation to another vote that took place in the same year, this time in the UK – the European Union referendum of 23 June.[116] These twin incidents encouraged more general concerns. Might online campaigning create the potential to compromise free elections and, by extension, democracy itself, of which they are a central defining feature? If so, the implications were grave.[117] (It is, however, the case that such apprehensions had greater resonance among those who disliked given outcomes such as the Trump presidency and UK exit from the European Union than those who did not.)

One commonly raised concern was that the Internet, or particular applications of it, served to compromise the quality of political discourse and deliberation, rather than enhancing it as some supposed it would. At the root of this perceived problem lay the commercial model on which the Internet functioned – suggesting products to people individually on a basis of their previous habits. In the political field, the effect was to present them with content that reinforced rather than challenged their views, selected to please them. In some accounts, the Internet consequently reinforced a tendency known as 'homophily', describing a tendency for people to engage with those that shared their outlooks. Cocooned by technological 'filter bubbles' that preselected material for them in accordance with their displayed tastes, the potential for them to take part in meaningful discussion and consideration was lessened.[118] Candidates, parties, and other politically orientated groups could deliberately utilise this technological feature through a practice known as 'microtargeting'. This technique involved aiming political material at individual voters chosen to appeal to the pre-existing preferences they revealed through their own online activities.[119]

113 Van Dijk and Hacker, *Internet and Democracy in the Network* Society, p. 63.

114 See e.g. Benjamin Kentish, 'Donald Trump Says He Is "Victim" of Dossier on His Russia Links that Was Paid for by Clinton Campaign', *The Independent*, 25 October 2017, available at: www.independent.co.uk/news/world/americas/us-politics/donald-trump-russia-dossier-hillary-clinton-campaign-latest-victim-us-election-a8019036.html, last accessed 17 February 2020.

115 Ott, 'The Age of Twitter'.

116 For an overview of issues that arose in relation to the Trump and EU referendum campaigns, see Jamie Bartlett, *The People vs Tech: How the Internet Is Killing Democracy (and How We Save It)* (Penguin, London, 2018), pp. 69–101.

117 For an overview of issues that arose in relation to the Trump and EU referendum campaigns, see Bartlett, *The People vs Tech*, pp. 99–101.

118 Andrew Blick, *Stretching the Constitution: The Brexit Shock in Historic Perspective* (Bloomsbury/Hart, Oxford, 2019), pp. 265–6.

119 Ibid., p. 271. Julianne Kerr Morrison, Ravi Naik, and Stephanie Hankey, *Data and Democracy in the Digital Age* (Constitution Society, London, 2018), pp. 50–2.

The same campaign could send contrasting or even contradictory messages to different people according to their discerned predilections. This approach, critics held, undermined the concept of democracy as involving choices between coherent, transparent programmes presented publicly. Two voters selecting the same party might, according to this analysis, have done so on a basis of pledges that were incompatible with those made to the other voter, without being aware of the contradictory commitments being offered.[120]

As well as creating democratic problems through the way in which it enabled the construction of communications networks, the Internet, some held, could impact negatively upon the quality of the messages themselves, and on wider discourse. As the Hansard Society *Audit of Political Engagement 15*, published in 2018, put it: '[s]ocial media, whatever the platform, provides an easy outlet for impulsive and reactive comment. An engagement culture governed, for example, by 280-character contributions does not lend itself to nuanced views or thoughtful deliberation.'[121] Online political content might be simplistic or misleading in nature, and intended to motivate by appealing to (and heightening) negative emotions rather than to reason.[122] Practices in the targeting of communications and the manner in which they were presented had implications for the content itself and the reception it was likely to receive. The overall environment, some believed, was conducive to more extreme and divisive messages, magnifying problematic political and social cleavages.[123] With such tendencies in mind, observers have presented the Internet as a vehicle for the phenomenon known as 'populism'. This term, often used in a derogatory sense, generally describes political movements which present themselves as championing the people – however defined – against supposed exploitative elites, challenging the established methods and structures of representative democracy.[124] It is possible to place both Trump and the movement that congealed around the 'leave' campaign of 2016 and later captured the UK government under Boris Johnson within this category (though such categorisations are open to discussion).

Such concerns connected with other criticisms of the political use of the Internet, and contrasted with aspects of the optimistic view Clinton had presented in 2010. For instance, while she had depicted it as a source of

120 Bartlett, *The People vs Tech*, pp. 84–5.

121 Hansard Society, *Audit of Political Engagement 15: The 2018 Report* (Hansard Society, London, 2018), p. 30.

122 Blick, *Stretching the Constitution*, p. 271; Morrison, Naik, and Hankey, *Data and Democracy in the Digital Age*, pp. 50–2; Ott, 'The Age of Twitter', pp. 59–68; Oliver Wright, 'Are We Being Dumbed Down by "News" from Social Media', *The Independent*, 16 December 2014, available at: www.independent.co.uk/voices/comment/are-we-being-dumbed-down-by-news-from-social-media-9929623.html, last accessed 19 February 2020.

123 Blick, *Stretching the Constitution*, pp. 265–6.

124 Sven Engesser, Nayla Fawzi, and Anders Olof Larsson, 'Populist Online Communication: Introduction to the Special Issue', *Information, Communication & Society* 20(9) (2017): 1279–92.

economic opportunity, critics held that the Internet exacerbated inequality; and they also noted that the US-based technology firms (which Clinton portrayed as her allies in the spread of democracy) were willing to comply with the requirements of authoritarian states. An increasing number of commentaries appeared expressing such concerns, a good example of which was the 2019 publication *Don't Be Evil: The Case against Big Tech*, by Rana Foroohar, an economics and business journalist.[125]

In fact, though events of 2016 prompted the voicing of concerns of this type, they had antecedents. Analysts had long postulated a number of ways in which the Internet might contribute to a weakening of democracy.[126] In the earlier years, a commonly expressed concern related to the existence of a so-called 'digital divide'.[127] The Internet might empower those who had access to it. But it would leave behind those who did not – and people who were not able to use the technology were likely to come from social groups that were already to some extent excluded.[128] Over time the Internet became more pervasive within the UK and internationally. But, as is discussed in Chapter 2 of this volume, access did not become universal and differential patterns of usage were an issue. Moreover, other concerns intensified.

From the outset, assessments of the Internet questioned how far it was supportive of democracy. For instance, they noted that it might be used for purposes such as entertainment, and not for promoting political awareness among the population. Indeed, it might serve to distract the public from issues regarding their governance in which they should be taking an interest.[129] Commentary drew attention to a range of possible abuses of the Internet. They included the potential for the invasion of personal privacy[130] and that it might be a suitable vehicle for demagogic or authoritarian political ends.[131] In pessimistic accounts, forces hostile to democracy, both within and without a given state, were able to deploy the Internet to pursue their malign ends.[132] In enduring non-democratic states, the Internet was not sufficient in itself to overturn the prevailing order.[133] There were doubts about the extent of the

[125] Rana Roroohar, *Don't Be Evil: The Case Against Big Tech* (Penguin, London, 2019). A summary of the case is found in ch. 1 of that book.

[126] For a prototypical example from within the post-1990 period assessed here, see Neuman, *The Future of the Mass Audience*, p. 28.

[127] Mansell, *Imagining the Internet*, p. 24.

[128] For analysis, see Wilhelm, Democracy in the Digital Age, pp. 69–72.

[129] Neuman, *The Future of the Mass Audience*, pp. 29–30.

[130] Howard Rheingold, *The Virtual Community: Finding Connection in a Computerised World* (Martin Secker & Warburg, London, 1994), pp. 280–1; Schmidt and Cohen, *The New Digital Age*, pp. 80–1.

[131] Paul Grosswiler, 'Historical Hopes, Media Fears, and the Electronic Town Meeting Concept: Where Technology Meets Democracy or Demagogy?', *Journal of Communications Inquiry* 22 (2) (April 1998): 133–51, 148.

[132] Mansell, *Imagining the Internet*, p. 20.

[133] Breindl and Francq, 'Can Web 2.0 Applications Save e-Democracy?', p. 18; Walton, 'Is Modern Information Technology Enabling the Evolution of a More Direct Democracy?', pp. 378–80.

diversity of political content that, in practice, it might or did provide to users.[134] Another possible problem identified with digital media involved that they might provide an excess or 'overload' of content to consumers that it would be difficult for them meaningfully to process and retain.[135] The Internet was held potentially to replicate pre-existing power structures.[136] It might serve to alienate already excluded groups, thereby denying them the opportunities for empowerment it could supposedly create. For instance, some research has identified social barriers to women using the Internet, and to gaining full benefits from it when they do so.[137]

By 2016, a substantial body of work questioning the social value of the technology was already developing.[138] In a 2015 report, the Intelligence and Security Committee of Parliament noted an episode that helped precipitate rising concern. It described how '[t]he extent to which our communications on the internet can be (and should be) accessed by others, particularly the intelligence Agencies, came into sharp focus in June 2013'. At this time 'a contractor working for the National Security Agency (NSA) in the United States, Edward Snowden, stole a cache of classified material'. Snowden went on to disseminate this content to 'media outlets around the world'. This episode gave rise 'to allegations that government agencies were engaged in blanket surveillance of the internet'. (The Committee, however, exonerated UK agencies from illegality.)[139]

After 2016 a narrative about the supposed toxicity of the Internet became more prevalent still. Though connected to them, it extended beyond the immediate issues of Trump or the EU referendum and its aftermath. Some of the foremost exponents of variants on this thesis were people who had once been more enthusiastic about the democratic potential of the Internet, and might have hopes that – were appropriate corrective action taken – such benefits could yet be achieved.[140] One perception that developed was that the network was a source of international instability and vehicle for authoritarianism, populism and terrorism, rather than a means of achieving a more

[134] Rheingold, *The Virtual Community*, pp. 277–8.

[135] A concept discussed early on in this period in Neuman, *The Future of the Mass Audience*, pp. 90–2.

[136] Breindl and Francq, 'Can Web 2.0 Applications Save e-Democracy?', p. 18; Evans, *Maintaining Community in the Information Age*, pp. 49–51; Hindman, *The Myth of Digital Democracy*, p. 9; Walton, 'Is Modern Information Technology Enabling the Evolution of a More Direct Democracy?', pp. 377–80.

[137] e.g. Vinitha Johnson, 'Women and the Internet: A Micro Study in Chennai, India', *Indian Journal of Gender Studies*, 17(1) (2010): 151–63, 151–2.

[138] For the immediate pre-2016 period, see e.g. Andrew Keen, *The Internet Is Not the Answer* (Atlantic, London, 2015); Lanier, *Who Owns the Future?*; Evgeny Morozov, *To Save Everything, Click Here: Technology, Solutionism and the Urge to Fix Problems that Don't Exist* (Penguin, London, 2013).

[139] Intelligence and Security Committee of Parliament, *Privacy and Security*, p. 9.

[140] Lanier, for instance, fits within this category. Lanier, *Who Owns the Future?*, p. xi.

democratic global unity.[141] Criticisms were partly based on claims about the impact of social media applications.[142] As well as being presented as conduits for the dissemination of simplistic messages, distortion, falsehood, and hostility, they were depicted as a vehicle for surveillance of individual behaviour by both corporations and governments.[143] Communication on social media could take the form of personal abuse, for which women – and especially women from ethnic minority groups – were frequently a target. Such messaging was often more likely to be shared by others and therefore disseminate more widely, both amplifying and creating an incentive for extreme, personalised hostility. The potential for anonymity seems to have aggravated this trend.[144]

The contrast with previously expressed optimism was stark. In 1995, Sadie Plant had seen the ability to conceal true identity online as potentially beneficial for women, and hoped that the Internet would help release marginalised social groups from oppressive social structures. There were cases, she recognised, of 'virtual sexual harassment' and misogynistic behaviour. Men using the network outnumbered women. Nonetheless, the qualities characterising the Internet that she discerned – while not necessarily 'positively feminine' – nonetheless went 'against everything dear to the heart of all power structures – and the phallic principles that keep them secure'.[145] In 2017, the Committee on Standards in Public Life described evidence it had received from the office of Diane Abbott, a black woman Labour MP, that '[t]he first thing we do in the morning is to block and delete online abuse, usually whilst having breakfast. Porridge with one hand, deleting abuse with the other.'[146] Members of the institution that is the focus for this study had become targets.

The Internet was perceived to have had the effect of undermining the business model on which professional journalism rested, with negative consequences for the standards of political reporting to the public.[147] Far from being an open medium, it had come under the control of a small group of entities, some of which were governments, others of which were commercial corporations managing to evade appropriate forms of regulation because of their immense wealth and transnational status. (The WikiLeaks organisation, formed in 2006, set out to utilise the Internet as a means of exposing some of these perceived abuses, through disseminating confidential information.[148]) Early in the period under examination some accounts depicted digital

[141] House of Lords Select Committee on International Relations, *UK Foreign Policy in a Shifting World Order*, p. 5.
[142] Bartlett, *The People vs Tech*, p. 12.
[143] Roroohar, *Don't Be Evil*, pp. 10–11.
[144] Committee on Standards in Public Life, *Intimidation in Public Life*, pp. 33, 27, 34.
[145] Plant, 'Babes in the Net', p. 28.
[146] Committee on Standards in Public Life, *Intimidation in Public Life*, p. 38.
[147] See e.g. Martin Moore, *Democracy Hacked: Political Turmoil and Information Warfare in the Digital Age* (Oneworld, London, 2018), ch. 6.
[148] For a critical assessment of Wikileaks, see e.g. Schmidt and Cohen, *The New Digital Age*, p. 43.

communications as likely to challenge the privileged position of 'middlemen'.[149] But an increasingly pervasive account depicted a small group of corporations that had inserted themselves into economic processes, extracting much and generating little. Between them, this analysis held, they had achieving unprecedented market dominance, extracting at unimaginable magnitude the personal information of their users and exploiting it by means including selling it to advertisers, at vast profit. They included Alphabet (the Google parent company), Facebook, Apple, Netflix, Amazon, and Chinese equivalents such as Alibaba.[150] They supposedly had the effect of hollowing out the economy, undermining the position of skilled workers or the 'middle class', however defined, and concentrating wealth in a tiny group.

In 2019, Shoshana Zuboff made an important contribution to this school. She argued that a new economic model – 'surveillance capitalism' – had developed. Its practitioners – such as Google – were able to monitor on a mass scale the minutiae of individual behaviour, translating the data acquired into social, economic, and political power to an extent not previously witnessed. Through the use of algorithms – sets of instructions that modelled likely future decisions on a basis of past behaviour, that could in turn create new algorithms of their own – they were able to anticipate personal choices and make their predictions become reality. Zuboff depicted this phenomenon as a threat to many key aspects of human existence, including to meaningful democratic self-government. The ubiquity of the technology meant that people were trapped within a system of exploitation from which a realistic means of escape was not apparent.[151] The potential for self-fulfilling prophecy even raised questions about the concept of free will itself. Theses of this kind in a sense reversed a previous premise that already dominant forces would monopolise and subordinate the Internet for their own ends. According to this newer outlook, entities that had become pre-eminent in the use of digital communications were able to translate this ascendancy into a more general hegemony. If we were to apply the analogy of the Internet as environment, then it provided a base from which incursions into the offline world were possible – literally in the case of the development of the 'Internet of things', through which physical devices became additional means of data collection.[152]

Nonetheless, a more positive outlook had important and considered advocates, such as Stephen Coleman. He continued to hold that – while political authorities had failed to capitalise on the engagement potential of this technology – the possibility remained for them to do so, and that recent threats to the system added to the urgency of such action.[153] Furthermore,

[149] Gates, *The Road Ahead*, p. 272.
[150] For a recent version of this thesis, see Roroohar, *Don't Be Evil.*
[151] Zuboff, *The Age of Surveillance Capitalism.*
[152] Ibid., p. 203.
[153] Coleman, *Can the Internet Strengthen Democracy?*

circumstances arising from the coronavirus pandemic of 2020 encouraged to some extent the adoption of a different narrative. The widespread physical containment and urgent need for access to information characterising this episode served to promote more favourable assessments of the Internet. David Omand, a former senior UK intelligence and security official, captured this sense of a partial rehabilitation for the technology in a relatively early phase of the emergency. A self-isolator at the time, he suggested that events following the virus outbreak demonstrated immense value on the part of the Internet – though he also noted there were potential problems. The technology was 'coming into its own, a digital coming of age, during the Covid-19 pandemic'. In his judgement '[t]he world of interpersonal internet communication will never be the same again'. Omand regarded circumstances then prevailing as 'the first in which we can see how valuable internet purchasing and social media are in preserving the fabric of everyday life and the personal interactions that are at the heart of our shared humanity'. It was 'the first time in our history' that it was not necessary 'to face alone the isolation of ignorance, quarantine or social distance in the face of communicable disease'. Nonetheless 'with that welcome public reliance on digital connectivity comes a different vulnerability, especially for those most at risk from the disease. For criminal greed and authoritarian malice do not respect our difficulties, they thrive on them.'[154] This more pessimistic aspect would gain in force in the weeks and months that followed, with the spread of false information about the virus by hostile foreign states and groups, internal extremists, and profit-seekers: the so-called 'infodemic'.[155]

Representative Democracy

A sub-question of the general topic of the Internet and democracy involves what it means for the representative variant of this form of government.[156] Analysis in this area has drawn attention to this technology as a means of discerning the opinions of members of the public swiftly and with relative ease, and creating the possibility for the public to coalesce around, and exert force in support of, specific causes.[157] A possible conclusion arising from such observations was that intermediary institutions creating combined policy platforms and taking decisions on behalf of the public were less relevant. More direct methods, with the public taking views on a case-by-case basis, might come increasingly to the fore.[158] Dick Morris, previously an adviser to Bill Clinton, held in 2001 that there was 'potential for widespread

[154] Omand, 'Hackers Will Try to Exploit Covid-19'.
[155] See Introduction and Ch. 8 of this volume.
[156] This theme is central to Bartlett, *The People vs Tech.*
[157] Gates, *The Road Ahead*, p. 272.
[158] Neuman, *The Future of the Mass Audience*, p. 6.

participation in Internet direct balloting on issues'.[159] In his programme, the idea of this network as a force for a single, global, self-governing entity surfaced once more. While referendums had long been in use in a number of US states,[160] Morris noted, they were not employed for federal decision-making. Morris, who was president of an initiative working in this field, Vote.com, argued that, with the rise of the Internet, this practice would take hold not only at national level in the United States,[161] but eventually on a global basis. As he put it 'the Internet will provide a central nervous system for the global body politics'. The 'electronic linkages' it created meant that 'voters will bind together with people from other lands to create a global political entity that has never existed before. Bypassing national representatives and speaking directly to one another, the people of the world will use the Internet increasingly to form a political unit for the future.' Morris concluded '[d]emocracy is on its way'.[162]

In a 2007 article on the subject of the Internet and direct democracy, Douglas C. Walton cites *The Economist* asserting, in January 2003, that '[t]he growing expectations of an educated public for whom individual choice is an important value, combined with the technology of an increasingly pervasive internet, will challenge the structures of all western governments based on representative models of democracy'. The journal judged that '[o]nce reliable methods for validating electronic votes have been found and internet penetration rates approach saturation, the internet will remove the biggest single obstacle to direct democracy – the physical difficulty of distributing information to a large population, engaging it in debate and collecting its votes'. At this point, 'probably during the next decade, many people will come to see national elections every few years as an extraordinarily blunt instrument for expressing the popular will, a remnant from the age of steam, when most representative institutions were invented'.[163] Within this type of scenario, a legislature such as the UK Parliament, along with other bodies such as political parties,[164] might seem under threat. Christine Bellamy and Charles D. Raab wrote an entry in the 1999 collection on the Internet and parliaments, cited in the Introduction to this volume, of which Coleman was a co-editor. In their chapter – entitled 'Wiring Up the Deck-Chairs?' – they wrote that 'the democracy that ICTs may help to re-invent is not likely to take a *parliamentary* form . . . [t]he most convincing uses for ICTs arise from

159 Dick Morris, 'Direct Democracy and the Internet', *Loyola Los Angeles Law Review* 34 (2001): 1033–54, 1041.
160 Ibid., pp. 1036–9.
161 Ibid., pp. 1048–9.
162 Ibid., p. 1053.
163 Walton, 'Is Modern Information Technology Enabling the Evolution of a More Direct Democracy?', p. 376.
164 Neuman, *The Future of the Mass Audience*, p. 6.

the vastly increased opportunities for individuals to acquire the means for direct, umediated political communication'.[165]

Some have welcomed this prospect. In a 2014 book about the crypto-currency, Bitcoin, the comedian and financial journalist Dominic Frisby predicted that, suitably adapted, the online technology underpinning it 'will . . . bring into question our system of representative democracy. The tech is there for people's identity to be proven and for them to vote instantly on just about any issue that comes up.' His list of possible subjects was: 'gay marriage, abortion law, planning permission, military intervention'. Frisbee advocated '[l]iquid democracy – where people actually vote on decisions as they get made'. He perceived it as 'surely a far truer democracy. Why then do you need a congressman or parliamentary representative?' He anticipated 'a huge battle for control . . . as those who have been outdated try to cling on'. Frisbee found this scenario 'all very exciting'.[166]

Though the prospect of online direct democracy has thrilled some, others have proved sceptical or fully hostile towards it.[167] In 1991, Mulgan discussed the proposition that '[e]lectronic democracy offers the removal of control from parliaments and governments into the home'. He held that '[t]he personalization of politics, and the bypass of intermediaries echo the consistent theme of network utopias, the idea that the only authentic control is direct unmediated'.[168] Mulgan added that advocates of 'electronic democracy' saw 'direct legislation by the people' as a means of quickening 'the long-term decline of political parties. If representation was to continue, representatives would be immediately and publicly accountable to their constituents.'[169] Mulgan took the view that '[i]deas of this kind raise enormous and probably unanswerable questions about implementation, about the framing of questions and about how governments would cope with inconsistent decision [sic], indeed with most of the basic questions of public policy that are at least formally solved in representative systems'.[170] He held that, in isolation, schemes of electronic democracy 'fail to ask how agendas of political discussion will be formed and how the network will bring people together rather than isolating them in their own homes'. Mulgan judged that '[d]emocracy depends also on media for argument, information and debate, mediations that sustain a public sphere of communication. Unmediated relationships between the individual citizen and the state will tend to be unbalanced and unequal.'

[165] Christine Bellamy and Charles D. Raab, 'Wiring Up the Deck-Chairs?' in Stephen Coleman, John Taylor, and Wim van de Donk (eds.), *Parliament in the Age of the Internet* (Oxford University Press, 1999), p. 157.

[166] Dominic Frisby, *Bitcoin: The Future of Money?* (Unbound, London, 2014), e-book location 2682–90.

[167] Coleman and Gotze, Bowling Together, p. 5.

[168] Mulgan, *Communication and Control*, p. 66.

[169] Ibid., p. 66.

[170] Ibid., p. 67.

The conclusion he reached was that 'proponents of electronic democracy fail to address . . . the need for diverse flows of information, for political education and an active, argumentative civil society'.[171]

In 1992, the independent US presidential candidate, Ross Perot, advocated the use of electronic technologies to facilitate exercises in direct public engagement and voting.[172] This proposal attracted criticism. A variety of media commentators denounced the idea as of demagogic and authoritarian implications, likely to debase political discourse and inflame divisions.[173] In some ways this episode was a rehearsal for the controversies that surrounded Trump from 2016 in his use of Twitter and other digital techniques.[174] A potential concern was that electronic technologies might empower one constitutional branch, the executive, at the expense of another, the legislature, through enabling the former to liaise directly with voters, excluding the latter.[175] As Howard Rheingold, an advocate of digital communications who also saw in them potential difficulties, put it in 1995: '[i]f the United States is on the road to a version of electronic democracy in which the president will have electronic town hall meetings, including instant voting-by-telephone to "go directly to the people" (and perhaps bypass Congress?) on key issues, it is important for American citizens to understand the potential pitfalls of decision making by plebiscite'. Rheingold cautioned that '[m]edia manipulated plebiscites as political tools go back to Joseph Goebbels, who used radio so effectively in the Third Reich'.[176]

Writing in the same year as Rheingold, Gates anticipated that '[s]omeone will doubtless propose total "direct democracy," having all issues put to a vote'. But he did not 'think direct voting would be a good way to run a government'. Gates maintained there was a need 'in governance for representatives – middlemen – to add value. They are the ones whose job it is to take time to understand all the nuances of complicated issues.' Noting that '[p]olitics involves compromise', he argued it could only be achieved through 'a relatively small number of representatives making decisions on behalf of the people who elected them'. This system allowed for the development of 'nonobvious solutions' that would not be possible under a system of 'direct democracy', since 'voters might not understand the trade-offs necessary for long-term success'.[177] In the two-and-a-half decades since Gates wrote, the calls he

[171] Ibid., p. 68.

[172] Starr Roxanne Hiltz and Murray Turoff, *The Network Nation: Human Communication via Computer* (MIT Press, Cambridge, 1993), p. 480.

[173] Grosswiler, 'Historical Hopes, Media Fears, and the Electronic Town Meeting Concept', p. 148.

[174] See e.g. Michael D. Shear, Maggie Haberman, Nicholas Confessore, Karen Yourish, Larry Buchanan, and Keith Collins, 'How Trump Reshaped the Presidency in Over 11,000 Tweets', *New York Times*, 2 November 2019, available at: www.nytimes.com/interactive/2019/11/02/us/politics/trump-twitter-presidency.html, last accessed 24 February 2020.

[175] Neuman, *The Future of the Mass Audience*, p. 6.

[176] Rheingold, *The Virtual Community*, p. 287.

[177] Gates, *The Road Ahead*, p. 272.

anticipated for online popular decision-making were made but they have not yet been implemented, giving rise to doubts about whether they ever will come into practice.[178]

Some analysis has suggested that, rather than being a means of supplanting or circumventing representative organs, the Internet is a means of interacting with and pressurising them.[179] This technology might also provide the basis for creating a new intermediary institution alongside the others, offering means by which the public can engage more fully with representatives.[180] A further variant on the prognosis for representative democracy is that its institutions can utilise the Internet for themselves, strengthening their interactions with the people they are supposed to serve, and performing their roles more effectively.[181] Such was the premise of the Speaker's Commission on Digital Democracy considered at the head of this chapter. Two advocates of variants on participatory mechanisms other than direct decision-making by the public presented them as a means of avoiding this more radical, and undesirable variant on digital participation. As they put it: 'one of the reasons for promoting e-democracy is to strengthen representative structures so that the allure of "technopopulism" remains resistible'.[182] There was debate about the compatibility of the representative system with electronic forms of participation. One view was that it was might enthusiastically employ the Internet, but that it was not necessarily well-advised to do so. In 2004, Karen F. Evans held that governments, including in the UK, were adopting digital engagement too eagerly and without the necessary degree of critical scrutiny.[183] Nearly a decade later, Evgeny Morozov depicted various uses of the Internet as debilitating to representative democracy, through subjecting it to transparency and targeted political pressure in ways with which it struggled to cope.[184]

Political Perspectives

During the period since 1990, a variety of political movements have attached significance to the Internet and connected technologies. They have variously promoted it as a vehicle for socially desirable outcomes and utilised it for their own purposes. It has attracted interest from different parts of the spectrum. In the early 1990s, Al Gore, running mate to Bill Clinton in 1992 and again in 1996,

178 Walton, 'Is Modern Information Technology Enabling the Evolution of a More Direct Democracy?', p. 366; Van Dijk and Hacker, *Internet and Democracy in the Network* Society, pp. 4–5.

179 Walton, 'Is Modern Information Technology Enabling the Evolution of a More Direct Democracy?', pp. 377.

180 e.g. Coleman and Blumler, *The Internet and Democratic Citizenship*, pp. 169–97.

181 See analysis in Blick, *Stretching the Constitution*, pp. 278–81; Van Dijk and Hacker, *Internet and Democracy in the Network* Society, pp. 174–88.

182 Coleman and Gotze, *Bowling Together*, p. 5.

183 Evans, *Maintaining Community in the Information Age*, pp. 65–6.

184 Morozov, *To Save Everything, Click Here*, esp. ch. 4.

Vice President from 1993, and unsuccessful presidential candidate in 2000, famously advocated the construction of an 'Information Superhighway'.[185] In his rhetoric, a digital communications network took on the appearance of public sector infrastructure programme.[186] The Internet could also have appeal to the Left in the UK. For instance, it was perceived as a possible a means of achieving social inclusion for hitherto marginalised groups.[187] The UK Labour government of Tony Blair presented the utilisation of internet-related technologies as important both to attaining more effective government[188] and to addressing issues of social inequality.[189] Later in this period, in Opposition, Labour came under the radical-Left leadership of Jeremy Corbyn (2015–20). His use of the Internet included the novel method of deriving the content of questions he put to the Prime Minister during the weekly parliamentary slot from members of the public, submitted to Corbyn online.[190]

Towards the other end of the political spectrum, in the 1990s, digital communications also appealed to Republicans in the United States, most notably Newt Gingrich.[191] In their 1996 account of what they termed 'The Californian Ideology', Barbrook and Cameron described how 'a loose alliance of writers, hackers, capitalists and artists from the West Coast of the USA have succeeded in defining a heterogeneous orthodoxy for the coming information age'.[192] The outlook they discerned had a strong libertarian character, and in their view had become increasingly associated with the free market variant of this school. The authors detected an irony in this trend, in that the development of internet technology had been heavily reliant upon government policy initiatives and subsidies.[193] More recent historical analysis of internet-related political attitudes has noted a tendency to emphasise the minimisation of governmental intervention as an end.[194] Dominic Frisby captured some of the potential appeal of such technologies in his work on Bitcoin, when asking: 'If everything can be dis-intermediated and decentralized, what about the

[185] Mansell, *Imagining the Internet*, p. 42.
[186] See Wilhelm, *Democracy in the Digital Age*, p. 68.
[187] Samantha Hellawell, *Beyond Access: ICT and Social Inclusion* (Fabian Society, London, 2001).
[188] See Prime Minister and Minister for the Civil Service, *Modernising Government*, ch. 5, 'Information Age Government'.
[189] e.g. Social Exclusion Unit, *A New Commitment to Neighbourhood Renewal: National Strategy Action Plan* (Cabinet Office, London, 2001), p. 37, available at: www.bris.ac.uk/poverty/downloads/keyofficialdocuments/Neighbourhood%20Renewal%20National%20Strategy%20Report.pdf, last accessed 9 February 2020.
[190] Jon Stone, 'Jeremy Corbyn Is Crowdsourcing Questions to ask David Cameron at PMQs', *The Independent*, 13 September 2015, available at: www.independent.co.uk/news/uk/politics/jeremy-corbyn-is-crowdsourcing-questions-to-ask-david-cameron-at-pmqs-10498633.html, last accessed 16 February 2020.
[191] Flichy, *The Internet Imaginaire*, pp. 156–68.
[192] Barbrook and Cameron, 'The Californian Ideology', p. 44.
[193] Ibid., pp. 44–72.
[194] Z. Isadora Hellegren, 'A History of Crypto-Discourse: Encryption as a Site of Struggles to Define Internet Freedom', *Internet Histories* 1(4): 285–311.

services governments provide – healthcare, welfare and education? The bureaucratic middleman megalith that makes them so expensive could be circumvented altogether.'[195]

As I have shown in a 2019 monograph, the Internet has appealed to the political Right in the UK. In a 1995 Bow Group pamphlet, Julian Roche proposed means by which digital communications technologies could strengthen existing institutions and practices.[196] His was a programme for strengthening traditions by new methods. Late in the first decade of the twenty-first century, a group of Conservative politicians – among whom Douglas Carswell, Member of the UK House of Commons (who subsequently joined the UK Independence Party) and Daniel Hannan, a Member of the European Parliament, were prominent – developed a more radical platform, that overtly drew on the Gingrich agenda. Within it, they presented the Internet as means by which candidates and policies previously excluded by the established political and media elite could appeal to voters, especially during referendum campaigns.[197] Their broad agenda would come into ascendancy in the UK (and elsewhere), especially from 2016. This political shift took place in a context generated by a popular vote on EU membership held in this year – in which the role played by social media became, after the fact, a subject of pronounced controversy. Dominic Cummings, head of the official lead campaign group for the 'leave' side and subsequently a senior adviser to Boris Johnson as Prime Minister from 2019 (up to his forced departure in 2020), made himself a prominent advocate of the effectiveness of political communication techniques employing the Internet, attracting critical scrutiny in the process.[198]

Other, more extreme, political groupings and ideologues have become associated with online technology. In the UK, the British National Party – an organisation of fascist heritage that made significant political gains around the mid-2000s – despite its ambivalence towards technological advancement, was noted for the effectiveness of its online presence.[199] Various terrorists, for instance of the religious[200] or Far Right[201] variety, have utilised the Internet for promotion and recruitment. As we have noted, the term 'revolution' has frequently been employed – with differing connotations – in accounts of the impact of digital networks. One belief system associated with the overthrow of

[195] Frisby, *Bitcoin: The Future of Money?*, e-book location 2682–6.
[196] Blick, *Stretching the Constitution*, pp. 278–84.
[197] Ibid., p. 138.
[198] Ibid., pp. 284–6.
[199] Peter John, Helen Margetts, David Rowland, and Stuart Weir, *The BNP: The Roots of Its Appeal* (Democratic Audit, Essex, 2006), p. 10.
[200] Jaime M. Freilich, 'Section 230's Liability Shield in the Age of Online Terrorist Recruitment', *Brookings Law Review 83* (2017): 675.
[201] Maura Conway, 'Determining the Role of the Internet in Violent Extremism and Terrorism: Six Suggestions for Progressing Research', *Studies in Conflict & Terrorism* 40(1) (2017): 77–98.

political systems is anarchism. The idea that it might somehow manifest itself through the Internet has attained currency.[202] The 'cypherpunk' or 'crypto-anarchist' movement already existed in some form by the beginning of the period assessed here,[203] as analysed by Robert Gibson in his MA dissertation written while studying at King's College London.[204] The conception of the Internet as an environment free from controlling authorities has encouraged references to the ideology associated with this idea. In their 2013 work, *The New Digital Age*, Erich Schmidt and Jared Cohen of Google claimed that '[t]he Internet is the largest experiment involving anarchy in history' and that the Internet was 'the world's largest ungoverned space'.[205] The ironies of two authors in their position making such claims are plain. Providers of glowing endorsements placed at the front of the text included Tony Blair, Bill Clinton, and Henry A. Kissinger, whose careers had been as operators within established political structures, and none of whom were known for their anarchist leanings.[206] Google often figures in accounts of the Internet as an environment dominated by a small number of wealth-hording powerful interests that between them pose a threat to freedom. Moreover, the version of anarchism presented here is presumably more of the libertarian than socially egalitarian variety. Wealthy people – even billionaires – associating with an ideology advocates of which once sought the abolition of private property might seem incongruous and intellectually somewhat vulgar. But it should be recorded that certain Russian aristocrats – who were from the nineteenth century among the most powerful advocates of anarchism in its Leftist form – were themselves unlikely proponents of their chosen cause (though for them the pursuit of their cause meant discarding a comfortable lifestyle, unlike their twenty-first century internet would-be successors). As we will see, where the subject of the role of science and technology in transforming power relationships is concerned, there is some continuity between the ideas of the more considered anarchists and those who adopted the term in a seemingly casual fashion later.

In some cases, the Internet became less a means of achieving a pre-existing ideological goal, and more the central focus or even the end in itself. The authors of 'Cyberspace and the American Dream' presented in 1994 a specific political programme for the technologically induced new era (a 'Third Wave')

[202] Kelly, *Out of Control*, p. 464.

[203] See e.g. the account by Timothy May of his 'Crypto Anarchist Manifesto', dating to mid-1988 and circulated at two gatherings in that year, that May continued to promote thereafter, available at: www.activism.net/cypherpunk/crypto-anarchy.html, last accessed 9 February 2020.

[204] Robert Gibson, '"Cypherpunks Write Code": What Is Crypto-Anarchism, Has It Been Distinctive during the Post-Internet Era, and What Impact Has It Had on Wider Society?', submitted to King's College London, 10 September 2018.

[205] Schmidt and Cohen, *The New Digital Age*, p. 3.

[206] Ibid., p. 2.

they perceived. They identified a 'need ... to revamp the policies and programs that are slowing the creation of cyberspace'. There should be a 'focus on removing barriers to competition and massively deregulating the fast-growing telecommunications and computing industries'. While the size of government would reduce drastically, 'smaller government does not imply weak government; nor does arguing for smaller government require being "against" government for narrowly ideological reasons'. In fact, the transition they depicted would necessitate 'a level of government activity not seen since the New Deal'. The authors made five recommendations for 'Creating a Third Wave Government'. It needed to avoid the 'factory model' of 'standardization, routine and mass-production' and move towards promoting 'uniqueness'. It ought not to 'centralize control' and should instead 'work to spread power – to empower those closest to the decision'. There should not be inducement to 'geographic concentration'. Rather, government of the Third Wave should pursue programmes that 'permit people to work at home, and to live wherever they choose'. Rather than being 'based on the idea of mass culture', 'Third Wave policies' should 'help transform diversity from a threat into an array of opportunities'. These five principles should be applied throughout government – 'from the defense and intelligence community to health care and education' – and would lead eventually to 'a complete transformation of government as we know it'.[207]

The direct purpose of the Barlow manifesto of 1996 was to oppose governmental efforts to regulate the Internet. He referred to a specific intervention by the US authorities to which he objected, that had prompted him to issue the declaration. The 'Telecommunications Reform Act' – passed the day he published his statement online – contravened, he held, the US Constitution and 'insults the dreams of Jefferson, Washington, Mill, Madison, De Tocqueville, and Brandeis'. Suggesting that the movement he espoused was a continuation of a historic political project, the author insisted '[t]hese dreams must now be born anew in us'. Faced with such 'increasingly hostile and colonial measures', participants in cyberspace were, Barlow supposed, in an analogous position to 'those previous lovers of freedom and self-determination who had to reject the authorities of distant, uninformed powers'. The contemporary heirs to this challenge had to 'declare our virtual selves immune to your sovereignty, even as we continue to consent to your rule over our bodies'. They would 'spread ourselves across the Planet so that no one can arrest our thoughts'.[208]

In the following decade, the tendency for the Internet in itself to become the focus for political programmes asserted itself in a fashion that was – in form, if not content – more traditional: with the (swift but relatively brief) international rise of the Pirate Party movement. A loose grouping, the core Pirate platform focused on internet-related issues: the right to privacy and freedom

[207] Dyson et al., 'Cyberspace and the American Dream'.
[208] Barlow, 'A Declaration of the Independence of Cyberspace'.

from governmental surveillance carried out on security grounds, and to share material online without being restricted by excessive copyright regulations. In this sense, it focused both on realising the freedoms that the Internet promised and preventing the abuse of this technology by oppressive authorities (parallels might be drawn here with the WikiLeaks cause). The Party launched in Sweden in 2006, where it secured two places in the European Parliament in 2009. It spread elsewhere, reaching Australia and the United States as well as other parts of the European continent. Notable electoral progress occurred for the party in Germany, including securing nearly 9 per cent of the vote share in elections to the Berlin state parliament in 2011.[209]

This tendency suggested a possibility that the Internet could form the basis for a political movement or even ideology in its own right. Two decades previously, few had heard of or used this technology. The rise was dramatic. But what did it mean in practice? Views differed on both what the Internet was and its implications, good or bad. They were difficult to reconcile. Moreover, as the preceding discussion of the role of printing demonstrates, uncertainty might well remain long after the Internet has ceased to be a new device. Interpretations of the Internet, however, whether they leant towards optimism or concern, tended to regard it as important – or even revolutionary. Some of the more excited projections were similar in tone to Andrew Marvell in his account of the printing press. Perhaps one day historians will be more dubious on this count. They may also be reluctant to regard this technology as a single defined entity arriving at a specific point, and stress its amorphousness and mutability. But – again like printing – regardless of its position in chains of causality, the Internet has been connected to important events. They include the supposed surge of populism and associated events such as the Trump ascendancy and 'leave' result in the 2016 EU referendum. The Internet has been hard to ignore. It has impacted upon perception and consequently influenced judgements and actions. If only for these reasons, it has made a difference.

Historical analysis of the political significance of communications technologies suggests a need to give proper regard to context. The Internet appeared and was adopted within a particular environment. This social surround shaped the way the technology manifested itself, which in turn impacted upon and became a part of it. A better understanding of such processes can be obtained from the particular standpoint of entities that formed an important part of this setting. The UK Parliament is a good starting point for such study. Within the UK political and constitutional system, it lay at the intersection of the perceived tendencies that the Internet generated. It was responsible, in theory, for their domestic legal and political management and was required to respond to and utilise the Internet as an institution. In studying Parliament,

[209] Martin Fredriksson, 'The Pirate Party and the Politics of Communication', *International Journal of Communication* 9 (2015): 909–24, 911–13.

we can also derive the benefits of historical perspective. It has roots lying arguably as far back as the Anglo-Saxon era, and is certainly as old as the UK itself. Before the Internet, the legislature had experienced, regulated, and adapted to a series of previous technological changes and the ideas and forces connected to them. Now it had to engage with this new invention. To begin this analysis, the next chapter focuses on direct parliamentary engagement with the Internet in the period from 1996.

2

The Permanent Platform

Parliament Online, 1996–2020

On 25 March 2020, the House of Commons entered Easter Recess.[1] It did so, on a proposal from the government, a week earlier than originally planned. This decision took place in the context of the coronavirus pandemic. Cessation of physical meetings was a logical step at a time of global efforts to contain the outbreak through mass confinement.[2] (The House of Lords, given the age profile and consequent vulnerability of its membership, faced even greater disruption.[3]) But the circumstances that placed obstacles in the way of the operation of the Commons (and Parliament generally) also heightened the need for some of the very functions that had become more difficult to perform. Before dispersing, Parliament had swiftly passed the *Coronavirus Act 2020*. Using this legislation and other laws, the executive took on immense discretionary powers that were widely judged to be of unsurpassed extent in peacetime.[4] Given the swollen authority attached to the UK government, it was important that the body with principal responsibility for holding it to account should be able to continue operating in some way.[5] The Commons authorities turned to digital communications technology to assist them in sustaining this function. In doing so, they contemplated what might turn out to be a moment of transition in the history of Parliament (with the Lords pursuing similar options[6]). At the very least, they would provide a precedent for the future.

[1] 'House of Commons in Recess, Not "Shut Down"', 25 March 2020, available at: www.parliament.uk/business/news/2020/march/house-of-commons-in-recess-not-shut-down/, last accessed 5 April 2020.

[2] 'Commons Could Close Early Due to Coronavirus', *BBC News*, 23 March 2020, available at: www.bbc.co.uk/news/uk-politics-52012377, last accessed 5 April 2020.

[3] Lord Fowler, Lord Speaker, statement, 19 March 2020, available at: www.parliament.uk/business/news/2020/march/lord-speaker-statement-on-covid-19/, last accessed 13 April 2020.

[4] Daniel Kraemer, 'Coronavirus: What's in the Emergency Legislation?', *BBC News*, 25 March 2020, available at: www.bbc.co.uk/news/uk-politics-52004116, last accessed 13 April 2020.

[5] Andrew Blick and Clive Walker, 'Why Did Government Not Use the Civil Contingencies Act?', *Law Society Gazette*, 2 April 2020, available at: www.lawgazette.co.uk/legal-updates/why-did-government-not-use-the-civil-contingencies-act/5103742.article, last accessed 13 April 2020.

[6] 'Lord Speaker's Statement on UK Parliament's Response to the Spread of COVID-19', Lord Fowler, Lord Speaker, 7 April 2020, available at: www.parliament.uk/business/news/2020/march/lord-speaker-statement-on-covid-19/, last accessed 13 April 2020.

As noted in Chapter 1, the coronavirus pandemic created a widespread need both for access to up-to-date information, and for means of maintaining social contact while adhering to distancing rules. The Internet could help fulfil both requirements. Usage of this system increased in parts of the world applying restrictions on movement, testing its ability to cope under pressure, and demonstrating its value and the extent of dependency upon it (as well as its potential use for dis- and mis-information).[7] In turning for additional support to a network of which it already made extensive use, the Commons was therefore part of a global tendency towards more intense and innovative utilisation of that technology. Inevitably, there was (and would continue to be) debate about how far the pandemic response simply accelerated developments already underway, or actually triggered changes that might never have occurred otherwise. But, this question aside, there was at least a case for arguing that the sum of the repercussions was likely to be immense.[8] Developments within the UK Parliament would form part of them.

The day after entering Recess, the House of Commons – utilising the Internet – issued a statement on its website insisting that this decision 'does not mean that the House of Commons is shut down. Far from it.' It set out a variety of measures, relying heavily on digital communications, that would enable it to carry on performing its core functions. (Similar developments were taking place in other sectors of the constitution, including, on 31 March 2020, for the first time ever, a Cabinet meeting – via Zoom – for which no ministers were in physical attendance.[9]) Many MPs would 'be holding virtual surgeries'. The Commons had 'already passed a motion to allow Select Committees to work remotely, so they can safely continue to scrutinise Government during this time of national crisis'. A collaboration between the Parliamentary Digital Service and the Parliamentary Broadcasting Unit had facilitated 'Parliament's first ever remote oral evidence session', held by the Health and Social Care Committee on that day, 26 March.[10]

A letter from the Speaker of the House of Commons, Sir Lindsay Hoyle, to all MPs, specified more detailed rules around this practice. He explained that members of select committees could take part 'in proceedings through email, conference calls, and digital conferencing', so long as they met certain

[7] Matt Burgess, 'No, Coronavirus Isn't Going to Break the Internet', *Wired*, 21 March 2020, available at: www.wired.co.uk/article/coronavirus-internet-speed-shut-down, last accessed 5 April 2020.

[8] For a US perspective on this point, see Jason Abbuzzese, David Ingram, and Sawyer Click, 'The Coronavirus Pandemic Drove Life Online. It May Never Return', *NBC News*, 28 March 2020, available at: www.nbcnews.com/tech/internet/coronavirus-pandemic-drove-life-online-it-may-never-return-n1169956, last accessed 5 April 2020.

[9] Andrew Woodcock, 'Coronavirus: UK's First Digital Cabinet Meeting Takes Place as Three Ministers Self-Isolate', *The Independent*, 31 March, available at: www.independent.co.uk/news/uk/politics/coronavirus-boris-johnson-matt-hancock-alister-jack-chris-whitty-cabinet-zoom-a9438921.html, last accessed 5 April 2020.

[10] 'House of Commons in Recess, Not "Shut Down"'.

requirements, including that technical and procedural specifications were fulfilled, and it was possible for officials to 'support the session'. This arrangement was intended to be 'temporary', lasting in the first instance 'until 30 June'. The Speaker could extend it if required. Hoyle did 'not envisage this facility being made permanent'. But, 'once the current crisis passes, colleagues will no doubt wish to evaluate whether there is merit in permanent authorisation of some form of remote participation in committee proceedings'. Hoyle noted that '[f]or hundreds of years Parliament has relied on the physical presence of Members in the Chamber and in Committee rooms to conduct its business'. In doing so he conveyed the immense historic significance of this institution acquiring the ability to proceed without convening in a single place.

Hoyle noted that recent measures swiftly taken had shown that there was 'more the House can do to facilitate agile working while enabling legislation, democratic scrutiny and representation'. After 'this crisis', he would 'establish a Speaker's Working Group to analyse the lessons we can learn and establish what solutions are needed (technologically, procedurally and logistically) to make us more robust in the future'.[11] The Speaker seemed to envisage that any repetition of these practices was likely mainly to be confined to emergencies, whenever they might happen. There would be pressure from some sources to return to more traditional methods as soon as was practically possible. But – as his comment about post-hoc reviews seemed to suggest – expedients adopted at this time might have wider influence upon regular as well as extraordinary practice. For instance, solutions reached at pace, that might seem to be mainly technical in nature (for instance, over whether to use Microsoft Teams or Zoom), could have lasting implications that were difficult to predict. Furthermore, as Hoyle recognised, events had furnished precedents, crucial from the point of view of the UK constitution, and perhaps especially Parliament. The potential use to be made of them in time to come was, again, hard fully to anticipate, but could be significant. Practices that had once been beyond the realm of practical experience had now become real.

A further measure the Speaker then advocated seemed potentially more dramatic still. In a letter to the Leader of the House of Commons (whose initiative was needed for this proposal), dated 1 April 2020, Hoyle, alongside other requests for government co-operation with the work of MPs, explained that '[o]nce the House returns, if we are still in the grip of the crisis where the physical presence of Members, or too many Members, in the Palace is not appropriate' he was 'keen that they should be able to participate in key parliamentary proceedings virtually, for example, oral questions, urgent

[11] 'Letter from the Speaker of the House of Commons, Sir Lindsay Hoyle, to MPs on Coronavirus', 27 March 2020, available at: www.parliament.uk/business/news/2020/march/letter-from-the-speaker-of-the-house-of-commons-sir-lindsay-hoyle-to-mps-on-coronavirus/, last accessed 5 April 2020.

questions, statements and PMQs'.[12] The press release accompanying this letter (issued online, naturally) summarised it as urging the introduction of a '"virtual" Parliament'.[13] This term and the measures taken at this time generated substantial media interest.[14] Hoyle had come to the office of Speaker amid expectations that he would prove to be a more restrained holder of the post than his forthright and controversial predecessor, John Bercow.[15] Yet he was now avowedly challenging a tradition as old Parliament itself – that it was of necessity a physical gathering. On 21 and 22 April, the Commons agreed to proposals for a temporary hybrid arrangement. 'Chamber' Proceedings could be attended either in person or remotely.[16] Emphasising the significance of the shift, on 12 May, the parliamentary website reported that 'the first ever remote division in the House of Commons' had taken place.[17] The willingness of Hoyle and others to countenance such a change was partly attributable to the severity of circumstances. But it also derived from the status already attained by the Internet, in society in general and in Parliament in particular. By what stages of development and over what period of time had the preconditions necessary to this occurrence come about?

This chapter approaches these questions by charting the progress of parliamentary use of the Internet over a span of nearly a quarter of a century. It is concerned principally with what happened and when: I will concentrate more on how and why later in this book. The period under consideration commences at an early stage in the operation of the parliament.uk website, conceived of as a way of disseminating information to the relatively small number of people who then had internet access, in 1996. It ends in 2020, by which time this technology was (among numerous other uses) a principal means via which Parliament itself could continue to function in a global emergency. The focus for this consideration will be two versions of the

[12] 'Letter from the Speaker to the Leader Urging a "Virtual" Parliament', 1 April 2020, available at: www.parliament.uk/business/news/2020/april1/speaker-urges-virtual-parliament-to-keep-up-commons-scrutiny/letter-from-the-speaker-to-the-leader/, last accessed 5 April 2020.

[13] 'Speaker Urges "Virtual" Parliament to Keep Up Commons Scrutiny', 1 April 2020, available at: www.parliament.uk/business/news/2020/april1/speaker-urges-virtual-parliament-to-keep-up-commons-scrutiny/, last accessed 5 April 2020.

[14] Nick Eardley, 'Coranavirus: Speaker Outlines Plans for "Virtual" Parliament', *BBC News*, 14 April 2020, available at: www.bbc.co.uk/news/uk-politics-52282817, last accessed 14 August 2020; Andrew Sparrow, '"Hybrid" Virtual Parliament Plans to Be Put to MPs Next Week', *The Guardian*, 13 April 2020, available at: www.theguardian.com/politics/2020/apr/13/hybrid-virtual-parliament-plans-to-be-put-to-mps-next-week, last accessed 14 August 2020.

[15] Rajev Syal, 'Sir Lindsay Hoyle Promises Calm after Being Elected Speaker', *The Guardian*, available at: www.theguardian.com/politics/2019/nov/04/sir-lindsay-hoyle-promises-calm-after-being-elected-speaker, last accessed 5 April 2020.

[16] 'House of Commons Chamber Proceedings during the COVID-19 Pandemic', available at: www.parliament.uk/about/how/covid-19-proceedings-in-the-house-of-commons/, last accessed 14 January 2021.

[17] 'MPs Cast First Ever Remote Votes in Commons Chamber', available at: www.parliament.uk/business/news/2020/may/mps-cast-first-ever-remote-votes-in-commons-chamber/, last accessed 11 August 2020.

parliamentary homepage, a permanent entity, albeit in changing form, throughout the period. The first is the earliest available version on the Internet Archive 'Wayback Machine', from autumn 1996. The second is that available on the same service from the beginning of April 2020, shortly after the House of Commons entered early Recess. To link the two, the chapter will provide detailed consideration of developments in between.

A homepage – like any source – has limitations as a basis for historical assessment. It does not capture the whole of a public site or of internal networks, less still the entirety of a given organisation's interactions with the Internet, for instance via social media, or the external online coverage it receives. But it can provide useful indicators pertaining to these matters. Users may well come direct to another part of the site rather than via the homepage, which they may never see. But, even if bypassed, a homepage contains insight into the way in which the organisation for which it was an outlet perceived itself, and wished to present itself to the public. Further, it gives an idea of the fuller content available. A homepage certainly does not encapsulate the whole of a body such as the UK Parliament in all its complexity. But, properly deciphered, it can be the basis for a useful and potentially wide-ranging discussion of its nature, in ways that may be unexpected. Indeed, it is precisely because of the defined limitations inherent within it that homepage analysis offers a manageable means of investigating subjects that might otherwise present an overwhelming task. The appropriate use of contextual information can help avoid an excessively constrained outlook. It is possible to augment the technique further by drawing comparisons between different homepages over time. To do so makes possible dynamic observations about continuity and change, better to understand that which came before and that which followed, by attention to the other. Having performed this task, the chapter will then consider the implications of this assessment for an understanding of the Internet and the UK Parliament.

1996

An institution as venerable and important as the UK Parliament adopting a new way of expressing itself is in itself an important development. However, as with some other significant historic occasions, precise dating is difficult. The earliest version of parliament.uk available on the Wayback Machine was captured on 3 November 1996.[18] The version of the homepage archived on this date itself states (in the bottom left-hand corner) that its most recent update was on 9 October 1996, although the earliest point for content added to the site as recorded on 3 November seems to be 23 October, the day of the State Opening of Parliament. (This event, as is discussed below, seems to have

[18] 'United Kingdom Parliament', captured 3 November 1996, available at: https://web.archive.org/web/19961103045305/http://www.parliament.uk/, last accessed 2 April 2020.

been the occasion for the relaunch of an upgraded version of the website, crucially to include Hansard, probably of both the Commons and the Lords.)[19] Links on the archived homepage take the user to pages some of which were also captured on 3 November,[20] others later.[21] For this reason, while meaningful analysis of the homepage must consider where its internal links lead, this task needs to be approached with caution, taking into account the date of capture of a given internal page. If later than 3 November, though it might have had the same appearance on this earlier date, there could be room for doubt on this point.

This Wayback Machine capture seems to be as early as it is possible for the researcher to go. The collections in other archives commence far later. The chronologically first 'snapshot' of parliament.uk on the UK Parliament Parliamentary Archives Web Archive took place on 1 July 2009.[22] On the UK Web Archive, a joint initiative of all Legal Deposit Libraries in the UK, the earliest version dates from 24 April 2013.[23] But though the 3 November 1996 capture may be the earliest that can be found, the website existed before then, and before 23 October and indeed 9 October of that year. Confirmation of this point is found in a report that the House of Commons Information Committee finalised on 27 March 1996, *Electronic Publication of House of Commons Documents*. It included within it a text the Committee had received from the Electronic Publishing Group (EPG), a group of Commons officials.[24] The EPG was charged with investigating practical issues connected to the external electronic dissemination of Commons material, and the possible consumers and uses of such outputs.[25] It noted in its report that, late in 1995, an experiment had already commenced with the posting on the Internet of content produced by the parliamentary Public Information Office.[26]

[19] e.g. 'Hansard on the Internet', Information Committee Press Notice No. 1 of Session 1996–97, Philip Moon, Clerk of the House of Commons Information Committee, 23 October 1996, captured 23 February 1997, available at: https://web.archive.org/web/19970223114954/http://www.parliament.uk/commons/selcom/INFOPN1.HTM, last accessed 14 April 2020.

[20] e.g. 'House of Commons', captured 3 November 1996, available at: https://web.archive.org/web/19961103045321/http://www.parliament.uk/commons/HSECOM.HTM, last accessed 15 April 2020.

[21] e.g. 'Visits to both Houses of Parliament', captured 13 November 1996, available at: https://web.archive.org/web/19961113120049/http://www.parliament.uk/parliament/TOURS.HTM, last accessed 15 April 2020; or 'House of Lords', captured 13 February 1997, available at: https://web.archive.org/web/19970213110323/http://www.parliament.the-stationery-office.co.uk/pa/ld/ldhome.htm, last accessed 15 April 2020.

[22] Available at: http://webarchive.parliament.uk/20090701092058/http://www.parliament.uk/, last accessed 15 April 2020.

[23] Available at: www.webarchive.org.uk/wayback/en/archive/20130424114044/http://www.parliament.uk/, last accessed 15 April 2020.

[24] House of Commons Information Committee, *Electronic Publication of House of Commons Documents*, First Report of Session 1995–96, HC 328 (Stationery Office, London, 1996).

[25] Ibid., p. v.

[26] Ibid., p. vi; and Annex, p. viii.

A report by the House of Lords Information Committee completed on 23 July 1996, called *Information Society: Agenda for Action in the UK*,[27] also referred to this embryonic website. It wrote that: '"The UK Houses of Parliament's Public WWW Service" provides, *inter alia*, factsheets about the House of Commons, lists of members of the House of Commons and information about visits to its gallery and about House of Commons business.' In its discussion, the Committee foreshadowed what would be an ongoing characteristic of parliamentary employment of the Internet: the existence of internal institutional discrepancies of approach and delivery, in this instance arising from the bicameral makeup of Parliament. The initiative was Commons-centric. In a passage suggestive of a degree of tension between the two Houses, the Committee noted that 'this home page at present makes no mention of the House of Lords'. However, it went on, 'under the heading "weekly information bulletin" information is provided about the business of both Houses, including forthcoming business in the House of Lords and public meetings of House of Lords Select Committees'.[28] Presumably to make up for its relative lack of online representation, the Lords was 'making arrangements to launch its own home page in autumn 1996'.[29] It intended a 'first phase', part of which would be 'Lords *Hansard* on-line', launching 'before the end of 1996'. Thereafter, 'publication of Bills and Committee Reports' was projected to take place in 1997. 'Some Acts', the Committee noted, were 'already available on the Internet on HMSO's [Her Majesty's Stationery Office] web site, and this service is to be expanded'.[30]

Perhaps serving to force more effective co-ordination, it seems that this plan came to be integrated with the revamped version of the existing website, first introduced at the time of the State Opening on 23 October 1996.[31] Hansard, 'together with various other House documents', became available online, probably in both its Commons[32] and Lords versions, the following day and thereafter.[33] This initiative followed the approval by the Commons

[27] House of Lords Select Committee on Science and Technology, *Information Society: Agenda for Action in the UK*, 5th Report of Session 1995–96, HL 77, available at: https://publications.parliament.uk/pa/ld199596/ldselect/inforsoc/inforsoc.htm, last accessed 15 April 2020.

[28] Ibid., para. 3.52.

[29] Ibid., para. 3.53.

[30] Ibid., para. 3.54.

[31] For an announcement specifically referring to the Commons text, see 'Hansard on the Internet', Information Committee Press Notice No. 1 of Session 1996–97, Philip Moon, Clerk of the House of Commons Information Committee, 23 October 1996.

[32] For an announcement specifically referring to the Commons text, see ibid.

[33] The earliest capture of the page containing links to House of Lords Hansard was on 13 February 1997. It states that it was '[p]repared 23 October 1996'. 'Hansard – House of Lords Debates', available at: https://web.archive.org/web/19970213110611/http://www.parliament.the-stationery-office.co.uk/pa/ld/ldhansrd.htm, last accessed 15 April 2020. The debates available, on a page captured on 13 May 1997, date from 10 June 1996 onwards. 'Past Editions [Debates]', available at: https://web.archive.org/web/19970513181926/http://www.parliament.the-stationery-office.co.uk/pa/ld199697/ldhansrd/pdvn/allddays.htm, last accessed 15 April 2020.

Information Committee of a recommendation from the EPG. Hansard had already been accessible in electronic form (in its Commons version at least) to those within Parliament connected to the Parliamentary Data and Video Network (PDVN) (through which it was also possible internally to view broadcasts of Commons and Lords proceedings), the introduction of which the Commons had agreed to in June 1994.[34] Making the electronic version of Hansard publicly available marked a key juncture in the history of parliamentary communications, following on from such events as the publication of the *Grand Remonstrance*, the introduction of printed Hansard and the commencement of radio and then television broadcasting.[35] Yet it does not seem to have received significant public attention at the time, unlike the 'virtual Parliament' episode of 2020, that this earlier development helped make possible.

We now turn to the 3 November 1996 capture of the homepage itself. A Crowned Portcullis logo sits in the top left-hand corner. It stands out on what is almost entirely a text-based site. This image (so an account on the 2020 parliamentary website informs us) is the 'principal emblem' of Parliament. Permission for the use of this 'royal badge' comes from the monarch. It signifies formal parliamentary publications and communications from members of either of the Houses of Parliament. It is, so the 2020 site states, 'an image of a grilled gate of the type found on medieval castles with a crown on top'.[36] It might be tempting at this point to detect and highlight a fierce juxtaposition: the deployment of pre-modern imagery through post-modern technology. The reality is more complex. An official factsheet (archived on the parliamentary website) confirms the long lineage of the portcullis. The future Henry VII took on the badge that had belonged to his great-grandfather, the Marquess of Dorset and Somerset, John Beaufort, who lived from around 1371 to 1410. Henry VIII also used the portcullis. It is believed that a connection between it and the Palace of Westminster began during the reign of this later Henry, probably as one of the decorative motifs employed for the reconstructed building following a 1512 fire.

[34] For an announcement specifically referring to the Commons text, see 'Hansard on the Internet', Information Committee Press Notice No. 1 of Session 1996–97, Philip Moon, Clerk of the House of Commons Information Committee, 23 October 1996. Hosting of Hansard for both Commons and Lords seems to have been on the basis of an arrangement with the Stationery Office, since when the link is followed, the address switches from parliament.uk to parliament.the-stationery-office.co.uk; e.g. for the Commons, see 'Hansard (House of Commons Debates)', captured 13 February 1997, available at: https://web.archive.org/web/19970213110441/http://www.parliament.the-stationery-office.co.uk/pa/cm/cmhansrd.htm, last accessed 15 April 2020.

[35] There was Stationery Office involvement, since some of the content to which the parliament.uk links as though part of its own service has a *parliament.the-stationery-office.co.uk* address; e.g. for the Commons, see 'Hansard (House of Commons Debates)', captured 13 February 1997.

[36] 'The Crowned Portcullis', undated, available at: www.parliament.uk/site-information/copyright-parliament/the-crowned-portcullis/, last accessed 2 April 2020.

Yet the Portcullis was not the sole symbol of the Palace at the time, the other features of which included the Tudor Rose. Moreover, the Palace was not synonymous with Parliament – by tradition a mobile entity – to the extent it would later be, though it became by the Tudor period the default venue. Furthermore, the Tudors used the Portcullis for other premises, such as King's College Chapel, Cambridge. Nor was the image entirely consistent – it did not necessarily have a crown on it. At the point of another fire, in 1834, the Portcullis was just one image alongside others that adorned Parliament. The co-creator of the new building, Charles Barry, set about elevating its prominence, using it in thousands of places in his design.[37] If we are to view this architectural project as having fabricated a neo-Gothic aura, then the logo was appropriate. Perhaps Barry made a crucial difference. Following him, the Crowned Portcullis gained ascendancy as a symbol of Parliament. Yet a royal licence formally granting it for use by the Commons and the Lords only appeared in 1996.[38] (In 2001 the link between the Portcullis and Parliament became further entrenched – in words – with the opening of the Portcullis House building.[39]) As the fully official emblem of Parliament, therefore, the Portcullis is roughly the same age as the parliament.uk website. Tradition is often a far from straightforward proposition. So is innovation.

To the right of the Crowned Portcullis on the 3 November 1996 capture homepage are the words 'United Kingdom Parliament'. Below them a centred block of text reads: 'Welcome to the United Kingdom Parliament's World Wide Web Service'. The homepage offers no explanation of what the UK Parliament is. Underneath a horizontal line, in a smaller font size, are the words: 'Here you will find information about the United Kingdom Parliament, the House of Commons and the House of Lords.' In other words, the principal purpose of the site was to disseminate, not to receive or engage in two-way interaction. (For instance, website content linked to from the homepage included the Order Paper, which sets out a schedule of forthcoming business, and, as noted above, Hansard.[40])

Nine links to subsections within the site then run down the left-hand side of the homepage. They are blue, providing rare colour on the homepage (the portcullis uses shades of grey, while most of the rest is black or white). When clicked on, they turn red while the viewer moves to the new location, and become purple when the user navigates back to the homepage. The titles for the links, each of which has a diamond shape to the left of it, are: 'House of

[37] House of Commons Information Office, *The Portcullis*, Factsheet G9, General Series (House of Commons Information Office, London, 2009, revised August 2010), pp. 2–3.

[38] Ibid.

[39] Portcullis House: Key Dates, available at: www.parliament.uk/about/living-heritage/building/northern-estate/portcullishouse/key-dates/, last accessed 15 January 2021.

[40] 'What's New', captured 3 November 1996, available at: https://web.archive.org/web/19961103045355/http://www.parliament.uk/commons/CMNEW.HTM, last accessed 14 April 2020.

Commons', 'House of Lords', 'Visits to both Houses of Parliament', 'Education Unit, providing a service for schools', 'Parliamentary Bookshop', 'Parliamentary Office of Science & Technology', 'Parliamentary Archives', 'Search the Parliamentary Publications Database', 'Enquiries', and 'The Information Offices of both Houses of Parliament'. There are no overt links to external organisations on the homepage (though some of the links on this list lead to pages, such as the House of Lords 'Home Page',[41] that are hosted by parliament.the-stationery-office.co.uk).

Underneath a horizontal line, the homepage states: '[v]isit these pages regularly to keep up to date with the United Kingdom Parliament'. It fell to users, therefore, to ensure they remained abreast of developments. The site attributes maintenance to '[t]he Communications Directorate, United Kingdom Parliament, Westminster, London', and instructs the viewer to report any difficulties to 'webmaster@parliament.uk' (another part of the text that is in blue). The only electronic contact from users for which the homepage allowed, then, concerned notifications about – presumably – whether it was functioning properly on its own terms. (Further emails and other contact details were available for various internal parliamentary offices elsewhere on the site.[42]) Finally, under a further horizontal line, also in blue, the site asserts that it is copyright of the UK Parliament, 1996; and directly below contains the aforementioned reference to the most recent update.

Main Developments, 1996–2020

A report, commissioned by Parliament and reviewing its online services, that appeared in March 2014 (discussed further below), captured the nature of change over nearly two decades of usage. It noted that '[l]ike many organisations, Parliament started working on online, internet based services as an addendum to its core business of producing and publishing documents'. This activity was 'an experiment started in the 1990s to keep up with the times'. The report recognised that '[t]he early commissioners of the Parliamentary website could not have known that in a period of time which was, by historic standards, extraordinarily brief, the internet would come to be the primary mechanism through which not just information but tools and services would be delivered to professional and amateur users alike'.[43] Much

[41] 'House of Lords', captured 13 February 1997.

[42] For instance, the parliamentary bookshop, captured 13 November 1996, available at: https://web.archive.org/web/19961113120057/http://www.parliament.uk/parliament/bookshop.htm, last accessed 14 April 2020.

[43] mySociety, *Review of Parliament's Online Services: A Strategic Review Containing Strengths, Weaknesses and Recommendations*, undated, published online 17 March 2014, p. 22, available at: www.parliament.uk/documents/news/2014/mysociety-report-on-online-services.pdf, last accessed 4 April 2020.

had transpired in a relatively compressed period. The development the report described involved both quantitative and qualitative alteration.

To deal with the first of these aspects, during the time that elapsed from 1996, there was a substantial increase in public use of the technology. As of July 1997, 2% of the UK population had internet access, a figure that rose to 33% by the close of 2000.[44] A survey conducted late in 2004 found that 63% 'have access to a PC [personal computer] at home' and that 53% 'had used the internet in the previous 3 months'.[45] The extent of internet access for the UK population had reached 60% by April 2006,[46] and the figure for households with access was 87% as of 2019.[47] From the perspective of Parliament (as of other organisations in the UK and elsewhere) this trend was a source of both threat and opportunity. As a body, it drew legitimacy from its role as representative of the public. If people were using a particular form of communications technology in rising numbers, then there was a case for utilising it as a means of maintaining contact with them. It might seem that, if Parliament wished to retain relevance, it needed to make effective use of the Internet, and that doing so, moreover, might enable it to introduce innovative practices through which it could perform more effectively: falling into the second, qualitative, category of change suggested above. Discussions around these points are explored further in Chapter 7.

One way in which the use of the Internet could strengthen links with the public was by providing the growing number of users of the network with information about the work of Parliament. In January 2002, a significant development in terms of visibility occurred when webcasting of the Commons, Lords, and some of their individual and joint committees commenced, initially on a pilot basis of twelve months.[48] Later in the same year, the House of Commons Information Committee judged that the introduction of the parliament.uk website had 'dramatically improved public accessibility to documents used by Parliamentary bodies, the record of what is said in Parliament, and decisions taken by Parliament'. It held that the site was 'increasingly recognised as the prime source of information about the activities of the two Houses'.[49]

Parliament began to experiment with activities that went beyond simply providing information to members of the public, and sought to involve them

[44] Ross Ferguson and Laura Miller, *Parliament for the Future: Forecasting the Form of a Digitally-Enabled Parliament* (Hansard Society, London, 2007), p. 5.

[45] See analysis in Warner Lusoli, Stephen Ward, and Rachel Gibson, '(Re)connecting Politics? Parliament, the Public and the Internet', *Parliamentary Affairs* 59(1) (2006): 24–42, 30.

[46] Ferguson and Miller, *Parliament for the Future*, p. 5.

[47] Ofcom, *Online Nation: 2019 Report* (Ofcom, London, 2019), p. 3.

[48] House of Commons Information Committee, *Digital Technology: Working for Parliament and the Public*, First Report of Session 2001–02, HC 1065 (London, Stationery Office, 2002), para. 28, p. 11.

[49] Ibid., para. 29, p. 11.

in discussions. It began hosting online forums, with support from the Hansard Society (initially in collaboration with UK Citizens Online Democracy, as is discussed in Chapter 5).[50] Stephen Coleman, who was closely involved in promoting and helping to organise these exercises, has described how they began in 1998, and that ten such 'online consultations' had taken place by 2002.[51] They could involve feeding into a general select committee inquiry, or commenting on a draft bill before it was formally introduced into Parliament.[52] The approach followed was that rather than 'simply creating a web forum and inviting the public to have its say, rather like an online phone-in programme, these consultations were designed to recruit participants with experience or expertise in relation to specific policy issues'. Their purpose could be to obtain evidence from people who could make a knowledgeable contribution on a particular subject or whose perspective might not normally be taken into account by Parliament. These forums could also make it possible for those who took part to 'interact and learn from ... one another over an extended period of asynchronous discussion'. They might also lead to the consideration of issues that would, without such a process, be overlooked. There would be an opportunity for parliamentarians themselves 'to participate in the online discussion, raising questions and responding to citizens' comments'. Finally, forums could be distilled into an evidence submission to a given inquiry.[53]

A later example of an initiative in this general area came in 2007. Commencing in August of this year,[54] Parliament began a programme of 'web forums', used to source evidence for Commons select committees. Their purpose was to obtain accounts of personal experience relevant to the given investigation taking place. For instance, in 2008, more than 200 users registered with a forum for people upon whom domestic violence had made a direct impact, through which they were able to submit evidence anonymously to a Home Affairs inquiry into this subject.[55] By May 2009, there had been at total of 120,200 visits to these forums by 63,600 individual users.[56]

50 Ferguson and Miller, *Parliament for the Future*, p. 3.

51 Stephen Coleman, 'Connecting Parliament to the Public Via the Internet: Two Case Studies of Online Consultations', *Information, Communication & Society* 7(1) (2004): 1–22, 2.

52 Ibid., p. 4.

53 Ibid., pp. 2–3.

54 'The Public Engagement Strategy in Parliament since 2006', Memorandum on behalf of the Group on Information for the Public, Elizabeth Hallam Smith, Director of Information Services and Librarian, House of Lords, and John Pullinger, Chairman, Group on information for the Public and Librarian and Director General, Information Services, House of Commons, in House of Lords Information Committee, *Are the Lords Listening? Creating Connections between People and Parliament*, vol. II: *Evidence* (Stationery Office, London, 2009), HL 138–II, First Report of Session 2008–09, p. 119.

55 Matt Instone, 'Parliament Web Forums', 7 December 2015, available at: https://pds.blog.parliament.uk/2015/12/07/parliament-web-forums/, last accessed at 8 April 2020.

56 'The Public Engagement Strategy in Parliament since 2006', Memorandum on behalf of the Group on Information for the Public, p. 119.

The forums were pre-moderated and made subject to a set of parliamentary 'Online Discussion Rules'.[57] More than twenty such initiatives ran between 2007 and 2015.[58]

A further means by which Parliament sought to incorporate the public into its activities was electronic petitioning (e-petitioning). The establishment of an online system for the House of Commons was a convoluted, faltering process, gaining ground during the second decade of the twenty-first century,[59] discussed in more detail in Chapter 7. There were also efforts from within Parliament to engage more widely by finding outlets beyond the website, with cognisance of changes such as the emergence of social media. A 2010 account described how '[n]ew channels more recently introduced are beginning to establish themselves as useful means to experiment with low cost new ways of reaching new audiences'. The list it produced included some services that remain prominent today: YouTube ('220,000 views . . . since launch in May 2008'); Twitter ('6,700 followers'); Facebook ('550 fans'); but one that is now defunct, 'FriendFeed' ('150 subscribers'). A bespoke Second Chamber site, 'Lords of the Blog', had reached '150,000 views including over 64,000 comments from the public in its first year from March 2008'.[60]

Another aspect to the relationship between Parliament and the Internet was employment of the technology by individual MPs. A timeline produced by Ross Ferguson and Laura Miller in a Hansard Society report published in 2007 gave an overview of the progress towards ubiquity made up to that point across a number of uses: hardware, websites, and email. In 1998, 200 MPs – slightly under a third of the total – had computers.[61] Changes allowing for central provision, facilitating increased take-up, would follow.[62] The first MP with a personal website seems to have been Anne Campbell (Labour), from 1994. By 1998, 60 MPs had followed Campbell, rising to 280 by 2003, and 520 by 2007 (along with 7 members of the House of Lords). By the close of 1996, the year of the full launch of the parliamentary website, fifty MPs had taken up a parliament.uk email address. By 2003, 430 had done so.[63] There were important implications in these changes for the way in which MPs worked and interacted with their constituents. The House of Commons

[57] For the rules, see 'Online Discussion Rules', undated, available at: www.parliament.uk/get-involved/have-your-say/online-discussion-rules/,last accessed 8 April 2020.

[58] Instone, 'Parliament Web Forums'.

[59] See e.g. Lucinda Maer, *Proposals for an e-Petitions System for the House of Commons* (House of Commons Library, London, 2010), esp. pp. 4–17.

[60] John Pullinger and Elizabeth Hallam Smith, 'The Public Engagement Strategy in the UK Parliament since 2006', *76th IFLA General Conference, Gothenburg, Sweden* (2010), p. 7.

[61] Ferguson and Miller, *Parliament for the Future*, p. 3.

[62] See House of Commons Information Committee, *The Supply of Members' Information Technology Equipment, Software and Associated Services*, First Report of Session 1998–99, HC 76 (Stationery Office, London, 1998), para. 29, p. ix; para. 48, p. xi.

[63] Ferguson and Miller, *Parliament for the Future*, pp. 3–4. The number of MPs elected to House of Commons in 1997 and 2001 was 659; in 2005, 646; from 2010, 650.

Information Committee estimated in 2002 that 'typically, 10 to 20 per cent of a Member's correspondence might be received electronically, but this figure seems set to climb'.[64] The use of email had by this point became accepted as a standard feature of the work of MPs and their staff.[65] Trends towards more extensive utilisation by MPs of the Internet in its different manifestations intensified. The authors of a further Hansard Society publication, appearing in 2011, found MPs making increasing use of the Internet, through email, blogs, websites, and social media. In the 2005–10 Parliament, 92 per cent of MPs had 'used email, 83% had a personal website and 11% had blogs'. They anticipated that such take-up was likely to increase, especially because of the turnover of MPs at the 2010 General Election, with a fresh intake more likely to employ these methods.[66] Other Hansard Society research confirmed that members of the 2010 cohort of newly elected MPs were more inclined towards use of the Internet than their predecessors.[67]

People working within Parliament became increasingly familiar and adept with digital technology. As the authors of an external review of parliamentary online activity published in 2014 and cited elsewhere in this chapter remarked, '[a] neutral observer might expect Parliamentary staff to be suspicious of new technologies and processes, given that they work for a very venerable institution, with many traditions'. However, the text went on, 'this . . . was not a problem'. The authors, in their investigation of the subject, had 'heard repeatedly and from a wide range of staff that they are keenly aware of the importance of online services in the modern world'. Moreover, they 'heard staff talking in sophisticated terms about the importance of supplying raw data, an even more difficult, hightech concept, and one that one would not necessarily expect to hear in an ancient institution'.[68]

Even for those who were not particularly proficient, using the Internet (and the internal network) became a part of day-to-day life for MPs and Peers, their staff, and officials. It was a device for internal communication. For instance, from 2002, electronic tabling of written parliamentary questions was introduced.[69] The network was a means by which they gathered information for research purposes. Wider social patterns in the way people accessed the Internet were reflected in the habits of parliamentarians. During the twenty-

64 House of Commons Information Committee, *Digital Technology*, para. 16, p. 9.

65 See House of Commons Committee on Standards and Privileges, *Conduct of Mr Iain Duncan Smith*, Fourth Report of Session 2003-04, vol. 1, HC 476-I (Stationery Office, London, 2004), pp. 42–3.

66 Andy Williamson, Matt Korris, Freddy Fallon, and Beccy Allen (eds.), *Connecting Citizens to Parliament: How Parliament Can Engage More Effectively with Hard to Reach Groups* (Hansard Society, London, 2011), p. 16.

67 Matt Korris, *A Year in the Life: From Member of Public to Member of Parliament* (Hansard Society, London, 2011), pp. 9–10.

68 mySociety, *Review of Parliament's Online Services*, p. 8.

69 House of Commons Procedure Committee, *e-Tabling of Written Questions*, Third Report of Session 2012–13, HC 775 (Stationery Office, London, 2012), para. 1, p. 5.

first century, for example, use of mobile devices for this purpose became normal: by 2019, 84 per cent of adults reported doing so.[70] This trend impacted within Parliament as it did elsewhere. Both the House of Lords and the House of Commons had to make various adjustments in their rules over time, seeking to accommodate the use of such technology by Peers and by MPs both in the Chamber and in Committees, but at the same time to avoid objections from colleagues about breaches of etiquette.[71]

Some influential internet engagement projects involved Parliament but were not initiated by it. In 2006, Richard Allan, a Liberal Democrat MP from 1997 to 2005 with a strong interest in this area, referred to the importance of efforts from within 'the technology community'. FaxYourMP, for instance, launched in 2000 with the purpose of facilitating online contact with MPs (its immediate spur was the Regulation of Investigatory Powers Bill, containing proposals that were controversial among people in this field). One of its services was to receive emails and send them on to MPs in fax form, meaning that those representatives who did not have public email addresses could nonetheless be contacted indirectly via the Internet. FaxYourMP then began publishing 'performance data' based on response times of MPs via this platform – a practice to which some MPs objected. A further online project, Public Whip, gathered information already in the public domain about the parliamentary activities of MPs, presenting it in a fashion more comprehensible to users, and which made possible comparisons between MPs. Then came TheyWorkForYou.com, which repackaged the online version of Hansard alongside other content in ways intended to be more comprehensible and useful to users than the official parliament.uk.[72]

To focus on the second of these projects, the earliest capture of the Public Whip website on Wayback Machine is dated 2 August 2003.[73] An FAQ (frequently asked questions) page describes the purpose of the initiative as being: 'to monitor the voting records of Members of the United Kingdom Parliament, so that the public (people like us) can better influence their voting

[70] Office for National Statistics, *Internet Access – Households and Individuals, Great Britain: 2019*, section 5, available at: www.ons.gov.uk/peoplepopulationandcommunity/householdcharacteristics/homeinternetandsocialmediausage/bulletins/internetaccesshouseholdsandindividuals/2019, last accessed 12 August 2020.

[71] For the House of Lords, see House of Lords Administration and Works Committee, *Use of Electronic Devices in the House*, First Report of Session 2010–11, HL 92 (Stationery Office, London, 2011), para. 16, p. 6. For the House of Commons see *Use of Hand-Held Devices in the Chamber and Committees*, Third Report of Session 2010–11, HC 889 (Stationery Office, London, 2011).

[72] Richard Allan, 'Parliament, Elected Representatives and Technology 1997–2005 – Good in Parts?', *Parliamentary Affairs* 59(2) (2006): 360–5, 362–3.

[73] What appears to be the homepage is 'The Public Whip: Counting Their Votes on Your Behalf', captured 2 August 2003, available at: https://web.archive.org/web/20030802155705/http://publicwhip.org.uk/, last accessed 13 April 2020.

patterns'.[74] It explained that '[a]ll the House of Commons debate transcripts (Hansard) back to 1988 are published electronically on the World Wide Web. We've written a program to read it for you and separate out all the records of voting. This information has been added into an online database which you can access.' Posing to itself the question '[w]hat organisation is behind the Public Whip?', the site responded: 'None. Just two guys Francis and Julian who had an idea and made it happen.'[75] A link leads to an external site containing details of the 'Francis' in question – Francis Irving, 28 years old. With a first in mathematics from Oxford (graduating in 1995), Irving was, in his professional life, a computer programmer, and an '[i]nternational development campaigner who works to make a fairer world'.[76] The 'Julian' referred to was Julian Todd, a fellow computer programmer.[77] Both Irving and Todd went on to other projects in the online gathering, processing, and presentation of data about Parliament and other political institutions, for use by the public including for campaigning purposes, such as TheyWorkForYou.[78]

The data presented on the Public Whip site pertained to rebelling (that is, MPs voting against the instructions of party whips) and the rate of attendance of MPs at votes. A user of the site would first encounter a list of the five 'Top Rebels' (with the top two positions taken by Jeremy Corbyn and then John McDonnell at this point) and then a list of the top five MPs with 'Best Attendance', followed by a list of five 'Interesting Divisions' – a list chosen 'at random from divisions with more than 10 rebellions'.[79] The effect of the site, therefore, was to emphasise the voting behaviour of individual MPs, and to measure it by participation and propensity to disobey directions. This focus leads to some significant observations about the nature of representative democracy. Public Whip appeared at a time of long-term increase in back-bench rebellion. Whether one regards such a tendency as desirable is a matter of perspective. On the one hand, it could be held that MPs should display independence of mind and not simply follow orders if to do so is to compromise important principles. On the other hand, it might be argued that respect for hierarchy is important and group loyalty is necessary because – as well as particular politicians – the public votes for parties, requiring their cohesion within the Commons. The importance one attaches to obedience

[74] 'The Public Whip – FAQ', 'What Is the Public Whip?', captured 2 August 2003, available at: https://web.archive.org/web/20030802200733/http://www.publicwhip.org.uk/faq.php, last accessed 13 April 2020.

[75] 'The Public Whip – FAQ', 'What Organisation Is behind the Public Whip?', captured 2 August 2003, available at: https://web.archive.org/web/20030802200733/http://www.publicwhip.org.uk/faq.php, last accessed 13 April 2020.

[76] 'Francis Irving', captured 12 July 2003, available at: https://web.archive.org/web/20030712013026/http://flourish.org/cv/, last accessed 13 April 2020.

[77] 'The Public Whip', available at: www.publicwhip.org.uk, last accessed 13 April 2020.

[78] 'TheyWorkForYou Makes Parliament Easier to Understand', available at: www.theyworkforyou.com/about/, last accessed 13 April 2020.

[79] See what appears to be the homepage, 'The Public Whip: Counting Their Votes on Your Behalf'.

might also vary in accordance with the view one takes of a particular leadership and its overall direction. On specific votes, whether resisting the whips is regarded as desirable or not might depend on the position one takes on the issue at stake on that occasion. The application of a communications technology, in this instance the Internet, could not fully be separated from such considerations, involving differences of opinion about crucial constitutional issues. It might – if only by implication – tilt perceptions in a certain direction, in this instance towards an emphasis on MPs as individuals rather than as members of groups. Scrutiny mechanisms cannot in themselves be entirely neutral. Structural decisions must be made by those who create them, with implications for appearances and outcomes.

Data, moreover, have limitations as a means of assessment. For instance, they could not reveal activities that were arguably more effective at changing outcomes than rebelling in divisions, such as seeking to influence policy before it is brought before the House. The Public Whip would later recognise difficulties its approach could create (though not in relation to rebelling), when – in October 2008 – it recorded that: 'We have found that people take the attendance in divisions too seriously, when it is really pretty meaningless. At Public Whip, we'd rather an MP actually scrutinised law and made it better, and voted well on it, rather than voted more often. Therefore, we have removed attendance from the main MP table.'[80]

The online activities of Parliament were subject to frequent and frequently critical assessment, with efforts at renewal often following. Both the services themselves and the structures for and approaches to delivering them could be found wanting. The homepage as captured on 3 November 1996 seems to be the product of an overhaul that came about after – and perhaps partly because of – criticism from within Parliament. The House of Lords Information Committee report *Information Society: Agenda for Action in the UK*, completed in July 1996, opened by noting that it was 'the first Select Committee report from either House of the United Kingdom Parliament to be published electronically', via the Stationery Office.[81] The Committee described its publication as being 'about one of the most important technological developments of this century. Directly or indirectly, the digital and communications revolution will affect us all.'[82] Among other observations, the Committee held that Parliament had not yet responded fully to this prospect. It remarked that the institution had 'not been an "early adopter" of Internet technology either in its use to promote the dissemination of a wide range of parliamentary information both to the UK electorate and worldwide, or in the use of e-mail to

[80] 'The Public Whip – FAQs', available at: www.publicwhip.org.uk/faq.php#clarify, last accessed 13 April 2020.

[81] House of Lords Select Committee on Science and Technology, *Information Society: Agenda for Action in the UK*.

[82] Ibid., para. 1.1.

facilitate two-way communication and citizens' feedback'.[83] As we have seen, the Committee also wanted more representation of the Lords online. On 2 April 1996, the Second Chamber had agreed a set of principles pertaining to electronic publishing, including that 'the House should make its publications available free of charge in electronic form' and that 'the medium for free distribution should be the Internet'. In pursuit of these objectives, the Committee announced plans for dissemination of material that would become part of parliament.uk in the autumn of 1996.

Scrutiny and change continued. The House of Commons Information Committee noted in its 2002 assessment of the website that it was 'shortly to be relaunched with a different "look and feel" both in terms of navigation and terminology. These revisions have been recognised as necessary for some time, and we very much welcome them.' It expressed the 'hope' that 'the public' would find the renewed website 'more accessible and easier to use'.[84] The Committee suggested that the site could expand usage by 'improving links from other websites, including media and government department sites'. They could, it observed, be from one homepage to another. But possibly more effective, the report suggested, would be 'subject based links'. It offered an example: a user could follow a news item about adoption directly to a section on parliament.uk dealing with an Adoption Bill before Parliament.[85]

Changes brought about gained praise. The redesigned site won a number of prizes. The British Web Design and Marketing Association found it 'simple, elegant and business-like' and 'the best example of "open government" adoption of internet technologies that we have seen'.[86] But, in an illustration of the pace of change in the technology and the rising expectations that come with it, criticism soon revived. In May 2004, the House of Commons Modernisation Committee produced a report on the subject of parliamentary interaction with the public. It included an assessment of the website, or rather what it described as 'three Parliamentary websites: the main site at www.parliament.uk, the educational site for schools and colleges, www.explore.parliament.uk and the webcasting site, www.parliamentlive.tv'. Content was plentiful: the sites contained: 'a vast archive of material including virtually every official parliamentary publication since the mid-1990s'. There was also 'a directory of MPs, Peers and staff, general information for the public about how Parliament works, Library Research Papers, practical information for visitors, live audio-visual coverage of both Chambers and Westminster Hall, and audio-only and audiovisual recordings of recent committee meetings'. In total there were 'over 9,000 pages hosted directly on the Commons site alone, and over a million

83 Ibid., para. 3.520.

84 House of Commons Information Committee, *Digital Technology*, para. 29, p. 11.

85 Ibid., para. 30, p. 11.

86 House of Commons Select Committee on Modernisation of the House of Commons, *Connecting Parliament with the Public*, First Report of Session 2003–04, HC 368 (London, Stationery Office, 2004), p. 17.

pages of linked publications'.[87] But the Committee found public dissatisfaction with the way in which the site (or sites) functioned, reporting in particular that the search facilities were difficult to use. It recommended another overhaul, and the Commons passed a resolution to this effect by 375 votes to 14 in January 2005.[88] An external inquiry, by the Hansard Society Commission on the Communication of Parliamentary Democracy, followed in the same year. Finding the website 'confusing and poorly designed'[89] it called for it to be 'radically improved. At a minimum, it should be consultative, interactive, and easily navigable.'[90]

The Management Boards of the House of Commons and of the House of Lords decided to pursue rationalisation. Previously, reflecting the general way in which Parliament tended to function, approaches towards digital communications had been disparate in form.[91] There were 'only two staff dedicated to co-ordinating content on the website, both shared between the two Houses. Most content is generated in a decentralised way by various staff throughout the two Houses, as a by-product of their other duties.'[92] In future, responsibility for both the website and the Intranet would fall to a single Web Centre, under a Managing Editor. Dominic Tinley was appointed to this post in October 2005. Slightly confusingly, however, the Web Centre would report to two different oversight bodies: an *Internet* Strategy Board and an *Intranet* Strategy Board. Further consolidation occurred with the formation of a Parliamentary Information and Communications Technology Service (PICT), among the responsibilities of which was supporting the Web Centre. In the spring of 2006, Tinley records, committees of each House 'finally approved in principle' a proposed 'radical redesign of the website'. Planning then commenced for 'a five-year programme of improvements'.[93]

Those who devised the approach to the website at this point seem in part to have drawn motivation from a desire to escape a cycle of vaunted relaunches that were soon condemned as outmoded, followed by further overhauls themselves of inevitably limited lifespans. Two officials with responsibility in this area subsequently explained that '[a] key feature was that a radical redesign would not be simply a "big bang" change but would instead be the development of an ongoing capability'. As a consequence, 'continuous adaptation as the medium itself developed' would be possible', and '[n]ew content

[87] Ibid., pp. 16–17.

[88] For an account of this process, see Dominic Tinley, 'The UK Parliament in the Digital Age: A Personal Perspective' in *Parliaments in the Digital Age*, Forum Discussion Report 13 (Oxford, Oxford Internet Institute, 2008), pp. 45–8, 45.

[89] Hansard Society Commission on the Communication of Parliamentary Democracy, *Members Only? Parliament in the Public Eye?* (Hansard Society, London, 2005), p. ix.

[90] Ibid., p. 69.

[91] Tinley, 'The UK Parliament in the Digital Age', p. 45.

[92] House of Commons Select Committee on Modernisation of the House of Commons, *Connecting Parliament with the Public*, p. 18.

[93] Tinley, 'The UK Parliament in the Digital Age', p. 45.

and functions would be released regularly each parliamentary term. This approach would maximise flexibility and control cost.'[94]

The mid-2000s project may have achieved a degree of success in this regard. A Hansard Society report from 2011 praised the 'online strategy' pursued since this point, describing it as 'focusing on Parliament as a whole, rather than on the Houses'. But it also referred – approvingly – to 'the 2010 redesign of the website', judging that it had secured enhanced 'usability'.[95] Had, then, the 2006 programme failed in its objective of making only incremental alteration necessary? Where (to use the terminology cited above) 'continuous adaptation' ends and 'radical redesign' begins is partly a matter of opinion. But it is clear that keeping pace with changing expectations in a fickle environment was a continuous challenge.

By 2014, there were around 400 staff members working on the website and the intranet across both Houses of Parliament.[96] Overall responsibility for internet-related work came under a bicameral Web and Intranet Service.[97] The task of 'improvements' to the 'presentation and functionality' of different aspects of the site was ongoing.[98] More change soon came. The previous year, Parliament had commissioned mySociety, an organisation for the promotion of online engagement into which projects including TheyWorkForYou.com were subsumed, 'to undertake a review of Parliament's online channels, including governance, strategy, and delivery'.[99] The consequent report, published in March 2014, found some positives. It judged that Parliament was attracting a respectable quantity of users to its various internet-based services.[100] The authors, moreover, found evidence suggesting reasonable levels of satisfaction among users of parliament.uk.[101] They noted further that parliamentary staff were committed to serving the public, and that they regarded 'better online services' as being 'essential, not optional'.[102] However, mySociety recorded, it took too long to update information or place new features on the site.[103] The report, furthermore, identified basic problems with the usability of parliament.uk. It warned that '[e]xpectations of what is normal on the internet change very fast'. The problem was that '[w]hat would have counted as an elegant, usable,

[94] 'The Public Engagement Strategy in Parliament since 2006', Memorandum on behalf of the Group on Information for the Public, p. 118.
[95] Williamson et al. (eds.), *Connecting Citizens to Parliament*, p. 75.
[96] Aileen Walker, Director of Public Engagement, House of Commons, 'Parliament and the Public: Public Information/Engagement Services in the House of Commons', February 2014, para. 4.4.1, p. 5, available at: www.parliament.uk/documents/speaker/digital-democracy/Digi094AileenWalker.pdf, last accessed 3 April 2020.
[97] Ibid., para. 4.4, p. 5.
[98] Ibid., para. 4.4.1, p. 5.
[99] mySociety, *Review of Parliament's Online Services*, p. 2.
[100] Ibid., p. 5.
[101] Ibid., pp. 6–7.
[102] Ibid., p. 7.
[103] Ibid., p. 9.

interesting webpage just five years ago will now come across as clunky, unhelpful and perhaps hard or impossible to read on a smartphone or tablet (devices that did not exist until recently)'.[104] The authors made various recommendations for updating the site and its features.[105]

The mySociety report appeared in March 2014, by which time the parliamentary Management Boards had agreed that they would put into practice the two central proposals contained within it. They would form a single Digital Office, integrating Information and Communications Technology (ICT) and online into one service, and recruit a Head of Digital to lead it, who would answer for achieving enhanced satisfaction with its performance among members of the public, parliamentarians, and staff.[106] In advocating this shift, the report had presented a historic argument. It held that 'the debate as to which medium would be used to deliver significant computer applications and information services to users is over, and the internet has emerged as the winner'. For this reason, 'separating "the internet" from "ICT" is now a division that serves only to increase friction and decrease the ability of Parliament to serve internal and external user needs'. mySociety found that '[t]he current structure of Parliament, with the Web and Intranet (WIS) team separated from the ICT team (PICT), reflects this legacy'.[107]

During the second half of 2015, Parliament developed a Digital Strategy, intended to apply not only to the Parliamentary Digital Service, but the whole of Parliament, that has formed a basis for subsequent internet-related parliamentary policy, based around 'eight aspirations', including transparency and efficiency, and nine 'principles' such as focusing on the requirements of users, being 'where people are', and 'continuous iteration'.[108] This programme sat within a wider managerial context. The official 'mission' of the House of Commons at present is 'to support a thriving parliamentary democracy'.[109] One of the means by which it formally sets out to achieve this goal is through '[m]aximising the potential of digital'.[110]

There were many different ways of measuring the online reach of Parliament. An opinion poll commissioned by the Hansard Society in 2002 found that 'one in four British users' of the Internet had accessed the

[104] Ibid., p. 17.

[105] Ibid., pp. 17–21.

[106] 'Review of Parliament's Online Services – Report Published', 17 March 2014, available at: https://old.parliament.uk/business/news/2014/march/review-of-parliaments-online-services-report/, last accessed 21 January 2021.

[107] mySociety, *Review of Parliament's Online Services*, pp. 22–3.

[108] Tracy Green, 'A Digital Strategy for Parliament – Making It Real', 12 November 2015, available at: https://pds.blog.parliament.uk/2015/11/12/a-digital-strategy-for-parliament-making-it-real/, last accessed 8 April 2020.

[109] House of Commons, *Administration: Annual Reports and Accounts 2018–2019*, HC 2434 (House of Commons, London, 2019), p. 12.

[110] Ibid., p. 13.

parliamentary site, already exceeding the number that had been to the physical estate.[111] According to research from 2004, about 10% of those asked had contacted their MP over the previous two or three years, of whom roughly 10% had used email to do so. To place this figure in perspective, more commonly used methods were post (41%) and telephone (20%).[112] Among users of the Internet, the 2004 survey found, over the past year, 40% had gone to a news website (21% of the public as a whole); 29% (and 15% for the wider public) to a local authority site; 21% (and 11%) to a government department; 2% (and 1%) to an MPs site; and 2% (and 1%) to Number 10 (i.e. the Prime Minister's Office website). The figures for the 'House of Commons' website were 5% among users of the Internet, and 3% for the total population.[113] In terms of absolute numbers using parliament.uk, during January 2004 there were 'over 2.5 million page requests on the main server and over 5 million hits (300,000 unique users) on the publications server'.[114]

Research for the mySociety review showed that during the three months that elapsed between 11 September and 11 December 2013, parliamentary 'online services' drew '4.9 million visitors in total' accounting for 7.15 million visits between them. Placing this latter figure in context, the report noted that it accounted '[v]ery roughly' for: 1% of visits to the *Mail Online* (the website of the *Mail* newspapers, a figure that included people beyond the UK), 20% of Gov.uk (i.e. the website of the UK government), and 50% of the Transport for London website. It was equal to Legislation.gov.uk (the official online law database), double the *Spectator* website (the Right-orientated weekly political journal), and ten times the number of online views of the Essex County Council site. The most common purposes of visiting the website related to: 'Bills and legislation' (approximately 15%, or 800,000 unique visitors over the three-month period), information about visits to Parliament (approximately 10% or 500,000), to find information about Members (approximately 10% or 500,000), to play video and audio (8% or 400,000), and committees (8% or 400,000).[115]

In March of the following year, 2014, parliament.uk received 2.3 million visits from 1.7 million unique visitors (i.e. more than five times the 300,000 unique viewers of January 2004), viewing 6.4 million pages between them. These figures represented approximately a 25% increase on the same month a year previously. Hansard was the most commonly accessed part of the site – 11% for the Commons version, 3% for the Lords. Next came committees (10%), people looking for information on members (5%), and video content (5%).

111 See analysis in Lusoli, Ward, and Gibson, '(Re)connecting Politics? Parliament, the Public and the Internet', p. 28.
112 See analysis ibid., p. 32.
113 See analysis ibid., p. 33.
114 House of Commons Select Committee on Modernisation of the House of Commons, *Connecting Parliament with the Public*, p. 17.
115 mySociety, *Review of Parliament's Online Services*, p. 5.

Of those viewing the site, 36% described themselves as members of the public, 31% as students. These categories had been the two most common since July 2011.[116]

Social media metrics were another means of measuring parliamentary online reach. mySociety recorded in 2014 that Parliament had 227,000 Twitter followers (comparable, the report held, with the US Congress) and that it had in excess of 18,000 and of 12,000 likes on, respectively, Facebook and YouTube. The Parliamentary Office of Science and Technology (POST) had more than 3,000 Twitter followers; the Parliamentary Archives, 4,000; and select committees had, variously, somewhere between the hundreds and 2,000.[117] In 2017, the Committee on Standards in Public Life received evidence informing it that each day MPs could receive 10,000 messages via social media.[118] As of October 2018, the 'UK Parliament's Twitter account ... [had] ... one of the biggest social media audiences across politics in the UK, with over 1.4 million followers.'[119] By January 2019, the parliamentary YouTube channel had reached 100,000 subscribers. Matt Instone, of the Parliamentary Digital Service remarked at the time that '[t]he top channels on YouTube have around 30 million+ subscribers'. While 'the UK Parliament channel is never going to compete with the likes of Justin Bieber, Katy Perry, and Ed Sheeran, we do measure up pretty well in terms of UK politics'. The parliamentary YouTube channel had 'more subscribers than all the Westminster political parties combined'. The Labour Party had 26,000 and the Conservative Party had 24,000. Parliament, furthermore, had 'more subscribers than all the government departments combined'. The 'most popular government department channel' was that of the Foreign Office, which had 12,000 subscribers. Instone noted that 'nearly a third of our subscribers' had been acquired during the previous twelve months.[120] The upward incline was sustained. By April 2020, UK Parliament on YouTube had approximately 213,000 subscribers – an increase of more than 100 per cent on the January 2019 figure.[121] It is tempting to conclude that parliamentary drama involving the process of UK withdrawal from the EU had driven this increase, suggesting

[116] Tracey Green, 'What Do We Know about Users of www.parliament.uk?', 8 April 2014, available at: https://pds.blog.parliament.uk/2014/04/08/what-do-we-know-about-the-users-of-www-parliament-uk/, last accessed 8 April 2020.

[117] mySociety, *Review of Parliament's Online Services: A Strategic Review Containing Strengths, Weaknesses and Recommendations*, pp. 5–6.

[118] Committee on Standards in Public Life, *Intimidation in Public Life: A Review by the Committee on Standards in Public Life*, Cm. 9543 (Stationery Office, London, 2017), p. 32.

[119] Kat Cimetta, 'Experimenting with a Twitter Takeover', 31 October 2018, available at: https://pds.blog.parliament.uk/2018/10/31/experimenting-with-a-twitter-takeover/, last accessed 8 April 2020.

[120] Matt Instone, '100,000 YouTube Subscribers but Where Next?', 18 January 2019, available at: https://pds.blog.parliament.uk/2019/01/18/100000–youtube-subscribers-but-where-next/, last accessed 8 April 2020.

[121] 'UK Parliament' YouTube channel, available at: www.youtube.com/UKParliament, last accessed 8 April 2020.

a close link between the impact of technology and the nature of the wider environment in which it operated.

There are many different ways of measuring quantitative impact. But it is clear that through its use of the Internet, Parliament connected with millions of people. My main interest is in the qualitative difference made, especially from a constitutional standpoint. There can be no doubt that, in the Internet, Parliament found new means of flexible, instantaneous, mass communication; and that over time it attached increasing priority to the task of exploiting it to the maximum. But doubts existed about whether such engagement was inherently good. Was it, for instance, entirely democratic? Behind the overall pattern of growth in usage of the Internet was differentiation of a type significant to any efforts at inclusive engagement. This point gained recognition from within Parliament. In 2001, the House of Commons Information Committee drew attention to figures (referred to above) showing that 38 per cent of UK households had access to the Internet, and that 51 per cent of adults had accessed the Internet either from work, from home or through a publicly available service (at the time, businesses such as internet cafés provided the use of terminals for this purpose, generally charging by time periods). Yet 35 per cent of those asked responded that it was 'very unlikely' they would utilise the Internet in the following twelve months – broadly stable from the year before. Usage tended to be concentrated among those of higher income and in younger age groups.[122] Such data might point to a conclusion that online interactions, depending on how Parliament handled them, could leave behind those who did not have access, entrench generational divisions, and possibly empower those who were already in a position of social privilege.

By 2019, 87% of households in the UK had access to the Internet. Adult internet users averaged three hours fifteen minutes per day online during September 2018 – an increase of eleven minutes on the year previously.[123] Yet 13% of adults in the UK said that they were not users of the Internet – a figure that had been static since 2014. There were generational and socio-economic divisions: 48% of people aged 75 and above, 33% of 65- to 74-year-olds, and 19% of 55- to 64-year-olds were non-users. Among adults from the DE social grade – that is, people from households whose chief income earner was a semi-skilled or unskilled worker, or was not in employment – 14% said they did not use the Internet, while the percentage for people not from the DE grade was only 4%.[124] The Hansard Society *Audit of Political Engagement 15*, published in 2018, included a specific focus on the use of the Internet. When it presented respondents with eight varieties of possible digital political activity,

[122] House of Commons Information Committee, *Digital Technology*, paras. 6–7, pp. 6–7.
[123] Ofcom, *Online Nation: 2019 Report*, p. 3.
[124] Ibid.

48% replied that they had not engaged in any.[125] Significantly, the chances that a person would do so increased in accordance with how interested they already were in politics. This characteristic overrode another tendency – for younger people to be more likely than older people to take part in politics via the Internet.[126] Like the 2001 data, this evidence suggested that, by connecting with the public online, Parliament might empower further those who were already involved, and widen the gap between them and those who were excluded. A further qualification is necessary when contemplating the impressively swift and extensive permeation of the Internet. It is important to avoid neglecting the persistence of other, older media (even though the digital network blurred the distinctions between all of these technologies). Data published in 2020 suggested that 65 per cent of adults in the UK used the Internet as a source for news. The figure for television was higher, at 75 per cent. Radio and newspapers, while employed less than the Internet, retained a presence, with, respectively, 42 and 35 per cent utilising them.[127]

There was a negative side to computer-based communications. Members of the public might abuse the ability to make contact with parliamentarians through the Internet. Evidence of this tendency came in a report published in December 2017, *Intimidation in Public Life*. In it, the Committee on Standards in Public Life found that all women MPs who were 'active on Twitter' had been targets for 'online intimidation'. Black and Asian women MPs received a disproportionate share of this type of communication. The person who received the most abuse of all was the black MP, Diane Abbott. She told the Committee that '[t]hirty years ago, when I first became an MP, if someone wanted to attack an MP, they had to write a letter – usually in green ink – put it in an envelope, put a stamp on it and walk to the post box'. But it had become possible for them to 'press a button and we read vile abuse that, 30 years ago, people would have been frightened even to write down'.[128]

Developments discussed in Chapter 1 created other unease about the social role of the Internet. In utilising the technology, Parliament was participating in a system – and requiring others who wished to engage with it by this route – which some found to have questionable aspects. From this perspective, a person who wished more fully to realise their democratic rights, was forced also to compromise them. A 2019 Amnesty International report captured this dilemma.[129] It noted that '[t]he internet has revolutionised our world on a scale not seen since the invention of electricity. Over half

[125] Hansard Society, *Audit of Political Engagement 15: The 2018 Report* (Hansard Society, London, 2018), p. 28.

[126] Ibid., p. 30.

[127] Ofcom, *News Consumption in the UK: 2020* (Ofcom, London, 2020), p. 6.

[128] Committee on Standards in Public Life, *Intimidation in Public Life*, p. 27.

[129] Amnesty International, *Surveillance Giants: How the Business Model of Google and Facebook Threatens Human Rights* (Amnesty International, London, 2019). All the extracts quoted here are from p. 5.

of the world's population now relies on the web to read the news, message a loved one, find a job, or seek answers to an urgent question.' The technology had 'opened social and economic opportunities at a scale and speed that few imagined fifty years ago'. Accordingly, the report went on, it was 'now firmly acknowledged that access to the internet is vital to enable the enjoyment of human rights. For more than 4 billion people, the internet has become central to how they communicate, learn, participate in the economy, and organise socially and politically.'

But the bulk of users depended 'heavily on the services of just two corporations'. They were Facebook and Google. However beneficial they were, their 'platforms come at a systemic cost'. The 'surveillance-based business model' these corporations employed obliged 'people to make a Faustian bargain'. They were 'only able to enjoy their human rights online by submitting to a system predicated on human rights abuse'. It amounted to 'an assault on the right to privacy on an unprecedented scale', with 'a series of knock-on effects that pose a serious risk to a range of other rights, from freedom of expression and opinion, to freedom of thought and the right to non-discrimination'. An ancient parliamentary tradition was that, as an entity, it existed to uphold the rights of the people, however defined. Increasingly enthusiastic engagement with the Internet meant that it was taking part in, seeking to benefit from, and encouraging others to use a system that was arguably compromised from this perspective. We will return to such concerns, from a specific parliamentary perspective, in Chapter 8. As we will see, parliamentary efforts to use the Internet (described in the present chapter) came to be accompanied by the end of the 2010s by growing reservations within the institution regarding the implications of the technology. Indeed, there were specific concerns about corporations providing the very platforms it valued so highly (that included Facebook and YouTube, owned by Google).

2020

A user navigating to parliament.uk (as archived for the Wayback Machine) on 1 April 2020[130] would encounter a multicoloured site, including a variety of photographic images of parliamentary architecture and other scenes. The top of the screen offers the option of finding 'out more about how we use cookies'. Cookies are devices that a site places on the equipment of users accessing it, that gather information about them for storage and processing. The more acceptable purpose of cookies is to help make the website function more effectively for the particular visitor, and more generally. They have also raised privacy concerns, regarding their possible improper deployment to track individual behaviour – hence the appearance of this message as the head item

[130] Available at: https://web.archive.org/web/20200401215324/https://www.parliament.uk/, last accessed 11 April 2020.

on the parliamentary homepage. The site asserts that proceeding to use it implies acceptance of the cookies policy. A sub-page within it reassures the user that the information gathered through cookies will remain anonymous, and is employed only for purposes such as efficiency improvements. It was open to anyone to prevent the use of cookies through their own settings.[131]

The cookies caveat illustrated that, as already discussed, the Internet had become a subject of controversy in the period since 1996. It was useful, indeed had become essential, to the functioning of institutions and their interactions with the outside world. It was part of the basic operational fabric of society in the UK and internationally. Within this context, ensuring that it was able to work with maximum efficiency and was capable of continuous improvement made sense. But achieving these outcomes involved deriving and processing data about the patterns of behaviour of the people who used it. This practice had led to concerns, the outcome of which had been changes of policy and law.[132] Parliament had increasingly recognised that it need not (and perhaps should not) just be a passive observer of arguable difficulties. As we will see in more detail later, it came to play a growing role in highlighting perceived problems, exerting pressure, and in some cases legislating to address them (though legislation is not a core issue for this book).[133] Furthermore, Parliament could adopt for itself protocols for protecting online users – as in the use of cookies.

The next row down starts on the left with the Crowned Portcullis. On the right of this previously discussed emblem is the title 'UK' and immediately below that 'Parliament'. Running from left to right are six tabs: *Business*, *MPs, Lords and offices*, *About*, *Get Involved*, *Visit*, and *More* (consisting of 'Learning' and 'Shop'), and then a search function. It is immediately apparent that, compared with the 1996 website, the overall volume of content had expanded enormously. Qualitative difference accompanied quantitative. The homepage places an emphasis on enabling users actively to engage with Parliament that is absent from its 1996 predecessor. Technological sophistication had advanced and expectations had grown in the intervening period. The drop-down menu produced by clicking on *Get Involved* offers links to guidance in various areas including forms of political participation such as voting, viewing parliamentary debates and contacting MPs and members of the House of Lords. Users of the website could employ it to arrange a physical visit or to view its proceedings – plenary and committees in both Houses – via parliament.tv.[134] It was possible to contact the office of MPs directly by a publicly available

131 www.parliament.uk/site-information/privacy/, last accessed 2 April 2020.

132 The legal framework for cookies initially derived from The Privacy and Electronic Communications (EC Directive) Regulations 2003. For an account see https://ico.org.uk/for-organisations/guide-to-pecr/what-are-pecr/, last accessed 2 April 2020.

133 For instance, the Data Protection Act 2018, creating a set of 'data protection principles'.

134 'Watch Parliament at Work', available at: https://web.archive.org/web/20200402210730/https://www.parliament.uk/get-involved/watch-parliament-work/, last accessed 11 April 2020.

personalised email address (they also generally had social media details of some kind and websites[135]) and every Peer either had an open email address or could be reached electronically via a central address (contactholmember@parliament.uk) from which messages were forwarded to the office concerned.[136] Further, more developed, forms of online interaction are discussed below. While facilitating contact with representatives, the site attempts to some extent to delimit the extent to which people do so. For instance, it presents as a given that interaction will be with the local constituency representative ('your MP'[137]). While acting on behalf of people within their particular geographical territory is an important part of the work of MPs, it is not their only function. For instance, they take interest in particular policy areas, which could properly engage them with networks stretching across and even beyond the UK.

The 'Have your say: Laws and debates' option links to a page which itself includes a link to a 'Digital Engagement Programme'.[138] This feature describes itself as: 'your chance to connect with the work of MPs and the House of Commons. We gather your knowledge and experiences and feed them back to MPs to help inform their work.'[139] It contains two main sections. The first is 'Digital debates and discussions'. It entails MPs who are about to hold a parliamentary debate on a particular subject canvassing the views of members of the public, using a variety of possible online media. Between 2015 and 2019, forty-two such initiatives took place.[140] For example, in response to an online petition advocating that the netting of hedgerows to prevent the nesting of birds become a specific criminal offence (receiving more than 350,000 signatures) Mike Hill MP 'led a Westminster Hall debate' on the subject on 13 May 2019.[141] The objection to this netting arose because of the threat it posed to birds and to biodiversity.[142] Hill engaged with a forum on Facebook on 7 May in which there were more than 4,000 participants. They broadly manifested support for the petition and for additional measures to safeguard the

[135] 'Contact your MP', available at: www.parliament.uk/get-involved/contact-an-mp-or-lord/contact-your-mp/#jump-link-1, last accessed 11 April 2020.

[136] 'Contact a Member of the House of Lords', available at: www.parliament.uk/business/lords/whos-in-the-house-of-lords/get-in-touch-with-members/, last accessed 11 April 2020.

[137] 'Contact your MP', available at: www.parliament.uk/get-involved/contact-an-mp-or-lord/contact-your-mp/#jump-link-1, last accessed 11 April 2020.

[138] 'Have your say: Laws and debates', available at: https://web.archive.org/web/20200402205302/https://www.parliament.uk/get-involved/have-your-say-on-laws/, last accessed 11 April 2020.

[139] 'Digital Engagement Programme', undated, available at: www.parliament.uk/get-involved/have-your-say-on-laws/digital-engagement/, last accessed 8 April 2020.

[140] 'Digital Debates Archive (October 2015 to October 2019)', undated, https://old.parliament.uk/get-involved/have-your-say-on-laws/digital-engagement/digital-debates/digital-debates/, last accessed 21 January 2021.

[141] 'Netting Hedgerows Digital Debate', undated, available at: www.parliament.uk/get-involved/have-your-say-on-laws/digital-engagement/digital-debates/netting-hedgerows-discussion/, last accessed 8 April 2020. Page no longer available.

[142] 'Petition: Make "Netting" Hedgerows to Prevent Birds from Nesting a Criminal Offence', date of closure 18 September 2019, last accessed, https://petition.parliament.uk/archived/petitions/244233, last accessed 8 April 2020.

environment, and expressed general concern about threats in this area.[143] In his speech opening the Westminster Hall debate, Hill specifically referenced the Facebook event and views emerging from it.[144] The government response to the petition noted that existing law already prohibited '[c]ausing suffering to birds', describing policy measures being taken in this area.[145]

The second main aspect of the Digital Engagement Programme was called 'Forums'. It involved promoting information to and soliciting views from a 'range of online communities'. Those listed on the site were: Mumsnet, Moneysavingexpert.com, Reddit, TES (Times Educational Supplement), The Student Room and RailUK Forums. It entailed Parliament having a specific presence of its own on the sites concerned, fitting within their formats, but utilising them as an outlet for its own work.[146] To give an example, the UKHouseOfCommons Reddit account page, has a green (i.e. the Commons colour) Crowned Portcullis in the top right-hand corner, with text underneath reading: 'This is the official Reddit account of the UK House of Commons. We'll be posting things we find interesting about the work, history and membership of the Commons and the UK Parliament more broadly.'[147]

The account has posted material such as news updates – for instance a notice announcing that Dame Eleanor Laing MP had become the first woman Chairman of the Ways and Means and Principal Deputy Speaker – and initiated Reddit discussions that would inform forthcoming Commons debates, for example on funding for post-16 education. In accordance with the Reddit template, users were able both to comment on posts and to debate with each-other. One participant in the post-16 education thread remarked: '[t]he biggest "hidden" issue is overcrowding. There are too many pupils in 6th Form and the financial strategy document specifically states that they need to take on more pupils than they would like so that they can get adequate funding.' A direct response to this comment read: '[t]his [a term signifying approval of the statement to which it was referring]. We have classes of at least 16ppl and up to thirty, it feels like being at high school. The complexity of A-level content means smaller class sizes are a reqiuirement [sic] so the teacher can dedicate more time to each student.'[148] The Digital Engagement Programme identified case studies of its work in practice, under the title 'Stories and Impact'. It presented three themes: 'Engagement in LGBT

[143] 'Netting Hedgerows Digital Debate'.

[144] 'Bird Nesting Sites: Protection', House of Commons (HC) Hansard, Westminster Hall, 13 May 2019, vol. 660, col. 1 WH, available at: https://web.archive.org/web/20190520023507/https://hansard.parliament.uk/Commons/2019-05-13/debates/4419D95F-AD1C-40B7-86FC-6564ED636AE6/BirdNestingSitesProtection, last accessed 9 February 20210.

[145] 'Netting Hedgerows Digital Debate'.

[146] 'Forums', undated, available at: https://old.parliament.uk/get-involved/have-your-say-on-laws/digital-engagement/forums/, last accessed 9 February 2021.

[147] Available at: www.reddit.com/user/UKHouseOfCommons, last accessed 8 April 2020.

[148] Available at: www.reddit.com/user/UKHouseOfCommons, last accessed 8 April 2020.

Issues', 'Mumsnet in the House of Commons', and 'Teaching Migration in the History Curriculum'.[149] The first entailed involving particular groups of people in discussion,[150] the second working with a specific online group that was also associated with a specific social category,[151] while the third focused on a given topic.[152] They included narratives of the processes that took place, data on public interaction, and testimonies from participants.

Returning to the parliament.uk homepage, repeating the heading of 'UK Parliament' it describes the institution to which it belongs in the following terms: 'The UK Parliament has two Houses that work on behalf of UK citizens to check and challenge the work of Government, make and shape effective laws, and debate/make decisions on the big issues of the day.' The tone of this description is relatively informal, presumably deliberately so. The account offered is assertive on behalf of Parliament as a bicameral body, both Chambers of which derive legitimacy from their role in serving the public (though only one of them is actually elected by it). In this depiction, they use the authority thereby acquired to function with a degree of autonomy, potentially offering resistance to the executive – from which they comprise a distinct entity – taking part in and potentially making 'decisions' on matters of substantial importance. This account of Parliament was not contentious in itself. But it is interesting to note what it chose not to include. It omitted the role of the monarch in, for instance, convening (and disbanding) Parliament and giving Assent to bills. There was no reference to Parliament being the basis (via the Commons) for the government of the day through the provision (and potential withdrawal) of confidence, that it was the place from which ministers were appointed or that most of its time and legislative agenda were under the control of the executive. No mention was made of the role of parties or whips, of financial functions or of the means by which parliamentarians came to hold their posts (by election to the Commons, or other means to the Lords).

There were limits to what could be included in what was, understandably, intended to be a succinct definition. But the decisions made were revealing. Most notably – particularly in omitting reference to extent to which government and Parliament were fused – they were suggestive of a desire to convey an assertive constitutional posture, an attitude for which the website and wider digital strategy provided an outlet and a stimulus. Further descriptive material on the homepage, in the 'Quick links' section, is discussed below.

[149] 'Digital Engagement Programme'.

[150] 'Digital Engagement with the LGBT Community', undated, available at: https://houseofcommons.shorthandstories.com/LGBT/index.html, last accessed 8 April 2020.

[151] 'Mumsnet Users in the House of Commons, 2019', undated, available at: https://houseofcommons.shorthandstories.com/mumsnet/index.html, last accessed 8 April 2020.

[152] 'Teaching Migration in the History Curriculum: Involving the Public in Education Policy', undated, available at: https://houseofcommons.shorthandstories.com/migrationhistory/index.html, last accessed 8 April 2020.

To the right of the 'UK Parliament' text is a logo comprising an image of what seems to be the Victoria Tower (representing the House of Lords) and the Elizabeth Tower (formerly the St Stephen's Tower, housing the Big Ben bell by which the structure itself is often known). The next row down presents the following message: 'Welcome to our new look homepage. We're introducing this new look to sections of our site such as MPs and Lords, Votes in Parliament, and MPs' Guide to Procedure. We'll be adding it to other sections soon. You can share feedback by emailing webmaster@parliament.uk.' These words confirmed an aspect of online technology generally, and the previously discussed experience of parliament.uk over the years since its instigation. The condition was one of constant transition. An end point could not be reached. Pressures from without and within Parliament combined to ensure continual overhauls. Those responsible for the site felt recurring compulsions to update, and to announce to the outside world that they were doing so.

The following row down is headed 'Featured News'. It highlights in three items that Parliament is at this point in Easter recess, but seeking 'new ways of working' during the coronavirus pandemic (that are considered at the outset of this chapter); it offers an 'Update' on what those measures are; and contains a link to a page dealing with parliamentary oversight of the substantial body of Statutory Instruments (secondary legislation) being passed to address the emergency. These items remind us that the Internet created opportunities for parliamentary functions to continue even when some of its formal proceedings were disrupted or interrupted, and when there were practical obstacles to participation in physical meetings. They also show that parliament.uk (alongside other online outlets such as parliamentary social media accounts) was a means of both communicating and embodying that continued existence.

Next come two rows of 'Quick links' to: House of Commons, House of Lords, MPs and Lords, Votes in Parliament, Hansard, Bills, Committees, and Brexit – a thematic collection of research papers by the Commons and Lords libraries and various committee reports. These categories show a recognition of the bicameral nature of Parliament combined with a desire to provide a range of information about the activities of the two Houses in a combined form. The two 'Quick links' respectively to the Commons and to the Lords offer descriptions of the roles of each of these chambers, supplementing the material in the 'UK Parliament' section further up the page and discussed above. The Commons, it is noted, is a 'Democratically elected House'; it 'makes laws and checks the work of government'. The account of the Lords omits reference to how its composition is determined. It tells the reader that the function of the second chamber is '[c]hecking and shaping draft laws and challenging the work of government'. These brief descriptions of each House draw attention to, but do not expressly state, a paradoxical feature of the UK Parliament and its constitutional role. The Commons is the more democratically legitimate of the two because it is elected. This quality enables it to form a basis for the government; but, as a consequence, it is less likely to use the special authority it possesses to challenge the executive. It is by definition normally broadly supportive of the administration of the day. The Lords, though it does not have 'primacy' and is less powerful than the Commons, is not invested in any particular government in the way that the Commons is. This dual position is reflected in the 'Quick links' descriptions. The act of 'challenging' the executive is allotted only to the Lords, not the Commons; and while the Lords checks and shapes laws, the Commons only 'makes' them. Overall, however, as in the 'UK Parliament' passage, the emphasis is on Parliament as a limitation upon the executive.

There are two parallel columns below the 'Quick links' rows: a wider one on the left ('Follow the latest business') contains a vertical series of 'News' items (with a tab enabling the user to toggle to 'What's on' – a schedule of forthcoming business. The narrower column on the right ('Watch') provides links to parliament.tv content, and to the UK Parliament YouTube channel. Various other links follow in a row below to two search facilities respectively for members of the House of Commons (by the postcode of the user, the name of the MP, and the constituency name) and Members of the House of Lords (by 'Name or title'). The third item in this row invites users to follow Parliament on Facebook, Instagram, Flickr, Twitter, and YouTube. The very bottom row of the homepage has 'Explore Parliament' – more internal links – on the left; and 'Site Information', including 'Email alerts' enabling people to learn of developments without necessarily having to check back in to the website.

Conclusion

From the outset, there were those who suspected that parliamentary use of the Internet had powerful implications. For instance, in 1996, at the time of the introduction of the online publication of Hansard, the Conservative MP Gary Waller, chair of the Commons Information Committee, saw harnessing of the Internet as a means of expanding awareness of the activities of Parliament, to the benefit of democracy.[153] Over the years and decades that followed – though it did not, and could not, entirely replace all other forms of communication – the ascendancy of the Internet was spectacular. Parliamentary engagement with this technology developed in multiple directions. The function identified by Waller and others – that of communicating information to the public – continued to be significant, and became more sophisticated. One aspect to this task was the dissemination of pre-existing outputs – such as Hansard or, subsequently, filmed debates – via a new medium, the Internet. Parliament also came to produce what were new types of artefact in their own

[153] For an announcement specifically referring to the Commons text, see 'Hansard on the Internet', Information Committee Press Notice No.1 of Session 1996–97, Philip Moon, Clerk of the House of Commons Information Committee, 23 October 1996.

right – such as tweets,[154] Facebook[155] posts, and informative audio-visual clips.[156] Indeed, the parliament.uk website was itself a novel form that at the same time subsumed or acted as a gateway to a myriad of other expressions, some of which were familiar, others of which were new.

A further purpose for which Parliament came increasingly to employ the Internet was that of two-way communication with the public, rather than simple dissemination. In some instances, this practice involved innovation – for instance, online forums that allowed group discussion of policy issues or draft legislation by outside participants. In other cases, it simply allowed people to engage in activities – perhaps more easily – that were already established, such as contacting their MP. In one important case, the Internet helped to revive an ancient practice that had been subject to a long-term decline (though that had experienced a slight upturn in the 1980s and 1990s). It is worth expanding upon this point because it helps illustrate the subtle impact of parliamentary use of the Internet. Petitioning – the submission of a 'formal written request from one or more people to the Sovereign, the Government or to Parliament' – probably has roots in Anglo-Saxon England and the concept of subjects in search of redress taking grievances to the ruler.[157] In this sense it lies at the historic core of what eventually developed into a system of representative democracy, characterised by mechanisms through which members of the public can have input into the way they are governed. *Magna Carta* itself originated in 1215 as a (soon reneged upon) series of commitments from King John issued after he agreed to demands from an alliance of aristocrats contained in a document known as the Articles of the Barons.[158]

Already long-established in practice and recognised in law,[159] the Bill of Rights 1688 included provision for a 'Right to petition'. The text condemns James II (James VII of Scotland) for various constitutional transgressions and stipulates '[t]hat it is the Right of the Subjects to petition the King'. Moreover, 'all Commitments and Prosecutions for such Petitioning are Illegall'.[160] Before the mid-seventeenth century, petitions tended to address more localised and personal complaints, but thereafter they became a means of exerting pressure

154 'UK Parliament' Twitter account available at: https://twitter.com/UKParliament?ref_src=twsrc%5Egoogle%7Ctwcamp%5Eserp%7Ctwgr%5Eauthor, last accessed 15 April 2020.

155 'UK Parliament' Facebook page available at: https://en-gb.facebook.com/ukparliament/videos/vb.16553417732/851389158577122/?type=2&theater, last accessed 15 April 2020.

156 Such as a clip on the restoration of the Elizabeth Tower, available at: https://en-gb.facebook.com/ukparliament/videos/vb.16553417732/851389158577122/?type=2&theater, last accessed 15 April 2020.

157 *Public Petitions* (House of Commons Information Office, London. 2010), p. 2.

158 Text and analysis available at: 'The Articles of the Barons', *The Magna Carta Project*, https://magnacarta.cmp.uea.ac.uk/read/articles_of_barons, last accessed 11 April 2020.

159 *Public Petitions* (House of Commons Information Office, London. 2010), p. 2.

160 'Right to Petition', Bill of Rights 1688, available at: www.legislation.gov.uk/aep/WillandMarSess2/1/2/introduction, last accessed 11 April 2020.

in relation to high-level political controversies. This campaigning technique was in part a method of participation for those who did not have the right to vote prior to realisation of a full franchise[161], a process not complete until 1928. Research by Richard Huzzey and Henry Miller shows that the UK Parliament received in excess of 960,000 Public Petitions between 1833 and 1918.[162] Individual initiatives could achieve supporters in the millions, over matters such as pensions (5 million in 1939, 4.1 million in 1943, and 6 million in 1945); payment for ambulance workers (4.5 million in 1989); the Chartist campaign for parliamentary reform (3.3 million in 1842); the level of entertainment duty (3.1 million in 1951); and sub post-office closures (3 million in 2000).[163] During the course of the twentieth century, however, petitioning measured by the number submitted, broadly went into decline, with a limited recovery in the 1980s and 1990s.[164]

Official e-petitioning at UK level began with the executive, not Parliament. The No. 10 website initiated a petitioning feature in 2006 (which moved to the DirectGov site five years later).[165] When Parliament developed its own system for handling e-petitions, it came to do so through in effect sharing the service the UK government had already established. In 2011, the House of Commons Backbench Business Committee was responsible for determining how to respond to petitions on the DirectGov site that had received 100,000 signatures or more and had sponsorship from an individual MP. In particular the Committee had to decide whether to provide space for a debate on the petition, from the limited amount of time available for backbench-initiated activities.[166] A Commons Petitions Committee formed in 2015 took over this function. The rules changed at this point. Previously, it was only possible to petition Parliament via an MP. Now direct submission was possible.[167] The Petitions Committee developed a variety ways of handling petitions received in addition to holding debates, such as seeking more information on the subject concerned from sources including the government, passing them on to a specialist select committee or calling for action from a relevant body. The government was supposed to respond to petitions that had received 10,000 signatures or more. If they reached 100,000, they could in theory be debated in

161 Philip Loft, *Petitions in the UK* (House of Commons Library, London, 2019), p. 14.

162 Richard Huzzey and Henry Miller, 'Exploring British History through a Popular Form of Political Participation', 2 November 2017, available at: www.proquest.com/blog/pqblog/2017/Documenting-the-Power-of-Petitions.html, last accessed 11 April 2020.

163 Loft, *Petitions in the UK*, pp. 15–16.

164 Ibid., p. 14.

165 Sarah Priddy, *Petitioning Parliament and Government* (House of Commons Library, London, 2020), p. 4.

166 Richard Kelly and Sarah Priddy, *e-Petitions* (House of Commons Library, London 2015), pp. 12–13.

167 Priddy, *Petitioning Parliament and Government*, pp. 4, 6.

Parliament, if the Petitions Committee chose to ask the Backbench Business Committee to allot the necessary time.[168]

The Internet facilitated a decisive revival in public participation in this political activity. Three petitions from 2015 onwards reached a million or more signatures. The largest, with 6.1 million supporters in 2019, called on the UK government to abandon departure from the European Union by revoking the process it had initiated under Article 50 of the Treaty on European Union. While the petition became the subject of a Westminster Hall Debate, the government (unsurprisingly in the political context) was unmoved.[169] In 2016, 4.1 million people supported a call for the EU referendum to employ a threshold requirement, and for the vote to take place again if it were not met.[170] Another petition also instigated in 2016 with 1.9 million supporters called for the UK government to prohibit a state visit by Donald Trump.[171]

A third dimension of parliamentary use of the Internet was that of its internal operations. Email, for instance, became core to its day-to-day functioning. While this practice was in some ways simply a new and possibly more convenient version of other older forms of communication (such as letter-writing, speaking in person or using a telephone), it possibly represented qualitative change in the speed combined with potential for mass but at the same time selective contact for which it allowed. e-Tabling of written questions was an adaption of an established practice, though making it easier to carry out (perhaps too much so, as we will see). Similarly, as is discussed later, there were efforts to ensure that, though members of either House might use mobile devices in the Chamber or elsewhere, they did so in a way that did not fundamentally alter the nature of their participation. Accounts have emerged in recent years of rebellious factions within the Conservative and Labour parties operating through WhatsApp groups.[172] In every case, whether technology has actually made a substantive difference, or just made it more convenient for people to carry out activities they would have engaged in anyway, is difficult to establish.

We can view the history of parliamentary employment of the Internet in the period from 1996 in part as one of a number of manifestations of the rise of this digital network. As mySociety put it in its 2014 review document, 'the internet' was 'the winner' in a competition over 'which medium would be used to deliver significant computer applications and information services to users'.[173] Parliamentary take-up was to a large extent a consequence of this outcome.

[168] Kelly and Priddy, *e-Petitions*, pp. 37–8.

[169] Loft, *Petitions in the UK*, p. 8.

[170] Ibid., p. 10.

[171] Ibid., p. 12.

[172] Stuart Dredge, 'Why Political Rebels Love WhatsApp', *The Observer*, 5 March 2017, available at: www.theguardian.com/technology/2017/mar/05/political-rebels-whatsapp-encryption-technology-mps-security, last accessed 15 April 2020.

[173] mySociety, *Review of Parliament's Online Services*, pp. 22–3.

As an institution, it was not necessarily exceptionally swift to act. As we will see, it was slower than some legislatures worldwide. But we should not caricature Parliament and the people who made it up solely as archaic, detached from the public they were supposed to serve, and inherently resistant to the incorporation of changes and innovations taking place elsewhere, including those represented by a technology such as the Internet. A more satisfactory interpretation would be to see it and them as behaving in a way that was relatively representative of society.

They adopted the Internet, tentatively at first, then – as general use expanded and developed – attached increasing importance to it, in its many manifestations. There were varying degrees of understanding and enthusiasm within Parliament, just as elsewhere. Parliament may not have placed itself in the vanguard of internet experimentation. But should we be particularly surprised? It was a complex, long-established entity with a demanding and socially vital function to perform. It was not, for instance, a small enterprise established specifically to develop new uses of the Internet, the failure of which would be of little consequence except to those directly involved. Adapting to relatively novel technologies which were not at first essential to its continued operation was unlikely to be an objective of the highest priority. That its website and other online activities were not necessarily groundbreaking, and not always as useable as they might have been, did not set Parliament apart from other established institutions, such as universities. But it did absorb and utilise the Internet in various significant ways over time, sometimes taking calculated risks. In the process, it changed its own configuration and practices in certain notable respects.

If we overlay this period of technological adoption on the longer-term history of Parliament, it appears significant in a number of ways. The Internet engages key aspects of the development of this critical branch of the constitution. They include the following.

Parliament as a Gathering Historically, the UK – and before that English – Parliament always involved people meeting in a particular place. Before the mid-sixteenth century, it was mobile. Thereafter, it became largely fixed on the site of the Palace of Westminster. Of the last three occasions on which it met outside London, two were at times of plague. A later public health emergency, in 2020, also created difficulties for the full meeting of Parliament. Convening elsewhere was not a viable option this time. An impact of the Internet, the full implications of which are hard to discern so soon after it has manifested itself, is that it made it possible for Parliament formally to conduct proceedings without all the participants being simultaneously present in any one location.

The Relationship with the Executive Under the established UK system, the executive is formed out of Parliament. Interactions between the two entities contains countervailing tendencies in that the latter provides the basis for the former, while also holding it to account. In practice, Parliament is to a significant extent subject to the priorities of the government of the day, though not wholly subordinate. The nature and extent of parliamentary use of the Internet has in part been dependent upon government interest or at least acquiescence in possible initiatives. The complex development of the public petitions system helps illustrate the intertwined nature of the two constitutional branches. In this instance, a process that might lead to Parliament making demands upon government rested on a system shared with and initiated by the executive. The 'virtual Parliament' of 2020 further illustrates the subtle dynamics at play. Measures intended to ensure continued government accountability to Parliament required co-operation from ministers. Yet despite there being a degree of dependency in some respects, the Internet has nonetheless provided Parliament with a new medium by which it can promote an identity distinct from that of the executive, and various communication tools with which it can seek to apply pressure to government.

Parliament as an Institution In its formative stages in the medieval era, Parliament was perhaps more of an occasion – a gathering of notables by the monarchy to address specific issues – than an institution. But over time it developed structures as well as procedures and rules, and staff to implement them. Parliamentary use of the Internet had institutional aspects to it. Adoption of the technology, for instance, required the reconsideration and modification of regulations pertaining to matters such as the dissemination of official publications, the use of mobile devices, and the reception and handling of petitions. The technology made it possible for Parliament to carry out some of its procedures – such as policy inquiries and the scrutiny of draft bills – differently. Some of the ways in which Parliament employed the Internet entailed it relinquishing a degree of institutional control and submitting to the procedures of other bodies; for instance, conforming to the templates of social media sites in which it participated. External entities – such as the Public Whip – were able to extract information it made available online and process and present it ways that fitted with their agendas, rather than those of Parliament. Finally, use of the Internet was connected to structural reconfiguration. In particular, it was associated with pressures to create a single team of staff and unified online strategy for the whole of Parliament. This tendency ran counter to powerful trends within Parliament for the dispersal of functions, and the existence of a bicameral structure.

The Relationship with the Public Parliament has always in some sense been a representative institution, charged with bringing the views and interests of wider society to bear in decision-making. This role is both a responsibility and a source of authority for Parliament. Under the democratic system that emerged following successive expansions of the franchise from 1832 onwards, the principal link between people and Parliament is the election of Members of the House of Commons. But it has never been the only way in which such contact is maintained. The Internet has provided new means by which both Houses of Parliament can interact with those who they represent. Members of the public can obtain information about the institution and view its proceedings, in committees and plenary, online. Individuals and groups have been able to use the Internet to pressurise Parliament, by such means as contacting MPs and signing petitions; and Parliament could also enlist online input from outside to give its activities enhanced credibility – for instance, through sourcing views on appropriate subjects for select committee inquiries. A particular innovation in the conduct of ongoing relations with the public was the use of online forums. Pre-existing methods of accessing information about Parliament – through newspapers or broadcast media, for instance – persisted, as did traditional means of influencing it, such as demonstrating. But a new channel, with special qualities of its own, had attained considerable significance.

The Role of Parliament in Social Regulation A central function of Parliament is in the oversight of the functioning of society. It has two dimensions to it: legal and political. Parliament is a producer of law. According to prevailing traditional interpretations, it is 'sovereign', by which is broadly meant that an Act of Parliament is the ultimate source of authority and is not subject (unlike in many other jurisdictions) to higher authority in the form of a constitutional text interpreted by the judiciary. Parliament can also have a role in processing subordinate legislation issued under the authority of Acts it has already passed. The Internet has increased the external visibility of parliamentary legislative processes and made it easier for those within Parliament to monitor and engage with them. For instance, parliament.uk contains information pages providing access to the various stages of bills in both houses, and related documents and links;[174] and a service for tracking statutory instruments.[175] The texts of laws once passed are now also available online, making them far easier to access. The political aspect of Parliament as social regulator involves its investigation of topical issues and the application of pressure to government and other individuals and institutions. The Internet is relevant in this regard in various ways. For instance, it was incorporated into the work of select committees through their use of online forums, their receipt of individual evidence submissions online, and the webcasting of their proceedings. e-Petitions, on which Parliament might follow up in some way, involved calls upon government to address given issues. In exercising its regulatory function, political or legal, Parliament might not only use the Internet, but make this network and its various applications the subject of its interest, with a view to making it function in ways it deemed desirable. It might, for instance, pass legislation intended to promote or restrict given activities, seek to persuade the government to adopt particular policies in this field or, perhaps, draw attention to practices in the online technology sector that it regarded as problematic.

The Ongoing Operation of Parliament An important theme at various points in the history of Parliament has been its ability to function and the

[174] See 'Bills before Parliament 2019–21' available at: https://services.parliament.uk/bills/, last accessed 27 April 2020.

[175] 'Statutory Instruments', available at: https://statutoryinstruments.parliament.uk, last accessed 27 April 2020.

rights it possesses in this respect. Historically, it has been dependent to some extent on the executive being willing to convene it, or not to disband it. The attempted prorogation of 2019 and the controversy it generated demonstrated that this issue remains relevant. When dissolved pending an election, Parliament ceases to exist altogether. But ever since parliament.uk became operational in 1996, it has had a permanent platform, providing it with an outlet and a means by which it can interact with the public. Even in times of inactivity, it serves as an archive of past and vessel for future endeavours. Furthermore, the pandemic saw the Internet become more than a means by which Parliament can communicate about, and solicit input into, its business. It was – in these emergency circumstances at least – a means by which members could participate in its actual proceedings.

3

Technology and Transformation

Perspectives up to 1945

Revolutionary Invention

Mary Shelley published the first edition of *Frankenstein* in 1818.[1] The author and the work might seem remote subjects from the perspective of a twenty-first century discussion of Parliament and the Internet. But the personal and conceptual proximity is more immediate than they might on the surface seem to be. Shelley first told the story that would become *Frankenstein* in 1816 at a gathering near Lake Geneva of which the poet Lord Byron was the host. Byron and his wife, Annabella, a mathematician, had a single child. Ada Lovelace, as she later became, was a collaborator with Charles Babbage, famed for his two (incomplete) scientific projects, a 'Difference Engine' and an 'Analytical Engine'. Lovelace first came into contact with the ongoing work of Babbage in the 1830s, and became a close colleague. She has earned a powerful historic reputation.[2] In the words of Sadie Plant, '[a] hundred years before the hardware had been built, Ada ... produced the first example of what was later called computer programming'.[3] The associations of Shelley with more recent discourse are strengthened further by a consideration of the themes presented in *Frankenstein*. They link us to persistent traditions of thought that retain salience up to the present, that are the subject of this chapter. In particular, these characteristics help us to discern a lasting tendency to discern in technology the potential for abrupt social transformation or revolution, that manifested once more in relation to the Internet. The much-analysed *Frankenstein* drew on a controversy of its time within the Royal College of Surgeons about 'the origins and nature of life, now known as the vitalist debate'.[4] It also reflected a prominent cultural association between – on the

[1] Subtitled *or, The Modern Prometheus.*

[2] See e.g. Dr Arthur L. Samuel, 'The Banishment of Paper-Work' in Nigel Calder (ed.), *The World in 1984: The Complete New Scientist Series* (Penguin, Harmondsworth, 1965), vol. I, pp. 142–7, 142.

[3] Sadie Plant, *zeros + ones* (Fourth Estate, London, 1997), pp. 5–9.

[4] Marilyn Butler, 'Frankenstein and Radical Science' in Mary Shelley, *Frankenstein*, ed. J. Paul Hunter, Norton Critical Editions (W. W. Norton, London, 2012), pp. 404–16, 406.

one hand – scientific discovery, in particular involving electricity, and – on the other hand – radical, even revolutionary, political thought.

During the eighteenth century, the idea that the advancement of learning and invention were key to human progress had provided a basis for the broad intellectual tendency labelled the Enlightenment. To consider a classic text associated with this movement that originated in the British Isles, in the opening stages of *The Wealth of Nations*, Adam Smith stresses the importance of technological development. He set out various reasons as to why the process of specialisation he described as the 'division of labour' was able to achieve expansions in production. One was that it brought about 'the invention of all those machines by which labour is so much facilitated and abridged'. For Smith, this type of advance was not an elite project, but achieved by the people actually engaged in the tasks concerned: in this sense, he anticipated later views of science and invention that perceived it in a democratic sense (though future exponents of such views did not necessarily share his other perspectives). A focus on a single activity could lead someone to finding ways of performing it more efficiently. Smith wrote that '[a] great part of the machines made use of in those manufactures in which labour is most subdivided, were originally the invention of common workmen, who, being each of them employed in some very simple operation, naturally turned their thoughts towards finding out easier and readier methods of performing it'.[5]

The Wealth of Nations appeared in 1776, shortly before the American Declaration of Independence. Enlightenment ideas, particularly in their more radical form, became associated with actual political revolution. Key figures in the struggle for American independence, such as Thomas Jefferson and Thomas Paine, were also active inventors. Both of Shelley's parents were part of an intellectual circle that drew inspiration from the early stages of the French Revolution, commencing in 1789. Her mother, Mary Wollstonecraft, as a component of a broader programme of human advancement, was an advocate of science, including that it form part of the educational curriculum and career paths of women as well as men.[6] While her mother is regarded as a prototypical feminist, Shelley's father, William Godwin, is seen as progenitor of the anarchist philosophy. He too saw immense potential in science, opposing its retardation by religious or governmental oppression.[7]

Within this general linkage between science and political radicalism there was an important sub-theme. As the literary scholar Jane Goodall puts it '[t]hrough the later decades of the eighteenth century, electrical experiment became symbolically associated with revolutionary energies and ideals'.

[5] Adam Smith, *The Wealth of Nations Books I–III* (Penguin, London, 1999), Book I, p. 8.

[6] Lois N. Magner, 'Women and the Scientific Idiom: Textual Episodes from Wollstonecraft, Fuller, Gilman and Firestone', *Signs: Women, Science and Society* 4(1) (Autumn 1978): 61–80, 61–6.

[7] A theme of his 1793 work *Enquiry Concerning Political Justice and Its Influence on Morals and Happiness* (Penguin, London, 2015).

Benjamin Franklin and Joseph Priestley, for instance, embodied this connection.[8] The drama and dislocation that the concept of electricity conveyed takes us back to the sources of *Frankenstein*, of which Goodall is an analyst. Shelley's husband, the poet Percy, also had a keen interest in this area, carrying out experiments from a young age.[9] His friend and subsequently biographer, Thomas Jefferson Hogg, provided an account of seeing Percy in his quarters at university and finding him filling himself with an electrical charge that made his hair stand on end. Hogg recalls Percy exclaiming: 'What a mighty instrument would electricity be in the hands of him who knew how to wield it, in what manner to direct its omnipotent energies.' Percy went on: '[w]hat a terrible organ would the supernal [sic] shock prove, if we were able to guide it: how many of the secrets of nature would such a stupendous force unlock!'[10]

While electricity and science generally were a subject of enthusiasm among people with whom Mary Shelley was associated, her work suggested a sinister potential to it. Possibly, she drew on the experience of Priestley – whose laboratory an anti-revolutionary mob destroyed in 1791 – to discern potentially destructive outcomes from experimentation.[11] Frankenstein's monster remains a powerful cultural symbol, adapted in many forms (perhaps most notably the James Whale film of 1931): it represents the idea of an artificial scientific construction that becomes a threat to its human creators. We can see it as an ancestor of, for instance, the robot in the 1927 film *Metropolis* (discussed below), or the recurring science fiction theme of rogue 'Artificial Intelligence' (as depicted, for instance, by Stanley Kubrick in the 1968 film *2001: A Space Odyssey*). Mary and Percy are grouped as part of the Romantic artistic movement. Key exponents of this school, such as William Blake and William Wordsworth are interpreted as reacting negatively to the technological developments and industrialisation of their era.[12] As the nineteenth century continued, bleak depictions of this socioeconomic transition continued, for instance in *Shirley* by Charlotte Bronte. Appearing in 1849 and set around 1811–12 at the time of the Luddite disturbances, it gave an account of unemployed workers who 'hated the machines which they believed took their bread from them ... hated the buildings which contained those machines ... hated the manufacturers who owned those buildings'.[13]

Many accounts of industrial society depicted technology as integral to a system depriving the mass of the population of their full humanity. But a nuanced approach to its role was possible, regarding it – if suitably harnessed –

[8] Jane Goodall, 'Electrical Romanticism' in Mary Shelley, *Frankenstein*, ed. J. Paul Hunter, Norton Critical Editions (W.W. Norton, London, 2012), pp. 490–506, 490–2.

[9] Richard Holmes, *Shelley: The Pursuit* (HarperCollins, London, 2005), pp. 17–18.

[10] Goodall, 'Electrical Romanticism', pp. 492–3.

[11] Ibid., p. 497.

[12] See e.g. Leo Marx, *The Machine in the Garden: Technology and the Pastoral Ideal in America* (Oxford University Press, 1964; 2000), pp. 18–19.

[13] (Penguin, London, 2012), p. 28.

as potentially of considerable benefit. For instance, Thomas Spence, a less renowned contemporary of the likes of Wollstonecraft and Godwin, was a prescient radical democrat. Like Francis Bacon in *A New Atlantis*, discussed in the Introduction, Spence projected certain ideas onto an imaginary island community, that he labelled 'Spensonia'. Also like Bacon, Spence envisaged technological development in this ideal society as being subordinate to the collective interest. The parliament of Spensonia was required to purchase any 'invention, or secret, in medicine, or other science, or art, or importance to mankind' and make details of it publicly available for the common benefit.[14] Percy Shelley, fascinated by science, sought through the innovative use of technology to pursue his political goals. He used balloons and miniature boats in his efforts to disseminate his radical writings at a time, in 1812, when to dissent was to risk official surveillance and perhaps persecution. Percy combined this affinity for experimentation and the new with an attraction to the rural lifestyle, attempting on various occasions to form an agrarian community based on principles of social equality.[15]

In this latter project, Percy anticipated the activities of groups connected to Robert Owen, the textiles manufacturer and social reformer.[16] Owen shared philosophical ground with Godwin, with whom he had frequent intercourse in the relatively early stages of his philosophical development. Through the ideas he promoted and his practical attempts to develop his mills into ideal communities, Owen achieved great fame. The rise of industrial production was, in his view, a source of mass suffering. He sought to replace competition with co-operation, introducing a system that provided for the welfare of workers and their families in the fullest possible sense. He sought a completely reconstructed society in which every aspect of life – work, welfare, the physical environment, education, and morality – was transformed in accordance with humane first principles.[17] Owen opposed the idea of people inhabiting densely populated urban areas.[18] In 1849 he set out a detailed scheme for 'Townships' of between 500 and 3,000, surrounded by enough open land to support their needs. Self-governing, the Townships would group together, 'federatively united' with one another to the point where 'they shall extend over Europe, and afterwards to all other parts of the world, uniting all in one great republic, with one interest'.[19]

14 Thomas Spence, 'A Further Account of Spensonia (1794)' in G. I. Gallop (ed.) *Pigs Meat: Selected Writings of Thomas Spence, Radical and Pioneer Land Reformer* (Spokesman, Nottingham, 1982), pp. 80–90, 90.

15 Holmes, *Shelley: The Pursuit*, pp. 85–6.

16 Ibid., p. 150.

17 For a description of the society he envisaged, see Robert Owen, 'From "The Revolution in the Mind and Practice of the Human Race", 1849' in *A New View of Society and Other Writings* (Penguin, London, 1991), pp. 365–76.

18 Gregory Claeys, 'Introduction' in Robert Owen, *A New View of Society and Other Writings* (Penguin, London, 1991), pp. xii–xxxii, xxv.

19 Owen, 'From "The Revolution in the Mind and Practice of the Human Race"', pp. 371–2.

Where did technology fit within this conception? In one sense Owen took a bleak view of recent advances, perceiving them as having created a need for the reforms he promoted. For instance, in an 1815 discussion of the impact of 'mechanical inventions which introduced the cotton trade into this country',[20] he concluded they had left the 'lower orders … in a situation infinitely more degraded and miserable than they were before the introduction of these manufactories'.[21] However, as J. F. C. Harrison argues in his analysis of Owen and the movement he inspired, it was part of Owenite philosophy 'that given a "rational" arrangement of society machinery could be a blessing instead of a curse. In all Owenite plans for community, machinery was posited as the basis for reduced hours of labour and the elimination of heavy or disagreeable types of work.'[22]

Owen conveyed this impression in 1820 when describing how '[t]he steam-engine and spinning machine, with the endless mechanical inventions to which they have given rise, have, however inflicted evils on society, which now greatly overbalance the benefits which are derived from them'. Such advances had 'created an aggregate of wealth, and placed it in the hands of a few, who, by its aid, continue to absorb the wealth produced by the industry of the many'. As Owen put it, 'the mass of the population are become slaves to the ignorance and caprice of these monopolists'. These victims were 'far more truly helpless and wretched than they were before the names of Watt and Arkwright were known'.[23] However, the apparent sources of this suffering were also the potential basis for its relief, and for social progress. Owen held that 'these celebrated and ingenious men [Watt and Arkwright] have been the instruments of preparing society for the important beneficial changes which are about to occur'.[24] He described the system he advocated itself as a 'machine', writing of 'this new machine, which is to perform so many important offices for society'. It would 'simplify and facilitate, in a very remarkable manner, all the operations of human life, and multiply rational and permanently desirable enjoyments to an extent that cannot be yet calmly contemplated by ordinary minds'.[25]

Owen, then, saw emerging technology as both the source of a problem and a means not only of transcending it, but achieving a world better than that which would have been possible before it had been introduced. In taking this attitude, he was an early exponent of a dual attitude to scientific advance that

[20] Robert Owen, 'Observations on the Effect of the Manufacturing System, 1815' in *A New View of Society and Other Writings* (Penguin, London, 1991), pp. 93–103, 93.

[21] Ibid. p. 95.

[22] J. F. C. Harrison, *Robert Owen and the Owenites in Britain and America: The Quest for the New Moral World* (Routledge and Kegan Paul, London, 1969), p. 69.

[23] Robert Owen, 'Report to the County of Lanark, 1 May 1820' in *A New View of Society and Other Writings* (Penguin, London, 1991), pp. 250–308, 263–4.

[24] Ibid., pp. 263–4.

[25] Ibid., p. 294.

continues to manifest itself in the time of the Internet. As such he prefigured a school of advocacy of reconstruction of the lived environment, aimed at achieving – with the assistance of new inventions – social transformation.[26] Alongside this general significance, Owen was important for his anticipation of, and contribution to, socialism. Later participants in this intellectual and political movement would display similarly variegated attitudes towards modern contraptions.

William Morris, for instance, working later in the nineteenth century, might appear in his artistic and social vision to favour the assertion of rustic values over industrial existence. But as his biographer, E. P. Thompson, explains, Morris had a sophisticated position in this regard. Thompson notes that '[t]here is a very widespread opinion . . . that he [Morris] was an uncompromising enemy of all machinery as such, and that his chief motive in becoming a Socialist lay in a Utopian desire to return to a society of handicraftsmen'.[27] But, Thompson continues, '[t]he horror, for Morris, was not in the factory system itself, but in its subjugation to profit-grinding in its working conditions and social organization'.[28] Technology had a part to play. For instance, in his 1890 portrait of an idealised agrarian society of the year 2012, *News from Nowhere*, Morris referred to the employment of devices such as 'force-barges', with a mysterious form of propulsion.[29] He anticipated that, under socialism, machinery would come within the control of humans, rather than the other way around. It would be a critical component in a general social reconstruction, allowing people to divide their time more evenly between manual and intellectual pursuits.[30]

Technology, then, performs an important – and not wholly negative – role in theories of socialist transformation or revolution. It is conspicuous in the work of Karl Marx. In his 2014 critical study of the social role of digital technology, Jaron Lanier recounts a story about how 'many years ago when I was driving in Silicon Valley . . . some Internet startup was on the radio trumpeting the latest scheme to take over the world'. Believing he was hearing 'a lot of the usual filler about innovation breaking through traditional market boundaries, the globalization of technical talent, and so on', Lanier 'was just about to turn the radio off, muttering something about how I couldn't take even one more pitch from one of these companies'. But then 'the announcer intoned "This has been an anniversary reading of *Das Kapital*." I had been

[26] e.g. Lewis Mumford, *The Culture of Cities* (Secker & Warburg, London, 1938, 1946 reprint), pp. 392–3.

[27] E. P. Thompson, *William Morris: Romantic to Revolutionary* (Pantheon Books, New York, 1976), p. 649.

[28] Ibid.

[29] William Morris, *News from Nowhere and Other Writings* (Penguin, London, 1993), p. 185.

[30] Thompson, William Morris: Romantic to Revolutionary, pp. 649–50.

listening to the lefty station KPFA without realizing it.'[31] Lanier duly judges that 'Marx was one of the first technology writers.'[32]

As Lanier suggests, the similarities between – on the one hand – recent discussions of internet-related technologies and their purveyors and – on the other hand – Marx's presentation of capitalist production and the bourgeoisie engaged in it are striking. Both create the impression of irresistible forces restructuring global society and overriding previous gradations, concentrating wealth and power in a tiny group while all others are lowered to the same unfortunate level. In his 2015 book *The Internet Is Not the Answer*, Andrew Keen distilled a strand of recent attitudes towards his subject when writing that '[i]n today's digital experiment, the world is being transformed into a winner-take-all, upstairs-down-stairs kind of society'. The 'networked future is characterised by an astonishingly unequal distribution of economic value and power in almost every industry that the Internet is disrupting'.[33] Marx had identified similar tendencies long before, and also saw technology as central to them. *The Communist Manifesto*, written with Frederick Engels in 1848, described how 'steam and machinery revolutionized industrial production', facilitating '[m]odern industry', that had in turn 'established the world market'.[34] They stressed the importance of advances, including 'machinery, application of chemistry to industry and agriculture, steam navigation, railways, electric telegraphs, clearing of whole continents for cultivation, canalization of rivers'.[35] Like later internet commentators, they perceived an economic polarisation effect: '[t]he lower strata of the middle class – the small tradespeople, shopkeepers, and retired tradesman generally, the handicraftsmen and peasants' would 'all ... sink gradually into the proletariat'. One reason for this outcome was that 'their diminutive capital does not suffice for the scale on which Modern Industry is carried on, and is swamped in the competition with the large capitalists'. Another was that 'their specialized skill is rendered worthless by new methods of production'.[36]

Like Spence, Owen, and Morris, Marx and Engels saw technology as more than a source of inequality. They supported its being harnessed for social goals. Moreover, like Owen (though of whom, it should be noted, they were disparaging), they envisaged an associated transformation of the lived environment entailing population dispersal. The *Manifesto* advanced a ten-point programme, including within it: 'centralization of the means of communication and transport in the hands of the State'; '[e]xtension of factories and instruments of production owned by the State; the bringing into cultivation of wastelands'; and '[c]ombination of agriculture with manufacturing industries;

31 Jaron Lanier, *Who Owns the Future?* (Penguin, London, 2014), pp. 126–7.

32 Ibid., p. 126.

33 Andrew Keen, *The Internet Is Not the Answer* (Atlantic, London, 2015), e-book location 181.

34 Karl Marx and Frederick Engels, *The Communist Manifesto* (Penguin, London, 2015), p. 4.

35 Ibid., p. 9.

36 Ibid., p. 13.

gradual abolition of the distinctions between town and country, by a more equable distribution of the population over the country'.[37]

The reference in the *Manifesto* to 'electric telegraphs' was noteworthy. This invention, coming into commercial use from the 1830s, would make possible the near-instant long-distance transmission of messages. Marx displayed a long-standing interest in the impact of developments in communications technology. In the collection of manuscripts written in late 1857 and early 1858, discovered and properly published under the title *Grundrisse* nearly a century later in 1953, Marx discussed the cultural significance of an earlier invention in this field, asking: 'Do not the song and the saga and the muse necessarily come to an end with the printer's bar, hence do not the necessary conditions of epic poetry vanish?'[38] The telegraph attracted the interest of Marx partly because of its potential role in the dissemination and indeed distortion of political information. He detected conflicting media accounts of the Vienna uprising that commenced in October 1848. Observing discrepancies regarding the progress that the Imperial forces had made in restoring control, in a German press article Marx speculated about the dissemination of 'false rumours' in some of the press and the part that the 'state telegraph' might have played in them.[39] He depicted premature claims regarding the surrender of Vienna as the consequence of a 'false telegram' that was 'deliberately or as a result of a *misunderstanding* issued to the world'. Compliant journals had, Marx held, 'like an orthodox, multilingual echo, willingly repeated the message'.[40] Scenarios in which new media formats are deployed in campaigns of dis- and misinformation are familiar today, now involving the Internet.

Beyond its use as a means of disseminating news, reliable or otherwise, Marx saw the telegraph as contributing to the formation of a global network for the transfer of information and physical goods, with immense social consequences. In the third volume of *Capital*, drafted between 1863 and 1867 and which Engels posthumously compiled and published in 1894, Marx held that '[t]he colossal expansion of means of communication – ocean-going steamships, railways, electric telegraphs, the Suez canal – has genuinely established the world market for the first time'.[41] In the years that

37 Ibid., p. 34.

38 Karl Marx, *Grundrisse: Foundations of the Critique of Political Economy (Rough Draft)* (Penguin in association with New Left Review, London, 1993), p. 111.

39 Karl Marx, 'The Viennese Revolution and the Kolnische Zeitung', 3 November 1848, published in German in *Neue Rheinische Zeitung*, No. 133, 3 November 1848, in Karl Marx and Frederick Engels, *Collected Works*, vol. VII: *Marx & Engels 1848*, e-book (Lawrence & Wishart, 2010), pp. 496–7, 497.

40 Karl Marx, 'The Outlook Brightens', 4 November 1848, published in German in *Neue Rheinische Zeitung*, No. 135, 5 November 1848, in Karl Marx and Frederick Engels, *Collected Works*, vol. VII: *Marx & Engels 1848* (Lawrence & Wishart electric book, 2010), pp. 498–9, 498.

41 Karl Marx, *Capital, Book III: The Process of Capitalist Production as a Whole* (Penguin, London, 1991), p. 620 fn. 8, p. 1086.

had elapsed since the time of Priestley, Franklin, and the Shelleys, electricity had progressed beyond being a curiosity, and was beginning to acquire something of the importance that Percy Shelley predicted it would. In comparison to steam, it was a new and exciting form of energy, which Marx – like many others of his time – viewed with fascination until the end of his life. Speaking at the burial of Marx at Highgate Cemetery on 17 March, 1883, Engels stressed that his colleague's approach was 'scientific' in character, involving the discernment of laws determining the development and operation of society. Engels went on: '[s]cience was for Marx a historically dynamic, revolutionary force. However great the joy with which he welcomed a new discovery in some theoretical science whose practical application perhaps it was as yet quite impossible to envisage, he experienced quite another kind of joy when the discovery involved immediate revolutionary changes in industry, and in historical development in general.' Providing an example of this trait, Engels described how Marx 'followed closely the development of the discoveries made in the field of electricity and recently those of [pioneer of the transmission of electricity] Marcel Deprez'.

A great rival of Marx, the anarchist, Michael Bakunin, also took a close interest in science. His major work, written in 1871 and published in 1882 under the title *God and the State*, six years after he had died, presented science as a potential tool of oppression in the hands of a monopolistic elite. But through measures such as mass education it could become the means by which the people could free themselves from religious and governmental subjugation. He wrote that: '[t]he government of science and of scientists … cannot fail to be impotent, ridiculous, inhuman, cruel, oppressive, exploiting, maleficent'.[42] Bakunin therefore called for '*the revolt of life against science*, or rather against the *government of science*, not to destroy science – that would be high treason to humanity – but remind it to its place so that it can never leave it again'.[43]

A fellow-Russian anarchist, Peter Kropotkin, was – like other earlier thinkers of revolutionary inclination – focused on a particular area of scientific advance. He shared with Marx not only in interest in electricity, but its transmission over distance. Kropotkin viewed technology from a democratic perspective. He took the same view as that proposed by Adam Smith: that it was practitioners engaged in working in a particular field who were the sources of inventions, and he observed that their work preceded that of theoretical advance.[44] In a work that was published in its first edition in 1898, he noted that '[i]t was not the theory of electricity which gave us the telegraph. When the telegraph was invented, all we knew about electricity was but a few facts

[42] Michael Bakunin, *God and the State* (Dover, New York, 1970), p. 43.
[43] Ibid., p. 47.
[44] Peter Kropotkin, *Fields, Factories and Workshops, or Industry Combined with Agriculture and Brain Work with Manual Work* (G. P. Putnam & Sons, London, 1898), p. 194.

more or less badly arranged in our books; the theory of electricity is not ready yet'. A 'Newton' in this field had yet to appear, and '[e]ven the empirical knowledge of the laws of electrical currents was in its infancy when a few bold men laid a cable at the bottom of the Atlantic Ocean, despite the warnings of the authorised men of science'.

As shown in his work from the late nineteenth century onwards, Kropotkin saw in recent developments a tendency to move beyond the division of labour that Smith had identified. The distribution of electricity made possible a dispersal of previously concentrated economic – and by extension political – power and the introduction of more effective farming techniques. Different activities – industrial and agricultural, manual and cerebral – while remaining discrete as tasks, might thereby be integrated, so no one person was confined to a particular function. Countries, and regions within them, could also diversify across kinds of production, without needing to specialise. This unity of varied activities, Kropotkin judged, was more in keeping with the proper condition of humans and their needs.[45]

Excitement about the socially transformative potential of electricity extended beyond revolutionary circles. Ebenezer Howard, a pioneering town planner, developed a programme he perceived as transcending political divisions, since it sought to provide an end to which no one would object: prevention of further overpopulation of cities and depopulation of rural areas.[46] In a work first published in 1898 and reissued under the title *Garden Cities of Tomorrow* in 1902, he proposed a model for society of the future in which (like that which Owen among others favoured) people live in more geographically dispersed units ('a new distribution of population'[47]), designed and organised with their welfare in mind. He described to this end a planning project which would: 'raise the standard of health and comfort of all true workers of whatever grade – the means by which these objects are to be achieved being a healthy, natural, and economic combination of town and country, and this on land owned by the municipality'.[48]

Technology and its possibilities lay at the centre of the Howard concept. He wrote, as he saw it, in the context of ongoing and rapid development driven by invention. Howard asked, 'can any reasonable person, who reflects for a moment on the recent unexampled rate of progress and invention, doubt that the next sixty years will reveal changes fully as remarkable?' He invited the reader to consider 'what possibilities are opened up by . . . the discovery of new motive powers, new means of locomotion, perhaps through the air, new methods of water supply'.[49] Such advances would have specific

[45] See generally ibid.
[46] Ebenezer Howard, *Garden Cities of Tomorrow* (Swan Sonnenschein & Co., London, 1902), p. 2.
[47] Ibid., pp. 88–9.
[48] Ibid., p. 10.
[49] Ibid., pp. 88–9.

application within the environment Howard envisaged. He described how '[t]he smoke fiend' would be 'kept well within bounds in Garden City; for all machinery is driven by electric energy, with the result that the cost of electricity for lighting and other purposes is greatly reduced'.[50] In other words, Howard envisaged a newer technology being used to overcome the problems associated with an older. Above ground, Garden City was a carefully laid out landscape of boulevards, public buildings, high-quality housing, commerce, and parkland, surrounded by countryside.[51] Beneath it would be a network of tunnels for a range of purposes, reflecting 'the rapid growth of invention'. Their functions would include the conveyance of communications with 'telegraph and telephone wires' and 'pneumatic tubes for postal purposes' running through them.[52]

We can view Howard as both continuer of an earlier tradition that included within it Owen, and as a contributor to an emerging movement that gained in force as the twentieth century progressed. It manifested itself in the garden city movement in the UK and had powerful adherents in the United States. An important figure in the drive to adopt a holistic approach to environmental planning was Patrick Geddes. Operating across fields including biology, architecture, philosophy, and sociology, Geddes drew inspiration from the work of Kropotkin (who wielded influence far beyond anarchist circles).[53] One of the most prominent Geddes projects was the Outlook Tower in Edinburgh. From 1892 he developed the site into an exhibition intended to encourage contemplation of the urban environment and how it might become restructured to reflect the needs of the people living within it – a core Geddes objective. The camera obscura already in place at the summit when Geddes took on the building projected a live overview of the city in miniature onto a screen for visitors to view.[54]

Through this exhibit, Geddes employed technology to provide an encapsulation of the urban setting. The objective was to enhance understanding and the potential for people to effect change in the world around them. This concept has proved recurrent, across diverse contexts. Stewart Brand – later a promoter of the use of the Internet for purposes of social interaction and community building – campaigned in the 1960s for the space programme to capture and make available a photographed image of the planet, as a means of bringing about altered public consciousness. Underlining the countercultural flavour of this exercise, Brand has recounted how he conceived of the idea

50 Ibid., p. 13.
51 Ibid., p. 10.
52 Ibid., pp. 10–13.
53 James W. Carey with John J. Quirk, 'The Mythos of the Electronic Revolution' in James W. Carey, *Communication as Culture: Essays on Media and Society* (Routledge, London, 1992), pp. 113–41, 128.
54 Alex Wright, *Cataloging the World: Paul Otlet and the Birth of the Information Age* (Oxford University Press, 2014), pp. 108–11.

while under the influence of LSD early in 1966.[55] The *Whole Earth Catalog*, which Brand launched in 1968, derived its name from this cause. This publication promoted various forms of technology as supportive of alternative, communal lifestyles: they ranged from the ancient, such agricultural tools, to the advanced – including computers.

In some respects, the Geddes Outlook Tower initiative also anticipated the aspirations of later digital theorists, who regarded their technologies of interest as a means of generating realities that could be employed by members of the public as participatory devices. In the early 1990s, for instance, David Gelernter expounded the 'mirror worlds' concept. He insisted that 'some day soon' it would be possible to 'look into a computer screen and see reality. Some part of your world – the town you live in, the company you work for, your school system, the city hospital – will hang there in a sharp color image, abstract but recognizable, moving subtly in a thousand places'. A user activating such a device would 'turn the world … inside out. You stuff the huge multi-institutional ratwork that encompasses you into a genie bottle on your desk. You can see over, under and through it. You can see deeply into it.' The effect, Gelernter held, would be one of empowerment rather than capture. As he put it, '[a] bottled institution *cannot* intimidate, confound or ignore its members; *they* dominate it'.[56]

James W. Carey and John J. Quirk have recounted how the ideas Geddes advanced, including his favouring of electricity as replacement for steam power, were subsequently incorporated into the philosophy of the Regional Planning Association of America. The Association, Carey and Quirk write, pursued 'the goals of public electric power and community planning', seeking 'to integrate the new technology with conservationism and democratic localism'.[57] Its ideas persisted and found a degree of expression in real-world policy. During the economic depression of the 1930s, the presidency of Franklin D. Roosevelt appropriated this approach, presenting electricity as central to public infrastructure projects such as the Tennessee Valley Authority.[58] Alongside his influence on American perceptions of environmental development, Geddes associated with a number of thinkers from the European mainland who now appear in accounts of theoretical developments that predated but anticipated the Internet. They include Paul Otlet, the Belgian promoter of international co-operation and systematic collation of human knowledge. Otlet envisaged a global network of information, that users could access via screens onto which text would be projected. Moreover, as Alex

[55] Andrew Brown, 'Whole Earth visionary', *The Guardian*, 4 August 2001, available at: www.theguardian.com/education/2001/aug/04/artsandhumanities.highereducation, last accessed 20 August 2020.

[56] David Gelernter, *Mirror Worlds: Or the Day Software Puts the Universe in a Shoebox … How It Will Happen and What It Will Mean* (Oxford University Press, 1992), p. 1.

[57] Carey with Quirk, 'The Mythos of the Electronic Revolution', p. 129.

[58] Ibid., p. 131.

Wright puts it, Otlet 'imagined that individuals would be able to upload files to central servers and communicate via wireless networks'. Otlet 'foresaw the possibilities of social networks'. He envisaged, Wright observes, the creation of 'a social space around individual pieces of media, and allowing a network of contributors to create links from one to another, much the way hyperlinks work on today's Web'.[59]

When considering a figure such as Otlet, a temptation exists to succumb to the cliché of visionary not fully appreciated in his own time, an isolated prophet the significance of whose ideas we can only appreciate in the light of recent developments. We need not wholly dismiss such perceptions, but it is also important to recognise that Otlet was part of a circle of mutual influence that included within it, among others, Geddes, and that his views about the prospects for technology in assisting social reconstruction were – though in one sense original – a variant on a recurring tendency. Seeking out the person who first anticipated the Internet might lead us to Otlet, alongside a number of other people, some of whom are discussed elsewhere in this chapter. But it is not necessarily the most worthwhile of exercises. More useful is an assessment of the range of perceptions of inventions and their consequences that were engrained long before the appearance of the Internet, and the difference they made to the way in which this later technology was understood and deployed.

Sound and Sight

While Otlet built his ideas on inventions yet to come into being, others in the first half of the twentieth century responded to actual developments in communications and media technology. Their hopes rested more on the possible uses of devices already in existence and in use. Expectations for radio, for instance, were high. The first public inquiry into broadcasting in the UK, chaired by the Unionist politician Frederick Sykes, took place in 1923. The Broadcasting Committee identified expansive possibilities, that in turn called for a careful approach to the technology. It concluded that: 'The outstanding feature of radiotelephony is that it enables a single voice to reach innumerable ears. It can carry speech and melody into every home. It can bring isolated towns and villages into close touch with the great centres of population.' The report went as far as to hold '[i]t may be that broadcasting holds social and political possibilities as great as any technical attainment of our generation'.[60]

Possible future uses of the new medium included government statements and '[d]ebates in Parliament and other public bodies'.[61] The Committee saw radio as able to perform an educational service, and the members were 'much

[59] Wright, *Cataloging the World*, pp. 8–9.

[60] Broadcasting Committee, *The Broadcasting Committee: Report* (His Majesty's Stationery Office, London, 1923), August, Cmd 1951, para. 4, pp. 5–6.

[61] Ibid., para. 8, pp. 6–7.

impressed with the widespread enthusiasm which broadcasting has aroused'. Their report remarked that '[l]arge numbers of persons who have never before taken any interest in such matters are now acquiring knowledge of the principles of wireless telegraphy and telephony, and of the construction and working of wireless receiving sets'. Furthermore, '[a] new class of literature on the subject has sprung up and is widely read. This new interest and study will, we are convinced, have good effects from the educational point of view, and will stimulate experiment and research.' The technology had inclusive potential: '[t]he listener may perhaps become an experimenter; the experimenter may possibly become an inventor'.[62] (While this inquiry was optimistic about the potential of radio to bring about social improvement, including through the dissemination of culture, different views were possible at this time and thereafter, including that it vulgarised that which it sought to communicate.[63])

The Committee detected immense persuasive – or even manipulative – force on the part of the medium, that it described as possessing 'such a potential power over public opinion and the life of the nation'. Consequently, it saw a need for action by public authorities to ensure that it did not become subordinate to a single private interest. It judged that 'control ... ought to remain with the State, and that the operation of so important a national service ought not to be allowed to become an unrestricted commercial monopoly'.[64] This claim demonstrated how views about the appropriate role of government with respect to the media could vary significantly according to the particular technology involved. As discussed in the Introduction, opposition to the idea of subjecting printing to such 'control' had become deeply ingrained. A major reason that attitudes regarding radio differed was the restricted bandwidth, which created far greater vulnerability to domination by a single entity. Public regulation in this context was conceived of as a means of avoiding monolithic control, rather than securing it. Even in the case of newspapers, despite being a medium without the same practical constraints on output, the commercial environment could lead – if not to single owner dominance – a decline of diversity. Devising an acceptable response to such a tendency, given sensitivities about interference in press freedom, was a problematic task. We have seen how – by the early twenty-first century – concerns were growing about subjugation of the Internet to a small number of corporations such as Facebook, Apple, and Google. This medium provided – in theory – an unprecedented capacity to communicate to anyone with the appropriate hardware and connection to the network. Yet its diversity was – in some senses – vulnerable. There were risks for print, broadcasting,

[62] Ibid., para. 9, p. 7.

[63] See e.g. the fantasy of a conversation with Mozart in Herman Hesse, *Steppenwolf* (Penguin, London, 2012), p. 232, though the purposes of the novel is not necessarily to endorse such criticism.

[64] Broadcasting Committee, *The Broadcasting Committee: Report*, para. 6, p. 5.

and the Internet. The problem – and one that Parliament would face in its response to each of these forms of communication – was that official regulation might be regarded as being as objectionable as the problem it sought to address, and perhaps more so.

A parallel development to radio, film, was also a subject of claims regarding supposed epochal importance. A good illustration comes in a work published in 1923, the same year of the first Broadcasting Committee, entitled *That Marvel – The Movie*. In it, the author, Edward S. Van Zile, argued that film – then existing in what we now term its 'silent' form – could, if approached properly, be a force to enable humanity to unify and overcome 'the Four Horsemen of the Apocalypse, War, Famine, Poverty and Disease'.[65] According to Van Zile, '[t]he race' had 'found at last its universal language, its Esperanto not of the ear but of the eye'. He held that '[t]he evolution of the motion picture, developing in a few years from a toy kinetoscope to a [director D. W.] Griffith wonder-worker, has made possible, for the first time in the history of humanity, an appeal to the heart and mind and soul of man that overcomes the ancient handicap of the confusion of tongues'. The emergence offered the prospect of overcoming 'the check to human progress given at the Tower of Babel . . . at the entrance to the motion-picture palace'. The medium could circumvent such barriers, making it 'possible at last for history to reveal its secrets, and vouchsafe its warnings, not to the comparatively few who read scholarly books but to the millions who, as democracy conquers the earth, have become masters of the destiny of nations'.[66] Van Zile called for major investment to establish an institution for the better realisation of these ends.[67] This proposal suggested that the potential of film was not necessarily self-realising, and required concerted and conscious action.

Television inspired similar excitement. In a 1932 work, *The Outlook for Television*, Orrin E. Dunlap asserted that '[t]he world is on the threshold of a great forward movement in mass communication – transmission and repetition of sound and sight combined'. Dunlap located this invention in a technological-historical continuum. He wrote: '[j]ust as the incandescent lamp guided man out of the dark ages and the motor-car extended his highways, so radio came to introduce a kind of armchair civilization'. This latter device meant that '[t]he snap of a switch brings music, drama, and speech delivered wholesale to a multitude who tap the electrical flow on a slender copper wire. The science of broadcasting presents the world with new instruments for reaching a populace of many millions.' For Dunlap, radio meant that 'the machine age has ushered in an era of electrical entertainment'. Television represented 'the next act' in this process. Dunlap represented this new

[65] Edward S. Van Zile, *That Marvel – The Movie: A Glance at Its Reckless Past, Its Promising Present, and Its Significant Future* (G. P. Putnam's Sons, New York, 1923), p. 208.

[66] Ibid., p. 8.

[67] Ibid., pp. 11, 211–12.

technology as 'a gigantic force looming to take its place beside the press, the talking picture, and radio broadcasting as a powerful instrumentality for entertainment and education'.[68]

As Van Zile had for film, Dunlap stressed the idea of universality when describing the impact of his favoured device. 'Television', he argued, would 'enable a large part of the earth's inhabitants to see and to hear one another without leaving their homes'. The medium was, Dunlap held, an educational device and as such a progressive force: a familiar Enlightenment theme. He called television 'an easy, quick, and economical means of spreading knowledge and information'. Ultimately it would 'bring nations face to face' and was 'a new weapon against hatred and fear, suspicion and hostility'.[69] The familiar idea of technology as source of upheaval recurred once more. Dunlap wrote that '[r]evolutions in modes of communication have always made the world more interesting. The word of mouth, the scratch of a pen, the metallic clicks of the telegraph, the spoken words of the telephone, the buzzing dots and dashes of wireless, the music and voices of broadcasting, all worked vast changes for individuals and institutions.' The latest instalment – that of 'transmission of sight by invisible waves in space' – would have similarly dramatic impact.[70]

In an Epilogue to the book, Theodore Roosevelt, son of the US President of the same name, discussed the implications of television for politics. For him, it was a potentially democratising device. It could bring about better informed and independent-minded public involvement in politics; and it would allow for a more competitive contest, with the possibility for a greater number of viable candidates. Roosevelt remarked that: 'whereas thirty years ago only an infinitesimal number of people in the nation ever heard the voice of the President or saw his picture outside of a few lithographs or some mediocre newspaper reproduction, now the vast majority of [the] country will see him as well as hear his voice'. Roosevelt judged that this change would 'have a great effect', and that it would 'stir the nation to a lively interest in those who are directing its policies and in the policies themselves'. The outcome he foresaw was that 'normally . . . we may expect more intelligent, more concerted action from an electorate. The people will think more for themselves and less simply at the direction of local members of the political machines.' One specific change would be that of opening up political competition. At present it was 'difficult for a man to become a national leader'. Attaining the degree of exposure required was a considerable challenge. Yet 'television and radio' would alter this position, with 'the number of leaders known to the general public multiplied many times'.[71]

68 Orrin E. Dunlap, *The Outlook for Television* (Harper & Brothers, New York, 1932), p. 3.
69 Ibid., p. 3.
70 Ibid., pp. 3–4.
71 Colonel Theodore Roosevelt, Governor General of the Philippines, ibid., pp. 264–5.

Twelve years after Dunlap, Robert Edwin Lee somehow managed to suggest his expectations for the device were even higher (with accompanying fears), in a book entitled *Television: The Revolution*. Once more, technological advance, in this instance involving electrical media, had prompted use of the word 'revolution'. Further familiar themes were those of universality, inclusiveness, and education. Writing in the context of ongoing world war, Lee proclaimed that: '[t]elevision is humanity's farthest step forward in mass communication'.[72] One consequence of the device Lee anticipated was that '[t]elecasting will make provincialism almost impossible'. There would be 'much greater *awareness* on a world-wide scale', leading to 'a great deal of stress on certain traditions which have always seemed cozy and comfortable'.[73] Television would mean that 'everybody ... will have a fairly equal chance to observe what's going on, while it is going on. And an equal chance to see means an equal chance to judge.' Lee anticipated that '[t]ens of millions – previously cut off because they were too far away to be informed – will find through their television screens a competence to contribute to the world's thinking and doing'.[74] The medium would 'encourage more sympathetic and generous understanding among people of all nations'.[75]

Television, as Lee perceived it, was an intellectual and emotional force so powerful that it could bring about great change in the condition of humanity. The outcome, he believed, might be good. But – reflecting the concerns of his time, and the use that the Nazis (along with other authoritarian regimes) made of mass media – Lee recognised that the technology might serve negative ends. Like many who came before him, he believed that '[k]knowledge has freed men from enslavement to superstition, disease, inclement environment, fear of the physical unknown'.[76] Television was 'so direct and fluid' as a means of dissemination that it could bring 'the realization – in concrete terms – in every nation on the planet – of the Four Freedoms defined by the leaders of the democracies'. Moreover, it could 'transmit *feeling* as well as information ... *emotion* as well as knowledge'.[77] Lee asked: '[w]hen these simultaneous nation-wide – or even world-wide – swells of feeling are channelled in the best interests of humanity, who can measure the resulting good?' He recognised the potential for abuse of this 'momentous force', which could be 'a force for freedom, or it can break faith with humanity; it can lift us toward a working world society, or drag us into worse chaos than before'.[78] Elaborating on this theme, Lee remarked of television that '[i]n the hands of conscientious men, it can make living a more worthwhile experience for every

[72] Robert Edwin Lee, *Television: The Revolution* (Essential Books, New York, 1944), p. 219.
[73] Ibid., p. 221.
[74] Ibid., p. 222.
[75] Ibid., p. 226.
[76] Ibid.
[77] Ibid., p. 227.
[78] Ibid., p. 228.

human being in the world. As a lever for vicious exploitation, it can pry us loose from the way of life we long to believe in, and let us fall into uncertainty'.[79] While warning of the threat of '[a] glib Goebbels' able to 'stampede a continent into animalism', Lee nonetheless concluded that, if deployed for the promotion of 'human decency ... television will be the greatest force for good and for freedom that this planet has ever known'.[80]

Fictional Perspectives

An important contribution to discourse about the implications of communications technology came from works of fiction, which had a powerful effect in shaping perceptions.[81] A variety of literary contributions helped shape attitudes towards the role of inventions in this field, including eventually the Internet. Advances such as the telegraph, telephone, and moving pictures encouraged thought about what might come next and what it might mean. Mark Twain, for instance, produced in 1898 a short story centring on a device he described as 'the telectroscope'. Twain depicted it as coming into 'public use' early in the twentieth century, whereupon it was 'connected with the telephonic systems of the whole world'. This 'improved "limitless distance" telephone' rendered 'the daily doings of the globe ... visible to everybody, and audibly discussable, too, by witnesses separated by any number of leagues'.[82] The narrator provides an account of a user of the device who – confined to custody at the time – becomes compulsive. He recounts how '[t]he connection was made with the international telephone-station, and day by day, and night by night, he called up one corner of the globe after another, and looked upon its life, and studied its strange sights, and spoke with its people'. The viewer 'realised that by grace of this marvellous instrument he was almost as free as the birds of the air, although a prisoner under locks and bars. He seldom spoke, and I never interrupted him when he was absorbed in this amusement.'[83]

Some writers went beyond focusing on specific imagined inventions and constructed entire worlds employing them. Such speculations might be optimistic in tone. A classic in this genre was *Looking Backward: 2000–1887*, by the US author Edward Bellamy. First appearing in 1888, it depicted what was in effect a socialist world order[84] which has 'abolished poverty and the fear of

[79] Ibid., pp. 229–30.
[80] Ibid., p. 230.
[81] For an overview of Bellamy, Wells and others from the first decade of the twentieth century, see Rev. James Wood, 'Some Utopias Past and Present' in Dorothea Hollins (ed.), *Utopian Papers: Being Addresses to "The Utopians"* (Master and Co., London, 1908), pp. 17–44, 33–44.
[82] Mark Twain, 'From the London Times of 1904' in *Steam Punk Six-Pack* (Enhanced Media Publishing, Paris, 2015), pp. 270–9, 271.
[83] Ibid., p. 273.
[84] Edward Bellamy, *Looking Backward: 2000 to 1887* (Wisehouse, Sweden, 2016), p. 60.

it, and inordinate luxury with the hope of it'.[85] The urban environment includes ample provision for open spaces between buildings.[86] Advanced technology plays a facilitating role for this social system. Bellamy described the use of 'devices for lightening the burden ... labor-saving inventions in all sorts of industry', improving the quality of life for all, and in particular for women. 'Electricity', we are told, 'takes the place of all fires and lighting.'[87] A telephone network transmits music into homes in accordance with the tastes of users, with a pre-set timing mechanism.[88] Religious preachers can use this system to reach large numbers. One character explains that while attending church is an option, 'I really don't believe you are likely to hear anywhere a better discourse than you will at home. I see by the paper that Mr. Barton is to preach this morning, and he preaches only by telephone, and to audiences often reaching 150,000.' The book then describes the experience of such a service, with 'the tinkle of a bell' followed by 'the voice of a man, at the pitch of ordinary conversation ... with an effect of proceeding from an invisible person in the room'.[89]

Bellamy had considerable and lasting influence on politics and public life, including through providing inspiration for those who sought to affect social reconstruction through technology. For instance, Arthur E. Morgan, the inaugural chair of the Tennessee Valley Authority from 1933 to 1938, was an admirer of the author, of whom he subsequently produced a biography.[90] Others were critical of Bellamy, as we will see. *Looking Backward* also helped inaugurate a wider literary movement of speculation about idealised polities of the future. For instance, in 1889, the year after the Bellamy work appeared, Elizabeth Burgoyne Corbett (under the name Mrs George Corbett) published *New Amazonia: A Foretaste of the Future*, depicting a matriarchy. In this novel, Corbett anticipates technological developments. Among them are a telephone system through which it was possible to order electrically delivered goods and listen to concerts and speeches.[91]

A persistent contributor to the genre of novels about scientifically advanced societies, also of expansive literary and social influence, was H. G. Wells. He produced a number of works containing speculation about the impact of technological developments to come. He is often remembered for taking a positive view of the likely outcomes. Works fitting this mould include *A New Utopia*, that appeared in 1905. In it Wells described a parallel, scientifically sophisticated planet. A single world state controls economic activity, with an elite group known as 'Samurai' carrying out the business of government.

85 Ibid., p. 42.
86 Ibid., p. 19.
87 Ibid., p. 51.
88 Ibid., pp. 49–50, 59.
89 Ibid., p. 113.
90 Arthur E. Morgan, *Edward Bellamy* (Columbia University Press, New York, 1944).
91 Mrs George Corbett, *New Amazonia: A Foretaste of the Future* (Tower, London, 1889), ch. XV.

All people have a 'certain standard of education and a certain minimum of nutrition and training' and are 'insured against ill-health and accidents'.[92] As in many other such blueprints, there is a 'mingling of homesteads and open country'.[93] Cities are carefully designed to provide space, and are pollution free. Machinery has eliminated the need for many menial activities. The population utilises sophisticated telephone systems. The network they comprise, combined with the availability of other utilities, means that even people living in geographically isolated areas do not suffer exclusion. Wells notes that '[h]ere and there ... will stand quite solitary homesteads'. Yet they would 'have their perfected telephonic connection with the rest of the world, with doctor, shop, and so forth, and may even have a pneumatic tube for books and small parcels to the nearest postoffice'.[94]

During his career Wells engaged repeatedly in speculation involving technology. His projections were not all optimistic. In *The Sleeper Awakes*, for instance, the final version of which appeared in 1910, he depicted a future society characterised by authoritarian rule, economic exploitation, and social inequality. As one character, Ostrog, puts it: '[t]he day of democracy is past ... Today is the day of wealth. Wealth now is power.' Dwellers in an advanced urban environment lack personal privacy. So-called 'Babble Machines' positioned in public spaces emit amplified political propaganda employing crass, simplified language and terminology. Devices known as 'kineto-telephotographs' enable simultaneous audio-visual broadcasting to global audiences. When using such mechanisms to issue political transmissions, it has become the custom for speakers to use 'just one sentence, six or seven words'.[95]

Men Like Gods appeared in 1923. In an optimistic frame again, Wells depicted a planet called Utopia, dwelling once more on its technological aspects. Before arriving at a condition of egalitarian paradise, the range of devices and techniques that facilitated this society had initially triggered immense and destructive destabilisation. In the ideal community eventually established, various inventions play a significant role. A mobile device comprising 'a little bundle of wires and light rods' connects to a 'pillar', providing 'the Utopian equivalent of letter and telephone'. Messages are stored via a network which a user can access at a point convenient to them, playing repeatedly if necessary, and can issue replies or new communications in the same form. Telephone conversations as such are not a normal occurrence. Wells notes '[t]he transmission is wireless'. The storage stations for messages have only minimal personnel, with most of

92 H. G. Wells, *A Modern Utopia* (Penguin, London, 2005), p. 68.
93 Ibid., p. 98.
94 Ibid.
95 H. G. Wells, *The Sleeper Awakes* (Thomas Nelson and Sons, London, 1910), ch. 12.

'the connexions . . . automatic'. Communications 'came and went from any part of the planet'.

Wells then discusses the political ramifications of this network. In doing so he identified problems that such technology might bring from the point of view of personal privacy and the potential for intimidation. He perceived dis- or misinformation as threats, while sensing that their suppression had to be reconciled with freedom of expression. Wells notes that the 'organization' responsible for communications 'had a complete knowledge of the whereabouts of every soul upon the planet. It had a record of every living person and it knew in what message district he was. Everyone was indexed and noted.' Such data in the possession of 'earthly governments' could lead to 'unending blackmail and tyranny', leaving everybody 'open to espionage'. Abuse of this kind was prevented on Utopia by adherence to 'Five Principles of Liberty'. The first was that 'all individual personal facts are private between the citizen and the public organization to which he entrusts them'. They could be 'used only for his convenience and with his sanction'. While 'available for statistical uses' this information could not be individualised. The second was 'Free Movement': while it was possible to track people using the communications network, there should not be restrictions on where they could go. Third came 'Unlimited Knowledge'. All information that existed – except of a personal nature – was readily accessible to everybody.

This stipulation linked to a fourth rule. As well as being available, information should be free from misrepresentation. Demonstrating that complaints about the nature of online communications have precursors, Wells made pointed reference in this context to the 'London newspapers' of his day. One character complains that they 'had ceased to be impartial vehicles of news; they omitted, they mutilated, the misstated. They were no better than propaganda rags.' Utopia had once suffered from similar problems. Accordingly, it had established the fourth Principle: 'that Lying is the Blackest Crime'. In Utopia, 'Lying' was interpreted broadly, to include 'the inexact statement of facts' and 'the suppression of a material fact'. The abiding maxim on Utopia was that '[w]here there are lies there cannot be freedom'. But another equally important component of 'freedom' came with the fifth Principle: 'Free Discussion and Criticism'. How could both the fourth and fifth be guaranteed together? Wells suggested a system in which there was an agreed body of facts, upon which it would then be possible to place differing interpretations. It was achieved through Utopia making 'a complete distinction between news and discussion'. Provision of factual content was insulated from commercial concerns and from any need to provide a particular quantity of coverage at given intervals; that is, the pressures of needing to attain a wide audience and keep up with the news cycle. Content eschewed sensationalism, but it was a source of stimulation through the discussion it generated. People were entitled to express their views 'however subversive' in any form that suited them, and had access to means of mass distribution of their output. They were subject to one limitation: that they 'refrain from lying'.[96]

Wells had discerned – and envisaged the solution of – a technologically connected dilemma that exists today in relation to the Internet, and with which Parliament has grappled. Freedom of expression is necessary to the conduct of meaningful public discourse. But this right can allow those exercising it – wilfully or otherwise – to create doubt about the agreed factual basis that the conduct of a functioning debate requires. Yet to seek to regulate contribution to discussion is to risk stifling it inappropriately – and indeed perhaps to prevent the dissemination of useful (and reliable) information. How can the sometimes conflicting but also interdependent goods of access to accurate knowledge and the ability to transmit views be attained together? That Wells judged a satisfactory answer to this question was possible was an illustration of his hopeful side. This characteristic manifested itself on his part again in the late 1930s, when Wells came to advocate the creation of what he termed a 'World Brain'. Utilising microfilm technology, users would be able request their chosen content from a central archive of world knowledge, viewing it on a screen at their desk once they had received it. This 'world-wide network' would promote international understanding and peace, Wells anticipated, and help bring about a global federal government. His reputation as prophet of the Internet rests to a significant extent on this project.[97] But the sum of his writing over the preceding four decades shows a far longer and wider engagement with issues that would arise around this technology.

The enthusiastic embrace of technology was central to a powerful artistic movement of the twentieth century. An inaugural moment for this tendency came in 1909 with the dissemination of what is known as the 'Futurist Manifesto' (the first of a number of such texts), in which F. T. Marinetti extolled an aesthetic, aggressively masculine revolution inspired by fast cars, aeroplanes, electric lighting, trains, steamships, and industrial machinery, and disdaining supposed vestiges of the past such as museums and libraries.[98] But countervailing attitudes were also apparent. An (earlier) example of a reaction against the glorification of the scientific future came in *News from Nowhere* by William Morris, written partly as a riposte to Bellamy. Morris objected to what he saw as the centralised nature of the society Bellamy envisaged, its urban focus, and its emphasis on technological advance as achieving improvement in itself. Morris complained: 'a machine-life is the best which Mr Bellamy can

96 H. G. Wells, *Men Like Gods* (Gateway, London, 1917), ch. 2.

97 For analysis of the 'world brain' concept and reactions to it, see Andrew Blick, *Stretching the Constitution: The Brexit Shock in Historic Perspective* (Bloomsbury/Hart, Oxford, 2019), pp. 262–6.

98 F. T. Marinetti, 'The Foundation and Manifesto of Futurism (1909)' in Alex Danchev (ed.), *100 Artists' Manifestos: From the Futurists to the Stuckists* (Penguin, London, 2011), M1.

imagine for us'.[99] Published in 1890 and set in 2012, the idealised agrarian society presented in *News from Nowhere* (though one in which technological innovation could have a supportive role) helped acquire for Morris the misleading reputation discussed above.[100]

Seeking to rebut Bellamy, Morris presented his own version of the good society. Others who were uncomfortable with models that the likes of Bellamy and Wells (in his more sanguine mode) presented took another approach. They imagined appalling worlds in which technology played a key role. Futuristic conurbations, for instance, might appear in a sinister light. In the 1908 Jack London novel, *The Iron Heel*, the 'wonder cities' of Ardis and Asgard exemplify the exploitative, oppressive 'Oligarchy' that orders their construction after taking power.[101] Though they differ in some respects, certain themes are common to many of the works of this type considered here. They depict polities of the future that divest people of their individuality and in which their lives become shells. A form of officially mandated happiness is imposed on or artificially induced within them. Naturally formed relationships – as the authors perceive them – are discouraged. The social system in question subdues those within it either through positive inducements or more naked force, threatened or actual. Another shared characteristic of many of these nightmare communities is that they do not allow for political pluralism and democracy (at least of the liberal variety). There is a tendency for those in control to engage in psychological manipulation, and distort truth and the nature of reality to serve their purposes. The stories tend to involve a person in some way challenging the prevailing norms, and suffering for doing so. Science and technology are prominent within and possibly central to these societies and the way they operate. Often, advanced communications techniques support the system in question. All of these depictions seem intended as commentaries on trends contemporary to the time they were written. They share close similarities with more recent critical accounts of the Internet, and have helped provide a conceptual framework for the formulation of these concerns.

E. M. Forster first published his short story, *The Machine Stops*, in 1909 – the year that also saw the appearance of the first Marinetti manifesto, a work presenting a fundamentally different approach. Forster depicts a future Earth in which members of a population dwelling underground in automated homes have little physical contact with one another. The 'Machine' of the title is a system made by humans, on which they have become dependent. It is in part a communications network, enabling people to order products such as clothes

[99] William Morris, 'A review of *Looking Backward* by Edward Bellamy', published in *Commonweal*, 22 Jun 1889, reproduced in Morris, *News from Nowhere and Other Writings*, p. 357.

[100] Morris, *News from Nowhere and Other Writings*.

[101] Jack London, *The Iron Heel* (Penguin, London, 2006), p. 174.

and food, and transmitting music to them on request. It provides for remote audio-visual contact using hand-held devices. Someone can have 'several thousand' acquaintances with whom they interact by this means. Such is the volume of communication via the Machine that those engaged in it can become overwhelmed, and irritable in their replies. As the narrative ironically remarks: 'in certain directions human intercourse had advanced enormously'. Academic seminars take place without anyone leaving their personal space. One of the central characters, Vashti, gives a lecture on music. Forster notes: '[t]he clumsy system of public gatherings had been long since abandoned; neither Vashti nor her audience stirred from their rooms. Seated in her armchair she spoke, while they in their armchairs heard her, fairly well, and saw her, fairly well'. As this passage suggests, the reproduction quality over this network makes it an inferior substitute for physical presence. But the ease it offers means that people find this less-than-perfect system sufficient. (Here is a distinction from the pandemic experience of 2020 onwards, when electronic communication was forced upon us, rather than chosen out of convenience.) When talking to her son, Kuno, Vashti 'fancied that he looked sad. She could not be sure.' Forster informs the reader that 'the Machine did not transmit nuances of expression. It only gave a general idea of people – an idea that was good enough for all practical purposes . . . Something "good enough" had long since been accepted by our race.' (Forster was not the first to anticipate such a scenario of technical limitation: Corbett in *New Amazonia* had recounted that public events channelled via the telephone system were such poor surrogates for actual presence that people had reverted to attendance in person.)

In the system Forster portrays, behind the comfort and utility lies a pronounced conformism. The products available, such as furniture, have a single design for all that may not fit with the needs of some users. Strict social rules apply. Those who fail to comply face retribution from the Committee of the Machine, which is able to render them destitute. The Machine itself is a subject of near-religious worship. Initially akin to an instruction manual, the 'Book of the Machine' has taken on the character of a holy text, with the following statement printed on its opening page: 'The Machine . . . feeds us and clothes us and houses us; through it we speak to one another, through it we see one another, in it we have our being. The Machine is the friend of ideas and the enemy of superstition: the Machine is omnipotent, eternal; blessed is the Machine.'[102] In 1905, in *A New Utopia*, Wells also depicted a device that could provide for social interaction and material needs without people needing to leave their place residence. For him it was gift, and a means of overcoming isolation. Four years later, Forster portrayed a similar mechanism as having the opposite effect, and as being of sinister connotation. The view taken of a particular technological prospect could change radically according to the

[102] E. M. Forster, *The Machine Stops* (Penguin, London, 2011).

perspective of the observer and the context. This potential for differing outlooks persisted in a later era when real systems delivering the functions imagined by Wells and Forster began to appear.

The Russian author, Yevgeny Zamyatin, wrote *We* during 1920–1.[103] A political radical, he nonetheless detected worrying tendencies in the wake of the 1917 revolution and Bolshevik ascendancy. As though determined to prove him correct, the Soviet authorities would later persecute Zamyatin for his unreliability and non-conformist ideas. Set in an authoritarian, scientifically advanced system some centuries from the then-present, the inhabitants of the world of *We* are known by alphanumeric codes. Individuality is supressed, with people living in 'transparent houses' denying them privacy. Government by a 'One State', with a 'Benefactor' at its head, takes place in accordance with mathematical formulas. Early in the novel, the central character, D-503, a rocket engineer, describes 'our life' as 'the mathematically perfect life of the One State'. The message of *We* is not one of outright opposition to the new, however – on the contrary, it emphasises the need for continual revolution, rather than fossilisation of a new order once established.

Other seemingly bleak – but potentially nuanced – views of the technological future came in the medium of film. In *Metropolis*, an adaptation of the Thea von Harbou novel that was first released in 1927, the German director Fritz Lang portrayed a mechanised city characterised by immense social inequality, with a privileged elite living above ground, supported by machine-workers toiling beneath the surface in appalling conditions. The Master of Metropolis, Frederson, who seeks to maintain strict control of the society, utilises devices comprising consoles and visual screens displaying data, as well as audio-visual communications systems. It is a male dominated society, but a woman, Maria, leads a covert, peaceful opposition movement. Technology is a foundation for the regime, but not wholly successful, and eventually serves to destabilise it. A robot impersonating Maria leads an uprising of workers. Science thereby appears as a political force. It is able to perpetrate deceit upon the vulnerable, deprived masses, using manipulative messages to drive them away from reformism and towards destructive extremes. As with *We*, the ultimate thesis of *Metropolis* is not the outright rejection of modernity. The message that Lang presents is that of a need to reconcile different groups and values within society.

The 1936 Charlie Chaplin film, *Modern Times*, explores some similar themes to *Metropolis*, though in a seemingly less distant time, and for comedic effect. It depicts advanced production-line processes as dehumanising in their consequences and harmful to the mental well-being of the workforce. The President of the 'Electro-Steel Corp.' uses an audio-visual screen device for communication with, and surveillance of, workers. The company experiments

[103] Yevgeny Zamyatin, *We* (Penguin, London, 1993).

with a mechanised system for feeding employees, to minimise break time and augment productivity. As in the United States and elsewhere at the time, there is mass unemployment and poverty, driving people to crime. The authorities persecute protestors.

Four years before *Modern Times* appeared, Aldous Huxley had published his novel *Brave New World*. Rather than employing brutality, in the futuristic system Huxley presented, the 'World Controllers' secure compliance through genetic engineering, recreational pharmaceuticals, the practice of group sex, and advanced electrical entertainment technologies. Henry Ford, a twentieth-century pioneer of production methods in the automobile industry, has become a subject of worship. There is a strict social cast hierarchy and a scientific approach to mind control. In one passage Huxley describes 'various Bureaux of Propaganda and the College of Emotional Engineering' based 'in a single sixty-storey building in Fleet Street'[104] (when Huxley wrote, and until late in the twentieth century, Fleet Street in London was the centre for the UK newspaper business). In another scene in a hospital, '[t]elevision was left on, a running tap, from morning till night'.[105] Further distractions come from the 'feelies'. This form of entertainment is an extension of the so-called 'talkies' that – by the time Huxley wrote – had largely supplanted what we know as 'silent' films (*Modern Times*, mainly without sound, being an exception to this general trend). In *Brave New World*, the 'feelies' enable an audience to experience the sensations of touch and smell as well as sight and sound.[106] Huxley would later seek to offer more positive perspectives. But as Chapter 4 will show, gloomy depictions of the technological future came increasingly to predominate in the following decade. They were shaped by actual historical developments, and would in turn influence perceptions of what had taken place – and what could do so in future.

'A Modernised, Electrified, Direct Democracy'

Regardless of the concerns motivating and promoted by these artistic statements, some commentators regarded future developments in communications technology as potentially creating opportunities, including for the adoption of methods of participatory democracy. The idea that electrical devices might facilitate the appearance of a large-scale, inclusive polity has deep roots. Samuel Morse himself expressed perceptions of this type. In the words of Carey, '[a]s early as 1838, Morse anticipated twentieth-century notions of the "global village"'. In his own words, Morse predicted that, in the near future 'the whole surface of this country would be channeled for those nerves which are to diffuse with the speed of thought, a knowledge of all that is occurring

[104] Aldous Huxley, *Brave New World* (Vintage, London, 2007), p. 34.
[105] Ibid., p. 101.
[106] Ibid., p. 85.

throughout the land: making in fact one neighbourhood of the whole country'.[107] Such concepts could have a democratically inclusive (by the standards of the time) aspect to them. In 1871, Carey and Quirk note, the poet James Russell Lowell remarked that 'the newspapers and telegraph gather the whole nation into a vast town-meeting'. This specific concept would have currency a hundred years later, as is discussed in Chapter 4. Like later advocates of this idea, Lowell saw advances in communications as a vehicle for high-quality deliberation, 'where everyone hears the affairs of the country discussed and where better judgement is pretty sure to make itself valid at last'.[108]

Such ideas strengthened with the advent of radio (and the prospect of television). The third and fourth decades of the twentieth century saw a number of commentators speculating on the democratic potential of broadcasting technology. In 1932 the German playwright Bertolt Brecht published an essay entitled 'The Radio as an Apparatus of Communication'. Already, in 1927, when considering options for this medium, Brecht had 'proposed the live broadcasting of law cases and Reichstag debates, as well as an increased proportion of interviews and discussion programmes'.[109] In this later work, he presented the idea that a new communications device, when it appears, might initially be employed to imitate established technologies, before more innovative uses are developed. He hoped that radio might be deployed for interactive purposes. Similar analysis would be applied to television and ultimately the Internet. As we have seen, the parliamentary website, when launched, was focused on the electronic dissemination of material such as committee reports and Hansard, that already existed in printed form. Subsequently, Parliament developed more original uses, including those that allowed for two-way engagement. Brecht remarked that it was possible to 'invent and perfect discoveries that . . . have to conquer their market and justify their existence'. When radio first appeared, 'society was not yet advanced enough to accept it'. The medium had therefore begun as 'a substitute for theatre, opera, concerts, lectures, café music, local newspapers and so forth'.[110] It would need to 'start looking . . . for an object in life'.[111] Brecht likened radio to a 'man' who begins 'asking at a certain age, when his innocence has been lost, what he is supposed to be doing in the world'.[112]

[107] James W. Carey, 'Technology and Ideology: The Case of the Telegraph' in *Communication as Culture: Essays on Media and Society* (Routledge, London, 1992), pp. 201–29, 207.

[108] James W. Carey with John J. Quirk, 'The History of the Future' in James W. Carey, *Communication as Culture: Essays on Media and Society* (Routledge, London, 1992), pp. 173–200, 192.

[109] Bertolt Brecht, 'The Radio as an Apparatus of Communication' in John Willett (ed.), *Brecht on Theatre: The Development of an Aesthetic* (Methuen, London, 1964), pp. 51–3, 53.

[110] Ibid., p. 51.

[111] Ibid., pp. 51–2.

[112] Ibid., p. 52.

This purpose should be more than 'prettifying public life' or 'bringing cosiness to the home'. A key problem at present was that 'radio is one-sided when it should be two. It is purely an apparatus for distribution, for mere sharing out.' Brecht therefore recommended changing 'this apparatus over from distribution to communication'. The device could thereby become 'the finest possible communications apparatus in public life, a vast network of pipes'. To achieve this outcome, radio needed to acquire the ability to 'receive as well as to transmit . . . to let the listener speak as well as hear . . . to bring him into a relationship instead of isolating him'. It should 'step out of the supply business and organize its listeners as suppliers'. Radio should seek to avoid the 'lack of consequences' from which literature and the educational system suffered. Listeners should become 'not only . . . pupils but . . . teachers'. Brecht conceded, however, that his proposal was 'utopian'.[113]

Brecht envisaged a communications medium facilitating new forms of mass participation, and perceived this development as containing political implications. Another author exploring this theme was the Conservative politician and jurist Lord Birkenhead (formerly F. E. Smith). In 1930, shortly before his death, Birkenhead published a work dealing in part with the prospects for technology. It was reminiscent of that which Francis Bacon had produced three centuries previously. Like Bacon, Birkenhead was a lawyer, parliamentarian, and former holder of the office of Lord Chancellor, a post also once held by Thomas More, who – through his 1516 essay *Utopia* – helped establish the speculative literary form of which Bacon and then Birkenhead were subsequent purveyors. Birkenhead differed from his two precursors in that, while they employed the device of depicting a parallel imaginary community, he – writing under the title *The World in 2030* A.D. – considered possible real outcomes in the society of the future. As he put it, the objective was 'to attempt a series of speculative predictions dealing with the possible development of the world during the next hundred years'.[114] Birkenhead overtly placed himself in a tradition that included Bellamy and Wells.[115]

Birkenhead envisaged a world divided into territorial power blocs[116] and predicted transformed relations between races[117] and sexes.[118] He anticipated that over the coming century '[a]pplied physics, which have given us the steam-engine, the internal combustion motor, as well as the wireless, telephones, and all the many other practical uses of electrical energy, will certainly make prodigious advances before the year 2030'.[119] Among many possibilities, Birkenhead anticipated advances in 'wireless telephony and television beyond

[113] Ibid.
[114] Earl of Birkenhead, *The World in 2030* A.D. (Hodder and Stoughton, London, 1930), p. vii.
[115] Ibid., p. xi.
[116] Ibid., pp. 146–7, 151–2
[117] Ibid., p. 156.
[118] Ibid., pp. 164–86.
[119] Ibid., p. 2.

our present most imaginative expectations'. It should become 'possible for any person sitting at home to be "present" at no matter what distant event. Stereoscopic television in full natural colours, and perfected wireless telephony will enable him to see and hear any event, which is broadcast, as effectively as if he stood beside the transmitting apparatus.' The technology, Birkenhead suggested, could be used between points anywhere in the world for the mass broadcast of events such as sports matches, or for personal contact between individuals.[120]

Inevitably, Birkenhead judged, there would be consequences for 'the future of politics'.[121] Like some later commentators on the Internet, Birkenhead saw potential for an elimination of intermediary institutions. Broadcast technology would make it 'feasible once more to revive that form of democracy which flourished in the city states of Ancient Greece'. Birkenhead expected that '[b]y 2030 the chosen spokesmen of each political party will be able to address every voter as effectively as he can now address Parliament'. Consequently, 'the electorate itself, rather than its representatives' would be able to 'decide each vital political issue. After the spokesman of each party has had his (or her) say, the votes of the entire country could be recorded and counted' using devices 'installed in the telephone exchanges. Within twenty minutes from the end of the last speech, the will of a national jury on any subject could be ascertained and announced.'[122]

Parliament as conventionally understood appeared to have no place within such a system. Elsewhere in the book, Birkenhead also suggested that parties might also eventually become redundant. He wrote that '[s]cientific psychology may destroy the possibility of conducting politics' on such a basis. The electorate 'educated in the light of the new psychology, will be immune from specious appeals to sentiment and illogical reasoning. They will be competent to support this or that project strictly on its merits, unswayed by rhetoric, unhampered by prejudice.' People would therefore divide on specific issues, rather than broader attachment to a wider group and platform.[123] Eventually, in place of the party system there would appear 'the rule of experts, who will seek popular sanction for each measure they purpose through a referendum'. They would be selected for 'the Parliament of skilled governors' on a basis of their personal 'qualifications'.[124] The 'Parliament' alluded to seems to be envisaged as a body that would discuss and then present proposals – or perhaps choices – using audio-visual broadcasting systems, followed by an electronic popular vote.

[120] Ibid., p. 8.
[121] Ibid., p. 8.
[122] Ibid., p. 8.
[123] Ibid., p. 87.
[124] Ibid., p. 88.

Birkenhead anticipated subsequent views of the democratic impact of technology in a variety of ways. For instance, he held that it would facilitate direct, popular decision-making; he regarded it as potentially leading to a better informed, rationally motivated public, reaching conclusions on a basis of evidence. Such propositions would surface in relation to the Internet. Yet contrasting views also manifested themselves – for instance, among those who argued that this digital network facilitated the exploitation of popular prejudice and emotional reactions to divisive effect. Just as the 1930s provide a precursor to more optimistic views, we can also find in this decade an embryonic version of the sceptical outlook. In a grand historical survey of technology and human civilization first published in 1934, Lewis Mumford, a Geddes protégé,[125] literary critic and commentator on architecture and society, argued that '[d]uring the last thousand years the material basis and the cultural forms of Western Civilization have been profoundly modified by the development of the machine'.[126] He divided the previous ten centuries into three broad periods: 'ecotechnic, paleotechnic, neotechnic'.[127] The third had begun in 1832, with 'the perfection of the water-turbine by Fourneyron',[128] and was 'marked ... by the conquest of a new form of energy: electricity'.[129] The communications technology that appeared in this era was, Mumford judged, of profound implication.

He discerned a cyclical pattern. Initially, '[c]ommunication between human beings' involved 'immediate physiological expressions of personal contact, from the howlings and cooings and head turnings of the infant to the more abstract gestures and signs and sounds'. There followed the development of 'hieroglyphics, painting, drawing, the written alphabet', that 'deepened and made more reflective and pregnant the intercourse of men'. The resulting 'lapse of time between expression and reception' made 'thought itself possible'. Then 'a series of inventions began to bridge the gap in time between communication and response despite the handicaps of space'. They were 'first the telegraph, then the telephone, then the wireless telegraph, then the wireless telephone, and finally television'. Consequently 'communication is now on the point of returning, with the aid of mechanical devices, to that instantaneous reaction of person to person with which it began'. A difference from this earlier form was that 'the possibilities of this immediate meeting, instead of being limited by space and time, will be limited only by the amount of energy available and the mechanical perfection and accessibility of the apparatus'.[130] Mumford held that 'television communication', when introduced, would

[125] Mumford, *The Culture of Cities*, p. v.
[126] Lewis Mumford, *Technics & Civilization* (University of Chicago Press, 2010), p. 3.
[127] Ibid., p. 109.
[128] Ibid., p. 213.
[129] Ibid., p. 221.
[130] Ibid., p. 239.

'differ from direct intercourse only to the extent that immediate physical contact will be impossible'.[131]

He foresaw 'a widened range of intercourse: more numerous contacts: more numerous demands on attention and time'. However, 'unfortunately, the possibility of this type of immediate intercourse on a worldwide basis does not necessarily mean a less trivial or a less parochial personality'. Mumford feared that 'the media of reflective thought and deliberate action' would 'be weakened'. The problem was that '[m]en often tend to be more socialized at a distance, than they are in their immediate, limited and local selves: their intercourse sometimes proceeds best, like barter among savage peoples, when neither group is visible to the other'. Observing these tendencies as already coming into being, Mumford saw the use of this new communications technology as being 'at the mercy of any strange person who seeks to divert it to his own purposes'. He noted the existence of 'a tendency to use' inventions regardless of 'whether or not the occasion demands'. For Mumford, '[t]he lifting of restrictions upon close human intercourse' had already 'increased the areas of friction' and had 'mobilized and hastened mass-reactions, like those which occur on the eve of a war, and it has increased the dangers of international conflict'.[132] Yet 'instantaneous personal communication over long distances' might nonetheless be a means of achieving 'those world-wide cooperations of thought and feeling which must emerge ... if our whole civilization is not to sink into ruin'.[133]

This technology had specific implications for 'politics', the field in which 'radio-communication' had had its 'greatest social effect' to date. It had achieved 'the restoration of direct contact between the leader and the group'. Through such media, it would be possible to recreate the ancient polity on a vast scale. Mumford noted that 'Plato defined the limits of the size of a city as the number of people who could hear the voice of a single orator: today those limits do not define a city but a civilization.' New technology could provide the basis for 'as close a political unity as that which once was possible in the tiniest cities of Attica' wherever they were in use and a common language was shared. He judged that 'possibilities for good and evil here are immense'. Stressing the more negative connotations, 'secondary personal contact with voice and image' might intensify 'the amount of mass regimentation', partly because there was less opportunity for resistance to a 'leader' not physically present at 'a local meeting'. Mumford held that, like many other aspects of the neotechnic era, 'the dangers of the radio and the talking picture seem greater than the benefits'. There was, in his view, in contradiction of the beliefs of 'the earlier

131 Ibid., pp. 239–40.
132 Ibid., p. 240.
133 Ibid., p. 241.

exponents of instantaneous communication', no reason to suppose 'that the results will automatically be favourable to the community'.[134]

Mumford expressly located his ideas in a historical continuum that included within it Owen,[135] Geddes, Howard, and Kropotkin, suggesting that their work might 'prove as important as the formulations of Leonardo, Galileo, Newton, and Descartes'.[136] In as far as he was part of such a succession, Mumford helped connect it to an era in which the Internet was coming into being. More than three decades later, he was still contributing to the debate about the role of electronic communications, and referring to this earlier intervention.[137] A further participant in the discussion at this later time – and one who exerted considerable influence upon other participants – was also a veteran, making his initial contribution in 1940. However, he came within the category of the firm optimist, members of which Mumford set out to question.

R. Buckminster Fuller, a US philosopher and architect, was best known for his association with the geodesic dome, a visually striking rapid-assembly shelter. In the decades following the Second World War this product was adopted by a range of users, including the military and subsequently the countercultural commune movement.[138] But his range of activity extended far further. Seeing both destructive danger and immense benefit in science, Fuller advocated a holistic approach to invention that would enable humanity better to fulfil itself and eliminate various ills from which it suffered, placing an emphasis on maximising the gains obtained from limited resources.[139] The language in which Fuller expressed himself could be difficult to decipher. In 1963, for instance, he described how:

> My continuing philosophy is predicated, first, on the assumption that in dynamical counterbalance of the expanding universe of entropically increasing random disorderliness there must be a universal pattern of omnicontracting, convergent, progressive orderliness and that man is that anti-entropic reordering function of universe and, secondly, upon the assumption that man is born with an extraordinary inventory of faculties within an extraordinary inventory of universal phenomena.[140]

[134] Ibid.

[135] Mumford, *The Culture of Cities*, pp. 392–3.

[136] Ibid., pp. 9–10.

[137] Lewis Mumford, *The Myth of the Machine: The Pentagon of Power* (New York, Harcourt Brace Jovanovich, 1970), p. 295.

[138] Hsiao-Yun Chu, 'The Evolution of the Fuller Geodesic Dome: From Black Mountain to Drop City', *Design and Culture* 10(2) (2018): 121–37.

[139] For a profile of Fuller, recognising the influence he had attained by the 1960s, in which he discusses his philosophy, see Calvin Tomkins, 'In the Outlaw Area', *New Yorker*, 1 January 1966, available at: www.newyorker.com/magazine/1966/01/08/in-the-outlaw-area, last accessed 22 August 2020.

[140] R. Buckminster Fuller, 'Preface', in *No More Secondhand God* (Anchor Books, New York, 1972), p. vii.

Though Fuller could be opaque, the impact he achieved creates a need for consideration of his work. As considered elsewhere in this book, he influenced movements and individuals that were associated with advocacy of the use of electronic communications devices – including the Internet – as means of democratic empowerment. His pollination of the US counterculture and individuals within it that became proponents of digital networking is already established.[141] (The geodesic dome featured in the *Whole Earth Catalog.*[142]) Chapter 4 identifies points of influence for Fuller within the UK, both at high political and activist level. We can see Fuller as having had a general influence on later thought about such technology. He also anticipated specific ideas about its political applications.

In 1940, Fuller wrote a 'poem' entitled 'No More Secondhand God'. In a 1963 reissue of the work, he described his purpose as being to 'discipline my mind into the development of tools of communication which might render democracy more effective in the era of the increasing political dictatorships'. He therefore put forward 'practical means for daily or hourly telephone voting by democracy'. In the intervening period, the idea had 'evoluted into my invention of two-way locally beamed television'. The concept, Fuller held, had now attained 'technical feasibility'. It was now possible, as well as to 'beam to each household', for 'each household' to 'beam right back to central computers, saying, I like it or I don't like it'.[143] This proposition was similar to that which Brecht had made in 1932 for radio that would 'let the listener speak as well as hear'.

Fuller wrote the poem in response to news of the Nazi attack on Oslo of 9 April 1940, remarking that the 'phoney war' had come to an end. In the wake of present threats, he held that:

> . . . Democracy must be structurally modernized
> must be mechanically implemented
> to give it a one-individual-to-another
> speed and spontaneity of reaction
> commensurate with the speed and scope
> of broadcast news
> now world-wide in seconds.[144]

[141] Stewart Brand, 'We Owe It All to the Hippies', *Time Magazine* 145(12) (1 March 1995); Jacques Vallee, *The Network Revolution: Confessions of a Computer Scientist* (And/Or Press, Berkeley, 1982), p. 198. See further Ch. 4 of this volume.

[142] Theodore Roszak, *The Cult of Information: A Neo-Luddite Treatise on High-Tech, Artificial Intelligence, and the True Art of Thinking* (Berkeley, University of California Press, 1994), p. 143.

[143] Buckminster Fuller, 'Preface', pp. xi–xii.

[144] '*No More Secondhand God*' in R. Buckminster Fuller, *No More Secondhand God* (Anchor Books, New York, 1972), pp. 1–30, 9.

To this end, it was necessary to:

> Devise a mechanical means
> for nation-wide voting
> daily and secretly
> by each adult citizen
> of Uncle Sam's family:
> Then – I assure you
> will Democracy 'be saved,'
> indeed exist,
> for the first time in history.

A form of '[e]lectrified voting'[145] could combine 'the speed of decision which is the greatest strength of the dictator (a boon if he's godly, a death-ray if he is not)' with 'additional advantages which can never be his'. These '[a]dditional advantages' would include that they would supply 'an instantaneous contour map of the workable frontier of the people's wisdom'. The system would secure 'spontaneous popular co-operation in the carrying out of each decision'. It could provide for 'continuous correction of the course . . . without political scapegoating'.[146] A source of strength for the state that practised it, the process would establish 'unified might . . . invoked through the thrilling mystical awareness of multimillions of individuals that they personally have taken responsibility for the course'.[147] Were the United States to adopt electrified voting, Fuller held, it would gain enhanced internationally credibility as a state.[148] As a 'direct evolution' of existing methods, it would avoid 'the possibility of revolution'. Fuller concluded that this 'modernized, electrified, direct Democracy', if 'not tried now' would be advocated by 'future generations'. He held that 'world civil wars' would continue 'until it receives adequate trial'. Under this system:

> God will be handling the radio-telegraph
> for such a mandated dictatorship; and
> Democracy is not challenged by such a dictator
> whose very first move must and will be
> tidal-waved with Demos authority.[149]

Fuller envisaged technology creating a true democracy, with direct decision-making supplanting representative mechanisms. His thesis fulfilled multiple categories of determinism. He seemed to regard it as fated that a particular invention would come about, would be adopted and applied to a particular social purpose, and would have certain impacts. Fuller also regarded these outcomes as desirable. As the decade in which he wrote developed, more negative perceptions would come to the fore, partly derived from observations of the practices of the dictatorships to which he hoped to offer an answer.

145 Ibid., p. 11.
146 Ibid.
147 Ibid., pp. 11–12.
148 Ibid., p. 12.
149 Ibid., p. 26.

4

Disillusion and Expectation, 1945–1990

The Computer Age: A Twenty-Year View was a collection that first appeared in 1979. The editors were Michael L. Dertouzos and Joel Moses, both Massachusetts Institute of Technology (MIT) computer scientists. It contained a series of essays by prominent commentators discussing the possible impact of the technology over coming decades. Dertouzos and Moses conceived of the work during the mid-1970s. At the time, they explained, they and others had 'conflicting impressions of the field'. While technical progress was taking place, 'many of the computer's early promises, some dating as far back as twenty-five years ago, remained largely unfulfilled. Yet such promises were being put forward again.' At what might now seem a fairly early point in its development, computing had already moved through a technological cycle from high expectation, to disappointment, to revival. Understandably, observers of and participants in this process could find it disorientating. Dertouzos and Moses discerned two possibilities. One was that 'the field of computer science was relatively mature and evolving slowly'. The other was that it was 'in its infancy, with a revolutionary impact yet to come'. In producing this book, they sought to discern which was correct.[1] It was difficult to know the future. This realisation should inform any consideration of the behaviour of participants in historical events, including those unfolding in our present.

The volume covered a span of subjects that had become common components of literature treating the consequences of technology. They included home and work life, the urban environment, education, business and the economy, the nature of knowledge and understanding, the structure of society and the distribution of power within it, and world relations. It contained discussions in which computers were perceived of as more than self-contained devices for the storage and processing of information, and considered their place within communications networks.[2] One article in particular took into account this aspect of the computer in the context of a discussion of its implications for the

[1] Michael Dertouzos and Joel Moses, 'Preface' in Michael Dertouzos and Joel Moses (eds.), *The Computer Age: A Twenty-Year View* (MIT Press, Cambridge, 1979), pp. ix–x, ix.

[2] B. O. Evans, 'Computers and Communications' in Michael Dertouzos and Joel Moses, *The Computer Age: A Twenty-Year View* (MIT Press, Cambridge, 1979), pp. 338–66.

operation of the political system. Entitled 'Computers and Government', the author was J. C. R. Licklider.[3]

The biography of Licklider included in the book described him as a Professor at MIT who had, early in the 1960s, directed the Information Processing Techniques Office of the Department of Defense Advanced Research Projects Agency (ARPA). It recounted that, in this role, Licklider had been 'instrumental in envisioning and funding the development of time-shared computers and advanced research in artificial intelligence and computer science'.[4] A summary of the career of Licklider written now would surely make explicit a precise achievement to his credit while at ARPA – helping instigate the project that would prove to be a direct precursor to the Internet, ARPANET. But as of 1979, though it was a well-known entity among practitioners and commentators, this system had not yet achieved the ascendancy – in absolute penetration and relative pre-eminence over other mechanisms – it would from the 1990s following the introduction of the World Wide Web. The contemporary view in 1979 was that it was one means of digital communication among others, such as Telenet.[5] Therefore, even those who anticipated immense progress in the field of networked computing did not expect the Internet necessarily to be the vehicle for it.

That Licklider – through his association with the Internet – now shares some of the historic credit for the system that achieved global ubiquity certainly adds to the piquancy of his essay. It also confirms an identifiable pattern surrounding the development of this technology. There was a tendency among those involved in it to perceive their work as contributing to potential social transformation. An important influence in this respect was a 1945 article by Vannevar Bush, a physicist who was Director of the Office of Scientific Research and Development during the Second World War, playing a major role in the co-ordination of military scientific research for the purposes of this conflict.[6] While the precise influences upon him are difficult to establish, Bush can be seen as writing in a tradition considered in the previous chapter of the present book, that encompassed Wells and his 'World Brain' concept, as well as Paul Otlet, and stretching through them far back into the nineteenth century and arguably earlier still.[7] Bush proposed a mechanism that might build upon advances achieved during the conflict for the purposes

[3] J. C. R. Licklider, 'Computers and Government' in Michael Dertouzos and Joel Moses, *The Computer Age: A Twenty-Year View* (MIT Press, Cambridge, 1979), pp. 87–126.

[4] Ibid., p. 87 fn.

[5] See ibid., p. 117. For an assessment of contemporary options, see Daniel Bell, 'The Social Framework of the Information Society' in Michael Dertouzos and Joel Moses (eds.), *The Computer Age: A Twenty-Year View* (MIT Press, Cambridge, 1979), pp. 163–211, 175–6.

[6] For the impact of the article, see e.g. John Markoff, *What the Dormouse Said: How the Sixties Counterculture Shaped the Personal Computer Industry* (Penguin, London, 2004), pp. 6–7.

[7] Alex Wright, *Cataloging the World: Paul Otlet and the Birth of the Information Age* (Oxford University Press, 2014), pp. 217–18.

of peacetime. He envisaged a 'future device for individual use, which is a sort of mechanized private file and library'. Bush described the technology – which he labelled a 'memex' – as 'a device in which an individual stores all his books, records, and communications, and which is mechanized so that it may be consulted with exceeding speed and flexibility. It is an enlarged intimate supplement to his memory.' The memex as he pictured it comprised 'a desk' that could 'presumably be operated from a distance' on the surface of which 'are slanting translucent screens, on which material can be projected for convenient reading. There is a keyboard, and sets of buttons and levers.' Utilising microfilm, it would provide access to a wide spectrum of human knowledge across different fields.[8]

The philosopher and mathematician, Norbert Wiener, was another key influence on the development of information technology, of which the Internet was an outgrowth. In the immediate post-Second World War period, he applied the term 'cybernetics' to capture his area of interest at the time – that is, the study of messages. He foresaw a technological system for their transmission, with political implications. In *The Human Use of Human Beings: Cybernetics and Society*,[9] first published in 1950 and then updated in 1954, Wiener postulated that 'society can only be understood through a study of the messages and the communication facilities which belong to it'. He anticipated that 'in the future development of these messages and communication facilities, messages between man and machines, between machines and man, and between machine and machine, are destined to play an ever increasing part'. In discussing this concept, Wiener presented an early incarnation of one pessimistic view of the Internet – that it was a means of gathering data for purposes of population control. He speculated about the possibility of 'a machine to collect this or that type of information', enabling it to predict social outcomes. It might, he went on, be 'a State apparatus covering all systems of political decisions, either under a regime of many states distributed over the earth, or under the apparently much more simple regime of a human government of this planet'. Some might welcome such a '*machine a gouverner*', Wiener felt. But potentially 'such machines, though helpless by themselves, may be used by a human being or a block of human beings to increase their control over the rest of the human race'.

Licklider himself had a sustained record of engagement with such issues, long predating his 1979 chapter. In 1960 he anticipated a 'Man–Computer Symbiosis', through which humans would co-operate with technology, with both achieving more than they could otherwise. As Licklider put it: '[t]he hope

[8] Vannevar Bush, 'As We May Think', *The Atlantic*, July 1945, available at: www.theatlantic.com/magazine/archive/1945/07/as-we-may-think/303881/, last accessed 9 May 2020.

[9] Norbert Wiener, *The Human Use of Human Beings: Cybernetics and Society* (Da Capo Press, Cambridge, 1988).

is that, in not too many years, human brains and computing machines will be coupled together very tightly, and that the resulting partnership will think as no human brain has ever thought and process data in a way not approached by the information-handling machines we know today'.[10] To return to his 1979 work, Licklider speculated about the potential roles of computing technology by 2000 if it continued to develop at a steady pace.[11] They included a scenario in which '[a]n international network of digital computer communications networks serves as the main and essential medium of informational intersection for governments, institutions, corporations, and individuals'. Licklider labelled this entity the 'Multinet'.[12] The account he presented of the operation of this system resembled that envisaged by E. M. Forster for his fictitious 'Machine' seven decades previously. For Forster this possible future was a nightmare in which the susceptibility of humanity to choose convenient options was a weakness that had allowed it to be trapped in a technological prison. For Licklider it was not. The Multinet would take over the functions of:

> the postal system for letters, the dial telephone system for conversations and teleconferences, stand-alone batch-processing and time-sharing systems for computation, and most filing cabinets, microfilm repositories, document rooms, and libraries for information storage and retrieval. Many people work at home, interacting with coworkers and clients through the Multinet, and many business offices (and some classrooms) are little more than organized interconnections of such home workers and their computers. People shop through the Multinet using its cable television and electronic funds transfer functions and a few receive delivery of small items through adjunct pneumatic tube networks. Routine shopping and appointment scheduling are generally handled by private secretary-like programs called OLIVERs which know their masters' needs [for OLIVERs, see below]. Indeed, the Multinet handles scheduling of almost everything schedulable. For example, it eliminates waiting to be seated in restaurants and if you place your order through it can eliminate waiting to be served.[13]

Licklider foresaw political aspects to this transformation. He judged that, over the next two decades, it was 'technically possible to bring into being … an informational environment that would give politics greater depth and dimension than it now has'. It 'would be a network environment, with home information centers … as widespread as television sets are now. The political process would essentially be a giant teleconference, and a campaign would be a month-long series of communications among candidates, propagandists, commentators, political action groups and voters.'[14] Licklider discerned some

[10] J. C. R. Licklider, 'Man–Computer Symbiosis', *IRE Transactions on Human Factors in Electronics*, Volume HFE-1, pp. 4–11, March 1960, available at: https://groups.csail.mit.edu/medg/people/psz/Licklider.html, last accessed 9 May 2020.

[11] Licklider, 'Computers and Government', p. 89.

[12] Ibid., p. 91.

[13] Ibid., p. 92.

[14] Ibid., pp. 115.

potential difficulties. He anticipated that: '[s]uch an environment and such a process would undoubtedly open-up new vistas for dirty tricks. However, by bringing millions of citizens into active participation through millions of channels, it would make it more difficult for anyone to control and subvert any large fraction of the total information flow.' In this case, Licklider failed to anticipate the prominence achieved by a small number of entities such as Google and Facebook. In as far as he did identify threats, they tended in his view to come from public authorities (domestic and foreign) as opposed to the private sector. Possible problems he identified included the use of the network for '[p]rogrammed ... brainwashing in favour of a regime in power'; '[p]-rogrammed monitoring and censorship' through the use of 'natural language understanding' systems; '[a]n automated system that appends the government's refutation to every article or program that is judged by the monitoring program to be critical of the government'; and monitoring of behaviour and interaction across social networks.[15] The population might have some doubts. There would be an occasional 'flurry of rumours about international espionage within the Multinet', though they would not achieve widespread credence. A more common complaint would be that 'a national government' was 'monitoring more assiduously than the law allows'.[16]

Communications Technology and Democracy after the Second World War

The view Licklider held regarding the prospects for the technological shift he helped bring about was one of general optimism tempered by recognition of the challenges. The downsides he discerned would certainly come to attract attention in the years and decades following the rise of the Internet. They also resonated in earlier times, including at the outset of the period that is the subject of the present chapter. Developments leading to the Internet in the post-Second World War period took place in a cultural environment that was not entirely hospitable to a device of this type. Partly as a response to world events culminating in the conflict of 1939–45, an influential narrative depicted the use of communications technology in a sinister light. Aldous Huxley conveyed this perception when he recounted how – 'at his trial' – Albert Speer, a senior figure in the regime of Adolf Hitler, stressed the importance of 'modern technical development' including 'the radio and loud-speaker' in creating the potential to subordinate 'eighty million people ... to the will of one man'.[17] The most powerful example of the technologically pessimistic strand, attaining immense and lasting international recognition, came in the form of the 1949 George Orwell novel *Nineteen Eighty-Four*. The work helped shape the way in which people developed and presented their views. It was a

[15] Ibid., pp. 115.
[16] Ibid., p. 93.
[17] Aldous Huxley, *Brave New World Revisited* (Random House, London, 2004), ch. 5.

standard point of reference, both among those who sought to deploy it as a warning and those who wanted to suggest that it was excessive in its pessimism. Within the specific context of communications technology, including computer networks, it was a recurrent theme, as this chapter (and others in this book) will demonstrate.

As the title suggested, Orwell set his work in the near future. But like the authors discussed in the previous chapter, Orwell sought to reflect tendencies he perceived in his own time. His observation of the Soviet Union was an important – but not the only – influence. In *Nineteen Eighty-Four* the world is divided into blocs. The UK – now renamed Airstrip One – forms part of one, named Oceania. In a militarised one-party system, the 'Ingsoc' government – presiding over an impoverished economy – maintains power through a combination of force and psychological manipulation. It promotes a personality cult around the leader known as 'Big Brother'; while the 'Thought Police' seek to ensure that even internal, mental dissent is eradicated. A central objective of the regime is to control the perception of reality. It promotes three contradictory slogans: 'WAR IS PEACE', 'FREEDOM IS SLAVERY', and 'IGNORANCE IS STRENGTH',[18] and has an official language – 'Newspeak' – designed to restrict independence of expression and conception. Full control is exercised across all media, with officials in the 'Ministry of Truth' creating output to fulfil political purposes, alongside deliberately crass material for the lower orders of society, the 'proles'. The authorities employ emotional manipulation, orchestrating mass hatred against constructed enemies.

Orwell gave a prominent role to technology in the world he created. In the opening pages we encounter the 'telescreen', described as 'an oblong metal plaque like a dulled mirror' built into a wall. These communications devices enable the dissemination of official announcements and the surveillance of the population. Orwell explains that a telescreen 'could be dimmed, but there was no way of shutting it off completely'. He goes on to describe how '[t]he telescreen received and transmitted simultaneously'. The two-way communications system – for some a device for democratic empowerment – was, as Orwell depicted it, sinister. He describes how '[a]ny sound . . . made, above the level of a whisper, would be picked up by it . . . There was . . . no way of knowing whether you were being watched at any given moment.' Uncertainty was part of the effectiveness of the telescreen: '[h]ow often, or on what system, the Thought Police plugged in any individual wire was guesswork. It was even conceivable that they watched everybody all the time. But at any rate they could plug in your wire whenever they wanted to.' The overall impact was that '[y]ou had to live – did live, from habit that became instinct – in the assumption that every sound you made was overheard, and, except in darkness, every movement scrutinized'.[19] The Ministry of Truth Records

[18] George Orwell, *Nineteen Eighty-Four* (Penguin, London, 2004), p. 7.
[19] Ibid., pp. 5–7.

Department is responsible for altering accounts of past events to bring them into line with the requirements of the present – for instance, ensuring that prior predictions made by Big Brother appear to have been accurate. Employees engaged in this function utilise a 'speak-write' device, pneumatic tubes and a remote system for ordering past editions of newspapers via telescreen. They consign superseded content to an incinerator known as a 'memory hole'.[20]

Pessimism regarding mass media and their social role was also found beyond the realm of speculative fiction. In January 1951, the Committee on Broadcasting, chaired by the distinguished social scientist Lord (William) Beveridge, reported to Parliament. Commissioned in 1949, it seems to have been influenced by some of the same recent uses of communications technology as Orwell, though allowing for hope alongside caution. The Committee expressed the view that '[b]roadcasting as an influence on men's minds has great possibilities, either of good or evil'. It held '[t]he good' to be 'that if broadcasting can find a serious audience it is an unrivalled means of bringing vital issues to wider understanding'. On the other hand, '[t]he evil is that broadcasting is capable of increasing perhaps the most serious of all dangers which threaten democracy and free institutions today – the danger of passivity – of acceptance by masses of orders given to them and of things said to them'. The report went on: '[b]roadcasting has in itself a tendency to encourage passivity, for listening as such, if one does no more, is a passive occupation. Television may be found to have this danger of passivity in even stronger form.'[21]

In the mid-twentieth century, broadcasting in the UK was a relatively recent phenomenon, having commenced on a regular basis following the formation of the British Broadcasting Company in 1922. This commercial operation was a predecessor to the publicly owned British Broadcasting Corporation (BBC), brought into being under Royal Charter in 1926.[22] Radio would achieve wide permeation. The number of licences to receive transmissions, an indicator of the popularity of the medium, grew from 35,774 in 1922 to 11,871,312 by 1950. This latter figure was augmented by a further 400,375 authorisations to receive sound and television, a dual licence first introduced in 1946.[23] By the time of the Beveridge committee report, on an evening in summertime, roughly 20 per cent of all adults listened to the radio (7.2 million of 36 million), rising to about 25 per cent in winter (9 million of 36 million).[24]

20 Ibid., pp. 33–4.
21 Broadcasting Committee, *Report of the Broadcasting Committee, 1949*, Presented by the Lord President of the Council and the Postmaster General to Parliament by Command of His Majesty, January 1951, Cmd 8116, para. 285, p. 75.
22 Ibid., para. 23, p. 6.
23 Ibid., Table 1, p. 18.
24 Ibid., para. 76, p. 20.

The 1949 Committee on Broadcasting saw immense future potential in broadcasting as a vehicle for social improvement (as well as the capacity for harm).[25] But its report attributed a significant failure to the short period of ascendancy since 1922. Providing 'education' was one of the three core purposes of the BBC, set out as such in its Charter alongside 'information' and 'entertainment'.[26] A section in Beveridge entitled 'Adult Education Radio' noted that, in the UK, like in the United States, 'broadcasting . . . started off with high hopes' that it could add value in this field. Fitting within the educational part of the BBC's remit, a Central Council for Adult Education, instigated in 1928, had promoted a model labelled the 'discussion group' – a unit of between about five and forty in total. Depending on its size, it might gather at the 'fireside' or in a 'public library'. After listening to a particular programme, members would 'discuss' its content, perhaps with facilitation from a 'group leader', with the broadcaster sometimes setting reading and questions for them. The Council had two high-profile chairs in succession, whose credentials suggested an aurora of progressive optimism surrounding the project: Lord Sankey, the jurist and Labour politician, and then William Temple, Archbishop of York and subsequently Archbishop of Canterbury. Yet despite such leadership and significant exertions by the BBC, programming for this purpose never achieved an audience of more than 20,000. By 1934, the Corporation began to scale down the project, and finally abolished the Group Listening Scheme in 1947.[27]

In analysing the performance of this initiative, the committee suggested that the impact of a communications technique was to a large extent shaped by the nature of the society into which it was introduced. In this sense it rejected technological determinism. Radio might provide a means of facilitating discussion networks, but was not in itself able to guarantee that they would operate. The Beveridge committee regretted that '[t]he bulk of listeners treat listening as a secondary activity, a background noise while they are doing something else, and most of them want from the radio not education but entertainment'. It remarked that people 'from the universities are ready to be curious listeners; those who have not passed beyond the elementary education stage at school are not easily brought beyond it by broadcasting'.[28] Moreover, in circumstances where it appeared to have been successful at stimulating discussion, broadcasting might not have been as useful as it seemed. The report described evidence it received to the effect that the success of a particular listening group depended on having an effective, informed leader and that if it did, then it did not need the radio.[29] The committee nonetheless

[25] Ibid., para. 285, p. 75.
[26] See ibid., para. 24, p. 6.
[27] Ibid., para. 280, pp. 73–4.
[28] Ibid., para. 284, p. 75.
[29] Ibid., para. 282, p. 74.

hoped that the BBC would renew its previous attempt at attaining more active listener involvement.[30] The Beveridge Report depicted the Group Listening Scheme as having been welcome in that it was 'a frontal attack on passivity'.[31] In the Beveridge narrative, then, broadcasting had failed to deliver on early hopes; and had instead become the source of a problem – but one that it might, if deployed differently, play a part in correcting. (A later, more substantial attempt to utilise the technology for educational purposes came with the Open University; established in 1969, the Labour Prime Minister, Harold Wilson, originally conceived of it as a 'university of the air'.) The Beveridge perspective helps place radio and television in a continuum of communications devices and perceptions of their potential that includes both earlier inventions such as printing, and later ones – notably the Internet.

More positive views were possible. As we have seen, with his 'Memex', Bush proposed a progressive role for new technology that influenced subsequent pioneers in the computing and internet-related fields. For instance, as W. Russell Neuman notes, in the decades following the Second World War there was a school of political scientists who took an Enlightenment-tinged view of communications mechanisms as a means of knowledge dissemination and political engagement and therefore a prerequisite for the emergence and sustenance of democracy.[32] Another prominent optimist – perhaps the most celebrated of all – was Marshall McLuhan, a Canadian philosopher of communications.[33] Like Orwell, he became a reference point, indicative of a broad attitude, even among those who might not have read his work. As we will see, he was invoked not only by those who wished to employ his concepts, but among commentators seeking to define themselves by distancing themselves from his ideas (or perhaps a generalised version of them). For them, he stood for determinism and an unquestioningly optimistic view of the democratising impact of technology. Among those who were more sympathetic, he correctly anticipated the technologically driven inception of an interactive global polity. McLuhan regarded successive inventions or 'media' as having shaped mental perceptions, and by extension human interactions and the societies in which they took place. His famous phrase 'the medium is the message' reflected this outlook. McLuhan was influenced by the concept of the 'noosphere', used to describe a universal layer of rational consciousness that emerges at a higher point of human development.[34] We can see in his ideas a precursor to the later tendency to present the Internet as comprising a world in its own right.

30 Ibid., para. 285, p. 75.

31 Ibid.

32 W. Russell Neuman, *The Future of the Mass Audience* (Cambridge University Press, 1991), pp. 33–5.

33 For McLuhan and his impact see e.g. Richard Barbrook, *Media Freedom: The Contradictions of Communications in the Age of Modernity* (Pluto Press, London, 1995), pp. 118–19.

34 Marshall McLuhan, *The Gutenberg Galaxy: The Making of Typographic Man* (University of Toronto Press, 2011), pp. 31–2.

The idea of communications technology determining reality would surface in the 1983 David Cronenberg film, *Videodrome*, in which some combination of video cassette and satellite television is able to subsume and control the existence of its victims. It features a character, Professor Brian O'Blivion, seemingly inspired by McLuhan, whose lines include the statements that 'there is nothing real outside our perception of reality'; and that '[t]he television screen is the retina of the mind's eye . . . television is reality, and reality is less than television'.

For McLuhan, devices introduced during the twentieth century were having the effect of creating – as he put it in 1962 – a single world polity or 'global village', resting on a 'new electronic interdependence'. The 'new electric culture', as he presented it 'provides our lives again with a tribal base . . . the world has become a computer, an electronic brain, exactly as in an infantile piece of science fiction'.[35] McLuhan saw political implications in this tendency. In a 1967 collaboration with the graphic artist Quentin Fiore, he argued that 'electronic technology' was 'reshaping and restructuring patterns of social interdependence and every aspect of our personal life'. He held that '[i]t is forcing us to reconsider every thought, every action, and every institution formerly taken for granted. Everything is changing – you, your family, your neighbourhood, your education, your job, your government, your relation to "the others." And they're changing dramatically.'[36] One of his observations regarding this tendency was that '[n]ose counting, a cherished part of the nineteenth century fragmentation process, has rapidly become a cumbersome and ineffectual form of social assessment in an environment of instant electric speeds'. For McLuhan, '[a] new form of "politics"' was 'emerging, and in ways we haven't yet noticed. The living room has become a voting booth. Participation via television in Freedom Marches, in war, revolution, pollution, and other events is changing everything.'[37]

In this passage McLuhan referred to existing 'electronic technology', as he put it. But by this time there was also discussion of newer inventions and different techniques in the field of communications. A sense of the kind of advances believed to be in prospect, and the questions they prompted, can be found in a series of short articles first published in 1964 in a UK-based journal, the *New Scientist*. They contained speculation by various international experts about possible developments in science and their implications over the coming two decades. In 1965 they reappeared in a two-volume work *The World in 1984* (a choice of year that was evidence of the cultural resonance that the Orwell novel had achieved).[38] The volumes covered a mass of subjects, among

35 Ibid., p. 32.

36 Marshall McLuhan and Quentin Fiore, *The Medium Is the Massage* (Penguin, London, 1967), p. 8.

37 Ibid., p. 22.

38 Nigel Calder (ed.), *The World in 1984: The Complete New Scientist Series* (Penguin, Harmondsworth, 1965), 2 vols.

them space exploration, food, energy, industry, the climate, chemicals, and forms of transport. Contributors included Wernher von Braun, then in a senior post at the US National Aeronautics and Space Administration (NASA), who made predictions including that: '[m]an may have landed on the surface of Mars by 1984. If not, he will surely have made a close approach for personal observation of the red planet. Likewise, manned "fly-bys" to Venus will have been made.'[39]

The diverse range of advances projected and discussed in these volumes leads to an important point. Though this book focuses on particular uses of technology in a specific context – that is, communications impacting upon politics and the constitution – we need to be aware that, at any given time, they were only one part of a wider setting. Given the breadth of apparent possibilities, it was difficult at a particular moment fully to anticipate such outcomes as which projected inventions might come to pass, the uses to which they might be put, the extent of their take-up, and the wider consequences. A failure to anticipate an important development might be fully understandable. When we consider the future there is likely to be an excess of variables involved. But there is consistency of a sort, involving thematic recurrence in debates about the nature of technology.

Ideas found in *The World in 1984* similar to those we have already encountered include views advanced by J. D. Clare of Standard Telecommunication Laboratories, Harlow. Clare described a new 'transmission network' that could be 'linked to active planning for decentralization of industry and population'.[40] In discussing communications technology in this way, the chapters often linked them with computers,[41] and saw implications for matters of politics and democracy. Arthur L. Samuel, of IBM, gave readers an idea of the historic sweep of his subject when noting that 1984 'will be celebrated as the 150th anniversary of the invention of the first computer, the Analytical Engine of the Englishman Charles Babbage', working with 'his almost equally famous interpreter, Lady Lovelace'.[42] He suspected that, two decades hence, it would be possible for anyone to have a computer of their own,[43] and anticipated what were, in effect, mobile phones, as well as 'video-communication'. People would be able to access a wide body of content, including 'large central files', books, 'any movie that has ever been produced', and statistical information 'all for the

[39] Dr Wernher von Braun, 'Exploration to the Farthest Planets' in Nigel Calder (ed.), *The World in 1984: The Complete New Scientist Series* (Penguin, Harmondsworth, 1965), vol. I, pp. 39–42, 39.

[40] J. D. Clare, 'Decentralization by Telecommunications' in Nigel Calder (ed.), *The World in 1984: The Complete New Scientist Series* (Penguin, Harmondsworth, 1965), vol. I, pp. 154–6, 156.

[41] Dr J. R. Pierce, 'Private Television Instead of Travel' in Nigel Calder (ed.), *The World in 1984: The Complete New Scientist Series* (Penguin, Harmondsworth, 1965), vol. I, pp. 150–3, 151.

[42] Dr Arthur L. Samuel, 'The Banishment of Paper-Work', Nigel Calder (ed.), *The World in 1984: The Complete New Scientist Series* (Penguin, Harmondsworth, 1965), vol. I, pp. 142–7, 142.

[43] Ibid., p. 144.

asking via one's remote terminal'. The public library would become obsolete 'and most of the world's knowledge will be in machine-readable form'. Assisting this compilation of readily retrievable information would be 'computers' programmed 'to read printed and handwritten material'. The 'consequences' would be 'profound in many diverse fields'.[44]

One area in which Samuel expected impact was the political. He seemingly perceived computers as creating the possibility for individual activism. In Communist countries personal ownership of the technology would be forbidden, since it would bring with it the potential for 'private, or, perhaps some would say, clandestine operations'. In its place all people would have 'access to a small terminal connecting him with one or more large state-owned computers giving him most of the advantages of a small privately-owned computer' without the scope for more subversive uses. Samuel doubted, however, that authoritarian states would reach a level of intrusion depicted by Orwell, writing that 'even in these countries the "big brother is watching" aspect will be very much less pronounced than was predicted'.[45] In these passages we can see – in gestational form – some of the later debate about the Internet. A variety of questions developed. What might communications mechanisms mean in the respective contexts of more democratic or of more authoritarian societies? In any type of system would such devices strengthen or undermine personal freedom and the ability to participate politically? Would they enhance the control of those in positions of authority, or make them more subject to influences produced by popular participation? Such queries and differing perspectives upon them were already forming long before a viable version of the technology they revolved around had come into being, let alone into mass usage. Ideas (however vague) had formed before the occurrence of inventions and their take-up. This sequence suggests that rather than being subordinate to technology, conceptual interpretations can help determine the context within which it is employed.

While Samuel conveyed the idea of computer-based communications as personally empowering and a potential challenge from the point of view of more oppressive regimes, another contributor leant more towards presenting such mechanisms as a threat to the individual. M. V. Wilkes of the Cambridge University Mathematical Laboratory predicted the imminent presence in 'shops and offices, laboratories and factories' of 'keyboards looking very like typewriters, but connected to a computer'. They would include 'graphical display devices on which diagrams may be drawn either by the user or by the computer itself'. With considerable storage capacity, one of the purposes of these devices would 'be to act as a "data base", that is to hold files of information, some public, some private'. Furthermore, '[s]oon computers in different areas will be talking to each other so that any user can

[44] Ibid., p. 145.
[45] Ibid., p. 144.

interrogate any file available to any of the computers'. Wilkes went on: '[o]nce a network of computers exists – and by 1984 it will be an international network – it will be the obvious thing to use computers for the transmission of messages ... Speech will also be transmitted as data and reconstituted at the far end.'[46] He identified a possible problem arising from this development. While arguing that 'machines are not to be feared in themselves, they will make it possible for those in authority to keep much closer tabs on what people are doing, and there are signs that governments are beginning to realize this'. Wilkes feared that '[m]any branches of life will lend themselves to computer surveillance, and I leave it to the readers to decide whether or not this is a pleasant prospect'.[47]

Gerald Barry, a journalist who had been Director General of the 1951 Festival of Britain, by this point of the Granada Television Network, contributed to the collection on the subject of 'Mass Communication in 1984'.[48] He held that 'twenty years from now there will have been accomplished a technical revolution in both the printing and the distribution of news comparable to the revolution caused by the invention of printing itself'.[49] Barry predicted that 'the "newspaper" of the future will be electronic ... People will probably get their news either on a television screen or on a wall panel or on a private teleprinter, or on some variant or combination of these devices.' The centre of gravity of journalism would shift 'firmly into the hands of television itself'. The attraction of this medium was that it could provide 'the actuality of event-plus-person summoned instantaneously together before the eye – there in the living room, though they may happen at the time to be on the moon'. Barry remarked that there was 'after all, nothing sacrosanct about a *newspaper* as such'. For him, 'if a full and free flow of news, comment, and criticism can be more conveniently and attractively supplied by television, then the needs of democracy will be served'.[50]

Multiple channels would broadcast in colour 'round the daylight clock'.[51] Remote education would become normal.[52] Politicians would be able to hold discussions without travelling to meet in person.[53] Furthermore, 'Parliament will be televised in one form or another. Most of the political restrictions now imposed on television but not on newspapers will be abolished.'[54]

[46] Dr M. V. Wilkes, 'A World Dominated by Computers?' in Nigel Calder (ed.), *The World in 1984: The Complete New Scientist Series* (Penguin, Harmondsworth, 1965), vol. I, pp. 147–50, 148.

[47] Ibid., p. 149.

[48] Sir Gerald Barry, 'Mass Communication in 1984' in Nigel Calder (ed.), *The World in 1984, The Complete New Scientist Series* (Penguin, Harmondsworth, 1965), vol. I, pp. 157–60.

[49] Ibid., p. 157.

[50] Ibid., p. 158.

[51] Ibid., p. 158.

[52] Ibid., pp. 158–9.

[53] Ibid., p. 159.

[54] Ibid., p. 158.

Such technology could promote 'the acceptance of One World' among the global population and help people adjust to coming social changes.[55] People could begin producing their own content, establishing 'a more indigenous and creative community life, a challenging corrective to the canned entertainment and mass persuasion that make us all the passive victims of output from a central pumping-station'. The existence of 'universal ... do-it-yourself electronic equipment' might 'encourage locally and regionally a more vigorous cultural and political life'. New technology could in this account help correct problems with the use of existing devices. But 'the virtually limitless powers of centralized supply will pull in the opposite direction'.[56] This caveat demonstrated a sense that, though diversification was a possibility, there were potentially countervailing tendencies, perhaps in the direction of uniformity and monopoly. Such conflicting possibilities would come to characterise the debate about the Internet and its political consequences.

V. K. Zworykin, of the RCA Laboratory at Princeton, made a specific proposal for the democratic use of communications technology that was reminiscent of ideas expressed by Brecht, Birkenhead, and Fuller set out in Chapter 3. He held that: '[g]overnment, to be good, must be informed; to be democratic it must be controlled by an informed citizenry'. It was only possible to achieve these qualities through 'an efficient system' achieving 'two-way communication between the people and their governmental agents'. While television and radio enabled government to direct its statements to the public, 'the ways open to the people for making their wishes known to their representatives appear quite inadequate'. The only means of such contact was 'the vote'. But it was a 'cumbersome business' involving ballot papers, polling stations, and opening times, all of which served to restrict 'both the frequency of such public expressions of public opinion and the range of issues covered by them'. Elections tended to focus on personalised clashes, with a lack of clarity about popular views on specific matters. Opinion research was a response to this uncertainty but was not necessarily reliable and precluded proper consultation on urgent matters.

Zworykin held that such limitations could be overcome. He wrote: 'modern technology makes it possible to give the people the ability to communicate their wishes and opinions to the government with a strictness and immediacy comparable with that realized at present only in the opposite direction'. Zworykin recognised that there was scope for 'doubt' regarding 'the desirability of direct popular control of public policy'. He recorded that 'past experience with the direct democracy of ancient Athens and the town meeting may be interpreted either favourably or unfavourably or even regarded as irrelevant, in view of the greater complexity of the questions presented to modern governments for decision.' But in the system he envisaged, 'only broad policy

[55] Ibid., p. 160.
[56] Ibid.

decisions would be made by laymen' while experts would deal with the complexities. As he saw it, this way of operating applied within government already. Moreover, continuous engagement in these processes would 'stimulate in the citizen an increased sense of responsibility and a desire to inform himself on public questions'. Public authorities would benefit from being able to discern popular opinion on given issues. Zworykin suspected, therefore, that by 1984 'governments will have availed themselves of the technical possibility of accurately gauging popular response to current and projected policies'. This goal was attainable through a combination of the broadcasting and telephone networks. Votes held by this means could occur swiftly and frequently, with registered participants taking part from home. The collation of results would also be rapid. The benefits would be a closer correlation between the views of the public and the policies of government, people feeling more empowered and encouraged to expand their political knowledge, and a more 'effective democratic government'.[57] Once again, speculation about the prospects for communications devices had led to consideration – and advocacy – of their use to facilitate direct democracy on a mass scale.

Cable Television and Beyond

Depictions of such technology as a possible means of social transformation continued into the 1970s and thereafter. A common theme was that the full potential of television had not yet been realised, and that cable television could help achieve this end, the benefits of which could include democratic enhancement. In his 1972 book – which first appeared that year as a special edition of the US journal *The Nation* – Ralph Lee Smith anticipated the 'information superhighway' concept of later decades. The title of the Smith work was *The Wired Nation: Cable TV: The Electronic Communications Highway.* He explained that cable television, 'originally called community antenna television' had begun 'as a minor adjunct to the present system of over-the-air commercial broadcasting'. Some still referred to it as CATV, but it was also known as 'broadband communications'. It was, Smith judged, 'on the verge of becoming a major medium in its own right. As cable systems are installed in major cities and metropolitan areas, the stage is being set for a communications revolution – a revolution that some experts call "The Wired Nation."'[58]

Cable, Smith held, was a supplement to radio, television, and telephone. It could provide for domestic and commercial use 'audio, video and facsimile transmissions' offering services including 'newspapers, mail . . . , banking and

[57] V. K. Zworykin, 'Communications and Government' in Nigel Calder (ed.), *The World in 1984, The Complete New Scientist Series* (Penguin, Harmondsworth, 1965), vol. II, pp. 51–3.

[58] Ralph Lee Smith, *The Wired Nation: Cable TV: The Electronic Communications Highway* (Harper & Row, New York, 1972, first published in shorter form as a special issue of *The Nation*, 18 May 1972), p. 1.

shopping facilities, data from libraries and other storage centers, school curricula, complete course offerings leading to college degrees, cultural programs, community orientated TV fare', and much else. It meant that 'every home and office can contain a communications center of a breadth and flexibility to influence every aspect of private and community life'.[59] It was possible that there would eventually develop 'a single, unified system of electronic communications'.[60] Just as, in the 1960s, federal government provided financial support for the construction of 'a new interstate highway system', Smith argued that '[i]n the 1970s it should make a similar national commitment for an electronic highway system, to facilitate the exchange of information and ideas'. Proper co-ordination was needed to ensure that the motive of immediate commercial gain did not override public interest, a shortcoming that had afflicted broadcasting policy up to this point.[61] But whatever the outcome, Smith saw it as inevitable that 'the cable will be built'.[62]

Cable would expand the number of channels and lessen the cost of broadcasting, ending the grip on programming 'exercised by a small commercial oligarchy'. One of the consequences he discerned for television would be that it would become 'far more democratic'.[63] Smith believed that cable might 'arrest and reverse some ominous developments in American electoral politics'. The need for television coverage and its high expense, he held, were the main causes of 'the rapidly increasing trend, for politics, at all levels, to become a game of the privileged, wealthy few'.[64] Cable could make that exposure more widely available, thereby expanding political opportunities. As shown in Chapter 3, Theodore Roosevelt (son of the former president) had predicted in 1932 that radio and television would make electoral politics a less exclusive activity, with a broader field of potential candidates. The view Smith presented four decades later suggested that the opposite outcome had manifested itself. Nonetheless, Smith believed that yet another technological development would reverse the tendency that its predecessor had – contrary to predictions – stimulated. A cycle of optimism, disappointment, and renewed hope had played out again.

Smith saw some potential downsides. The trend for more affluent groups in society to move away from inner cities could accelerate, since services would readily be available via the network. This tendency might have a harmful effect on social solidarity.[65] Smith also suspected that the technology he envisaged could have negative consequences for privacy. Centrally connected cameras could be widely dispersed in public places, making intensive police

[59] Ibid., pp. 1–2.
[60] Ibid., p. 9.
[61] Ibid., pp. 83–4.
[62] Ibid., p. 98.
[63] Ibid., p. 8.
[64] Ibid., p. 19.
[65] Ibid., p. 97.

surveillance possible. Providers of cable systems would be able to monitor the viewing habits of users, as well as their financial transactions and other activities. The contents of messages sent via cable might also be accessible in this way. Moreover, if cable was used for the dissemination of information, decisions would need to be made about what material could and could not come within its scope. Smith held that '[u]nless the issues in these future uses of the cable are understood and faced, 1984 could easily come well in advance of George Orwell's prediction'.[66]

Another work published in 1972 made a still more strident case for cable as a corrective to 'the superficial standards and the shallow and oversimplified program content of mass communications, especially of television and radio'.[67] Entitled *Cable Television: A Guide for Citizen Action*, it held among other claims that the technology it advocated would make politics more inclusive and responsive. It would reduce the costs incurred by candidates for office when communicating and engaging in dialogue with voters,[68] and make possible wider participation in political debates.[69] The main authors, Monroe Price and John Wicklein, argued that '[c]able television can make it possible for your community organisation to conduct a meeting of all the people in your neighbourhood, without any of them having to leave their homes'. It was possible to 'organise to do something that needs to be done by *getting together* via cable'. Moreover, 'cable can become a two-way medium of communication, letting people in their homes respond to the issues being discussed'. At present, 'only a rudimentary response is possible by pressing "Yes" or "No" buttons on your television set'. But '[m]ore sophisticated response systems are being studied and may soon be developed'.

The authors saw cable as creating potential for the networking of home computer terminals.[70] They also referred to the possible importance of 'low-cost video cameras that can be operated by amateurs . . . when linked to a cable as a cheap form of transmission and distribution of images'.[71] The book then offered a vision of a future that the transformation in communications it advocated might bring about, in a chapter entitled 'What do the dreamers dream about the future of cable communication?'[72] They speculated that, in the year 2002, there would be less need to travel, meaning that pollution and traffic congestion could have eased, and the population could have dispersed from city centres, facilitating racial desegregation. People could hold business meetings by video links, and education could take place by the same means.

[66] Ibid., p. 98.
[67] Monroe Price and John Wicklein, *Cable Television: A Guide for Citizen Action* (Pilgrim Press, Philadelphia, 1972), p. vii.
[68] Ibid., pp. 2–3.
[69] Ibid., p. vii.
[70] Ibid., p. 3.
[71] Ibid., p. 96.
[72] Ibid., p. 106.

Newspapers would be transmitted electronically, with people receiving content tailored to their personal preferences. (In later discussion of the Internet, depiction of targeting of this type was often more negative in tone, with analysis suggesting it produced self-reinforcing, possibly polarised 'filter bubbles'.) Less privileged social groups would be able to organise politically and exert influence. Members of the electorate would 'know their political candidates better', enabling them to 'vote more intelligently'.[73]

Such claims are certainly familiar. In his 2004 work, *The Digital Sublime*, Vincent Mosco placed expectations attached to cable television in the early 1970s in an historical continuum, stretching back to the nineteenth century and the telegraph, and on to twenty-first and the Internet. He describes how in 1973 'I spent a summer doing research ... on trends in communication and information technology.' At this point, 'the typical conclusion' about cable was that it 'had the potential to connect people like no other technology. It would bring about ubiquitous two-way communication, and it would likely usher in a Wired Society governed by Electronic Democracy.' It would 'revitalize communities, enrich schools, end poverty, eliminate the need for everything from banks to shopping malls, and reduce dependence on the automobile ... In short, cable TV would transform the world.' Noting that these claims were 'familiar', Mosco remarked 'how little predictions about new technology have changed over the years'. Where once 'people ... hailed the Telegraph Age, the Age of Electricity, the Age of the Telephone, the Age of Radio, or the Age of Television, we are now said to be in the Age of the Computer'.[74]

The cable television movement was predominantly focused on the United States. But at this time the general potential for electronic communications technology was a subject of interest within the UK. A further 1972 publication was *Television and the People: A Programme for Democratic Participation*, by Brian Groombridge. He called for 'a development of a new kind of educational television, which I believe would have a benign influence on the medium as a whole and would certainly reduce the gap between those who make programmes and those who receive them'.[75] Groombridge recognised that he was relatively modest in his proposals,[76] which were certainly not as dramatic as some of the ideas advanced in the United States. Nonetheless, he saw himself as addressing a crisis in '[r]epresentative democracy'. If it did not develop into 'participatory democracy' – with the assistance of the more interactive programming he supported – there was a risk of descent into 'some

[73] Ibid., pp. 106–12.

[74] Vincent Mosco, *The Digital Sublime: Myths, Power, and Cyberspace* (MIT Press, Cambridge, 2004), pp. 1–2.

[75] Brian Groombridge, *Television and the People: A Programme for Democratic Participation* (Penguin, London, 1972), p. 7.

[76] Ibid., p. 7.

kind of autocracy, which could be bland and manipulative, but might well be brutish and tyrannical'.[77]

Yet another 1972 publication, by a UK-based, US-born journalist, Brenda Maddox, was entitled *Beyond Babel: New Directions in Communications*. It built on an earlier pamphlet issued by *The Economist*, 'Revolution in Communications'.[78] In it Maddox envisaged an unfolding future in which '[c]ommunications satellites and refinements in electronics . . . will give people more influence over the world around them, as they become able to talk across national boundaries, to pay close attention to a number of levels of the political process and even to vote without leaving their homes'.[79] Maddox anticipated that '[t]elephones, all with push-button dials and some with picture screens, will deliver and receive streams of electronic information. They will also become portable; telephone numbers will eventually be assigned to people, not to places.' She predicted that '[t]elevision will have dozens of channels, some for private communication with other television sets, some for communication with computers'. The technology would lead to an enhanced variety of programming. A further projected development was that '[t]he television set will also print out newspapers and deliver facsimiles of letters'.[80] This speculation is an example of anticipation of future patterns of development, but not the precise means – the Internet – by which they would come about.

Maddox gave consideration to whether 'a fully operational electronic network would give a dictator an easy life'. Her view was that it would probably not, because it was likely to facilitate 'mobile and two-way communications. A dictator relies on one-way communication. Big Brother wants to watch everybody; he does not want them watching him.' Nonetheless, Maddox recognised that 'the enormous capacity of electronic files presents a new temptation to the official surveillance of private citizens'.[81] Technology could not in itself cause dictatorship, though such regimes would use it to maintain control. There were benefits to be had from 'data banks', which might inform better public policy.[82] Moreover, she regarded it as 'possible that the worldwide sharing of information at enormous speeds will actually raise the collective intellectual potential of the human race, just as the printing press and the computer have done'.[83]

Computers, Networks, and Democracy

These 1972 discussions of electronic communications contained some references to computers. Other observers with similar interests were more specific

[77] Ibid., p. 18.
[78] Brenda Maddox, *Beyond Babel: New Directions in Communications* (Andre Deutsch, London, 1972).
[79] Ibid., pp. 15–16.
[80] Ibid.
[81] Ibid., pp. 252.
[82] Ibid., pp. 253–4.
[83] Ibid., pp. 254–5.

in their focus on this technology as part of some kind of information network. In 1967, for instance, Herman Kahn and Anthony J. Wiener, published *The Year 2000: A Framework for Speculation on the Next Thirty-Three Years*. In it they held that: '[t]he capacity of the computer ultimately to effect a dramatic extension of man's power over his environment, as well as many other social and economic changes, is by now obvious to all'.[84] They speculated that '[e]ventually there will probably be computer consoles in every home'. They might be 'linked to public utility computers and permitting each user his private file space in a central computer, for uses such as consulting the Library of Congress, keeping individual records, preparing income tax returns from these records, obtaining consumer information, and so on'.[85]

The general idea of computers being revolutionary in their potential had currency at this time. Shulamith Firestone, for instance, made a claim of this type in *The Dialectic of Sex: The Case for Feminist Revolution*, that first appeared in 1970. In this work, Firestone held that 'cybernation' – by which she meant the appearance of machines with creative and 'problem-solving' capacity on parity with or greater than that of 'man' – might help trigger the 'feminist revolution'. Firestone recognised the existence of concerns about: 'Technocracy, 1984: the increased alienation of the masses, the intensified rule of the elite (now perhaps cyberneticians), baby factories, computerized government (Big Brother), and so on.' She held that '[i]n the hands of the present establishment there is no doubt that the machine could be used – is being used – to intensify the apparatus of repression and to increase established power.' But, Firestone went on, the technology would have the effect of eliminating differences since it would supplant all workers. She wrote that '[w]e will be beyond arguments about who is "bringing home the bacon" – no one will be bringing it home, because no-one will be "working". Job discrimination would no longer have any basis in a society where machines do the work better than human beings of any size or skill could.' A period of disruption and 'revolutionary ferment' would develop, leading to a changed social system.[86] Firestone did not specifically address the idea of the computer as communication device. But *The Dialectic of Sex* provided a particular variant on a thesis occurring frequently in the present book: that of a technology that is part of a problem in a given political context, but that also contains the seeds of a solution and of a possible transformation of that same framework.

Also in 1970, Nigel Calder, editor of the *World in 1984* collection discussed above, published *Technopolis: Social Control of the Uses of Science*. He held that: '[f]uture historians will probably be able to match the importance of the

[84] Herman Kahn and Anthony J. Wiener, *The Year 2000: A Framework for Speculation on the Thirty-Three Years* (Macmillan, New York, 1967), pp. 86–7.

[85] Ibid., p. 90.

[86] Shulamith Firestone, *The Dialectic of Sex: The Case for Feminist Revolution* (Verso, London, 2015), ch. 10.

computer with nothing that preceded it, back to the invention of writing; even the invention of the steam engine and other heat engines will seem like a runner-up'. Calder judged that '[t]he computer opens pathways to achievements in the realm of information and ideas previously denied to us'. The 'political and social implications' were 'already staggering'.[87] Calder anticipated the emergence of a 'grid or network of computers, analogous to electricity supply systems. Huge "data banks" for recording information of all kinds will be built into the network'.[88] This merging of 'computers with modern communications' would amount to 'a system incorporating the computing, publishing, newspaper, broadcasting, library, telephone and postal services of the country, together with larger slices of teaching, of government, of industrial and commercial operations, and of many professional activities'. Each of these components, 'subsumed in one system (or a small number of alternative systems) will together outstrip in magnitude and importance any industry or collective activity in which human beings have previously been engaged'. Every person would have, at home or work, 'a console' linking them to 'the system'. Calder labelled it the 'World Box'.[89]

In the scenario Calder set out, the World Box might have many dramatic impacts. For instance, like numerous other analysts of the likely social consequences of technology over time, Calder expected it to bring about reductions in the size of urban population centres.[90] In his analysis, Calder suggested that the 'grid' he expected to come into being could not be neutral. The way in which it functioned had implications for outcomes; and the system itself could be a source of power for those positioned advantageously within it. He posed a series of questions about this network, including: '[w]ill political propaganda be censored or rationed? ... who will control the system and what will the rules be?' He concluded that '[d]ecisions on these points will affect the character of the available information. Even if they are not government hacks, the men organizing the content on the system will be immensely influential.'[91] The technology might appear to have a levelling effect, undermining 'the domination ... of big companies in the mass-communication field; in theory any individual could publish a book or article merely by typing it or having it automatically read into the system'. Yet 'the trouble in drawing it to the attention of subscribers redresses the situation ... The power and importance of advertisers, like that of editors, can only tend to increase – unless advertising is confined to information requested by the subscriber.' As Calder put it, '[i]t is a question of who is in charge of information about the information'.[92]

87 Nigel Calder, *Technopolis: Social Control of the Uses of Science* (Simon and Schuster, New York, 1970), pp. 204–5.
88 Ibid., p. 207.
89 Ibid., p. 208.
90 Ibid., p. 211.
91 Ibid., p. 209.
92 Ibid., p. 210.

These remarks were significant in that they anticipated aspects of later commentary on the Internet that were not as prominent a feature of communications technology discourse at this time. Discussion of the political implications of computer networks from this earlier period tended to focus on the relationship between the public and governmental institutions. Calder included this point, but added to it consideration of the possible role of private corporations. Furthermore, he provided an associated argument that again comprised a precursor to certain views of the Internet. He suggested that those with access to the underlying operational mechanisms of this system – to the 'information about the information' – could use it as source of immense leverage, serving to concentrate rather than disperse power. If regulation (or the lack thereof) allowed them to do so, advertisers could employ this privileged position to present users with content they had not knowingly solicited, intended to shape behaviour in particular ways that suited the interests of those already entrenched within the network.

Calder also saw potential consequences for the political system. Computer networks might lead to a centralisation of authority, or the opposite.[93] As Calder put it: '[a]ll forms of transport and communications are a potential aid to central government. But they can operate the other way, too, making it easier to organize a revolution.'[94] He expected that 'control of the networks and transport systems will itself be the prime means by which general control is exercised – as it was in the days of the horse and the sailing ship'. Once again, for Calder, the network was more than a conduit, and was a means of control: '[t]he channels may become politically more significant than the senders or receivers of the messages, even as the significance of the message grows with the augmentation by the computer'.[95] Calder foresaw technology leading to an internationalisation of issues involving the power balance. He remarked: '[w]hen the world is encased in an electronic cocoon of interconnected computer networks, and more and more administration and business is international in scope, the issue of centralization versus decentralization will be a global one.'[96] He recognised that such technology could be used for the accumulation by government of personal information, a fact that was a source of 'fears that the computer system may turn into Big Brother'.[97] A further concern was that, were authoritarian leaders to take office, they would be able to deploy 'data banks' for malign purposes.[98] But on the positive side, it would be possible to establish two-way communications, '[a]n "electronic loop" between rulers and citizens'.[99]

93 Ibid., p. 211.
94 Ibid., p. 212.
95 Ibid., p. 215.
96 Ibid., p. 217.
97 Ibid., p. 218.
98 Ibid., p. 222.
99 Ibid., p. 335.

Ongoing observation of developments in electronic communications occurred in parallel with another trend.[100] The idea that the public should be more fully involved in the political system grew in salience, with discussion of mechanisms that might achieve this outcome. A tendency developed among political scientists to consider the overlap between technological advances and democratic needs.[101] In 1973, Ithiel de Sola Pool edited a collection entitled *Talking Back: Citizen Feedback and Cable Technology*, to which Pool's contributions included a chapter joint-authored with Herbert E. Alexander, 'Politics in a Wired Nation'.[102] The authors discussed the potential uses of cable television for the broadcasting of the proceedings of institutions, including Congress; for news services; for more targeted electoral campaigning (sometimes defined as a problem rather than an opportunity in the context of the Internet); and for stimulating local activism.[103] They judged that, by the 1990s, cable would become a means of two-way communications.[104] Alexander and Pool foresaw that, eventually, '[w]ith advanced computerized information systems, the viewer could request the candidate's views on a given subject and receive them immediately on demand in his home'. Another possibility involved 'digital feedback', which meant 'that the viewer can push a button on his set or tap a code on his touch-tone telephone and thereby record some simple coded message into a computer at the other end'.

Unlike some others who speculated on this subject, Pool and Alexander were resistant to the substantial expansion of direct democracy. They remarked that '[t]he most common science fiction notion about the use of digital feedback in politics is that of the instant referendum. The notion is that the ancient dream of direct democracy, in which the people themselves vote on the issues instead of merely periodically choosing representatives, can at last be made a reality.' The authors rejected this idea as 'sheer fantasy. It rests upon a total misunderstanding of the legislative process.'[105] Alexander and Pool argued that the complexity of most legal measures meant that even representatives needed to divide specialisms between them, and the public could not be expected to pronounce on such matters. In their view, there could be a proper place for occasional referendums on a small number of matters of great significance. But they need not involve cable technology: '[v]oting is a major event, and so there is no particular reason why it should be done by pressing a button in one's home'. It would be possible, however, to employ digital

[100] For a popular work that includes discussion of both, see John Naisbitt, *Megatrends: Ten New Directions Transforming Our Lives* (Warner, New York, 1982).

[101] For the concept of 'deliberative democracy' and the Internet, see Matthew Hindman, *The Myth of Digital Democracy* (Princeton University Press, Princeton, 2009), ch. 1.

[102] Ithiel de Sola Pool, 'Politics in a Wired Nation' in Ithiel de Sola Pool (ed.), *Talking Back: Citizen Feedback and Cable Technology* (MIT Press, Cambridge, 1973), pp. 64–102.

[103] Ibid., pp. 65–78.

[104] Ibid., p. 79.

[105] Ibid., p. 79.

feedback for purposes of opinion polling and for ascertaining or demonstrating the existence of a body of support for a particular cause.[106] While speculating about the future uses of technology, Alexander and Pool were resistant to any notion that its qualities entailed predetermined outcomes. They took the view that '[e]ach physical medium – print, cinema, radio, TV – has shaped the message by its material form'. Nonetheless, they held that 'Marshall McLuhan overstates the case. The molding effect of the medium is small. The diversity of uses of which any medium is capable is great.'[107]

Interest in these areas was sustained into the 1980s, and on into the 1990s and the era that saw the rise of the Internet. Concepts developed in relation to other technologies such as cable television, or which considered computer-based communications in a more general sense, were carried over and applied more precisely to this specific digital technology. Some academics, such as Benjamin R. Barber, straddled the earlier and later periods, engaging with both.[108] The idea of 'teledemocracy' was a subject of much consideration, with academic studies focusing on the theory of initiatives such as 'electronic town meetings', and on various attempts to put them into practice, for instance in Hawaii from the late 1970s.[109] A theme that recurred was that the political system was experiencing problems of some kind, and that the potential of technology to help solve them required assessment. As F. Christopher Arterton wrote in his 1987 book, *Teledemocracy: Can Technology Protect Democracy?*: 'American democracy is beset with problems that threaten its vitality ... at the same time, the United States is undergoing a rapid and sustained transformation in communication technologies.'[110]

In the UK, the Oxford academic, Iain McLean, published *Democracy and New Technology* in 1989. In it he discussed various electronic networks that might be used for public engagement purposes. In his words '[p]art of the IT revolution is not about computers, but about communications'.[111] When discussing the introduction of 'electronic switching, fibre optics and satellites'[112] into the telephone network, he remarked that: '[o]nce a telephone network is seen as a network of digital messages, it becomes obvious that it is

[106] Ibid., pp. 65–78.
[107] Ibid., p. 64.
[108] For an earlier contribution first published in 1984, see Benjamin R. Barber, *Strong Democracy: Participatory Politics for a New Age* (University of California Press, Berkeley, 2003), pp. 273–8. For later work, see Benjamin R. Barber, 'The New Telecommunications Technology: Endless Frontier or the End of Democracy?' in *A Passion for Democracy: American Essays* (Princeton University Press, 1998), pp. 258–82.
[109] e.g. F. Christopher Arterton, *Teledemocracy: Can Technology Protect Democracy?* (Sage, Newbury Park, 1987), p. 54. See also: Starr Roxanne Hiltz and Murray Turoff, *The Network Nation: Human Communication via Computer* (MIT Press, Cambridge, 1993), p. 197.
[110] e.g. Arterton, *Teledemocracy*, p. 13.
[111] Iain McLean, *Democracy and New Technology* (Polity, Cambridge, 1989), p. 81.
[112] Ibid., p. 81.

well adapted for communications between computers'.[113] McLean discussed the Prestel system that the Post Office had introduced in the 1970s, and its use as a means of conducting opinion research. He considered possible applications of cable television, including as a way of holding a 'town meeting' in which all those who had the relevant equipment could participate remotely.[114] But McLean saw more potential elsewhere, arguing that 'direct democracy will come in ... as a by-product of technology that has been installed for some other purpose'. Private financial interests and organisations engaged in scientific research had invested in electronic mail, so that it could fulfil their need for the transfer of large quantities of information. The advances achieved now meant that higher-education institutions in the UK were connected to one another and to US universities, that were similarly networked. Users could now deploy the technology for purposes other than those originally intended for it. They might, for instance, employ it to post political messages on electronic '[b]ulletin boards'.[115]

McLean saw 'no insuperable technical obstacle to having the Athenian Assembly in our living-rooms and workplaces'. Furthermore, an 'Assembly could hold only 6,000 people, most of whom cannot have been able to hear the speeches, let alone take any real part in the discussion.' He detected equalising potential: '[t]hose who could get heard were likely to be the fit and extrovert. But unfit and/or introverted people have opinions too, and in a democracy they should have an equal right to have them heard. The new information technology could put them on an equal footing for the first time.'[116] Yet McLean did not see direct democracy as supplanting the representative variety. While the former system was more suited to government in smaller groups, the latter worked better on a mass scale.[117]

The idea that computers, especially when networked in some way, might bring with them social – and within that, political – benefit was given wide attention. But the views on offer could be ambivalent, sceptical, or even hostile regarding such notions. In 1978, Starr Roxanne Hiltz and Murray Turoff published *The Network Nation: Human Communication via Computer*, a work that attained prominence as an important statement of the prospects in this area. In it they described what they termed a 'computer conferencing system (CCS)', that 'uses the computer to structure, store, and process written communications among a group of persons. When something is entered through one terminal, it may be obtained on the recipients' terminals immediately or at any time in the future until it is purged from the computer's memory.'[118] They went on: '[w]hen such systems become widespread, potentially intense

[113] Ibid., p. 82.
[114] Ibid., pp. 82–4.
[115] Ibid., p. 85.
[116] Ibid., p. 94.
[117] Ibid., pp. 148–56.
[118] Hiltz and Turoff, *The Network Nation*, p. 7.

communication networks among geographically dispersed persons will become actualized'. Hiltz and Turoff foresaw that '[w]e will become the Network Nation, exchanging vast amounts of both information and social-emotional communications with colleagues, friends, and "strangers" who share similar interests, who are spread out all over the nation'. The outcome would be that 'as communication satellites and international packet switched networks reach out to other cities and villages around the world, these social networks facilitated by computer-mediated communications will become international'. In what was presumably a conscious echo of McLuhan, they predicted that 'we will become a "global village" whose boundaries are demarcated only by the political decisions of those governments that choose not to become part of an international computer network'.[119]

In their interpretation of the political uses of computing, Hiltz and Turoff subscribed firmly to the direct democratic school. For them, '[t]he most exciting and potentially revolutionary political application of a CC system is the facilitation of the direct participation and voting of citizens on important state or national issues'.[120] They also saw digital networks as dispersing power more fairly, widening participation, and facilitating collective action. Computer conferencing would make it easier for 'groups that do not participate as effectively in the political process as other groups that are smaller but better funded'. People who were previously more marginalised and who were 'interested in the same objective' would in theory be better able 'to find one another and to organize as a group'. The outcome might be 'a much more fluid situation with respect to political alignments. Needless to say, we do not understand all the implications for the political process of this potential for uniting like-minded people.'[121] There was a possibility for the formation of 'computer-linked community councils consisting of representatives of neighbourhoods, ethnic, or other groups'.[122]

Alongside the potential for electronic referendums and popular organisation, Hiltz and Turoff saw implications for the operation of the institutions of representative democracy. Different tiers of government would be able more readily to consult with members of the public,[123] who could obtain access to technical expertise to help them provide their contribution.[124] The authors noted that 'Congress now has an on-line system to inform its members of the status of pending legislation.' There was, furthermore, 'no reason why the *Congressional Record* could not be produced and distributed through such a data base, to provide same-day access to anyone with a terminal'.[125] Here they

[119] Ibid., p. xxv.
[120] Ibid., p. 195.
[121] Ibid., p. 198.
[122] Ibid.
[123] Ibid.
[124] Ibid., pp. 198–9.
[125] Ibid., p. 197.

foreshadowed the early functions of the UK parliamentary website, as we have seen. Computer conferencing might be a means by which elected representatives could liaise with staff and hold negotiations remotely. Again, it was hard to predict what the consequences of this shift might be. It might simply mean engaging in the same activities more effectively. The authors noted that '[u]ltimately, one could imagine legislative sessions being held through a computerized conference, particularly special sessions or emergency sessions called to deal with a specific issue'.[126] In 2020, such predictions proved prescient for legislatures around the world – including the UK Parliament – when they employed the Internet to support their continued functioning during the pandemic.

There were – as Hiltz and Turoff saw it – potential problems with 'the coming computer information-communication technologies', which brought with them a 'unique element for abuse'. In identifying drawbacks, they went beyond the possibility of restrictions on content and the violation of privacy that others had already detected, to consider the use of the network for more active inappropriate shaping of outcomes. In doing so, they anticipated more recent concerns about so-called 'fake news' or dis- and mis-information, and the potential for online foreign interference in political processes. The technology the authors envisaged would make it far easier, they held, 'to monitor activities and potentially to interfere with and attempt to direct them'. These systems raised the possibility that 'an unscrupulous person or organization' might be able 'to electronically "frame" a dissident', through generating 'a fake trail of electronic circumstantial evidence linking a person to a criminal act'. Abuse could take place on a transnational basis. The authors cited a conference paper from the previous year by Stewart Umelby warning that:

> [t]hree new technologies – computer networks, electronic newspaper typesetting machines, and covert propaganda operations – could converge in the future to produce a deleterious effect on the freedom and autonomy of the press. With 'paper' travelling at the speed of light, the writer or editor could be located half way around the globe without encountering significant delays in getting out a daily newspaper ... It offers the opportunity for interference in the press of other nations, particularly the developing countries [by making] it much easier for the intelligence agencies of large countries to coordinate propaganda themes and disinformation campaigns in other countries.[127]

Hiltz and Turoff saw potential for 'manipulation on an unprecedented scale'. Moreover, it was 'just one example of a potential application' for computer conferencing 'that could detrimentally affect the quality of life, if not

[126] Ibid., p. 199.

[127] Cited from Stuart A. Umpleby, 'A Potential Negative Secondary Effect of On-Line Intellectual Communities', Paper presented at a workshop on On-Line Intellectual Communities, Soc. for General Systems Research (Denver: Colorado, 1977). Hiltz and Turoff, *The Network Nation*, p. 446.

prevented by policy decisions and legal safeguards'.[128] Nonetheless, along with this downside they stressed that 'computer-based communications can be used to make human lives richer and freer, by enabling persons to have access to vast stores of information, other "human resources," and opportunities for work and socializing on a more flexible, cheaper, and convenient basis than ever before'. This prospect comprised what they labelled 'a Network Nation'. But were careful regulation not formulated, the technologies might 'become the basis for a totalitarian network of control much more comprehensive and efficient than any that has ever been developed'.[129]

Jacques Vallee published *The Network Revolution: Confessions of a Computer Scientist* in 1982. It contained another version of the thesis that computing – 'the most powerful force changing human society today' – in networked form would be a vehicle '[o]ver the next generation' either for immense individual empowerment or great oppression.[130] Vallee discerned two possible futures. The first was a 'Digital Society' in which 'massive amounts of computer technology are used to control people by reducing them to statistics. In the Digital Society, computers would be repressive tools and their use for private communication discouraged'.[131] Vallee feared that '[w]e might even end up living in some version of the world describer by Forster in "The Machine Stops": his characters spend their entire lives in little cells underground supported by every imaginable form of communications, controlled and regulated by numbers'.[132] In such a system 'our civilization would become nothing more than a giant, clean, well-ordered Disney World, where Presidents, activated by invisible machines, get up and make predictable speeches before well-behaved children whose every possible move has been anticipated'.[133] (It seems Vallee did not foresee the phenomenon of a President heavily deploying digital communications technology who made a virtue of volatility in public pronouncements, prompting disorderly behaviour among members of the public.)

The second scenario was 'the Grapevine Alternative'. In presenting this optimistic version of the future he referred to the employment 'of computer networks for group communication'. Presumably referring to the Internet, he described this practice as 'a dynamic force that began in obscure research organizations ten years ago'. It would be possible for mass users to 'discover in these networks gateways to other minds, windows to unsuspected vistas, bridges across their loneliness, and precious understanding'.[134] This use of

[128] Hiltz and Turoff, *The Network Nation*, p. 446.
[129] Ibid., pp. 447–8.
[130] Jacques Vallee, *The Network Revolution: Confessions of a Computer Scientist* (And/Or Press, Berkeley, 1982), p. 4.
[131] Ibid., pp. 4–5.
[132] Ibid., p. 38.
[133] Ibid., p. 42.
[134] Ibid., pp. 4–5.

technology could enable society to take on 'the beautiful distribution of tension realized in the dome'. In a reference to the famous product associated with Fuller, Vallee advocated '[a] geodesic organization' that 'would demand an information system that could instantly tie together all its segments when a collective decision was required'. It would not operate 'in the sense of a broadcast or a mass rally, where masses of people are at the receiving end of a giant, one-way channel'. Nor would it function 'in the sense of voice or television conferencing, which demands the simultaneous presence of the parties at a few designated sites'. Rather, 'the geodesic structure requires an information medium in which participants can join the dialogue at any time, and in which past statements are not lost as the interaction progresses'. Vallee held that '[c]omputer conferencing is a first step towards the creation of such a medium: a revolutionary network where each node is equal in power to all the others'.[135]

It is notable that – for Vallee – there was a dichotomy between the use of computers for 'private communication' and their employment as 'repressive tools', 'reducing' the individual 'to statistics'. In contrast, more recent concerns about the Internet have depicted 'private' online activities, when monitored by corporations such as Google and Facebook (alongside other entities such as domestic or foreign intelligence agencies), as in themselves the very basis for 'reducing' people 'to statistics' – or big data, employed for purposes of predictive analytics. Vallee regarded 'group communication' systems as the route to personal empowerment and a balanced distribution of power within society. But some more recent analysis has depicted the actual outcome of such technology as being in practice to produce the opposite results, with concentrations of manipulative power.

Some found the idea that networked computers might be a force for democratisation dubious. In 1984, Langdon Winner, deliberately recalling Marx and Engels in the *Communist Manifesto*, described how '[a] specter is haunting modern society – the specter of computer revolution'. He recounted how '[c]ountless books, magazine articles, and news-media specials declare that this upheaval is underway' and 'that nothing will escape unchanged'. Benefits projected by 'the visionaries' included that 'existing differences between rich and poor' and between 'advantaged and disadvantaged, will begin to evaporate. Widespread access to computers will produce a society more democratic, egalitarian. and richly diverse than any previously known.' Furthermore, '[b]ecause "knowledge is power"' and 'because electronic information will spread knowledge into every corner of world society, political influence will be more widely shared'. The 'personal computer' according to such theses would serve 'as the great equalizer', and 'rule by centralized authority and entrenched social elites will gradually fade'. Ultimately '[t]he

[135] Ibid., p. 198.

marvelous promise of a "global village" will be fulfilled in a worldwide burst of human creativity'.[136]

As we have seen, some of those who promoted optimistic views about networked computers often balanced them with cautionary content for which this description of such views does not allow. But while there might have been a degree of caricature in the account Winner presented, he nonetheless identified generally existing strands of opinion. He presented the views he had described as amounting to what he labelled 'mythinformation: the almost religious conviction that a widespread adoption of computers and communications systems and broad access to electronic information will automatically produce a better world for humanity. It is a peculiar form of enthusiasm that characterizes social fashions of the later decades of the twentieth century.'[137] Winner recognised that '[i]t is not uncommon for the advent of a new technology to provide an occasion for flights of utopian fancy'. He recounted how, '[d]uring the last two centuries the factory system, railroads, the telephone, electricity, automobiles, airplanes, radio, television, and nuclear power have all figured prominently in the belief that a new and glorious age was about to begin'.[138]

Winner took the view that, as was often the case with powerful mythology, the enthusiasm for computers he identified had some basis in reality. But while 'computer and telecommunications systems' might be used to facilitate 'participatory democracy, decentralized control, and social equality', the technology could not facilitate such outcomes in itself, which would require wider changes.[139] A more likely scenario was one in which those who were already in an advantageous position would utilise these devices further to consolidate and strengthen their status.[140] Winner questioned in particular whether there was a genuine problem of a lack of information, whether information was synonymous with knowledge, whether possession of knowledge equated with having power, and whether enhancing the ability of people to acquire information would be democratically beneficial.[141] He regarded 'mythinformation' as an ideology that reflected primarily the interests of those involved in the production of the technologies involved.[142]

The Counterculture and Networked Computers

From the 1960s onwards, then, there was much consideration of the socially transformative potential of electronic communications technology, including

[136] Langdon Winner, 'Mythinformation in the High-Tech Era', *Bulletin of Science, Technology & Society* 4(6) (1984): 582–96, 582–3.
[137] Ibid., p. 585.
[138] Ibid.
[139] Ibid., p. 587.
[140] Ibid., pp. 586–7.
[141] Ibid., p. 588.
[142] Ibid., p. 593.

its political and democratic implications. Some of it included reference to the use of computers, possibly as part of networks, and even the embryonic internet (though not necessarily named precisely). Special impetus for interest in these particular technologies derived from social trends of the era. A consideration of this tendency demonstrates the importance of the relationship between – on the one hand – the development and uses of technology and – on the other hand – wider changes in patterns of behaviour and thought. Chapter 1 noted that accounts of enthusiasm about the Internet and its supposedly democratic potential in more recent decades have attributed them to a significant extent to the influence of the so-called 'counterculture' that originated in the 1960s. It is now appropriate to examine this proposition and its significance more closely. In doing so, I treat the loose concept of the counterculture as embodying a tendency occurring in the United States and internationally, especially in the 1960s and 1970s, with a strong youth component. It entailed the conscious challenging of established social structures and values, through such means as the adoption of unorthodox lifestyles or direct political action.

The development of the counterculture occurred roughly in parallel to key processes of technological advance leading to what became the Internet as later understood. But on the surface, as the historian Fred Turner has observed, though they were contemporaneous, the cross-pollination that came about between the two phenomena was far from inevitable. Indeed, they have been interpreted as in tension with one another.[143] From the vantage point of the early 1990s, two commentators – noting the contemporaneous development of the computer and the counterculture in the 1960s – described the 'hippie movement' as characterised by 'a bitter technophobia' alongside 'a wide-spread interest in mysticism, drugs, Eastern cults, astrology, and off-brand religion'.[144] Computing had associations with the US military, with strict social organisation, and with domination by a single, hierarchical and centralised corporation, IBM, 'a high tech colossus that stood astride the world, suave, aloof, and imperial'.[145] In late 1964, the student protester Mario Savio, a leader of the Berkeley Free Speech movement, famously attacked the 'operation of the machine' – by which he meant manifestations of social authority – and called for those who opposed it to 'put your bodies upon the gears and upon the wheels' in order 'to make it stop'. In an interview with *Life* magazine the following year, Savio gave an idea of how this perspective might lead to a negative perception of

[143] Fred Turner, *From Counterculture to Cyberculture: Stewart Brand, the Whole Earth Network, and the Rise of Digital Utopianism* (University of Chicago Press, 2008), Introduction.

[144] Heidi and Alvin Toffler writing as Alvin Toffler, *Powershift* (Bantam, London, 1991), p. 365.

[145] Theodore Roszak, *The Cult of Information: A Neo-Luddite Treatise on High-Tech, Artificial Intelligence, and the True Art of Thinking* (Berkeley, University of California Press, 1994), pp. 136–7.

digital technology. He complained of a system in which 'you're little more than an IBM card'.[146]

Further analysts identified direct tension between the counterculture and scientific advance, including the fields of communications and computers. Lewis Mumford, who we encountered in Chapter 3, is an important linking figure in this work. Over a period of more than four decades he consciously operated within an intellectual tradition concerned with the connection between technology and social improvement that dated back at least as far as Robert Owen in the early nineteenth century.[147] He had, in 1934, urged caution about the political impact of possible future devices; a position he reasserted decades later. In his 1970 work, *The Myth of the Machine: The Pentagon of Power*, Mumford reserved special criticism for McLuhan, and his insistence on 'treating the planet as a "tribal village"' achieved 'by instant electronic communication'. He feared instead a conjunction that 'united the crippling limitations of a pre-literate culture, which made the scattered, farming population of the world an easy prey to military conquest and exploitation, with the characteristic historic mischief of "civilization": the subjugation of a large population for the exclusive benefit of a ruling minority'.[148]

The misgivings Mumford expressed about technological prospects extended to the computer. He presented this device as 'an attempt to exercise control, not only of the mechanical process itself, but of the human being who once directed it: turning him from an active to a passive agent, and finally eliminating him altogether'.[149] For him, 'the most serious threat of computer-controlled automation' was not 'the displacement of the worker in the process of manufacture' but 'the displacement of the human mind and the insidious undermining of confidence in its ability to make individual judgements that run contrary to the system – or that proceed outside the system'.[150] Mumford placed the social unrest of his time in this context. For him, 'the increasing number of mass protests, sit-downs, and riots – physical acts rather than words' could be construed as 'an attempt to break through the automatic insulation of the megamachine, with its tendency to cover up its own errors, to refuse unwelcome messages, or to block transmission of information damaging to the system itself.' He saw '[s]mashed windows, burning buildings, broken heads' as a way of restoring 'two-way communication and reciprocal intercourse'.[151] Computers were, in this analysis, a blockage to rather than a

[146] Jack Fincher, 'The University Has Become a Factory', *Life*, 26 February 1965, pp. 100–1. See Turner, *From Counterculture to Cyberculture*, Introduction.

[147] See e.g. Lewis Mumford, *The Culture of Cities* (Secker & Warburg, London, 1938, 1946 reprint), pp. 9–10, 392–3.

[148] Lewis Mumford, *The Myth of the Machine: The Pentagon of Power* (New York, Harcourt Brace Jovanovich, 1970), pp. 297–9.

[149] Ibid., p. 189.

[150] Ibid., p. 192.

[151] Ibid., p. 183.

means of conducting such interaction. Mumford called for 'a profound reorientation of our vaunted technological "way of life"' that would 'replace the mechanical world picture with an organic world picture'.[152]

Theodore Roszak, a historian who popularised the term 'counterculture' (though at this stage treating it as two separate words) had similarly depicted this tendency as a reaction to scientific development. He did so the previous year in a work with the self-explanatory title: *The Making of a Counter Culture: Reflections on the Technocratic Society and Its Youthful Opposition.* Roszak discussed 'the interests of our college-age and adolescent young in the psychology of alienation, oriental mysticism, psychedelic drugs, and communication experiments'. For him, these individuals made up 'a cultural constellation that radically diverges from values and assumptions that have been in the mainstream of our society at least since the Scientific Revolution of the seventeenth century'.[153] Roszak saw this youthful group as the final line of resistance against 'a technocratic totalitarianism'[154] of which the computer was a component factor.[155] He judged that: '[i]f the resistance of the counter culture fails, I think there will be nothing in store for us but what anti-utopians like Huxley and Orwell have forecast'.[156]

As we have seen, Roszak would later present a revised view of this relationship, depicting digital technology as a potential vehicle – rather than simply a target – for the movement. Other assessments of the counterculture would depict it as prone to utilising science and invention in accordance with human values, rather than simply rejecting it. In a widely read book that appeared in 1970 in the United States and in the UK the following year, *The Greening of America*, the Yale legal academic, Charles Reich, insisted '[t]here is a revolution coming'. It would be of a peaceful kind. In the vanguard would be 'the new generation' with '[t]heir protest and rebellion, their culture, clothes, music, drugs, ways of thought and liberated life-style'.[157] For Reich, a transition to a new consciousness of historic significance approached. It involved movement away from an order that subordinated 'man's nature to his role in the economic system' and facilitated 'the domination of environment by technology'.[158] The coming mode of being, by contrast, 'seeks restoration of the non-material elements of man's existence'. But '[i]t is by no means anti-technological, it does not want to break machines, but it does not want machines to run men. It makes the wholly rational assertion that machines

[152] Ibid., p. 413.
[153] Theodore Roszak, *The Making of a Counter Culture: Reflections on the Technocratic Society and Its Youthful Opposition* (Garden City, Anchor Books, 1969), p. xii.
[154] Ibid., p. xiii.
[155] Ibid., pp. 287–9.
[156] Ibid., p. xiii.
[157] Charles A. Reich, *The Greening of America* (Allen Lane, London, 1971), p. 1.
[158] Ibid., p. 258.

should do the bidding of man, of man who knows and respects his own nature and the natural order of which he is a part.'[159]

The counterculture, as Mumford and Roszak (at first) observed it, was a forceful and negative response to a system within which technology was the defining component. Yet a strand that developed within this movement hoped to utilise invention, for different purposes (as Reich suggested). The following discussion focuses on the United States, since it was there that the precise collision between social upheaval and the emerging internet technology occurred. But the general attitudes outlined could reveal themselves elsewhere, as in France, where violent unrest centring on student protests broke out in May 1968. Impetus for this revolt came partly from the Situationists, an artistic-political grouping. The most prominent figure within this school was Guy Debord, author of the 1967 book *Society of the Spectacle*. The ideas he presented here find an echo in more recent times, for instance in the work of Shoshana Zuboff, with her portrayal of the Internet as a vehicle for social subordination and intensified economic exploitation. Debord presented electronic media as means of manipulative oppression, that he collectively labelled the 'spectacle'. He defined the 'spectacle' as 'not a collection of images' but 'a social relation between people that is mediated by images'.[160] Debord defined the 'particular manifestations' of the spectacle as 'news, propaganda, advertising, entertainment'.[161] For Debord, the centralised nature of the mass media was a critical aspect of their make-up. He argued that '[t]he concentration of these media . . . amounts to concentrating in the hands of the administrators of the existing system the means that enable them to carry on this particular form of administration'.[162]

But Debord suggested elsewhere (in the 1960 'Situationist Manifesto') that these channels could be utilised for different ends. Their very centralisation made them vulnerable to a single act of revolutionary seizure. Through perpetrating such an act, Debord explained, the Situationists could bring about a 'new culture' involving 'total participation . . . collective participation . . . everyone will become an artist . . . a producer–consumer of total culture creation'.[163] Participants in the 1968 Paris uprising shared some of this attitude and prioritised seizing control of and utilising broadcasters in the city. In the years following these events, the political forces connected to them found an outlet in France through the alternative media movement, publishing their own journals and employing other technologies. Eventually they were able to utilise Minitel, the government-initiated project launched in the early

159 Ibid., p. 259.
160 Guy Debord, *Society of the Spectacle* (Rebel Press, London, 1994), p. 7.
161 Ibid., p. 8.
162 Ibid., p. 13.
163 Guy Debord, 'Situationist Manifesto (1960)', Alex Danchev (ed.), *100 Artists' Manifestos: From the Futurists to the Stuckists* (Penguin, London, 2011), M70.

1980s that provided France with an electronic communications and information network in a pre-mass internet era.[164]

An optimistic countercultural attitude towards technology could apply specifically to computers. 'Machines of Loving Grace', a poem by Richard Brautigan published in 1967, captured this possibility. Brautigan conveyed images such as 'a cybernetic meadow', in which 'mammals and computers live together in mutually programming harmony'; and 'a cybernetic ecology', in which people 'free of our labours' can be 'joined back to nature' and exist alongside other mammals, 'all watched over by machines of loving grace'. Roszak himself would come to observe, from the standpoint of the 1980s, an important intersection between countercultural tendencies and the development of the computer industry. He noted that the idea of employing technology to access 'the ancient, the primitive, the tribal'[165] had always underpinned the movement – whether through electronic production of music or the use of LSD, 'itself a technology, a laboratory product'.[166] Roszak recounted a narrative that is now common in the literature. Its outline is that, as early as the late 1950s, a so-called 'hacker' culture developed around computer science (the term 'hacker' initially applied to someone for whom computing embodied an approach to life, rather than – as it later came to imply – a specialist in obtaining illicit access to digital systems).[167] Groups of people working in the field came to form an ethos which ran counter to the more orderly reputation of the sector in which they operated. Then, from the 1960s onwards, the counterculture began to emerge in its various manifestations, some of which intersected with computing. There was a geographical aspect to this association: California became both a focus for the new social movement, and global centre for the digital technology. Within it, the same educational institution – for instance, Stanford – could be the site of anti-military protests and of defence-funded computer research.[168]

Depictions of the career of one particular person, Stewart Brand, have come to serve as an emblem of the pattern of interaction between these two spheres.[169] Brand was active at the core of the 1960s counterculture, even featuring in the opening pages of *The Electric Kool-Aid Acid Test*. This 1968 book by the journalist Tom Wolfe describes the expedition that the novelist Ken Kesey made across the United States with his group of 'Merry Pranksters'. It describes 'Stuart Brand, a thin blond guy with a blazing disc on his forehead . . . and a whole necktie made of Indian beads. No shirt however,

[164] Barbrook, *Media Freedom*, pp. 91–114, 180–2.
[165] Roszak, *The Cult of Information*, p. 152.
[166] Ibid., p. 151.
[167] See Steven Levy, *Hackers: Heroes of the Computer Revolution* (O'Reilly, Beijing, 2010), esp. ch. 2.
[168] Markoff, *What the Dormouse Said*, pp. 171–4.
[169] See e.g. Martin Moore, *Democracy Hacked: Political Turmoil and Information Warfare in the Digital Age* (Oneworld, London, 2018), ch. 1.

just an Indian bead necktie on bare skin and a white butcher's coat with medals from the King of Sweden on it.'[170] In 1968 Brand began publishing the hugely successful *Whole Earth Catalog*, containing lists of equipment chosen for being of potential use to the growing number of people taking part in communal living projects at the time. Roszack has written that, '[f]or the most part, the *Catolog* featured the wares of simple living and rustic ways'. Yet, from the outset, 'it had also been fascinated with certain forms of high tech: stereo systems, cameras, synthesisers, and, as early as its first issue, computers. The *Catolog* was, above all, inspired by the work of Buckminster Fuller, the maverick engineer who had patented the geodesic dome.'[171]

Also in 1968, Brand helped stage arguably the most important demonstration event in the history of computing. This occasion in San Francisco saw the first appearance of a number of inventions – including the mouse, windows, links, and graphics – that would subsequently become indispensable components of the technology. They were the outputs of the Augment project led by Douglas Engelbart, who sought to utilise science to expand human potential.[172] Brand demonstrated a sustained ability to participate in notable episodes in the development of computing and the Internet. For instance, he co-initiated a relatively early experiment in online social networking in 1985, called the WELL (Whole Earth 'Lectronic Link). Along with *Whole Earth Catalog* colleagues he was also involved, at the point of its inception in 1993, with *Wired* magazine, a publication with a focus on new technology that took special interest in the Internet.[173]

Beyond the focus on Brand, wider patterns are discernible. Pioneers in the field of computer technology – such as Engelbart – came into contact with participants in the counterculture to whom their ideas could have an appeal. Another figure whose views chimed with radical perspectives of the 1960s onwards was Ted Nelson. Berners-Lee describes how Nelson, 'a professional visionary, wrote in 1965 of "Literary Machines", computers that would enable people to write and publish in a new, nonlinear format, which he called *hypertext*'. This concept was intended to ensure 'a reader was not constrained to read in any particular order, but could follow links and delve into the original document from a short quotation'. Nelson, Berners-Lee went on, 'described the futuristic project, Xanadu, in which all the world's information could be published ... He had the dream of a utopian society in which all information could be shared among people who communicate as equals.'[174]

Participants in the counterculture initiated an early effort to facilitate the use of computing for social networking purposes, the so-called Community

[170] Tom Wolfe, *The Electric Kool-Aid Acid Test* (Black Swan, London, 1989), p. 8.
[171] Roszak, *The Cult of Information*, p. 143.
[172] Markoff, *What the Dormouse Said*, pp. 148–78.
[173] Turner, *From Counterculture to Cyberculture*, chs. 5 and 7.
[174] Tim Berners-Lee, *Weaving the Web: The Past, Present and Future of the World Wide Web by Its Inventor* (Orion, London, 1999), pp. 5–6.

Memory project. Operating in the Bay Area from 1973, its express motive was a desire to democratise the dissemination of information. In place of the one-way communication of predetermined content from above that television news services offered, it encouraged horizontal sharing of material chosen by those taking part. Community Memory replicated the bulletin board in electronic form, with members of the public able to post on subjects of their own choosing using networked terminals. The first such device was located in Berkeley, California, at the Leopold's Records shop. The 'founders ... were all involved, to varying degrees, in the Free Speech Movement at the University of California, Berkeley, protests of U.S. intervention in Southeast Asia, and countercultural movements in general'. Finally ceasing to operate in 1992, Community Memory is acknowledged as a precursor to the contemporary Internet and features of it such as social media.[175]

Lee Felsenstein, a Berkeley computer graduate, was a key player in the 'Community Memory' project. He provides a good illustration of the trajectory of countercultural activist into pioneer of personal digital technology. Brand described in 1995 how 'Lee Felsenstein, who designed the first portable computer, known as the Osborne 1, was a New Left radical who wrote for the renowned underground paper the *Berkeley Barb*.'[176] Felsenstein recollected in 1993 that his purpose in participating in Community Memory was to reverse a process of centralisation in the electronic media. The existing system, as he perceived it, entailed uniform messages being disseminated outwards, and people no longer being able to communicate with each other in a localised environment or 'agora'. During the 1960s he had hoped that the goal of 're-establishing functioning communities could be served by the newly established "underground press"'. However, he then formed the view that 'the structure of that medium' shaped 'its economics and thereby its content'. Nor did he feel that 'broadcast media' were suited to supporting 'the cause of decentralization of power within society'. Then in 1970 Felsenstein became aware of 'mainframe-based network computing'. His introduction to this technology 'alerted me to the fact that such a network had no geographical restrictions and that information items could be made accessible to variously defined groups of users'. He formed the firm view 'that through computer networks it would be possible to support the information needs of an overlapping set of communities of interest'. With the launch of Community Memory, 'an agora appeared, with an unknowable number of different needs, desires, suggestions, proposals, offers, statements, poems and declarations cropping up'.[177]

175 Bo Doub, 'Community Memory: Precedents in Social Media and Movements', *Computer History Museum*, 23 February 2016, available at: https://computerhistory.org/blog/community-memory-precedents-in-social-media-and-movements/?key=community-memory-precedents-in-social-media-and-movements, last accessed 24 May 2020.

176 Stewart Brand, 'We Owe It All to the Hippies', *Time Magazine* 145(12) (1 March 1995).

177 Lee Felsenstein, 'The Commons of Information', May 1993, available at: http://besser.tsoa.nyu.edu/impact/s94/speakers/felsenstein/felsenstein-article.html, last accessed 4 June 2020.

Felsenstein was also co-founder in 1975 of the 'Homebrew Computer Club'. Attended by enthusiasts in the San Francisco Bay Area, an underlying ethos of the club was the idea that, rather than being hugely expensive and useable only by experts working for government or large corporations, the machines should be affordable, widely available and accessible to the public, disseminating their potential benefits. Among its members were people who would become in the future prominent figures within the industry.[178] They included Steve Wozniak and Steve Jobs of Apple; and the first demonstration of the Apple-1computer, launched in 1976, took place at the club.[179] The connection with Apple is a reminder of the cycle of technological perception that would play out once again in relation to computers. A collection of individuals who saw themselves as challengers to an established system sought to find new approaches that would overcome problems associated with that existing order. Yet in time some among their number would come to be regarded as part of a new power elite, generating difficulties of its own. By the end of the second decade of the twenty-first century, Apple – as we have seen – was identified by critical observers as one of a small number of monopolistic and exploitative global technology companies. Moreover, by this time, the personal aurora surrounding the late Jobs had begun to fade. For instance, the central character in the *Mr. Robot* television series – a rebellious hacker figure – complains in the first episode, from 2015, that 'we collectively thought Steve Jobs was a great man even when we knew he made billions off the backs of children'.

Links between the counterculture and ideologies of computer technology continued into the era of internet ascendancy. John Perry Barlow, whose 'A Declaration of the Independence of Cyberspace' we encountered in Chapter 1, is a further example of an advocate of the Internet as vehicle for personal empowerment who possessed firm countercultural credentials. A lyricist for the Grateful Dead, a psychedelic San Francisco Bay Area band, from the early 1970s onwards, Barlow joined the WELL, in which many associates of the Grateful Dead participated, in 1986. In 1990, Barlow became co-founder of the Electronic Frontier Foundation, an organisation campaigning for the protection of rights in the context of emerging technologies, bringing legal cases over such matters as the privacy of electronic mail.[180]

The approach to computing and the Internet was an appropriate extension of a tendency characteristic of the counterculture: a desire to create a different reality, whether through such means as political protest, fashion choices, artistic expression and consumption, communal living, or drug use. But how, precisely, should we interpret the attraction to digital technology?

[178] For Homebrew, see Markoff, *What the Dormouse Said*, pp. 275–82.

[179] For background impressions of Jobs and Wozniak, see Brand, 'We Owe It All to the Hippies'. For Homebrew and Apple, see Roszak, *The Cult of Information*, p. 142.

[180] 'A History of Protecting Freedom Where Law and Technology Collide', *Electronic Frontier Foundation*, available at: www.eff.org/about/history, last accessed 24 May 2020.

Though many of his observations are astute, Roszack reaches a faulty conclusion regarding the originality of the philosophical standpoint of this particular subgroup within counterculture. As discussed in the Introduction to this book, he divides '[u]topian visions of the future ... between two philosophical camps'. They were 'the *reversionary* scenario' – one of 'wishing the world away' into which Roszack placed William Morris. The other type of utopian Roszack discerned was the technophile, who 'enthusiastically embraced the urban-industrial system'. He found among their number both Francis Bacon and H. G. Wells. Roszack claimed that the vision of 'the guerrilla hackers' was 'unique in its determination to synthesize these two seemingly contradictory images. They wanted to have it both ways.' While their 'tastes and talents' inclined them towards 'the expansion of high tech', they wanted it to be 'contained within an organic and communitarian political context'.[181]

We have already seen that Morris had a more sophisticated attitude towards technology than the 'wishing the world away' label might suggest; and Bacon and Wells, though certainly more enthusiastic than Morris, perceived potential problems with scientific invention and a need for careful regulation of its use. Furthermore, in their intention that 'new technology would be contained within an organic and communitarian political context' computer and internet enthusiasts from within the counterculture were not 'unique' in the way Roszak suggests. Morris, among many others discussed in the previous chapter, provided a model for this outlook. While contrasting views of the value of technology were possible, the firm division into two camps that Roszak proposed is difficult to sustain. Long before the appearance of the counterculture, syntheses were attempted.

Examples of a nuanced approach can be found in the work of two authors who exerted visible influence on the broad movement of which Roszak was an analyst. Both Herman Hesse and Aldous Huxley achieved an impact that continued after their deaths (respectively in 1962 and 1963) an indicator of which is found in musical groups of countercultural association taking names from the titles of their works. Steppenwolf drew on a 1927 Hesse novel,[182] while the name of The Doors came from a 1954 Huxley essay (which itself drew on William Blake), *The Doors of Perception*. Huxley also appeared – in 1967 – on the cover of *Sgt Pepper's Lonely Hearts Club Band* by The Beatles. (Huxley was in between Robert Peel and Dylan Thomas. Among the other cultural figures whom The Beatles featured in the artwork, both considered in this book, were Karl Marx and H. G. Wells.)

In *Steppenwolf* Hesse presented a complex discussion of the social role of radio, then a new medium, that is neither unquestioningly positive nor wholly condemnatory. In a fantasy sequence, Mozart – depicted 'assembling ... a

[181] Roszak, *The Cult of Information*, p. 146.

[182] David Horrocks, 'Translator's Afterword' to Herman Hesse, *Steppenwolf* (Penguin, London, 2012), p. 241.

wireless set' on which he then listens to a broadcast of a composition by Handel – tells the narrator, '[y]ou must learn to listen to life's damned radio music, to respect the spirit that lies behind it while laughing at all the dross it contains'.[183] But it is Huxley who expanded his attitude towards technology into a fuller philosophical perspective that (whether they were aware of the similarities with Huxley or not) supporters of the deployment of science for countercultural ends would echo.

Perhaps second only to Orwell in impact, through *Brave New World* Huxley had created in 1932 a work that exemplified the nightmarish society, in which technology played a facilitating role. In his 1958 *Brave New World Revisited*, he expressed the view that mass electronic media, combined with developing psychological techniques, were creating expanded possibilities for manipulation of the public. As he put it: '[s]ince Hitler's day the armoury of technical devices at the disposal of the would-be dictator has been considerably enlarged'. Alongside 'the radio, the loud-speaker, [and] the moving picture camera', it was now possible to utilise television. Paying tribute to the late Orwell, he warned that 'Big Brother can now be almost as omnipresent as God.'[184] In this respect Huxley was part of the pessimistic school of the post-Second World War era, which he had to some extent anticipated. But there was another side to Huxley. In a 1946 foreword to a reissue of *Brave New World* he expressed regret that in it he had only presented a binary choice between a society in which technology dominated, or one from which it was largely excluded. Were he writing the book again, he would have constructed a third variant, a system of co-operation and dispersed political power, in which science was harnessed for human ends.[185] In his 1954 work *The Doors of Perception* and its 1956 follow-up *Heaven and Hell* (this title also being taken from Blake), drawing on his experiences with the use of hallucinogenic substances, he considered the connection between chemical processes and consciousness.[186] Finally, with *Island*, a novel published in 1962, Huxley depicted an ideal community which utilises technology, but only in so far as it supports the purposes of a harmonious polity.[187]

Huxley not only influenced the counterculture, but his work demonstrated that, in its approach to scientific advance, including computing, rather than being wholly original, it was part of a tradition. Like many before them, participants in this movement saw invention as a means to a better society, potentially through correcting problems that were themselves connected with technology, which needed to be applied differently, or supplanted. Again following in an established pattern, they pursued this end both by practical

[183] For discussion of Hesse in this context, see ibid., p. 257. See the novel proper, pp. 231 and 236.
[184] Huxley, *Brave New World Revisited*, ch. 5.
[185] Aldous Huxley, *Brave New World* (Vintage, London, 2007), 'Foreword', 1946.
[186] Aldous Huxley, *The Doors of Perception: And Heaven and Hell* (Vintage, London, 2004).
[187] Aldous Huxley, *Island* (Chatto and Windus, London, 1975), e.g. p. 154.

action and by exposition. In earlier periods, among other artefacts, novels served as repositories of cultural perspectives; so it was for the counterculture. An example of this tendency is *Ecotopia* by Ernest Callenbach, which appeared in 1975. Set in the then-future of the late twentieth century, it provides an account of a West Coast US breakaway state, the name of which is the title of the work. Nearly four decades later, in a 2014 foreword to a new edition, Malcolm Margolin, a friend and colleague of Callenbach, described how on rereading it 'I . . . see the Berkeley of the 1960s and early 1970s, a seedbed of innovation and radical thinking.'[188] The Ecotopian system is organised around principles of environmental sustainability. The population has dispersed away from more concentrated cities; and political power, too, is decentralised, with women playing prominent roles. Black separatism has led to the formation of separate city states. Communications technology facilitates the broadcasting of the proceedings of elected representatives and the dissemination of information via 'electronic print-out terminals'.[189] (Another novel that appeared in the same year, *The Shockwave Rider* by John Brunner, depicted the future use of networked computers, including for mass consultation on decisions through '[t]hree hundred million people with access to the integrated North American data-net'.[190])

Ecotopia provides insight into the way in which countercultural attitudes led to prescriptions for social transformation which science could help facilitate. This tendency helped drive the development of technology and formulate perceptions of the uses to which it could be put. It was in these respects significant to the rise and application of the Internet, and in particular the idea that it was in some way of a democratising, even revolutionary character. An extension of this desire to employ technology for a changed world was the concept that a technology could create a plane of existence, removed from the physical, upon which a social order might form. Chapter 1 discussed the potency of such images of the Internet (or related concepts) in the period from 1990. Here was another aspect of the technology and its conception, the roots of which were partly countercultural. In particular, commentators have argued that online initiatives such as the WELL acted as the electronic equivalent of the physical commune movement of the 1960s: offering open spaces for the formation of experimental, free societies operating according to self-defined rules.[191] Evidence of this outlook is discernible, for instance, in 'A Declaration of the Independence of Cyberspace', which Barlow, whose countercultural credentials we have previously considered, produced in 1996. In this text, discussed in Chapter 1, he presented the idea of a 'global social space'.

188 Malcolm Margolin, 'Foreword', Ernest Callenbach, *Ecotopia* (Banyan Tree/Heyday, Berkeley, 2014), p. iv.

189 See e.g. Callenbach, *Ecotopia*, pp. 16–21, 24, 83–9, 98, 39, 111.

190 John Brunner, *The Shockwave Rider* (Del Rey, London, 1995), Bk 1.

191 See e.g. Moore, *Democracy Hacked*, ch. 1; Turner, *From Counterculture to Cyberculture*, Introduction.

The 'Declaration' described efforts at legal regulation as 'erecting guard posts at the frontiers of Cyberspace'. Rather than governmental regulation, participants in this environment hoped that 'from ethics, enlightened self-interest, and the commonweal, our governance will emerge'. They sought to construct a 'world' that was 'more humane and fair' than that brought into being by the conventional governments to which the text was addressed.

Once more, however, it is necessary not only to recognise the undoubted significance of the counterculture, but also to qualify it. Traces of the idea of a technologically generated reality, as already discussed, can be found in the ideas of McLuhan, who influenced participants in the countercultural movement, but predated and was not directly part of it. Another influence on the idea of a computer network as a universe was the growing use of commercial video games, which could make the idea of an electronic world easier to accept. Seeking to capitalise on the popularity of this medium, the 1982 Steven Lisberger film *Tron* portrayed a human transported into a video game reality, battling against a villainous sentient 'Master Control Program'. With his futuristic novel, *Neuromancer*, published in 1984, William Gibson popularised the concept of 'cyberspace'. A 'matrix' into which users, employing specific equipment, could insert their consciousness, the work described cyberspace as '[a] consensual hallucination experienced daily by billions of . . . operators . . . A graphic representation of data abstracted from the banks of every computer in the human system.'[192] Gibson came from a background that might be deemed countercultural. He has described how in 1967 he moved to Canada to avoid fighting in Vietnam, were he drafted, and partook of the associated lifestyle. Later, a direct influence on *Neuromancer* came when he saw a poster for an Apple personal computer, a company the founders of which had their roots in the Homebrew Computer Club, as we have discussed. But Gibson was not a prime mover in the counterculture, and seems not to have been especially ideological in his approach to it.[193] A key influence on *Neuromancer* was the same that inspired *Tron*. The 'matrix' upon which cyberspace rests, the Gibson novel explains, had 'its roots in primitive arcade games'.[194]

This chapter has shown that we can trace continuous patterns of thought about technology, communications and society, with a strong political strand, already clearly observable in the 1960s, continuing into the period of internet pre-eminence. They included both more and less optimistic interpretations, with many commentators combining elements of both in their analysis. Devices such as radio, television, and then cable figured in discussion, but computers began to feature increasingly from the 1960s, including the idea

192 William Gibson, *Neuromancer* (Gollancz, London, 2016), ch. 3.

193 Tim Adams, 'Space to Think', *The Guardian*, 12 August 2007, available at: www.theguardian.com/books/2007/aug/12/sciencefictionfantasyandhorror.features, last accessed 25 May 2020.

194 Gibson, *Neuromancer*, ch. 3.

that they might form part of networks for the transmission of information, and for interactive dialogue in which the audience became participants. It was a debate in which North Americans were prominent, but there were other contributors – including from the UK. More than simply recipients and recyclers of ideas, writers from the UK – perhaps most notably Orwell – but also Forster, Huxley, (Mary) Shelley, and Wells – helped create the very framework within which such discussion took place. What can broadly be classed as the counterculture, though it contained anti-technocratic aspects within it, was important to developing the idea and practice of computer-based communications as a means of personal empowerment. But the contribution this movement made needs to be located in a context longer and broader than itself.

In the discourse considered in this chapter, various themes and some of the people promoting them were remarkably persistent. They frequently linked new inventions with challenges to existing political methods and structures. There might be a direct democratic component to them, or perceived implications for the operation of representative institutions. Both considerations were relevant from the point of view of a body such as the UK Parliament, since they might threaten to bypass it, or lead to changes in the way it functions. To establish the continuity of such ideas that ran through the period and on into the mass internet era, it is worth considering the output of Heidi and Alvin Toffler. They provide a link between the debates of the 1960s and 1970s and those of the 1990s, eventually associating with Newt Gingrich,[195] himself an influence on radical twenty-first century UK Conservatives who saw the Internet as a possible vehicle for their ends.[196]

The Tofflers were a couple who produced a sequence of international bestsellers during the last three decades of the twentieth century (though for most of this time Heidi did not take a share of the credit for authorship[197]). The first, *Future Shock*, that appeared in 1970, was a discussion of a projected period of accelerated and disruptive technologically driven change in the developed world. One scenario they envisaged involved a networked computer system that would assist users in voting decisions. The device they presented as performing this function was known as an 'OLIVER'. While the initials supposedly signified the term 'On-Line Interactive Vicarious Expediter and Responder', it was named after Oliver Selfridge, originator of the concept (and son of the department store owner). An OLIVER was envisaged as a system to 'help us deal with decision overload'. It would 'be a personal computer programmed to provide the individual with information and to make minor decisions for him'. Then '[a]s computerized information systems ramify ... it

195 For a work by the Tofflers for which Gingrich wrote a foreword, see Alvin and Heidi Toffler, *Creating a New Civilization* (Atlanta, Turner, 1994).

196 See Ch. 1 of this volume.

197 Toffler, *Powershift*, pp. xviii–xix.

would tap into a worldwide pool of data stored in libraries, corporate files, hospitals, retail stores, banks, government agencies and universities. OLIVER would thus become a kind of universal question-answerer.' Furthermore, it might be 'possible to construct an OLIVER that would analyse the content of its owner's words, scrutinize his choices, deduce his value system, update its own program to reflect changes in his values, and ultimately handle larger and larger decisions for him'. It would be able to anticipate the decisions of the user, including 'whether its owner would vote for candidate X'.[198]

A decade later, a further work by the Tofflers, *The Third Wave*, appeared. Once again, it sought to convey a phase of revolutionary change, the 'Third Wave' of the title, entailing: 'a genuinely new way of life based on diversified, renewable energy sources; on methods of production that make most factory assembly lines obsolete; on new, non-nuclear families ... and on radically changed schools and corporations of the future'. This transition created a need for 'governments that are simple, more effective, yet more democratic than any we know today'.[199] The book judged 'that many of the decisions now made by small numbers of pseudo-representatives may have to be shifted back gradually to the electorate itself'.[200] This change could be achieved with the assistance of '[s]pectacular advances in communications technology' providing 'a mind-boggling array of possibilities for direct citizen participation in political decision making'.[201] The book contained an account of taking part in 'the world's first "electronic town hall"', held in Columbus, Ohio, using the Qube cable TV mechanism, with residents voting on local issues from 'their living rooms'.[202] It expressed the view that 'advanced computers, satellites, telephones, cable, polling techniques, and other tools' would at last enable 'an educated citizenry' to make 'many of its own political decisions'. It discouraged the idea of a dichotomy between direct and indirect democracy, however, and regarded the increased use of the former as compatible with and to the potential benefit of the latter.[203]

The third entry in the Toffler trilogy, *Powershift*, first appeared in 1990. In a similar tone to the earlier instalments, it tells the reader that 'the entire structure of power that held the world together is now disintegrating. A radically different structure of power is taking form. And this is happening at every level of human society.'[204] The book stressed the importance of 'electronic networks' that 'form the key infrastructure of the 21st century, as critical to business success and national economic development as the

198 Alvin Toffler, *Future Shock* (Bantam, New York, 1971), pp. 434–5.
199 Alvin Toffler, *The Third Wave* (Bantam, New York, 1981), pp. 10–11.
200 Ibid., p. 428.
201 Ibid., p. 430.
202 Ibid., pp. 429–30.
203 Ibid., p. 430.
204 Toffler, *Powershift*, p. 3.

railroads were in Morse's era'.[205] It anticipated the advent of an 'Electronic Activism'. Computer-based technology could allow for large-scale public participation in 'political polling or collective decision-taking – and political organizing of a new kind'. *Powershift* foresaw a 'spread of network interactivity' placing 'tools for political' engagement 'in millions of living rooms. With them, citizens could, in principle at least, conduct their own polls, and form their own "electronic parties" or "electronic lobbies" and pressure groups around various issues.'[206] The work expressed fear of governmental intervention, holding that '[j]ust as the state invented new forms of mind control when the industrial revolution brought mass media into being, it will search for new tools and techniques to retain at least some control over the images, ideas, symbols, and ideologies reaching its people through the new electronic infrastructure'.[207] In this context, the assertion of freedom of expression was essential.[208]

As the 1990s progressed, the Tofflers continued to contribute to discussion about the implications of electronic communications, including for politics and democracy.[209] Increasingly, the focal point for this discourse was the Internet, reflecting the practical reality of its growing international take-up. But the ideas raised were extensions of those which the Tofflers and others had promoted previously, without necessarily alighting specifically on this particular technology as a vehicle. To some extent replicating earlier thought (consciously or otherwise) they and their contemporaries helped in turn to create a framework for future debate. Key features of both more and less optimistic interpretations of the Internet therefore predated the ascendancy of this network. This realisation is important for a number of reasons. It shows that ideas – or myths – have a power of their own, and are not simply subordinate to material developments in technology. They can shape the approach taken to science and its application.

But the persistence of certain modes of thought also suggests that conceptions of and arguments about the Internet were in some ways rote, amounting to the imposition of general templates, more than being bespoke responses to the reality of the particular technology. In this respect, it is reasonable to question their genuine applicability to the subject they addressed. The extent to which a particular contributor was aware of the range of prior specialist work in this area might vary. But there was a general cultural background to which the likes of Orwell, Huxley, Forster, Wells, and Bellamy contributed. Furthermore, even if arrived at (relatively) independently, perspectives on the Internet might be seen more as expressions of general archetypes concerning

205 Ibid., p. 102.
206 Ibid., pp. 356–7.
207 Ibid., p. 361.
208 Ibid., p. 362–3.
209 See e.g. Alvin and Heidi Toffler, *Creating a New Civilisation: The Politics of the Third Wave* (Turner, Atlanta, 1995).

the role of technology in society than of meaningful analysis of a particular form of digital communications. The Internet provided a canvas for them. Yet the pre-existing discourse did more than simply detract from rational analysis. It offered, for instance, insight into legitimate reservations about the role of communications technology in areas such as surveillance and inappropriate interference in public debate. Some concerns recur for good reason. It also correctly anticipated some of the democratic purposes for which the Internet was ultimately employed, such as interacting with representatives and organising interest groups. However, in other areas predictions have not yet proved accurate – for instance, there has not so far been a decisive shift towards government by ongoing online referendums, in the UK or elsewhere. The extent of parliamentary awareness of these various issues and the ways in which it has engaged with them over time is assessed over coming chapters, in particular 7, 8, and 9. Though some indication of the future might have been found in the discussions analysed in the preceding pages, members of the UK legislature could not realistically be expected to be fully aware of it; nor would it have been easy to discern which of the sometimes contradictory aspects were likely to come to pass.

The prolonged gestation of ideas had a further significance. By the 1990s, electronic activism constituted an increasingly well-defined school of thought and practical engagement, to which internet activists could point and within which they located themselves. In mid-1994, for instance, the Morino Institute, an organisation formed in January the previous year to promote computer-based local level networking, produced an assessment of its work and the environment in which it operated. It included what it described as 'A Brief History of Community Networking'. This account took the form of a chronology of 'some of the key events in the history of community networking'. Like the story of the Internet itself, it meshed technological developments with deliberate efforts at social reorientation, and intersected work in scientific, academic fields with the radical fringes, including the counterculture. The first entry was for 1969 – which saw, it stated:

> ARPANET (precursor to Internet) created – first American networking community.

Further items on the Morino Institute list included:

> **1973**
> First international connections to ARPANET: England and Norway
> ...
>
> **1977**
> ... Publication of seminal Network Nation by Hiltz and Turoff
> ...

1979
… first dial-up computer service Berkeley Community Memory project established – public terminal-based communications service
…

1985
The Well established by Stewart Brand in Sausalito, California[210]

The ways in which this tradition, along with other internet-related concepts, filtered specifically into UK culture, and the political and constitutional context – including that of the UK Parliament – in which this process took place, is the subject of the next chapter.

[210] Morino Institute, 1994, 'A Brief History of Community Networking', Appendix A to 'Assessment and Evolution of Community Networking', available at: www.morino.org/assessment.htm#emergence, last accessed 22 November 2019.

5

The Political and Constitutional Context

'Electronic Referenda Will Be Feasible within a Generation'

On 25 May 1968, the Labour politician Tony Benn gave a speech entitled 'Developing a Participating Democracy'.[1] It provides us with a view of a parliamentarian holding ministerial office in the UK becoming an advocate of the employment of computers and electronic communications technologies for purposes of political inclusion. Benn both objected to some uses of such devices, but also saw them as radical – even revolutionary – in their implications. Addressing the Welsh Council of Labour at its Annual Conference, held in Llandudno, he was at the time Minister of Technology in the Harold Wilson government. Benn opened by noting the preoccupation the UK had with economic difficulties in the decades following the Second World War. He believed that 'we will never get our economic system right, unless the political processes of decision-making are right too'. He drew a connection between scientific development and the prospects for democracy, holding that '[j]ust as technology is revolutionising industry, so it is outdating our political institutions as well. Our educational system, our system of local government, the civil service and the legal system are all now under critical examination because technology has made them obsolescent.' Benn then moved to a specific focus on 'Parliament itself', asking: '[c]an we assume that it will go on, in exactly the same form as we now have it, for ever and ever? I very much doubt it.'[2]

Referring to the social convulsions and unrest of the era, Benn argued that 'the present wave of anxiety, disenchantment and discontent' was to a large extent 'actually directed at the present Parliamentary structure. Many people do not think that it is responding quickly enough to the mounting pressure of events or the individual or collective aspirations of the community.' Subscribing to a central criticism of representative democracy, Benn doubted whether 'people will be satisfied, for much longer, with a system which

[1] Tony Benn, 'Developing a Participating Democracy' in *Speeches by Tony Benn* (Spokesman, Nottingham, 1974), pp. 201–7.

[2] Ibid., p. 201.

confines their national political role to the marking of a ballot paper with a single cross once every five years'. They wanted 'a much greater say'. This desire was a motivation for various discontent groups: students; striking workers, especially those involved in unofficial action; Scottish and Welsh nationalists; and the 'Black Power movement'. In each case people were rejecting traditional structures and seeking to exercise power more on their own account. This collective tendency amounted to what would ultimately be an irresistible challenge to 'temporary authoritarianism that rests upon elected power'. The consequences for 'our system of Parliamentary democracy' and by extension the Labour Party would be immense.[3]

Shifts in the balance of power were coming, Benn held. In some instances, it would be centralised, owing to the nature of scientific development. But much movement would take place in the opposite direction – for instance, in the form of territorial dispersal, through devolution; and towards the individual and away from representative institutions.[4] Pre-eminent among such bodies, Parliament had altered much over the centuries, with various social groups forcing their inclusion. Similarly, radical development would now come to fulfil the demands 'of a new generation'. It would entail the development of a 'participating democracy'. Within the system Benn envisaged, information and communication technology of various kinds would play a central role. He placed a premium on making official information available to the public. By this means, Benn judged, it would be possible to ensure that political discourse centred on material issues at stake, in place of 'the obsession with personalities' and 'columns and columns of personal tittle-tattle masquerading as serious political comment'.[5] The idea that greater and wider dissemination of knowledge, perhaps enabled by technology, would lead to social improvement had been asserted before, and would be again, including among those who saw potential in the Internet. But complaints about low-quality debate also recurred.

Alongside the public having access of this type to official information, government in turn would need 'to know a great deal more than it does know about the community it was elected to serve'.[6] Describing what was a forerunner to the algorithm-based approach of today, Benn anticipated that, in the following decade, computer systems could enable sophisticated decision-making on a basis of a vast body of accumulated data. They would make it possible to conduct economic management and even the 'complete integration' of 'taxation and social security' payments. There were threats. Social surveillance on this scale 'could be the basis for a police state'. Protections against such abuse would be necessary. But this use of accumulated personal

[3] Ibid., p. 202.
[4] Ibid.
[5] Ibid., p. 203.
[6] Ibid.

information could also create a new form of individual empowerment. Whether or not a person was politically active, a compulsion would exist for 'government to take account of every single individual in the development of its policy. Just to exist will be to participate.'[7]

Benn saw problems with the operation of the 'mass media', which – he held – provided privileged access to large audiences for those already in positions of authority, and excluded others. He identified a particular need for change in the way in which broadcasting functioned. Benn complained that the editorial policies of the networks served to exclude more marginal viewpoints. An 'equivalent to the publishing function' was lacking. He anticipated a future scenario in which 'independent groups of publishers would be allocated so many hours of broadcasting a month and told to help those who have something to say, to say it clearly and well, to national audiences'. Failure to adopt such a practice would be to restrict a beneficial exposure to diverse viewpoints, 'good, bad and indifferent'.[8]

In the seventeenth century, in the context of the printing press, Milton had advocated the principle of allowing for the expression of a broad span of viewpoints. Benn – faced with a different communications environment – had inverted the Milton approach. Milton – on the one hand – called for official forbearance: that Parliament refrain from censorship, creating space for the dissemination of whatever ideas might be forthcoming (subject to some limits). Benn – on the other hand – advocated positive action by public authorities to ensure the wide promotion of differing perspectives alongside the more mainstream. Part of the reason for this contrast was the nature of the technologies involved. The practical limitations on the use of printing were less than those on broadcasting in the 1960s, which was subject to bandwidth constraints. For this reason, openings in the latter media had to be carved out from existing channels. Subsequently, the Internet would create the 'publishing function' to which Benn referred without these same practical constraints. This quality was one of the reasons that this digital network technology was a source of excitement in some quarters regarding its democratic potential. In this sense it might be seen as a vehicle for the type of discourse that Benn favoured. However, while the Internet could attract positive assessments for being supportive of diversity, there were also complaints about its domination by a limited number of entities, including corporations and governments, that could condition the transmission of information and messages that took place. Further objections arose regarding the system supposedly being structured in such a way that certain viewpoints predominated. In these accounts, however, it was often held that extreme views that challenged the existing order, rather than mainstream perceptions, were favoured. Finally, the theoretically open and free nature of the Internet meant that some could use it as a conduit for targeted

[7] Ibid., p. 204.
[8] Ibid.

abuse, deterring others from participating and thereby arguably limiting the extent to which they exercised the right to freedom of expression.

Benn saw a need to promote the formation of 'representative organisations of all kinds'.[9] They might include pressure groups, professional bodies, and trade unions. They were a means by which government could strengthen links with the public, and become more responsive in its policy formation.[10] Once again, Benn identified possible positive outcomes (as he saw them) that later exponents of the democratic potential of the Internet would promote. These later analysts sometimes held that a strength of this technology was that it lowered the resource barriers involved in the formation of coalitions of interest by people who might not otherwise be able to organise and assert collective objectives. Nonetheless, there were also suggestions that the Internet facilitated uneven concentrations of power rather than wider dispersals.

Perhaps the most striking aspect of the Benn speech from the standpoint of this work was his discussion of the possibility of 'direct sharing of decision-making with the electorate as a whole'. Making a standard case for referendums, Benn held that '[t]he five-yearly cross on the ballot paper is just not going to be enough. Inevitably we shall have to look again at the objections to the holding of referenda and see if they are still valid.' He was inclined towards holding popular votes, in the first instance on matters 'that are now decided by private Members' Bills'. He seems to have had in mind issues such as abortion and sexual offences. Benn conceded that '[w]e might not all like the result'. However, in his view, 'by sharing responsibility an interest in public policy would be stirred in every household'.[11] Benn then took the speech back to a core theme, speculating that 'technology may ultimately help us. Electronic referenda will be feasible within a generation and with it could come a considerable up-rating of the responsibility and understanding of ordinary people.'[12]

The Benn speech was significant to this book because of the ideas it contained, the person who was voicing them, the context in which he came to do so, and the reception he received. Through it, Benn placed himself in an intellectual tradition according to which the deployment in particular ways of existing or new inventions might be a means of addressing problems, including of a social and political nature, that were themselves associated with technology. Indeed, there is evidence he might have consciously drawn directly on at least one aspect of this heritage, or at least soon became aware of the precursors to his thought. Specifically, his idea about electronic referendums was reminiscent of similar proposals made in the 1930s and 1940s, in particular by Lord Birkenhead (F. E. Smith) and Buckminster Fuller. Benn does not

[9] Ibid., p. 205.
[10] Ibid., p. 206.
[11] Ibid., p. 204.
[12] Ibid., p. 205.

seem to have identified any direct influences for his similar 1968 suggestion. But he subsequently recorded high admiration for Fuller, and even met with him. It is possible that Benn had encountered Fuller's 'modernized, electrified, direct Democracy' concept prior to his Llandudno speech and found inspiration in it. In a diary entry for 1 March 1970, Benn recorded:

> In the evening Buckminster Fuller came to dinner at home with James Mellor who has just edited his work.
>
> I had read a little bit of Fuller's writing and had found it extremely difficult to understand; it is full of academic technological jargon, but I had been struck by his geodesic domes, by his speech to architects in Mexico City and by one or two other things. He is a short man of seventy-four and is very deaf. I got out my blackboard and he lectured to us from about 6.30 until after midnight, doing drawings, and describing his conception of comprehensive anticipatory change. He talked about the regenerative system, and the collection and use of waste. He was very optimistic about our capacity to deal with the population problem, saying that mankind had been born to be a success and that it was our job to see that it was. He was very anti-political and thought politics was just corrupt, but I liked him enormously, and found him a very impressive man ...[13]

This meeting took place nearly two years after the Llandudno speech, but Benn noted that he had 'read a little bit of Fuller's writing', which – though he struggled with it – he found sufficiently interesting to receive the author at his home. Whether his acquaintance with the work of Fuller predated May 1968, and whether the 'one or two other things' he had 'been struck by' included electronic voting remains, on the basis of this diary entry, open.

Benn made his admiration for Fuller public. In his Roscoe Lecture to the University of Manchester of 23 April 1970, Benn presented Fuller as a substantial figure, referring to him with him alongside Karl Marx and Henry Ford. Benn asked:

> What is technology? The best and simplest explanation that I have ever heard is one given by the American professor Buckminster Fuller, for whom I have a great deal of admiration, who said technology simply means getting 'more out of less'. If the central problem of the world, overall, is shortage, which it is, the need to get 'more out of less' is a rather more accurate way of describing the challenge facing us than can be deduced from the more limited and mechanical words that are used to describe technology.[14]

The interaction continued. A Benn diary entry for 16 October 1970 noted:

> Had a most stimulating breakfast meeting with Buckminster Fuller. He described the necessity throughout history for communities to come to terms

[13] Tony Benn, *Office Without Power: Diaries 1968–72* (Arrow, London, 1988), diary entry for Sunday 1 March 1970, pp. 244–5.

[14] Ibid., Appendix iv, 'Learning to Use Power', Extract from the Roscoe Lecture, delivered to the University of Manchester, 25 April 1970, p. 497.

> with their old timescale. For example in the agricultural timescale everything corresponded to the seasons through one year. Then the early arrival of ships had led people to say, 'when my ship comes in' which was a longer timescale than the one based on 'when the harvest is brought in'. His is a most creative and fertile mind.[15]

In subsequent commentary published in 1970, Nigel Calder, the former editor of the *New Scientist*, presented Fuller and Benn as within a similar school of thought.[16] Even if Fuller was not an overt influence on the Llandudno speech and its reference to electronic voting, the affinity Benn developed for him is of wider importance. It demonstrates the diverse parallel pathways that ideas about the democratic application of technology could take as they worked down through the decades: at once, Fuller was influential in countercultural circles in the United States,[17] and upon a senior figure in the UK Labour Party.

The analysis Calder provided also suggested that, alongside links to the past, in making this speech Benn joined a contemporary current which saw a potential for linking electronic media with a shift towards participatory mechanisms. Calder himself was probably an influence upon Benn in this regard. Calder was aware of the work of Vladimir Zworykin and his advocacy of 'instant polls'.[18] Zworykin had presented his ideas in a collection first published in 1964, discussed in the previous chapter, of which Calder was editor.[19] Calder – whose father, the socialist journalist and academic, Ritchie Calder, became a Labour Peer in 1966 – seems to have had some impact on policy thinking at high level within Labour.[20] It is plausible that Calder brought ideas such as those proposed by Zworykin and Fuller to the attention of Benn. A diary entry for 22 July 1966 demonstrates that Benn saw in Calder someone who shared his forward-looking disposition, and who was a potential source of innovative ideas regarding the application of science, suitable to adaptation in a political environment.[21]

During the 1960s, in both his Postmaster General and Technology briefs, Benn was a strong advocate of innovative application of scientific development.[22] For instance, soon after taking up office as Postmaster General he began to develop ideas about computers and 'the role of the telecommunications

[15] Ibid., diary entry for Sunday 16 October 1970, p. 309.

[16] Nigel Calder, *Technopolis: Social Control of the Uses of Science* (Simon and Schuster, New York, 1970), p. 334.

[17] Theodore Roszak, *The Cult of Information: A Neo-Luddite Treatise on High-Tech, Artificial Intelligence, and the True Art of Thinking* (Berkeley, University of California Press, 1994), p. 143.

[18] Calder, *Technopolis*, p. 335.

[19] V. K. Zworykin, 'Communications and Government' in Nigel Calder (ed.), *The World in 1984: The Complete New Scientist Series* (Penguin, Harmondsworth, 1965), vol. II, pp. 51–3.

[20] Tony Benn, *Out of the Wilderness: Diaries, 1963–67* (Arrow, London, 1988), diary entry for 30 May 1967, p. 28.

[21] Ibid., diary entry for 22 July, p. 459.

[22] e.g. ibid., p. 164.

network in meeting the requirements of industry for the transmission of data'.[23] He saw technology as generating social momentum of its own. In interviews given to the *New Scientist* published the month after Llandudno, Benn responded to questions upon the themes he had addressed. On the specific issue of referendums, he held that:

> [t]he technical means for undertaking referenda without disrupting people's daily lives are going to be available quite soon. Homes will be connected to central points for the supply of colour television programmes, telephone channels, and for the monitoring of electricity meters. There will be a two-way link – in and out. Almost certainly market research people will use it. When people suddenly wake up to the fact that they have an instrument for answering back in their hands, don't you think they'll want to use it? I think they will. Then we're going to have to decide whether to let them.[24]

The concepts Benn advanced certainly had many precursors, and were part of a developing trend at the time rather than being unique (though certainly towards the contemporary forefront). But it is significant that a parliamentarian was expressing these notions, especially given that they appeared to accept the expansion of bases of authority other than the Westminster legislature – for instance, at devolved level and through popular voting. Benn sensed a challenge to Parliament and the representative system to which it was central. Technology – in the Benn analysis – was transforming the entire basis on which individual incorporation into the political process took place, and it would continue to do so. This process, as he interpreted it, brought dangers and new openings; leaders, in his view, had to face both.

There was also a contemporary international political context. Benn spoke in the wake of unrest in Paris. When reproducing the text of his Llandudno speech in a collection issued in 1974, he specifically referred in an introductory note to its being 'delivered just after the Paris uprisings in May, 1968'.[25] As we have seen, one of the areas of interest of participants in these disturbances, and that the Situationists in particular had promoted, was to commandeer the mass media for their own purposes. The idea that the mainstream outlets were a vehicle for established power elites, and that there was a need to find space for marginalised groups and viewpoints, motivated the alternative media movement in France in the years that followed the events of 1968. Though a participant in government rather than an external protester against it, Benn found himself to a large extent in sympathy with radical activists across the world of the time.[26] In this sense he provided an example of how social and

[23] Ibid., diary entry for 22 October 1964, p. 169.

[24] Tony Benn, 'Politics in a Technological Age', interview published in *New Scientist* on 6 June and 13 June 1968, reproduced in Tony Benn, *Speeches by Tony Benn* (Spokesman, Nottingham, 1974), pp. 207–14, 211–12.

[25] Benn, 'Developing a Participating Democracy', p. 201.

[26] Benn, *Office Without Power*, diary entry for Sunday 7 May 1968, p. 65.

political forces of a countercultural character that developed in this time could channel into ideas about the employment of electronic communications technology for democratic ends.

Ideas he expressed, including over the potential of technology to bring about greater democratic engagement, would retain relevance in relation to the Internet. He identified some of the potential drawbacks that might develop, but optimism dominated to an extent that, from the standpoint of more recent times, appears dated. Moreover, in as far as Benn identified possible downsides in some of the developments he identified – in particular misuse of personal data – he attributed them to government, rather than commercial organisations, which have lately become the culprits in accounts of undesirable aspects of the Internet.

The Llandudno speech and its aftermath were retrospectively a significant change in the developing career of Benn. By the early 1970s, he had fully transitioned from a seemingly technocratic, modernising ally of Wilson, to a leader of the radical Left within the Labour, placing himself at the forefront of a movement that exerted pronounced pressure upon the party leadership.[27] The ideas Benn proposed regarding electronic direct democracy were not central to his later agenda – and his projections regarding the swift development of facilitating technology proved excessively optimistic anyway. But his attraction to such concepts seems to have played a part in his transition to a more dissenting stance. Earlier in his ministerial career communications and data were for Benn more a means of meeting the needs of industry; later they would become engagement tools. In the years after 1968, he would continue generally to advocate an opening up of the media to different groups; and – perhaps most importantly – exert pressure for a referendum on UK participation in European integration, though one that would ultimately be held by the traditional method, rather than using home-based devices. Here was evidence of the radicalising potential of thought about the political applications of communications technology.

Through his speech, Benn generated much controversy, among the wider public[28], and his own colleagues in the Cabinet and the Parliamentary Labour Party.[29] One source of comment arose from his being seen as criticising the policy of the very administration in which he was a participant. Another was constitutional. Arguably, by making a speech with such content, he challenged the doctrine of collective Cabinet responsibility, by which members of the government maintained a united front around policy.[30] He also touched on sensitivities regarding key tenets about the way in which the system worked,

[27] See e.g. Jad Adams, *Tony Benn: A Biography* (Biteback, London, 2011).

[28] See e.g. Brian Groombridge, *Television and the People: A Programme for Democratic Participation* (Penguin, London, 1972), pp. 163–4.

[29] Benn, *Office Without Power*, diary entry for 29 May 1968, p. 73.

[30] Ibid., diary entry for 30 May 1968, p. 73.

including the principle of representative democracy,[31] and freedom of expression[32] (since he was arguing for positive action with implications for the content of broadcast material, though he held it would entail opening up rather than closing off discussion). The ideas Benn presented in part amounted to a series of possible constitutional reforms, in areas such as freedom of information, referendums, and devolution. With this consideration in mind, the next section of this chapter considers the constitutional environment – both within Parliament and beyond – within which engagement with computers and the Internet would take place. It then considers two particular movements which provide examples of how concepts about the employment of such technology could gain traction among social and political activists, and their ultimate connection with Parliament.

The Constitutional Dimension

The chapters that follow will discuss how Parliament (in various manifestations) developed an increasing interest in computers – including their incorporation into communications networks – both for the specific use it could make of them, and for their wider potential implications. It then began to engage with this technology – including, eventually, the Internet – in a practical sense. A proper understanding of these developments requires an appreciation of their constitutional setting. Approaches taken to the technologies involved were both influenced by this broader environment, and in turn had an impact upon it. In this book, detailed discussion of parliamentary activity in this area commences in the 1960s. It ran broadly in parallel with a prolonged period of examination, criticism, and reform of aspects of the UK system of governance – including Parliament itself.

By the end of the 1950s, a number of commentators were becoming critical of various UK social and political institutions and the people who operated them, often grouped under the general heading of the 'establishment'. This term provided a title for a collection edited by the journalist Hugh Thomas. He defined it as meaning 'the English [sic] constitution, and the group of institutions and outlying agencies built round it to assist in its protection'.[33] First issued in 1959, the volume captures key aspects of this intellectual movement and the mood it generated. The underlying picture that emerges is one of a country that, moving into a post-imperial era, was a declining force in world politics; and seemed to be suffering from relative economic underperformance. Perceived difficulties led to a weakening of deference, with commentators more willing to scrutinise aspects of the elite (albeit of which they were

[31] Benn, 'Politics in a Technological Age', p. 210.
[32] See e.g. Benn, 'Developing a Participating Democracy', p. 201.
[33] Hugh Thomas, 'The Establishment and Society' in Hugh Thomas (ed.), *The Establishment* (Ace, London, 1962), pp. 7–18, 12.

arguably themselves members). Thomas himself was critical of the supposed 'establishment' as a whole, presenting it as an outmoded entity. He wrote: '[t]o those who desire to see the resources and talents of Britain fully developed and extended there is no doubt that the fusty Establishment, with its Victorian views and standards of judgement, must be destroyed'.[34] Other chapters in the volume focused specifically on the public school system, the armed forces, the Civil Service, the City of London and financial sector, and the BBC. Christopher Hollis, a former Conservative MP, contributed an essay entitled 'Parliament and the Establishment'. It demonstrated that – when blame was being apportioned for the supposed deterioration of the UK – the institution in which he had served could become a target. The general line of criticism Hollis mounted was that, within the system of two-party dominance that then prevailed, rigid discipline exercised by the whips constrained the autonomy of Parliament and prevented it from imposing meaningful accountability upon the executive.[35]

The Thomas work marked an early stage in a sustained process through which questioning led to reform proposals and in turn actual changes. Many of them had consequences – direct or indirect – for Parliament. Indeed, the idea that it should adopt new practices appeared early on in this period of self-examination and reform. Impetus came both from external observers and from those within the institution who sensed a need to respond to a perceived threat of fading parliamentary legitimacy. Within the latter group, in the same year that *The Establishment* first appeared, the leading Labour politician, Aneurin Bevan, described in the Commons debate on the Royal Address on 3 November the view that 'there was a considerable gulf growing between this House and the nation'.[36] He judged this interpretation:

> to be absolutely true. There is a lessening interest in our discussions. We are not reaching the country to the extent that we did. It can no longer be argued that the national newspapers are means of communication between the House of Commons and the public. The fact is that Parliamentary reporting has become a sheer travesty. Apart from a few responsible, solid newspapers with small circulations, the debates in this House are hardly reported at all, and such reports as take place are, as hon. Members on both sides know, a complete travesty of our proceedings.

Parliament had once resisted coverage of its activities. Now MPs were complaining that it was not sufficiently extensive. Bevan detected commercial pressures at work. He was 'not making a special attack upon the newspapers. It may be that the demands of circulation make it impossible for them to report our proceedings at any length.' But whatever was driving this tendency,

[34] Ibid., p. 18.
[35] Christopher Hollis, 'Parliament and the Establishment' in Hugh Thomas (ed.), *The Establishment* (Ace, London, 1962), pp. 158–74.
[36] Hansard, HC Debates, 3 November 1959, col. 865–7.

'there do not exist at present in Britain the normal processes of democratic education that make the people aware of the problems which lie ahead of us, and of their own responsibilities'. He took the view that '[t]he same can be said of the radio and even more can be said of television'. Bevan spoke at a time when the broadcast media had recently taken on an increased ability to cover matters of political controversy. The so-called 14-day rule had stipulated that they were not supposed to report on issues that might be discussed by Parliament at some point over the next two weeks. It was fatally undermined during the Suez crisis of 1956 and abandoned the following year.[37]

Bevan expressed discontent with aspects of political broadcasting. He objected in particular to the way in which 'Members of the House are picked out to take part in television broadcasts' by 'the bureaucracy at Broadcasting House'. He regarded as 'humiliating' the practice of 'Members of Parliament in responsible positions' being 'selected by unrepresentative persons to have an opportunity of appearing on the radio and the television'. There were also problems with MPs coming 'increasingly to rely upon fees provided by bureaucrats in the B.B.C.' – a tendency Bevan regarded as 'squalid'. At this point, an unnamed Member interjected '[a]nd I.T.V.' – a reference to the commercial television network that had begun its service in 1955, with a statutory basis in the Television Act 1954. Bevan concurred that the same criticism applied to it. He saw 'such a state of affairs' as 'inconsistent with the dignity of a democratic procedure'. Moreover, the particular decisions made about who should take part in broadcasts meant that 'political alternatives are not placed before the people in a realistic fashion'.

Bevan therefore supported 'a serious investigation ... into the technical possibilities of televising Parliamentary proceedings'. At the time he spoke there was no radio or television broadcasting of this type. In 1945, the BBC began transmitting the radio programme *Today in Parliament*, in fulfilment of the requirement in its Licence and Agreement that it would 'broadcast an impartial account day by day, prepared by professional reporters of the proceedings of Both Houses of Parliament'. But until 1978, when permanent sound broadcasting of Parliament began, it used accounts of debates rather than actual recordings. A year before Bevan made his speech, filming of the 1958 opening of Parliament and the Queen's Speech had taken place, an event that was presumably in the minds of parliamentarians at the point Bevan made his case. But it did not amount to ongoing coverage of debates and other business.

The inquiry, as Bevan envisaged it, would consider what was practically viable, preparatory to the taking of a decision on the 'principle' of

[37] For a timeline of developments, see House of Commons Information Office, *Broadcasting Proceedings of the House*, Factsheet G5, General Series (House of Commons Information Office, London, 2010), pp. 2–3, 5–7; Colin Seymour-Ure, *The British Press and Broadcasting since 1945*, 2nd edn (Blackwell, Oxford, 1996), pp. 278–9.

broadcasting. This proposal was controversial, prompting an interruption and causing Members, as Bevan noted, to 'shake their heads'. He noted he had not consulted with the Labour leadership before making this case, on the grounds 'that when one makes a suggestion . . . it passes through the interstices of the party machine so slowly that by the time it emerges it has only a meagre resemblance to its former self'. He recognised that his idea was 'not novel' and had 'been mentioned before'. In the past it had 'been brushed aside as something so unorthodox and unconventional that we ought not to think about it at all'. Yet he felt 'that the time has come when we should give it serious consideration'.

Dealing with the resistance to his idea, he asked MPs to consider: '[w]ould it not be an excellent thing if, instead of speeches being made in comparative obscurity, and, in fact, never heard at all except by the few Members who assemble here to hear them, they were heard by their constituents?' Bevan – whose party had suffered a heavy defeat by the governing Conservatives at the General Election of the previous month – insisted he was not claiming 'that the electoral results might have been different. Indeed, they might have been confirmed or might have been reinforced. I do not know.' But he was of the view 'that in these days when all the apparatus of mass suggestion are against democratic education, we should seriously consider re-establishing intelligent communication between the House of Commons and the electorate as a whole. That, surely, is a democratic process.' Bevan remarked that he had not previously been a frequent viewer of television. But lately he had given it his attention and had 'been impressed by it as a medium of communication. There is no doubt at all that it is a very powerful medium, but I think that the time has come when people should be able to switch over to a Parliamentary debate.' There would be no obligation to view such proceedings; but there should 'be a special channel that they can turn on and listen to us at any time'. He was not a supporter of having 'only special debates televised'. Rather 'there should be a special channel for the House of Commons itself, and, so that its position may be consolidated in the public esteem, there is no reason why the other place [the House of Lords] also should not be televised'.

Bevan – who described his view as 'not novel' – sat within an established pattern. Calls for broadcasting of Parliament dated back to the earliest days of the introduction of radio into the UK. In 1926, the Conservative Prime Minister, Stanley Baldwin, had informed the Commons that 'I have consulted with the leaders of the other parties, and have obtained information through the usual channels. I have come to the conclusion that there is a greatly preponderating body of opinion against broadcasting the proceedings of this House.'[38] In so doing, Baldwin confirmed that – already by this point – the proposal both existed and generated firm opposition. The idea Bevan

[38] Hansard, HC Debates, 22 March 1926, col. 866.

proposed – that an innovative use of technology might improve upon current unsatisfactory applications – was familiar too. But in other ways, he anticipated the future. His proposal eventually came into being, but not in full until 1992, with the launch of a specific parliamentary channel. Ongoing radio coverage of both Houses of Parliament began in 1978. The Lords (which Bevan thought could take part) had then led the way on television, with regular broadcasting of its proceedings commencing in 1985, the Commons following in 1989.

As well as anticipating the future of broadcasting, Bevan advanced views similar to those subsequently deployed by internet advocates. They, like he, discerned the emergence of 'a very powerful medium'. Both saw the potential to harness it for the purpose of bypassing existing conduits of information provision. Each could detect an increasing disconnect between Parliament and public, which existing communications could not reverse and were possibly aggravating. New techniques – whether using a purpose-designed television channel or the Internet – could enable direct communication with voters on terms that suited Parliament, and might enable the strengthening of the link between the two.

Some of the complaints that Bevan levelled at print and broadcast outlets were also similar to those eventually directed at the Internet – for instance, that it provided certain entities with influence without accountability, and compromised elected representatives and the democratic system itself. Both sets of arguments included the following components. A medium (for Bevan, television) had 'power', but it was not necessarily being used in a way that was socially beneficial. With regard to the press, the market led to unsatisfactory outcomes; and issues and debates were presented in ways that distorted their true nature. Consequently, Bevan judged, there was a need for a political authority – in this instance, Parliament – to take measures to ensure that the public had access to a fuller, more balanced source of information. The complaint that 'all the apparatus of mass suggestion are against democratic education' fitted with the tenor of some Internet analysis six decades later.

While seeing television as in possession of 'power' of some kind, Bevan judged that it was difficult to establish what difference it might make – for instance, to an election result. The idea that media might have an impact, but not necessarily in a straightforward or readily discernible sense, is more widely applicable, including to the Internet. It is not only hard to predict in advance of their being employed what difference they will make. There are often problems in determining what precisely the impact has been after adoption, even though we might suspect there have been significant consequences. Merely enabling people to access this kind of experience was surely important in itself. It was also arguable that broadcasting could not only provide coverage of an event, but perhaps play a part in the outcomes it achieved. Indeed, anticipation of the likely effect of a medium might encourage certain forms of behaviour. Early on in the era of the televising of the House of Commons, on

13 November 1990, the resignation speech of former Conservative Cabinet minister Geoffrey Howe attained wide publicity and possibly helped to undermine the Conservative Prime Minister, Margaret Thatcher, who conceded her office a little over a week later.[39] Discerning how events might have transpired differently had there been no broadcasting, however, is a speculative exercise in counterfactual analysis and of limited value. But it is important in itself that the incorporation of new media provided new ways in which political processes could play themselves out. Aside from more dramatic episodes, discussion of the idea of broadcasting proceedings often involved consideration of whether it would change the environment it sought to depict, through imposing a new awareness and set of priorities upon participants.

It is worth considering further the development of broadcasting of parliamentary proceedings. The Bevan speech was suggestive of important characteristics of this process. He noted the controversy of his ideas; and that they were not the official policy of his party. In other words, they were not a regular partisan matter, and they generated disagreements that cut across these more normal divisions. Perhaps because of these special characteristics, as Bevan seemed to recognise, progress was likely to be slow. Over time, the protracted nature of consideration attracted comment, including from those who noted specifically the time that had elapsed since Bevan made his intervention on the subject. For instance, in 1975, in a House of Commons discussion of the prospects for its being broadcast, Edward du Cann, a Conservative MP, held that:

> It is an astonishment to me that we should have talked about this matter for as long, I believe, as 15 years since the late Aneurin Bevan first mentioned it in a speech. It is an astonishment to me that it is 10 years since the Select Committee reported in favour, and it is an astonishment to me that we should have needed to discuss the matter some seven times.[40]

Then in a 1978 debate on sound broadcasting of the House of Commons, the Labour MP William Molloy remarked that:

> One would hardly believe that it is nearly 20 years since the late Aneurin Bevan almost casually in a debate on the Gracious Speech remarked that he felt that this House should be televised. That remark caused a great debate throughout the country. One would have thought that at least within a decade this proposal would have been under way.[41]

In 1977, the Joint Committee on Sound Broadcasting issued a report that provided an account of the tortuous process that finally led to agreement to permanent parliamentary radio broadcasting. It noted that the Select

[39] See Geoffrey Howe, *Conflict of Loyalty* (Pan, London, 1995).
[40] Hansard, HC Debates, 24 February 1975, col. 54.
[41] Ibid., 6 February 1978, col. 1130.

Committee on Publications and Debates Reports had investigated the prospects in this area during 1964–5; and the Select Committee on Broadcasting etc. of Proceedings in Parliament had continued this task in 1965–6. The latter inquiry reached the view that 'continuous live broadcasting' would not be viable or advantageous. But it recommended providing broadcasters with a 'feed' and that there should be a 'closed circuit experiment' of both video and audio. The House of Commons voted against this idea in 1966, while the House of Lords agreed. The Lords trial took place in 1968. The House of Commons consented to 'an experiment in closed circuit radio transmission' in 1967; it also occurred in 1968. Various discussions followed but no progress was made. Finally, on 24 February 1975, the Commons agreed to a trial radio broadcast. It was held during the following June and July. Following a recommendation from the Select Committee on House of Commons (Services), on 16 March 1976, the Commons decided in favour of permanent radio broadcasting. The Lords supported a similar proposal on the same day.[42]

The prolonged discussions that took place revolved around a number of issues. Bob Franklin – with a focus on the debate about televising the Commons, but broadly applicable to radio, also – identified them as predominantly 'constitutional' in nature. Supporters, he records, emphasised the potential 'democratic benefits' on offer. It would 'make ... [the Commons] ... more accountable to the public, enhance public participation in the political process, albeit vicariously' and play an 'educational' role with regard to the way in which the Commons operated, and the substantive issues with which it engaged. Televised proceedings 'might also serve to halt the twentieth-century decline of Parliament by publicizing, and thereby bolstering, its effectiveness as a checking mechanism on the executive'.[43] They would also ensure that the UK Parliament kept pace with international trends towards the broadcasting of legislatures. The extensive permeation of television technology meant there was a pre-existing potential mass audience, comprising the bulk of the population.[44] Objections to this proposed change included that the equipment required – such as microphones, cameras, and lighting – might be of an 'intrusive' nature, causing discomfort and unease among Members. Selective coverage might misrepresent or distort the Commons, to meet the 'entertainment' requirements of the television medium rather than the needs of the institution. It could have the effect of promoting larger parties at the expense of smaller. The priorities of television might create pressure for the Commons to alter its procedures, and Members might modify their behaviour in undesirable ways to achieve attention through the medium.[45]

[42] Joint Committee on Sound Broadcasting, *Second Report*, HL 123, HC 284 (Stationery Office, London, 1977), pp. v–vi.

[43] Bob Franklin, 'Televising the British House of Commons: Issues and Developments' in Bob Franklin (ed.), *Televising Democracies* (Routledge, London, 1992), pp. 3–26, 5.

[44] Ibid., p. 6.

[45] Ibid., pp. 6–10.

An important consideration for Parliament was control. How far could and should Parliament seek to determine the way in which it was presented? There were numerous options. They included the Bevan proposal, for a continuous parliamentary channel. Parliament might choose to create its own highlights, similar to *Today in Parliament*, but edited in accordance with its own priorities, whatever they might be. When discussing these options in a debate in May 1965, the Conservative MP Tom Iremonger raised the further possibility that:

> the House could simply throw the field wide open and take what came from accredited gallery observers and commentators entitled to make their own excerpts from video tape as they chose, when they chose and of what they chose and to use them at their discretion for the benefit of their companies. John Milton might possibly argue that this would be the way that free men unafraid of liberty should choose.[46]

He acknowledged a potential drawback that applied to this model: 'Its demerits are, of course, that what we do and say here would be susceptible to unfair representation and selection by anyone who wanted to be unfair.'[47]

In a 1985 memoir, the former Labour minister and Speaker of the House of Commons from 1976 to 1983, George Thomas, favoured a degree of freedom of coverage. He regretted what he saw as a decline in standards of behaviour in the Chamber, with aggressive heckling hampering the potential for proper debate. Radio allowed those 'who behave like shouting hooligans' to remain anonymous. He therefore welcomed the prospect of televising proceedings, in as far as it could reveal the identity of the perpetrators. This practice could, he felt, have an immediate positive effect, reducing the quantity of improper interruptions. It would also encourage higher levels of attendance in the House, since absences would be visibly exposed. But, Thomas noted, these benefits were dependent upon cameras being allowed to 'operate freely', rather than simply being 'focused on the man who is speaking'. To constrain what could be shown, he cautioned, 'could almost be misleading.'[48]

Ultimately, Parliament applied a variety of rules and guidance intended to ensure that both radio and television broadcasts of its proceedings did not damage its reputation. For instance, it sought to limit the type of shots used for television coverage and to ensure that parliamentary content was incorporated into other programming in ways that were appropriate.[49]

The idea that Parliament was somehow in decline, either in its objective performance or in popular perception and public confidence was a

[46] Hansard, HC Debates, 28 May 1965, col. 1038.

[47] Hansard, HC Debates, 28 May 1965, col. 1037.

[48] George Thomas, *Mr Speaker: The Memoirs of Viscount Tonypandy* (Century, London, 1985), pp. 194–5.

[49] Select Committee on Televising of Proceedings of the House, *First Report*, vol. 1, HC 141–I (Stationery Office, London, 1989), pp. xvi–xxii.

powerful motivation. But some disputed such concepts. In a Commons debate on broadcasting in 1972, Charles Pannell, a Labour MP, took issue with the proposition:

> that this place has fallen from a previous high level ... What is the point in history from which we have fallen? Where is the peak? ... What is the high point from which we have declined? Is it the 1880s? Is it the 1930s? Is it the 1920s? ... There is not a major literary figure who has ever written about this place – Pepys, Dickens, Hazlitt, Lamb, Carlyle, George Bernard Shaw – who has not always referred to it with the utmost contempt.[50]

As the analysis of Franklin noted, the prospect of broadcasting raised concerns for some that it would have an inappropriate distorting effect, rewarding undesirable qualities. In the 1972 Commons debate on broadcasting, the Labour MP Myer Galpern, with edited television coverage in mind, cautioned that: 'those who are less fortunate in appearance or approach may not get an innings'. Exclusions would apply to those judged 'dull' and failing to 'show sufficient anger'. An MP rejected for these reasons would be replaced by a colleague 'more flowery in style who has at his command the well-polished phrase, or somebody who gets up and creates a scene'. Coverage would fail 'to enable the public to have a better understanding of what happens in Parliament' and instead present them with 'the cranks and comedians. That is what we shall have. It will change this place from a debating chamber into a stage for performers.'[51]

Concerns of the type that appeared in the debate about radio and television broadcasting were of a recurring quality, arising in the context of different devices. As the Iremonger reference to Milton suggested, comparable viewpoints had manifested themselves with regard to the printing press. Such issues would assert themselves again with respect to the Internet – both its general perceived impact upon politics, and its specific implications for Parliament. This realisation is significant because it provides a revealing standpoint from which to assess the parliamentary approach to digital network technologies. We might wish, for example, to compare claims about the distortion of discourse attributed respectively to broadcasting and to online coverage. What is their relative veracity? What is the relationship between them?

Alongside pessimistic accounts, optimistic views of the Internet (as set out in later chapters) also mirrored earlier discussions about different communications technologies. For instance, an important motivation for parliamentary interest in networked computing was the perception of some form of democratic malaise, with negative consequences for Parliament, that it was hoped the use of this invention might help address. Yet the sense that it was in

[50] Hansard, HC Debates, 19 October 1972, cols 475–476.
[51] Ibid., col. 506.

reduced circumstances as compared with the past has been regularly asserted for decades or even centuries. This realisation does not necessarily refute claims that such a tendency has developed lately, but it does necessitate careful reflection upon them rather than immediate acceptance. Furthermore, it is important to note that broadcasting – like the Internet – was advocated as a solution to such supposed difficulties. It might be asked, if the adoption of other communications technologies in an earlier era had failed to avert the later perceived problems, why might the Internet have been expected to succeed? Again, to pose these questions is not to dismiss the significance of the digital network and some of its qualities, such as its potential to facilitate two-way interaction. Nonetheless, such consideration is useful. In parliamentary discussion of the Internet from the 1990s, that more attention was not given to the relatively recent adoption of radio and television, the debates surrounding it, and its implications is perhaps partly indicative of a tendency associated with technologies that were once regarded as of radical reforming potential but have been supplanted by others. They can become a subject of criticism. But they can also come to be overlooked, and their impact – though it might be great and possibly ongoing – not noticed or appreciated.

Such neglect might also lead to a failure to recognise the possibility that the acceptance of broadcasting helped make engagement with the Internet easier to implement. While it is useful to draw comparisons between the parliamentary incorporation of – on the one hand – broadcasting and – on the other hand – the Internet, we should avoid the perception that they were discrete processes. They occurred to some extent in overlapping periods and impacted upon one another. Radio and television were themselves two distinct media that have tended to be grouped into one overall category both by analysts and in parliamentary discussion – and were in the UK attached to the same public institution, the BBC, in a legal monopoly position over both until 1955, when ITV launched (following the 1954 Act). Over the three decades that followed the Bevan intervention, culminating in the introduction of ongoing television coverage of the Commons from 1989, the debate about the broadcasting of Parliament generated significant attention and was a subject of controversy within and outside the institution. Chapter 6 will show how, from the 1960s, in parallel to this tendency, increasing levels of interest developed inside Parliament about computing, including the use that the legislature itself could make of it. However, the subject of possible parliamentary employment of this technology did not achieve the same levels of interest as the broadcasting issue, either internally or in the outside world.

With hindsight, the adoption of computers was arguably at least as important a development for Parliament as its proceedings being disseminated by radio and television. It had substantial implications for the way in which it operated internally and its external interface with other institutions and the public. There were those – within Parliament and outside – who recognised some of the political potential of computing, including its being a means of communication, alongside data storage and processing functions. One obvious reason that it received relatively less attention than broadcasting was that its application as means of communication did not become fully apparent until the 1990s, while radio and then television had revealed this characteristic through mass permeation long before. During the 1970s, while Parliament argued about whether and how it should utilise radio and television, computers were coming increasingly into use in the workplace, and by the 1980s were finding their way into homes. But the linking of millions of people to a specific network through which they could both receive and disseminate content – the Internet – did not begin until the following decade. This shift prompted more widespread and intense interest in the uses and implications of this technology, in Parliament as elsewhere.

By this time, some important battles had been fought. Their outcome entailed a shift in the parliamentary posture. It is reasonable to regard the acceptance and then practical use of broadcasting as contributing to a cultural change. The idea that Parliament should use electronic communications devices to make itself more immediately and conveniently accessible to members of the public was easier to advance from the mid-1990s onwards than when, for instance, Bevan spoke in 1959. A long struggle had taken place between then and 1989, when continuous televising of the Commons began. A little over half a decade later, Parliament began tentative experiments with its own website. Debates about, and the employment of, earlier technologies – radio and television – had prepared the ground for the adoption of another. This pattern was already established. From the seventeenth century onwards, the printing press had played a part in the process whereby the English (and subsequently UK) Parliament had become an increasingly visible institution, a focus for intense scrutiny, eventually publishing a record of its own proceedings, which had once been secret. In this sense, later developments in broadcasting built on this earlier transition. Indeed, those who advocated it sometimes presented themselves as continuing in this tradition and promoting the values they attributed to it. Technological change could potentially provide a practical as well as principled basis for more such development. In discussion of the introduction of radio broadcasting to the Commons, consideration was given to the fact that microphones had already been installed in the Chamber for purposes of internal amplification using a Tannoy system.[52] Each technology had its own distinct characteristics and its adoption came about in specific circumstances with particular consequences. But certain common themes, as discussed above, arose. As if to establish that it was a successor to these earlier mechanisms, the Internet was able to absorb them within it. A feature of the parliamentary website from early on was its electronic reproduction of

[52] Select Committee on Broadcasting, etc., of Proceedings in the House of Commons, *First Report*, HC 146 (Stationery Office, London, 1966), pp. vii–viii.

Hansard, previously produced only in printed form; and parliament.tv provided an online version of television broadcasting of proceedings.

The discussion and adoption of broadcasting is just one of a number of strands of development involving the UK constitution that provide a context within which we should consider Parliament and the Internet. By the late 1960s, a number of potential reforms were on the agenda for Parliament and the political system more generally. Some of them had been under consideration as long ago as the nineteenth century; and earlier periods had also seen change.[53] Equally, Parliament is in many ways characterised by long-term continuities, and can prove resistant to change – as the decades-long prelude to the broadcasting of its proceedings demonstrates. Nonetheless, it is important to consider the shifting (though never completely transformed) environment within which parliamentary incorporation of computers and eventually the Internet took place. Processes leading to major constitutional reforms were already underway by the 1960s, and they would continue over the decades that followed.

Proposals included: enhancements to the research services available to MPs via the House of Commons Library; the establishment of permanently functioning Commons select committees systematically overseeing specific departments or policy areas; and some kind of alteration of the composition of the House of Lords (in addition to the introduction of Life Peers – who could be women or men – in 1958). There were calls to create devolved tiers of elected governance in different parts of the UK (there was already such a system in Northern Ireland, suspended from 1972), plans by the UK government to participate in the European integration project, and advocacy of the use of referendums (above local level, where they already took place, for instance on alcohol licensing rules). The supposed need for alterations in the Civil Service to make it more effective and better at supporting ministers became an ongoing theme. These various proposals came to be associated with certain principles about the future of democracy in the UK: that it should be more open; that public authorities – in particular the UK executive – should be subject to heightened levels of legal and political accountability; that it should be more effective and responsive to individual needs; and that the public should be more involved in its processes. An underlying motivation for such ideas was that of supposed declining public confidence in the system that their pursuit might halt or reverse. Proposals also sometimes arose from the premise that the UK political system was becoming subject to burdens that it was difficult for it effectively to manage. Often these constitutional issues – whether decided by free votes (as, for instance, was broadcasting of the Commons) or not – were matters that cut across normal political demarcations, creating divisions within parties.[54]

53 For an overview of the proposals that had accumulated by the beginning of the 1960s, see Hansard Society, *Parliamentary Reform: 1933–1960* (Cassell, London, 1961).

54 For constitutional reform from the 1960s onwards, see Andrew Blick, *Beyond Magna Carta: A Constitution for the United Kingdom* (Bloomsbury/Hart, Oxford, 2015), Pt 2.

An example of how such outlooks could apply in the specific case of the UK Parliament can be found in a 1964 work, *What's Wrong with Parliament?* The book was part of a 'Penguin Special' series that captured the pessimistic tone of the time. Titles within it – using the 'What's Wrong' moniker – sought to discern the supposed failings with different aspects of UK society such as the Church, business, and the health service. In the Parliament entry, the authors opened with the statement that '[i]n 1945 the reputation of the British Parliament stood as high as ever before in its long history'. They then asked '[h]ow high does Parliament's reputation stand today?'[55] After some discussion of the views of opinion formers and evidence of public opinion, they concluded that 'as one considers current attitudes to Parliament and then compares them with those of 1945, that the massive general goodwill towards Parliament has been gradually frittered away'. The evidence cited included opinions expressed in the media and declining sales of Hansard. Possible causes of this trend they identified included excessive subservience to the whips among MPs and 'innumerable false points of order'. They stressed that 'Parliament is not the only British institution which has come under severe criticism lately',[56] and noted that earlier eras, such as the 1930s, had also seen the effectiveness of Parliament called widely into question.[57] They hoped to remedy present problems, bringing about an improved public reputation for Parliament, and enabling it to hold the executive to account more effectively. To this end, the work advocated various measures, specifically focused on the Commons, including the establishment of specialist committees, mechanisms to ensure more satisfactory responses to petitions from the public, and the televising of proceedings.

Proposals of the type the authors supported were receiving wide support at the time, with advocates including the Study of Parliament Group. Coming into being in 1964, the Group advocated reforms such as expansions in the research capacity of the House of Commons Library; procedural changes intended to alleviate pressure on the parliamentary timetable; and – again – specialist committees for oversight of the executive.[58] In various ways, many of these ideas would – sometimes after prolonged debate – be implemented.[59] Parliament – both the Commons and the Lords – obtained enhanced means of performing its accountability role and became more willing to offer resistance to the executive. In the Commons, over the decades following the 1960s, there

[55] Andrew Hill and Anthony Whichelow, *What's Wrong with Parliament?* (Penguin, Harmondsworth, 1964), p. 9.

[56] Ibid., p. 11.

[57] Ibid., p. 94.

[58] Study of Parliament Group, *Reforming the Commons* (Political and Economic Planning, London, 1965).

[59] For an earlier entry in this field, see Bernard Crick, *Reform of the Commons* (Fabian Society, London, 1959). Also, by the same author, *The Reform of Parliament* (Weidenfeld and Nicolson, London, 1965).

was a general upward trend in rebelliousness, while the in the Lords – especially after the removal of most hereditary occupants in 1999 – Peers generally seemed to regard themselves as more legitimate and able to assert themselves in the legislative process.[60]

It was within this dynamic setting that Parliament eventually came to adopt and develop its approach to the Internet. A number of complex interactions were at play. A useful illustrative example, that will recur in following chapters, involves specialist parliamentary committees, and in particular House of Commons select committees. The main focus for consideration in this area tends to be on the period from 1979 onwards.[61] Yet – just as this study suggests is the case with computers and the Internet – it is important to consider a longer timeframe. Certainly, key developments in terms of political pressure and practical experiments were already underway during the 1960s.[62] They would eventually lead to the system of a group of Commons committees monitoring specific departments instigated in 1979. As we will see, the story of select committees and the subject of this book were intertwined. These parliamentary bodies were early users of computer technology, innovating in various ways in this field from the early 1970s. Furthermore, they could also explore the social potential of such devices and the networks they might form. We consider these matters in detail in Chapters 6–8.

In some significant cases, it should be noted, rather than 1979-model departmental committees, committees (in either House) concerned with the internal business of Parliament – such as Procedure, Services, Administration and Information – played a part in discussing the use that the wider institution might make of computers or the Internet specifically and making recommendations. The Committee on the Modernisation of the House of Commons, an executive-driven committee with a Cabinet minister, the Leader of the House of Commons, in the chair, provided impetus for innovation in use of the Internet early in the twenty-first century. Select committees universally came to utilise the Internet itself as a means of obtaining written evidence; they broadcast evidence sessions online and carried out some of their proceedings remotely via the Internet during the 2020–1 pandemic. Innovations in the use of digital forums were often linked to the work of select committees. That these mechanisms did not become more fully integrated into the legislative process is probably a reflection of the nature of the select committee system. In contrast to other jurisdictions, in the UK Parliament these bodies engage more with policy, administration and expenditure than the production of law. First the Backbench Business Committee and then – from 2015 – the purpose-created

60 See e.g. Meg Russell and Philip Cowley, 'The Policy Power of the Westminster Parliament: The "Parliamentary State" and the Empirical Evidence', *Governance* 29(1) (2016): 121–37.

61 See e.g. Gavin Drewry (ed.), *The New Select Committees: A Study of the 1979 Reforms* (Clarendon, Oxford, 1989).

62 For a reassessment of this period, see Philip Aylett, 'Crossman and Beyond: House of Commons Select Committees in the 1960s', *Parliamentary History* 38(3) (2019): 408–30.

Petitions Committee had the task of handling the Commons response to e-petitions. Select committees in the Commons and Lords came to take a pronounced interest in the social implications of the Internet, promoting options intended to maximise benefits and minimise harm.

Alongside committees, the topic of the Internet and Parliament intersects with numerous further areas of UK constitutional development. Within Parliament, for instance, the House of Commons Library – the expansion of which was a reform objective by the 1960s – was an early source of pressure for the adoption of computers and their use for remote access to information. Subsequently, the Internet would provide the Library with a public face, with many of its outputs made available online. Beyond Parliament, other constitutional developments were significant. For instance, membership of the European Communities from 1973 encouraged a perceived need for the use of computers, including to obtain remote access to information relevant to UK participation in the continental integration project. Devolution to Wales and Scotland and its restoration in Northern Ireland from the late 1990s led to the establishment of elected assemblies the practices of which – including in the field of the Internet – might influence the UK Parliament. Parliamentary use of computers and the Internet could also fit with prevailing ideas about the proper purposes of the UK constitution. For instance, it could facilitate public access to official information – and indeed encourage the view that such openness was proper. The Internet might, some hoped, make Parliament operate more efficiently and facilitate more rigorous accountability for the executive. A common motivation for parliamentary employment of the Internet was the theory that it was a means of enhancing public engagement and confidence in the political system and in Parliament itself.

A note that senior staff at the House of Commons Library submitted to the House of Commons (Services) Committee in 1977, making the case for the introduction of a computer index system, showed how various tendencies could combine to create a perceived need for the incorporation of digital technology. It read:

> **Changing needs of Members of Parliament**
>
> 1. The work of Parliament has increased in volume and complexity over the whole period since the Second World War, but the increase has become more marked in the last decade. Features of the increase have included:
>
> (a) a rise in the volume of legislation both primary and secondary;
> (b) a considerable increase in the activity of Select Committees, with the setting up of new types of Committee some ten years ago;
> (c) the adherence of the UK to the EEC, with a need for Parliament to keep itself informed of developments and review secondary legislation; and
> (d) the prorogation of the Stormont parliament, so that legislation for Northern Ireland is now handled at Westminster.

These have been among the factors in the rise in the volume of parliamentary business, and hence in making Members of Parliament much busier people; and their increased activity has impinged on the staff of the House of Commons, including that of the Library.

The increased pressure on the library staff results not only from the increased activity of Parliament as an institution described above but also from:

(a) the great rise in the flow of documentation from government departments, international organisations and other sources, all of which has to be dealt with;
(b) the tendency for a larger proportion of Members than previously to be full-time politicians and
(c) the heavier burden of constituency casework now handled by Members, compared with earlier periods, arising from the more extensive activities of the public services, on much of which it has come to be expected that the Library should supply assistance.

Another factor that has caused a considerable increase in the workload of the Library has been the large growth of the number of Members' personal research assistants. They both make direct use of the Library's indexes and holdings and occupy some of the time of Research Division staff. There has also been a rise in the amount of work carried out for Peers.[63]

Over time, some of the factors referred to in the paper would change – for instance, devolution would be restored to Northern Ireland, and introduced in Wales and Scotland. But the general pattern would continue: a desire to utilise technology arising in connection to patterns of constitutional development – actual or at least perceived – and the intention of responding appropriately to them. Yet development took place, within Parliament and across other parts of the UK constitution, within the context of a long-established institutions and their practices, which could shape and limit it, as we will see.

The present chapter provides a political and systemic context for the central subject of this book. It has so far identified how ideas about communications, technology, and democracy comparable to some that later appeared in the context of the Internet could appeal to a senior politician – namely Benn – in the late 1960s. It has also provided an overview of the constitutional context within which the legislature came to utilise networked computing from this period through to the present. The chapter will now move to considers how – beyond more established structures – concepts about the democratic application of the Internet could gain in salience and eventually become part of the mainstream in the UK. It does so through two case studies. They provide – rather than a comprehensive account of the movements to which they are connected, or of wider society – an indicator of the circumstances in which certain ideas could seed and develop. The first focuses on a particular aspect of environmentalism. This subject is of significance

[63] 'The Library's Proposals for Computer-Based Indexing', Memorandum by the Librarian and Deputy Librarian, Select Committee on House of Commons (Services), *Computer-Based Indexing for the Library*, Fifth Report of Session 1976–77, HC 377 (Stationery Office, London, 1977), Minutes of Evidence, 5 April 1977, Q. 35, p. 21.

because the rise of this cause (though it had clear precursors) in the UK (and internationally) took place broadly in parallel to the invention and permeation of the technology under consideration here. After a general discussion of the links between this movement and scientific advance and innovation, I focus on a particular aspect of environmentalism: the 'alternative technology' school of the 1970s and 1980s, and a particular journal that promoted it, *Undercurrents*. Secondly, the chapter examines the rise of online activism in the UK during the 1990s. It takes as its focus a collection of online activist initiatives operating during the second half of the 1990s. A central figure in this movement, David Wilcox, has left a significant imprint of material on the Internet that remains available in its original form. As is discussed below, this particular case study enables us to connect longer traditions of thought and practice involving technology and democratic empowerment with parliamentary employment of the Internet.

Alternative Technology, the Internet, and Politics

Environmentalism – that is, the cause of protecting the natural world against threats of human origin – can appear to have a powerful strand of hostility to technology within it. Yet within this school, scientific advance could also have an important positive role ascribed to it. In this sense it was another expression of the tendency noted in this book to present invention and innovation as a source of problems and the solutions to them. Indeed, some thinkers we might regard as precursors to contemporary environmentalism displayed this twin outlook. William Morris, for instance, disliked the industrial society of his day but valued technology directed to his preferred purposes and provided it with a role in the idealised alternative he proposed. Those who exercised influence on the development of the movement in more recent decades displayed a similar complexity of outlook. Through a 1962 work, *Silent Spring*, Rachel Carson generated significant public concern about the impact of chemistry as applied to the elimination of pests.[64] Her chief conclusion was that 'we should no longer accept the counsel of those who tell us that we must fill our world with poisonous chemicals'.[65] Yet Carson – like many of those who would follow her lead – was herself a scientist. She held that it was possible to preserve food supplies in less harmful ways: 'based on understanding of the living organisms they seek to control, and of whole fabric of life to which these organisms belong'. There were '[a] truly extraordinary variety of alternatives to the chemical control insects'. Some were in use already, others 'in the stage of laboratory testing' or 'little more than ideas in the minds of imaginative scientists'.[66]

Another influential figure on the environmental movement as it developed during the final third of the twentieth century was the economist E. F. Schumacher. In his work, published in 1973, *Small Is Beautiful*, one of his

[64] Rachel Carson, *Silent Spring* (Penguin, London, 2000), p. 241.
[65] Ibid., p. 240.
[66] Ibid.

themes was the social impact of technology. He found that in the 'modern world' it had led to three simultaneous 'crises'. They were, first, that of 'human nature' revolting 'against inhuman technological, organisational, and political patterns, which it experiences as suffocating and debilitating'. The second was the issue of 'the living environment which supports human life', which 'aches and groans and gives signs of partial breakdown'. The third were 'the inroads being made into the world's non-renewable resources ... such that serious bottlenecks and virtual exhaustion loom ahead'.[67] Nonetheless, rather than outright rejection, Schumacher proposed that '[i]f technology is felt to be becoming more and more inhuman, we might do well to consider whether it is possible to have something better – a technology with a human face'.[68] In his work, Schumacher – in a tone that contrasted with Benn – questioned the potential of computer data analysis. Specifically, he raised doubts about the possibility of modelling future behaviour and developments.[69] But, again, he was not wholly dismissive. He regarded computers as fulfilling an important basic function, making it possible to 'do in seconds what it would take clerks or even mathematicians a very long time, if they can do it at all'.[70]

Computing had already made a practical impact in the field of environmental thought. Coming into being in April 1968, the 'Club of Rome' was an international, informal grouping of various figures from academia and other research, business, and public administration, that took upon itself the ambitious task of analysing the main challenges facing humanity. In 1972 it published what would become a best-selling work entitled *The Limits to Growth*. It comprised computer-based modelling that suggested projected levels of global economic expansion would produce significant environmental strains.[71] In the same year, a work that made a particular impact in the UK was *A Blueprint for Survival*, the authors of which were the editors of *The Ecologist* magazine, among whom Edward Goldsmith was the pre-eminent figure.[72] They discerned that industrial society was generating an impending set of interlinked environmental cataclysms. Transition to a different kind of society would either be achieved before disaster came about, or be forced by its occurrence. They proposed a major decentralisation, with people living in politically self-governing and self-sufficient communities of around 5,000. This shift would involve a turn away from existing forms of production.

67 E. F. Schumacher, *Small Is Beautiful: Economics as if People Mattered* (Harper, New York, 2010), p. 156.

68 Ibid., p. 155.

69 For my analysis of this aspect of Schumacher, see Andrew Blick, *Stretching the Constitution: The Brexit Shock in Historic Perspective* (Bloomsbury/Hart, Oxford, 2019), pp. 274–5.

70 Schumacher, *Small is Beautiful*, p. 157.

71 Donella H. Meadows, Dennis L. Meadows, Jorgen Randers, and William W. Behrens III, *The Limits to Growth* (Universe, New York, 1972).

72 The editors of the Ecologist, *A Blueprint for Survival* (Penguin, Harmondsworth, 1972). For my discussion of Goldsmith and *Blueprint for Survival*, see Blick, *Stretching the Constitution*, pp. 180–5.

The authors held that 'science must address itself much more vigorously to the problems of co-operating with the rest of Nature, rather than seeking to control it'.[73] Yet it would have an important role, including in designing new forms of transport, in 'research into materials substitution' and in 'development of alternative technologies'.[74]

The term 'alternative technologies' came to be attached to a particular branch of the environmental movement. Participants within it sought a revised approach to science and invention. They regarded prevailing social approaches in this area as detrimental to the needs of humanity and the natural environment within which it existed. The first edition of a journal that promoted this cause appeared early in 1972. Called *Undercurrents*, it was an activist-driven rather than commercial publication. It had a fringe flavour, to which the contributors – through their determination to challenge existing practices and standards – seem to have consciously contributed. They appeared to conform to the clichéd pattern of excitedly forming groups the likely active membership of which – the reader might well suspect – was only in single figures, only to schism into even smaller entities.[75] Yet this peripherality, rather than being a reason for dismissing its contents, is the source of its importance. Change to the mainstream can only come about because of the incorporation of forces and ideas that were previously external to it and challenged its existing arrangements in some way. In this work, I argue that such a process of adaption can take place because outlying concepts, and their advocates, achieve direct influence upon established groups and institutions; or because concepts develop more spontaneously, taking hold in environments that are more receptive to them sooner before more general dissemination; or some combination of the two. If we are better to understand transformation at the centre then it is necessary to explore the margins. Apparent barriers between the two can prove permeable, and tendences observable in the former can come to appear in the latter.

Even in the 1960s and 1970s the environmental movement of which *Undercurrents* and the alternative technology school formed a part was capable of generating significant public attention and high-level endorsement internationally and within the UK. The reception of the ideas of Carson supports this point. More radical proposals – such as dispersal into communities of 5,000 – have not yet come to pass. But in time, the broad philosophical approach with which *Undercurrents* was associated – that technological development and the economic rationale underpinning it had to alter to reflect environmental needs – would become a commonplace. This transition makes a consideration of the concepts presented in the journal more than a historical

[73] The editors of the Ecologist, *A Blueprint for Survival*, p. 67.
[74] Ibid., p. 59.
[75] Steve Boulter, School of Environmental Studies, University College, London, 'A.T. Goes Boom', *Undercurrents* 7, July–August 1974, p. 4.

curiosity. They contained aspects of future social priorities to which most mainstream politicians, for instance, would today – at least in their public rhetoric – adhere. The Green Party – the original precursor to which was formed in 1973, as assessed by my former research student, Mitya Pearson – eventually secured representation at local, European (before UK departure from the European Union), and Westminster level. Within Parliament, from 1997, a specific initiative provided concerns in this area with both formal recognition and an outlet, in the form of the House of Commons Environmental Audit Committee, responsible for oversight of government and its policies in this field.[76]

Over a similar period, ideas presented in *Undercurrents* regarding networked computing would – in modified form – appear increasingly conventional, including within Parliament. While evidence of a direct causal relationship between the formation of ideas among exponents of alternative technology and their more general adoption is harder to find, *Undercurrents* is important in that it provides evidence of how certain concepts and discussions could incubate in an early phase in the UK.

In the February 1982 edition of *Undercurrents*, marking its tenth anniversary (it ran for a further two years), the founding editor, Godfrey Boyle, gave an account of his personal background and the thinking that led to the establishment of the publication. His interest in the 'idea of producing an "underground" science and technology magazine' dated to the late 1960s. Studying engineering at Queen's University, Belfast, he had 'developed an interest in the paranormal, altered states of consciousness, unorthodox philosophies, "disreputable" phenomena like UFOs and the strange occurrences chronicled by Charles Fort, and libertarian political ideas'. Boyle adds that such 'enthusiasms were strengthened' through time spent in the United States in 1966. He shared with 'many students at the time' sympathy for 'criticisms that were being voiced, especially after May 1968, on technology and the technocratic society'. On occasion Boyle wrote articles for student publications comprising 'onslaughts against the engineering profession for which I was being trained'.

Arriving in London at the beginning of the next decade he became increasingly exposed to some of the same countercultural elements that influenced advocates of democratised networked computing in the US around this time. Boyd 'was turned on not only by the more famous "alternative" papers like *Oz* and *IT*, but by other obscure specialised periodicals', including those that questioned the nature of the computing business. He took an interest in London-based activists and experimental multimedia projects, as well as 'the first *Whole Earth Catalog*, from California'. The environmental movement was also gaining in momentum, with the formation of 'the British branch of

[76] See www.parliament.uk/business/committees/committees-a-z/commons-select/environmental-audit-committee/?utm_source=dlvr.it&utm_medium=twitter, last accessed 20 July 2020.

Friends of the Earth and the British Society for Social Responsibility in Science'. Moving in circles associated with a journal called *Resurgence*, whose advocacy of 'decentralisation' Boyd found attractive, they in turn 'introduced me to the writings of an obscure economist called Schumacher', as well as the activities of 'an equally obscure group of US scientists', followers of Buckminster Fuller, known as 'the New Alchemists'.[77]

By 1971 Boyd was professionally engaged writing for *Electronics Weekly*, 'mainly about communications'. He launched *Undercurrents* with the assistance of a Labour councillor who owned a printing press. The first edition appeared early in 1972. Boyd began establishing contact with a wider group who were part of the emerging alternative technologies (AT) movement and became contributors to *Undercurrents*. The journal attained some notoriety in the mainstream media during its first year when it published an article discussing the prospects for the destruction of Parliament and the government using a homemade atomic device.[78] In an edition that appeared in November 1973, it presented an 'Undercurrents Manifesto 1973'. It complained that '[s]cience … has largely abandoned its original "quest for truth"'. Furthermore, '[t]echnology … while still masquerading as mankind's great emancipator, is increasingly becoming the instrument of our enslavement'. It was 'in practice … the means whereby the unjust economy and power structure of our industrial civilisation is kept intact and entrenched'. The text expressed regret that '[t]echnology no longer concerns itself with the satisfaction of individual human needs, but with the churning-out of cheaper and ever-more-sophisticated products which the masses can be persuaded they need, brainwashed as they are by the propaganda of advertising and the mass media'. While the system produced more, 'the overall distribution of wealth' remained unequal. The manifesto noted that this social arrangement had lately become subject to criticism, naming Theodore Roszak as an example of a sceptic.[79]

Meanwhile 'pollution, industrialisation, standardisation, the depletion of natural resources, and the other concomitants of the industrial way of life' were leading to growing disillusion regarding the supposed benefits of science. *Undercurrents* therefore called for 'a "sadder but a wiser" science, a science that is aware of its limitations as well as its strengths'. The manifesto insisted that 'technology can be reorientated to serve not economics and governments but individual human beings'. It could be employed 'to provide small-scale sources of basics like energy, food, shelter, clothing and tools, to provide unfettered communications between the smaller, more human communities

[77] See e.g. Steve Rose, 'The Circle of Life', *The Guardian*, 29 September 2019, www.theguardian.com/lifeandstyle/ng-interactive/2019/sep/29/the-new-alchemists-could-the-past-hold-the-key-to-sustainable-living, last accessed 20 July 2020.

[78] Godfrey Boyle, 'In the Beginning', *Undercurrents* 50, February 1982, 29–30.

[79] 'Undercurrents Manifesto 1973', *Undercurrents*, 1 November 1972 (no issue number), p. 1.

that our world must create if it is to avoid overpopulation, alienation, violence and all the attendant evils of the mass society'. Science might also 'provide simple data processing and automation facilities in a way that genuinely relieves human beings of boredom and drudgery without enslaving them to machines or to their owners'.[80] The latter passage suggested that computers – perhaps as part of networks – might play a part in the programme of *Undercurrents* and the AT movement. But there was some scepticism among adherents about these devices. One contributor, Alan Campbell, had produced an article in February 1972 entitled 'Alternative Uses of Computers', writing that: 'I'm not sure there are any . . . I see computers primarily as tools . . . They are neither good nor bad; they can only be put to good or bad uses.'[81]

Other contributors were more enthusiastic, promoting ideas about the potential of networked computing similar to those that had emerged from the US counterculture which had influenced the formation of *Undercurrents*. In the April–May 1978 edition, John Garrett and Geoff Wright produced an article, 'Micro Is Beautiful', which consciously adapted Schumacher to apply to analysis of developments in the 'computer industry'. The article suggested that structurally distributed technology could bring about an organisational dispersal of power that mirrored its decentralised architecture, thereby having a democratising effect. Computing, the authors remarked, had long been dominated by a single corporation, IBM, supplying equipment to 'organisations' that were 'cumbersome, inflexible ... [and] ... bureaucratic' – terms, the authors judged, that could also apply to the way in which its technology functioned. But this 'steady progress towards a computerised 1984' now faced a countervailing trend in the form of 'distributed processing', enabled since 1966 by 'low-cost ... mini-computers' and then – from 1972 – 'even lower cost ... micro-computers'. This process entailed 'the decentralising of computing power around a network of computers, instead of all computing power residing in one, usually large, central computer'.[82] Comprising a set of 'remote terminals' connected to powerful 'central computers', while these 'computer networks' had existed for some time, an important difference had appeared lately. The terminals had become more sophisticated and could themselves be used for 'simple programming'. Moreover, there were 'now full inter-computer networks, with mini-computers in place of terminals'. They used telephone lines at present but were likely eventually to utilise 'high-speed computer "grids"' or 'communications satellites'.

These systems, the authors held, were first designed for defence purposes, to allow government to continue to function following 'nuclear attack'. But now, '[i]ronically what was designed for the defence of the state could become the communications structure of a decentralised society'. They envisaged a

[80] Ibid., pp. 1–2.

[81] Alan Campbell, 'Alternative Uses of Computers', *Undercurrents* 1, February 1972, p. 35.

[82] John Garrett and Geoff Wright, 'Micro Is Beautiful', Undercurrents 27, April–May 1978, p. 33.

scenario in which '[c]ommunes, farms, workshops and factories in a region, each with a computer in the network, would be able to do their own computing to link to others or to update and use shared data-bases'. They could establish a system of barter-trading in 'goods and services'. This 'decentralised society' would require 'a very fast and efficient decision-making system, involving all those who might be affected'. The article called into doubt the effectiveness for this purpose of '[t]he traditional democratic method of delegate conference'. It suffered from 'being slower and ... hidebound by rules'. The authors anticipated that '[c]ommunication networks should allow decision-making to be faster, more responsive to events, and theoretically enable *all* members of a unit to be consulted rather than just one delegate'. In the scenario they envisaged, '[p]olitics could become the day-to-day occupation of the many rather than the personal gamesmanship of the few'.

Garret and Wright noted a need 'to avoid control of any computer network or control of information in the network being in any one unit's hands'. A means of preventing this outcome was through making 'data-bases themselves ... decentralised round the network'.[83] To make the enhancement of democracy meaningful it would be necessary to expand: 'the availability of information. At the moment both government and the controllers of industry hog information to help them maintain control.' Yet '[w]ith recent developments in computer networks, decentralised control with no loss of efficiency is possible'. The article therefore proposed that '[a]ll homes and workplaces in the country could be networked via the [Post Office] Viewdata system'. The authors hoped that '[i]f all available economic, social and political information were in the system, it would then be available to every citizen. Such a system makes possible decentralised, democratic, economic management on the feedback principle.'[84]

This article shows how ideas about networked computing could form during the 1970s in activist circles in the UK. They appeared in this instance as a means of achieving desired outcomes, and as a method of making political decisions – by direct as opposed to representative means. This technological advocacy prefigured some views advanced on behalf of the Internet, especially from the 1990s onwards. Subsequent scepticism about the same subject can also be found within AT circles as expressed in *Undercurrents*. Writing in the October–November 1978 edition, Campbell responded critically to Garrett and Wright. While acknowledging that the 'changes in the computer industry' they identified were taking place, he held that 'they are indulging in wish-fulfilling fantasies if they think those changes are going to lead to, or even make more probable, real and desirable social change'. He identified the example of 'distributed computing' noting that, once made viable:

[83] Ibid., pp. 34–5.
[84] Ibid., p. 36.

> I'm willing to bet an early application will be a computer-in-every-copshop, all linked together and talking back and forth amicably with the Police National Computer. Of course if the National Question has been solved by then, it will be the Police World Computer.

Campbell doubted the 'democratic metaphor in computing' and anticipated that the technology would destroy jobs or move them elsewhere in the world.[85]

At this point, discussion was not yet focused precisely on the Internet, but *Undercurrents* eventually drew attention to its immediate precursor. In the December 1980–January 1981 edition, Dave Kanner noted long-standing prophecies of 'an information explosion with the great improvements in communications technologies and the spread of cheap microprocessors', referring to 'Marshall McLuhan's *global village*, James Martin's *wired society* and Alvin Toffler's *electronic cottages*' as instances 'of over-optimistic assessments of the effect of these developments'.[86] Kanner then listed various varieties of digital networks that existed. Remarking that '[t]rue interactive networks allow participants to put information into store as well as assessing what's already there', Kanner acknowledged that:

> [t]he big daddy of them all is ARPANET, set up by the Advanced Research Projects Agency of the US Department of Defense. This links some 200 mainframe computers in universities, research centres and government facilities in the US and overseas. The network can be used to send and receive mail, establish direct contact or run programs on common databases.

He then went on to refer to '[t]he Community Memory Project' in the San Francisco Bay Area. It was, Kanner wrote, 'the nearest thing to a fully participatory network. The CM people are providing linked terminals in public places on which anyone can type in messages, notices, party invitations, or whatever'.[87]

Undercurrents had recently published accounts by AT advocates of a projected model society within which they anticipated such technology would play a part. The October–November 1980 issue contained a description of what its designers described as a 'Community for the Future', a physical scale model of which had been constructed, known as 'Protopia'.[88] The advocates of this project hoped to recruit participants and embark on such an experiment in practice, perhaps in the vicinity of the Milton Keynes new town.[89] It would be 'self-governing, running many of the social, educational and welfare services normally provided by larger local authorities'. Protopia would combine the use of 'high technology' in areas including 'information', and 'low

85 Alan Campbell, 'Hard Chips', *Undercurrents* 30, October–November 1978, p. 30.

86 Dave Kanner, 'Computer Networks', *Undercurrents* 43, December 1980–January 1981, p. 22.

87 Ibid., p. 23.

88 Guy Dauncey and Andrew Page, 'Blueprint for Greentown?', Undercurrents 42, October–November 1980, p. 9.

89 Ibid., p. 10.

technology in ... production'.[90] Among the devices available would be a 'Community Communications System' (CCS). Users would have 'at home a console consisting of two video monitors, channel selectors and dials ... a computer keyboard, and a special telephone linked directly to the co-ordinating centre'. There would also be 'CCS Consoles ... located throughout the community'. The CCS would serve to prevent 'the community from becoming cut off from the rest of the world'. It would also facilitate the new economic model for the community, in which low-technology-based forms of production would leave a variety of labour-intensive jobs requiring performance. The CCS would enable people to choose from a variety of tasks to avoid the monotony of carrying out only one.

Construction of a model society intended to combine the advantages of rural and urban, advanced and simple technology, was a project with many precursors discussed previously in this book. *Undercurrents* acknowledged this point when alluding to Karl Marx and his description in his 1845 *German Ideology* of how, in a communist system, it would be 'possible for me to do one thing today and another tomorrow, to hunt in the morning, fish in the afternoon, rear cattle in the evening, criticise after dinner, just as I have in mind'.[91] This veiled reference to Marx was indicative of awareness within the AT movement that it had forerunners. Another such acknowledgement came in the form of the title of a regular column in the journal: 'News from Everywhere' – a variation on *News from Nowhere* by William Morris. In 1976 the editorial team behind *Undercurrents* issued a collected volume, *Radical Technology*.[92] Jos Kingston contributed a chapter entitled 'It's Been Said Before and Where Did That Get Us'.[93] He wrote of:

> radicalism in early nineteenth century Britain, especially the socialism of the Owenites ... For anybody who's involved in today's making of an alternative culture (which excludes the large majority of academic historians studying the radical movements), the similarities between what went on then and what goes on now seem almost uncanny.[94]

Kingston noted: '[t]he Owenites were especially concerned about the role of science and technology in society. Science wasn't rejected, but acclaimed as the great improver of mankind.'[95]

But though proponents of AT might recognise such precursors, and while addressing the perceived inequity of capitalism might be an important feature

[90] Ibid., p. 9.
[91] Andrew Page, 'Convivial Computing', Undercurrents 42, October–November 1980, p. 12.
[92] Peter Harper, Godfrey Boyle, and the editors of *Undercurrents* (eds.), *Radical Technology* (Wildwood House, London, 1976).
[93] Jos Kingston, 'It's Been Said Before and Where Did that Get Us', in Peter Harper, Godfrey Boyle and the editors of *Undercurrents* (eds.) *Radical Technology* (Wildwood House, London, 1976), pp. 238–48.
[94] Ibid., p. 240.
[95] Ibid., p. 241.

of their programme, they were reluctant to identify specifically as of the Left as conventionally understood. Moreover, unlike the branch of the environmental movement that led to what became the Green Party, there was a tendency for AT activists to regard electoral politics as distasteful, though there was some discussion in *Undercurrents* of whether and how they should engage with them (in this reluctance to take part they were once again similar to Owen).[96] Geoff Wright voiced this reticence even while overcoming it in an article in the June–July 1979 edition, published following the Conservative General Election victory under Margaret Thatcher in May. Writing that '[t]he parliamentary charade isn't something *Undercurrents* takes too seriously', Wright had nonetheless interviewed the Conservative MP Ian Lloyd, who had been Vice Chairman of the House of Commons Select Committee on Science and Technology in the previous Parliament. In the interview, Lloyd predicted that 'any intelligent person, student, journalist, or whatever, who needs to acquire specific information, will very soon be able to go to a telephone in their own house and dial and say "I want..." They will then be presented with a branching system down which they can go to find it.' Lloyd judged that 'this is going to have an immense effect on the distribution of power in the community, a point which I think very few political people appreciate at the moment'.[97] When reminded that 'Tony Benn has come out in favour of instant referenda', in replying, Lloyd remarked that:

> Tony Benn is a populist ... and I don't denigrate him for that, populism has always been a very tempting political philosophy ... If you are a populist you say if it can be done, do it. You then justify it by saying 'Of course I trust the people, the people are wiser than the experts and will always show shrewd instinctive judgement when the experts get it wrong.'

Lloyd held that '[i]f you believe that on all issues, at all times, then you must be a populist'. However, he did not accept that public wisdom was superior on every occasion. Rather, he was 'a democrat, and I believe on some issues, on some occasions, the people are wiser than those who govern them'.[98] When participants in the AT movement had advocated the application of networked computers for political decision-making, they focused on their use in decentralised small units in which the whole community could take a direct part. The reference Wright made to Benn suggested an awareness among those proposing such systems of the May 1968 proposal that this Labour politician had made for holding such exercises on a countrywide basis, and was suggestive of possible influence it had. But both approaches – the local and whole UK – were envisaged exercises in direct democracy. The response received from Lloyd showed that the use of networked computers as a means of

96 See e.g. various articles in *Undercurrents* 32, February–March 1979.
97 Geoff Wright, 'Looking Forward to 1984', Undercurrents 34, June–July 1979, p. 31.
98 Ibid., pp. 31–2.

political engagement in the UK would necessarily take place within the context of a representative system. Within this established structure the supreme organ – of which Lloyd was a member – was Parliament. We return to his contribution later. The next case study considers, with a central focus on one individual, a collection of digital activists and groups that – like those associated with AT – tended not to align themselves with pre-existing political orientations. Their approach to computing was even purer than that presented in *Undercurrents* since, rather than being a means towards a particular goal, public participation via the Internet was the end in itself. Pursuit of this objective eventually led to a direct interface with Parliament.

Online Activism in the UK, 1995–9

In June 2006, David Wilcox posted on his 'Designing for Civil Society' blog an article entitled 'e-Democracy Projects Resurrects Its Parent'. He noted how, a decade previously, he, a friend of his (Richard Stubbs), and a collection of others including Irving Rappaport (the instigator of the initiative), had 'put enormous efforts into giving birth to e-democracy through an organisation . . . called UK Citizens Online Democracy [UKCOD]'. It was 'the world's first national online democracy experiment'. The key purpose was to facilitate official policy consultations, engaging members of the public via the Internet. At the time it was an innovative practice. Rather than simply disseminating information from above, it entailed soliciting views from below. The project, as Wilcox put it, 'connected politicians directly with the public they represented using the new internet technology'. In other words, it sought to create new ways in which people could participate, wielding influence upon and working with, but not seeking to supplant, representative institutions. It was radical, but within certain existing parameters. Adept at elite contact-building, UKCOD secured high-prestige connections. Its first work commission, Wilcox recounted, came from the European Union, to 'host and manage an online discussion' about the merits of the UK participating in the single currency. UKCOD also helped with 'research work contributing to the Freedom of Information Act 2000'. This project earned UKCOD 'a meeting with Tony Blair . . . in December 1997', then early in his period of office as Labour Prime Minister. As part of its promotional campaigning, UKCOD 'recruited celebrities from the world of film, TV, theatre and music . . . with the help of a lovely and very dedicated PR woman by the name of Sarah Macaulay', later married to Gordon Brown.[99]

Participants in UKCOD included Stephen Coleman, who – as discussed elsewhere in this work – was a key promoter and practitioner of internet-based

[99] David Wilcox, 'e-Democracy Project Resurrects Its Parent', *Design for Civil Society*, available at www.designingforcivilsociety.org/2007/06/edemocracy_proj.html, last accessed 9 December 2019.

forums to support parliamentary inquiries, especially in the late 1990s and early 2000s. In a 2004 article, he produced a list of ten such parliamentary exercises held up to 2002. The first, from 1998, commissioned by the Parliamentary Office of Science and Technology, was on the subject of the Data Protection Bill. The joint organisers were the Hansard Society and UKCOD. For subsequent consultations, Coleman brought the work wholly within the former organisation, and UKCOD was no longer involved.[100] However, as an innovator in this field, UKCOD, as we shall see, provides clear a link between many of the long-term tendencies discussed in this book and the specific subject of this work, that of Parliament and the Internet.[101]

A further connection is worth remarking upon. While UKCOD in its first incarnation had ceased to be active by the end of the 1990s, it was subsequently revived in 2003 and the following year became a parent organisation for the mySociety project. A registered charity, UKCOD as a legal entity provided a useful vehicle for this new purpose. Beyond this formal existence there was little direct continuity between UKCOD in its earlier and later forms. But the general objective of promoting democratic activity on the Internet remained the same. mySociety, as we have seen, would become important to the practice of online interactions involving Parliament. For instance, it came to incorporate TheyWorkForYou (launched in 2004, coming under the mySociety umbrella in 2006), and produced an influential review for Parliament of its digital services, published in 2014. Moreover, it provided the technical expertise that made the No. 10 petitions website possible – eventually shared with Parliament. The initial launch of this platform in 2006 provided the occasion for Wilcox to write under the headline 'e-Democracy Projects Resurrects Its Parent'.[102]

To trace the activist career of Wilcox and various initiatives with which he was involved, leading on to UKCOD, is to conduct a study in the developing interaction of technology, ideas, and civil society organisation. He began with an interest in engaging the public at local level in projects to bring about transformation of the spaces in which they lived, moving in circles in which the name of Patrick Geddes was referred to as an influence.[103] His focus subsequently expanded to encompass the use of networked computers for engagement purposes. Up to 1978, Wilcox was 'planning correspondent' for the London newspaper, the *Evening Standard*. He wrote about such subjects as 'housing, transport, property and the social and economic forces changing the capital's communities'. Thereafter, he became a 'consultant, writer and trainer,

[100] Stephen Coleman, 'Connecting Parliament to the Public Via the Internet: Two Case Studies of Online Consultations', *Information, Communication & Society* 7(1) (2004): 1–22, 4.

[101] Wilcox, 'e-Democracy Project Resurrects Its Parent'.

[102] Ibid.

[103] Mentioned by Wilcox unprompted in conversation with the author.

specialising in community engagement' – a set of skills he was able to apply to his internet activism.[104]

Wilcox began serious engagement with online communications in 1995, at which point he began developing contacts with a range of local activists and groups across the UK. Finding some like-minded people already working in the field, he went on to instigate and participate in a wide range of organisations and initiatives, including UK Communities Online and Partnerships Online, building links with industry and government. His account of this period is suggestive of a growing movement, driven by a network of enthusiasts, working to permeate the idea that the Internet had genuine political and democratic applications and was a means by which members of the public could organise and exert power. They were based in various diverse parts of the country, from the south coast of England, to Powys, to the north-east of England. Some projects were location-specific, while others dealt with themes, such as the Black Information Link and Youthnet.

Important impetus for Wilcox came from a visit to a 1995 US conference, entitled 'The Ties That Bind'. The organisers were the Morino Institute and Apple, and it took place at the Apple headquarters in Cupertino, California. This event demonstrates a clear link between Wilcox and the UK online activism movement, within which he was a central player, and the US tradition and its countercultural sources. For instance, participants in Morino events around this time, as discussed in Chapter 4, included Lee Felsenstein, in the 1960s a radical student activist, in the 1970s a participant in the Community Memory project, a member of the Homebrew Computer Club, and a pioneer of the personal computer.[105] A key US influence on Wilcox was Terry Grunwald and her 'community technology projects'.[106] Grunwald was a graduate in City and Regional Planning and author of an activist manual entitled *Making the Net Work*. Since 1990, through an entity called NCexChange in North Carolina, she had been working 'to promote and support electronic networking for nonprofit groups ... and low wealth communities in the state'. She was a general advocate and critical analyst of means of using the Internet to disperse power. Similarly to Wilcox, for Grunwald this online dimension was an extension of a longer personal history in the 'nonprofit' sector, 'working on issues such as housing, community development and crime victim assistance'.[107] A collection of groups with which Wilcox was

[104] 'About David Wilcox', 2 February 2003, available at https://partnerships.typepad.com/civic/2003/02/about_david_wil.html, last accessed 23 September 2020. See also 'Partnership History and Projects', reproduction of 1995 leaflet, available at http://partnerships.org.uk/partline/leaf.html, last accessed 22 October 2019.

[105] 'David Wilcox's Story', undated, available at: http://partnerships.org.uk/stories/main.htm, last accessed 2019.

[106] 'About David Wilcox'.

[107] 'Meetings with US Community Networker', 1998 undated, available at: http://partnerships.org.uk/sussex/terry.htm, last accessed 22 October 2019.

associated arranged for Grunwald to visit the UK in the summer of 1998 and take part in a series of events discussing means by which people could improve their lives through collective use of the Internet.[108]

In 1996, Wilcox attended a further US event at Taos, New Mexico, hosted by the local organisation, La Plaza Telecommunity.[109] Plans were made to launch an International Association for Community Networking. One participant, Dough Schuler, proposed that it should work in accordance with a set of 'Community Networking Principles' that were as follows:

+ Universal access to communication infrastructure
+ Civic society and civic values (the 'radical center')
+ Focus on the underserved, economically disenfranchised
+ Fundamental right to privacy
+ Opposition to media concentration
+ Support of diverse, alternative, and marginalized voices
+ Partnerships with civic organizations and institutions
+ Commitment to strong democracy
+ Freedom of speech and expression
+ Access to government information
+ Build the systems on local needs using local people and organizations as co-developers[110]

Ultimately this envisaged international project failed to progress. As Wilcox recalled, a focus on building up organisation in a single country was more realistic at this stage.[111] While much of the activity with which Wilcox and his extended network was associated was local and practical in its focus, it also scaled up to UK-level projects, including the parliamentary project discussed above, and participants proved willing to develop general programmes and engage in theoretical discussion. In 1999, Partnerships Online published 'A manifesto for online communities'. It was designed to promote the principle that 'the Internet and development in cyberspace should enhance rather than restrict democracy, enable us to be active citizens – and that everyone should have an opportunity to participate'. The key components of the 'draft manifesto' were that:

1. Every citizen, regardless of their economic circumstances, should be able to share the benefits of the Information Age – including better communications, greater participation, electronic life long learning, and e-commerce. To achieve this they should have access to local *community technology centres*, plus public online forums and services to create an *online community*.

[108] 'Online Sussex', 'prepared' 7 June 1998, but text seemingly written post-26 July 1998, available at: http://partnerships.org.uk/sussex/index.htm, last accessed 23 September 2020.
[109] Ibid.
[110] 'International Association for Community Networking', reproduction of text from 1996, available at: http://partnerships.org.uk/iacn/IACN.html, last accessed 23 September 2020.
[111] 'Online Sussex'.

The centres will provide technical support and help 'on the ground', the forums will be 'virtual spaces' for online communities related to localities.
2. Centres and online communities should be easy to find – signposted locally, and through a *national gateway*.
3. *Public support* should be available, particularly in low-income neighbourhoods, where the market is unlikely to provide facilities on a sustainable basis without public funding.
4. Development of centres and online communities should be piloted through *pathfinder projects*, with community participation.
5. There should be a *network* and support for the local champions and partnerships who will develop the centres and online communities.
6. A *virtual resource centre* should be developed to provide sources of advice for local champions and partnerships, and a neutral space online for discussion of the development of centres and online communities.[112]

A theoretical aspect could accompany such programmatic content. The manifesto linked to another page on the Partnerships Online site, by David Greenop, a technological strategist for British Telecom, containing a 'draft ... indicative' text, in the form of an essay entitled 'Scenarios for Cyberspace'. It built on research work carried out at the 'Euroscom research institute', for which European telecommunication corporations had provided financial support. Greenop speculated on a range of patterns of development in the use of online technology. He firmly subscribed to the idea of the Internet (or 'Cyberspace') as comprising a parallel and increasingly important reality in its own right. As Greenop put it:

> Cyberspace is a dynamic, developing concept ... Life experiences today are increasingly divided between the physical here and now and a 'someplace else' immanent in a virtual electronic space. The social, economic, and political lifelines of the world are now evolving almost exclusively within this electronic space. Here, for example, large corporate alliances busily co-ordinate their quest to balance efficiency, flexibility, and economies of scale. Here, data about consumer demand, production flows and finance is managed and shaped. Here is where our savings reside in bit form so that large banks and investment firms can fundamentally mould our lives. This virtual world is thus a place in which we already live.[113]

Greenop held the term 'Cyberspace' to entail 'the emulation of physical space in electronic environments. As the Internet continues to grow, electronically mediated environments will expand and "physical place" will become less important.' Conceiving of it as a 'place outside physical space', Greenop suggested that an 'analogy for Cyberspace might be that of a belief in

[112] 'A Manifesto for Online Communities', undated, probably 1999, available at: http://partnerships.org.uk/cyber/manifest.htm, last accessed 23 October 2019.
[113] David Greenop, 'Scenarios for Cyberspace', undated, probably 1999, available at: http://partnerships.org.uk/cyber/scene.htm, last accessed 23 October 2019.

Heaven where disembodied souls are freed from the moral or physical weaknesses of the flesh'. The enthusiasts of his time similarly 'hail their realm as a place where we will be freed from all physical limitations'. The possibilities Greenop proposed extended as far as the direct connection of the human brain to an enveloping simulated reality. He struck a slightly more pessimistic note than the general thrust of the campaigning of his time. Greenop suggested that there could be authoritarian outcomes, employing the term 'CyberBigBrother'. In this scenario, 'smaller numbers of increasingly larger suppliers' would come to 'control the provision of certain related services'. Political authorities would force these corporations to provide 'full access to all messages, transactions and addresses', analysing data and using it for social control purposes. But Greenop emphasised that it was for humans to design the environment. It remained possible to ensure that the electronic environment he depicted was supportive of their needs, rather than oppressive.[114]

By examining the surviving online imprint, it is possible to uncover accounts of various activities, groups, programmes, and theorising during the second half of the 1990s, for which the Internet was a focus. As opposed to a more specific and distinct policy objective, such as environmental protection, engagement through a particular technology was itself the defining goal of this tendency. Participants in it were a vanguard, but one that promoted wide inclusion. Though their ideas were in some senses radical, the participants proved adept at forging links with established governmental authorities (and the corporate world), accessing their financial and institutional resources, and persuading them to adopt new practices. It was an example of excitement about a technology contributing to flux. One such successful connection was with the UK Parliament. The ideas transferred by this means would help ensure that this ancient institution would seek to use the Internet for more than the dissemination of information, and would attempt to employ it for purposes of two-way interaction with the public. A technology and a concept came together, and found their way into the mainstream.

[114] Ibid.

6

Computers, Networks, and Parliament up to 1996

Computers and the Internet are closely related. To appreciate the nature and significance of parliamentary engagement with the latter, it is necessary to consider the way in which the institution came to adopt the former. The present chapter performs this task over a period running from the 1960s through to 1996. It assesses, over this timespan, the ways in which computers were perceived; the means by which they came into use; the pace of take-up; the forces that drove forward and resisted this process; what the key decisions were; and – most importantly – what was the connection between these issues and the Internet. It relates these various themes to the position of Parliament within the political and constitutional system of the UK.

An important moment came in January 1977, with the publication of the report of the Parliamentary Informal Joint Committee on Computers. As we will see, the members of this body, drawn (as the 'Joint' label suggests) from both Houses, saw the technology as of historic importance to their institution. It is worth considering the wider climate within which they reported. As we have seen, by this time, various commentators were speculating about the prospects for social transformation, driven by communications technology, in which computers could play a part. Such discussion often addressed the possibility of change in the political system, potentially involving a tilt towards direct democratic mechanisms – perhaps a threat from the point of view of an institution such as Parliament. It might also envisage new modes of operation for representative institutions. The extent to which either members or staff of the UK legislature were aware of such theories is open to question. But some of the work in this genre – such as that produced by the Tofflers – had attained wide publicity and circulation.

Moreover, since the 1950s, mainstream newspapers and periodicals had carried stories about some kind of computer-driven 'revolution'.[1] Indeed, such were the expectations that had been generated that, by the second half of the 1970s, some commentators were discussing the failure of computers in reality to match these predictions. A 1978 Fabian Society pamphlet by

[1] E.g. Jane Bown, 'Dr. Norbert Wiener', *The Observer*, 28 January 1951.

Tom Crowe and John Hywel-Jones discussed various aspects of the subject, including 'network techniques using communication technology and message switching programmes' that 'make it possible to connect computers and people around the globe'. (It made specific reference to 'the ARPA').[2] Yet the authors also cautioned that '[a]t the moment the public attitude towards computer technology is jaundiced; the initial eager aspirations of computer scientists have not been realised and people enjoy the recital of anecdotes showing up the computer as being more inconvenient that it was worth'.[3] In 1979, Nigel Hawkes wrote in *The Observer* that '[o]ne of the hazards of the twentieth century is the possibility of becoming bored by the future before it even happens. Told for the hundredth time that silicon chips are about to transform the world in new and startling ways, the temptation to yawn is almost irresistible.'[4]

We discuss general parliamentary engagement with computers later in this chapter. But what recognition was there from within the institution of the possible connotations for the legislature itself and for the constitutional system of which it was a crucial component? From the 1960s onwards, the issue of 'data banks' and their implications for personal privacy came to receive substantial international political attention, including among UK parliamentarians.[5] Eventually there was legislative action at UK level, in the form of the Data Protection Act 1984.[6] From this perspective, the technology was treated more as a problem to be managed than a democratic benefit. But the Informal Joint Committee in 1977 presented computers not as a problem but as a tool the adoption of which was a positive necessity. It wrote that:

> the introduction of computer-based systems into both Houses is essential if Parliament is to fulfil its proper constitutional role *vis-a-vis* the executive. Government is extending its control over an increasingly wide, complex and technical range of activities and Parliament must have access to information of a correspondingly wide variety to enable it to evaluate government policies and legislation and to anticipate the needs of the future. The quantity of information needed to fulfil this role efficiently is enormous, and it will place a growing burden on Members of both Houses and the officials who serve them. The Committee consider that Parliament's information services will be seriously impaired unless computer techniques are introduced as a matter of urgency, and that the offices of both Houses will

[2] Tom Crowe and John Hywel-Jones, *The Computer and Society,* Fabian Tract 457 (Fabian Society, London, 1978), p. 5.

[3] Ibid., p. 1.

[4] Nigel Hawkes, 'Chips on the Brain', *The Observer*, 23 September 1979.

[5] David Steel, 'When Men Are Subjected to Authoritarian Rule They Are Cramped in Spirit', *The Guardian*, 1 June 1970; Andrew Blick, *Stretching the Constitution: The Brexit Shock in Historic Perspective* (Bloomsbury/Hart, Oxford, 2019), pp. 293–4.

[6] Jon Agar, *The Government Machine: A Revolutionary History of the Computer* (Cambridge, MIT Press, 2003), pp. 359–66.

> become increasingly ill-equipped to carry out their work unless they also are able to take advantage of contemporary technology.[7]

These words reflected a developing interest within Parliament. Important impetus in this direction had come from the staff side.[8] In the early 1960s, officials in the House of Commons Library and Clerk's Department began to become interested in the potential of the technology – then relatively scarce, expensive, and requiring significant expertise to utilise. The Librarian 'talked to a number of computer companies about the possibilities, but it was not possible at that time to come to any firm conclusions – still less to make decisions'.[9] Later in the decade, in 1968, the Library trialled the use of computers to assist in creating 'Current Awareness Bulletins',[10] received by '300 Members and 70 outside organisations'. A subsequent account explained that:

> [t]he service provided was a series of 36 bulletins issued every week, each of which covered one area of British Domestic Affairs (eg agriculture) in which all the acquisitions made by the Library in the previous week in the subject area in question were listed. Members were able to request bulletins in the subjects which interested them. The bulletins also indicated what types of documents contained the information listed, so that it was possible to see where the information came from, for example, a Select Committee Report or a newspaper article.[11]

Such a service was only practically feasible with computer assistance.[12] Technical support for this project came from the United Kingdom Atomic Energy Authority (UKAEA), which facilitated in 1970 '[a] presentation of on-line retrieval of information, processed in the 1968 project'. Also in 1970, Aslib – the name for what used to be called the Association of Special Libraries and Information Bureaux – conducted a 'full-scale feasibility study' of options for computing in the Library. The report it produced the following year found in favour of a 'move towards automation' for the Library.[13] The authors anticipated the permanent provision of briefings for members of the type that

[7] Parliamentary Informal Joint Committee on Computers, *Report of the Informal Joint Committee on Computers to the Leaders of both Houses*, January 1977, p. 1.

[8] Ibid., p. 5.

[9] 'The Application of Computers to the Work of Parliament', *Paper Prepared by the Clerks to the Computer Sub-Committees of the Two Houses*, Appendix 2, Select Committee on House of Commons (Services), *Computer Applications for the House of Commons*, Seventh Report of Session 1977–78, HC 617–II (Stationery Office, London, 1978), pp. 45–5.

[10] D. Menhennet and D. J. T. Englefield, 'Outline History of the Library's Experiments with Computer Applications', February 1978, Select Committee on House of Commons (Services), *Computer Applications for the House of Commons*, Seventh Report of Session 1977–78, HC 617–II (Stationery Office, London, 1978), p. 50.

[11] 'The Application of Computers to the Work of Parliament', pp. 45–5.

[12] Ibid.

[13] Menhennet and Englefield, 'Outline History of the Library's Experiments with Computer Applications', p. 50.

the 1968 experiment facilitated. But the costs involved proved to be too great an obstacle to the implementation of this proposal.[14]

Further demonstrations of '[o]nline retrieval' took place in 1973. International Computers Limited (ICL) organised an event showing how use could be made of the 'macro-economic databank' of the Central Statistical Office, while IBM presented the 'STAIRS' package as a means of facilitating 'retrieval of Parliamentary Questions and Statute Law'.[15] The ICL session:

> provided access to 15,000 series of statistical data which were obtained from a computer readable databank compiled by the Central Statistical Office, and held on a 190IS model computer at ICL's Putney Headquarters. It was interrogated from the House of Commons over GPO telephone lines using a visual display screen and keyboard.

The material accessible in this way was still limited at this time. Nonetheless, the event was an indication to parliamentary officials that they could use computers not only for storing and processing information, but for communication with the outside, obtaining external material to support them in their work. It is important, however, to note the distinction between the establishment of individual links between terminals and a computer, comprising a single network, and the Internet as it developed, which made up a network of multiple such networks. Much of the discussion of computer-based communications in this chapter – especially in the earlier periods – refers to the former technique, which the Internet, combined with the World Wide Web, eventually displaced. Tim Berners-Lee captures the difference in the following terms:

> The Internet is a very general communications infrastructure that links computers together. Before the Internet, computers were connected using dedicated cables from one to another. A software program on one computer would communicate over the cable with a software program on another computer, and send information such as a file or a program. This was originally done so that the very expensive early computers in a lab or company could be used from different sites. Clearly, though, one computer could not be linked to more than a few others, because it would need tens or hundreds of cables running from it.
>
> The solution was to communicate indirectly over a network. The Internet is a network of networks. Its essence, though is a set of standardised *protocols* – conventions by which computers send data to each other. The data are transmitted over various carriers, such as telephone lines, cable TV wires and satellite channels. The data can be sent, an e-mail, a sound, an image, a software program – whatever.[16]

[14] 'The Application of Computers to the Work of Parliament', pp. 45–5.

[15] Menhennet and Englefield, 'Outline History of the Library's Experiments with Computer Applications', p. 50.

[16] Tim Berners-Lee, *Weaving the Web: The Past, Present and Future of the World Wide Web by Its Inventor* (Orion, London, 1999), p. 20.

Yet another demonstration took place in 1974, when UKAEA showed the Library how it could use computers for '[o]n-line retrieval of Statute Law and EEC documents', employing the 'STATUS' program. By 1974 the Library had recruited a Computer Officer. It had also come to rely on close co-operation with the Central Computer Agency (CCA) of the Civil Service Department.[17] That the legislature needed help from this source points to a complexity in power dynamics at the centre of the UK constitution, with consequences for the adoption of digital technology. An important function of Parliament is to hold government to account; and a recurring and crucial argument offered in favour of the parliamentary use of computers (and later the Internet) was that it would contribute – and was even essential – to effective performance of this role. The Informal Joint Committee, for instance, as noted above, made this case in 1977. Yet to make progress in the use of this technology, Parliament needed support (including via the CCA at this point) from the same executive it was responsible for overseeing. This relationship was illustrative of more general countervailing tendencies in the association between legislature and government in the UK. Parliament is in some respects dependent upon the executive. But the relationship is not wholly one of subordination. Governments, that are formed out of the legislature, can be susceptible to the influence of it. In support of this latter, balancing, observation, demonstrating the potential for Parliament to have an impact upon the executive, the CCA was established in 1972 following a recommendation by the House of Commons Select Committee on Science and Technology Committee in a report, discussed below, published the previous year.[18]

Alongside Library research, another early motivation for parliamentary interest in the employment of computers was its possible use in the legislative process. It did not generate the same enthusiasm as the Library experiments. As the Clerk of the House of Commons, Richard Barlas, subsequently recounted:

> The *Public Bill Office* was involved peripherally with an experiment mounted by IBM Ltd on the production of Bills by computer in 1973. The Badgers Bill was put on to magnetic tape, and a system using a programme, ATMS/STAIRS, developed by IBM which enabled the user to change the text of the Bill as displayed on a VDU [visual display unit, i.e. a screen]. By this means amendments could be inserted into the Bill using the VDU located in the Lords Public

[17] Menhennet and Englefield, 'Outline History of the Library's Experiments with Computer Applications', p. 50. For the files of the Central Computer Agency, see The National Archives (TNA) HN, Records of the Central Communications Agency and predecessors, 1956–1988. The Central Computer Agency was formed in 1972, adding 'Communications' in 1979.

[18] The National Archives, 'Records of the Central Communications Agency and predecessors' available at: https://discovery.nationalarchives.gov.uk/details/r/C149, last accessed 7 February 2021.

Bill Office. The two Public Bill Offices felt that the exercise showed that there was no real need for such a system.[19]

By the time the Informal Joint Committee report appeared in January 1977, a number of House of Commons select committees had utilised computers in the course of their inquiries. In mid-1976 a civil servant who was on secondment to the Select Committee on Abortion – that had been sent in excess of 300 evidence submissions – employed a computer for the analysis of this material. Around the same time, the Environment Sub-Committee of the Expenditure Committee, which was conducting an investigation into planning procedure, circulated a survey to 458 local planning authorities in England and Wales. The management of this survey was made possible by the support of the CCA of the UK government, based in the Civil Service Department. In both the 1976–7 and 1977–8 parliamentary sessions, Sub-Committee B of the Select Committee on Nationalised Industries engaged a specialist adviser who used a computer for a range of tasks related to an inquiry into the British Steel Corporation. They were: planning the work and future needs of the sub-committee, drafting correspondence, storing and processing the text of oral evidence sessions, producing briefing notes for the sub-committee, and analysing data. By the late 1970s, the General Sub-Committee of the Expenditure Committee regularly received advice from Cambridge economists. Making use of their access to a University computer, they assisted the sub-committee in the assessment of Treasury plans. The analysis Barlas provided in February 1978 suggested that not all of these experiments had been successful. The employment of computing for the forward planning of committee work, for instance, 'did not prove helpful', and word-processing functions did 'not appear to be a particularly economic use of computer time'. Furthermore, Barlas stressed 'the importance of clarifying the purpose and nature' of an activity 'before a computer is used'.[20] Nonetheless, possibilities were becoming apparent. Activities such as word-processing involved in these early experiments, even if the technology or perhaps the potential users were not yet ready, would eventually become normal parts of committee and general parliamentary work.

The House of Lords demonstrated its capacity to be a source of innovation. On 2 March 1976, the Administration Sub-Committee of the Offices Committee of the House of Lords had 'authorised the installation of computer facilities in the Parliament Office'.[21] It would also be available to the House of

[19] Richard Barlas, Clerk of the House of Commons, 'The Application of Computers to the Work of the Clerks' Department', Memorandum by the Clerk of the House, February 1978, Appendix 5, Select Committee on House of Commons (Services), *Computer Applications for the House of Commons*, Seventh Report of Session 1977–78, HC 617–II (Stationery Office, London, 1978), p. 56.

[20] Ibid., pp. 55–6.

[21] Parliamentary Informal Joint Committee on Computers, *Report of the Informal Joint Committee on Computers to the Leaders of Both Houses*, January 1977, p. 3.

Lords Library and the Record Office (attached to both Houses of Parliament). The House of Commons Library and the Vote Office were soon pressing for access.[22] The Lords itself consented to this plan on 13 April 1976. The formal adoption of computers by one of the Houses of Parliament is, in retrospect, a moment of immense significance. It led on to many changes in the way the institution as a whole functioned internally and interacted with the outside world. Computer technology would, during the pandemic that began in 2020, even help Parliament to continue functioning during a global emergency. None of this potential is apparent from the official record of the decision. The statement, under the heading 'Installation of Computer Facilities', 'that the Administration Sub-Committee had authorised the installation of computer facilities in the Parliament Office and the Library' was item two on a list of thirteen brought forward by the Chairman of Committees, the Earl of Listowel. Exemplifying the potential of the Lords to produce incongruous combinations of ancient and contemporary, other matters it addressed included expenses available to the Yeoman Usher of the Black Rod for purchasing Court Dress, the application of employment legislation to staff within the Lords, and the use of photocopying machines. All were approved as a group without discussion.[23]

The Informal Joint Committee signified an effort to establish a single approach towards computer technology within a diverse institution prone to developing varied and uneven practices. In later decades this pattern of variety coupled with efforts at standardisation would – as we have seen – be a feature of the parliamentary approach to the Internet. The Informal Joint Committee had come into being because, by mid-1976, 'the authorities of both Houses had given much thought to the possible introduction of computer systems'.[24] On 13 May 1976, the leaders of both the House of Lords and of the House of Commons – that is the Lord Privy Seal and the Lord President of the Council – informed both Houses through written answers that they had established an 'informal Joint Committee on Computers'. With the Labour Peer Lord (George) Darling of Hillsborough in the chair, its terms of reference were 'to consider and advise on the contribution that computer-based systems might make towards meeting the information and other requirements of both Houses'.[25]

That the subject was one of rising salience was further reinforced by the existence of parallel investigations (discussed below) into the use of computers in preparing legislation and in the printing of parliamentary material.[26] The Informal Joint Committee took oral and written evidence from the industry

22 Ibid., p. 4.
23 Hansard, House of Lords (HL) Offices, 13 April 1976, cols. 2034–7.
24 Parliamentary Informal Joint Committee on Computers, *Report of the Informal Joint Committee on Computers to the Leaders of Both Houses*, January 1977, p. 3.
25 Ibid., p. 1.
26 Ibid., p. 2.

itself, from public bodies in the UK, and legislatures abroad.[27] It reported in January 1977. As the quote at the head of this chapter shows, the Committee chose to view its subject matter as having decisive bearing upon the functioning of the political system. In this sense it shared ground with some of the literature discussed in earlier chapters (both predating and antedating the Committee report of 1977), that attached great importance to new technology. However, it often (but not always) tended to depict new inventions (or applications thereof) as connected to an overthrow of existing arrangements (either for good or ill) or at least the introduction of significant innovations – such as frequent electronic referendums – alongside more entrenched mechanisms. Within such scenarios, a long-established institution such as Parliament might be threatened or at least forced to accommodate change. The Informal Joint Committee proposed means by which Parliament could incorporate computers and use them to preserve its position within the traditional framework of the representative system. They would enable it more effectively to perform some of its core functions: holding government to account and discussing future policy prospects. In taking this perspective, the Informal Joint Committee presented a view of computers as augmenters of human capacity, stating: '[i]n the British Parliament, neither Members nor the officials that serve them will be able to keep abreast of essential information or continue to conduct their work efficiently without the assistance of computer techniques'.[28]

Another pattern of attitudes towards technology was to see it both as a source of and potential solution to problems. For instance, if a device was being deployed in a way that had undesirable consequences, it might be possible to overcome them either by applying it differently, or through the use of a further new invention. When referring to the expansion of government 'control over an increasingly wide, complex and technical range of activities', the Committee appears to have perceived this tendency as resting on the use of computers. It therefore concluded that to avoid the emergence of an increasingly unrestrained executive, Parliament had fully to appropriate this same technological resource for its own purposes. In this regard parliamentary motivation for the adoption of computers seems reactive and driven by fear of increasing irrelevance.

In later decades, a principal justification offered for the parliamentary use of computers – via the Internet – was that they would facilitate more meaningful and two-way interaction with the public public, acting as a medium for direct communication. This idea was a central component of the discourse around the democratic potential of communications technology discussed in previous chapters. But it was not yet a theme for discussions of this nature in Parliament in the way it would later become. The Informal Joint Committee

[27] Ibid., p. 1.

[28] Ibid., p. 8.

report focused on ways in which Parliament could perform existing internal functions and possibly gain access to external sources of information to support it in these tasks. The employment of computers by select committees to manage the gathering and processing of evidence, however, might be seen as entailing their use to assist engagement with the public. Furthermore, as is described below, the 1977 report suggested that outside users might have access (albeit for payment) to computer-stored information generated by Parliament. It could, moreover, be noted that a core purpose of Parliament is to act on behalf of the people. In this sense, any use it made of technology was potentially in service of that relationship. But express treatment of the idea of computers as forming part of an actual channel for dialogue between public and representatives was lacking in this report.

The Informal Joint Committee created the impression of a general dynamic at high constitutional level towards the adoption of computers. It noted that – broadly in parallel with its work – other bodies were investigating matters involving this technology and activities pertaining to Parliament. In 1973, the Lord President of the Council, Jim Prior, had established the Committee on the Preparation of Legislation, or 'Renton Committee'. With David Renton MP in the chair, its terms of reference were:

> with a view to achieving greater simplicity and clarity in statute law, to review the form in which public Bills are drafted, excluding consideration of matters relating to policy formulation and the legislative programme; to consider any consequential implications for parliamentary procedure; and to make recommendations.[29]

It had a specific sub-committee on the possibilities for the employment of computers for the purposes set out in this remit. In its report of May 1975 it made recommendations, including for electronic storing of machine-readable versions of laws.[30] The Statute Law Committee, a standing body charged with simplifying the presentation of legislation through consolidation, had a sub-committee on the application of computers, of which Lord Justice Scarman was chair.[31] The process of parliamentary printing was being computerised; and a Parliamentary Working Group of Her

[29] See TNA CAB 135, Committee on the Preparation of Legislation (Renton Committee): Evidence, Correspondence and Report, 1973-1975, available at: https://discovery.nationalarchives.gov.uk/details/r/C3942, last accessed 10 May 2020.

[30] Parliamentary Informal Joint Committee on Computers, *Report of the Informal Joint Committee on Computers to the Leaders of Both Houses*, January 1977, p. 2. For the government reception to the Renton recommendations, including on computers, see Hansard, HL Debates, 'Renton Committee Report on Legislation', 10 December 1975, cols. 945–1038, esp. 964, 973, 1030–1.

[31] Parliamentary Informal Joint Committee on Computers, *Report of the Informal Joint Committee on Computers to the Leaders of Both Houses*, January 1977, p. 2. For the files of this inquiry, see Parliamentary Archives: GB-061 SLC/99, Statute Law Committee Papers, Sub-Committee on Computer Technology (1974–1980).

Majesty's Stationery Office was considering the further uses that could be made of the data that would consequently be produced.[32] In other words, the employment of computers generated its own momentum, creating possible opportunities the realisation of which would require the further application of the same technology. Eventually, such material stored in this way could be made available over the Internet.

The Informal Joint Committee, then, was an emanation of certain patterns of development that it in turn observed and from which it drew influence. These tendencies were discernible both within the UK and elsewhere. The Committee described how in the United States in 1973, Congress had launched a system providing users with information about the progress of legislation. Titled the 'Bill Status system', it was a forerunner to the 'Bills before Parliament' feature on the website of the UK Parliament today.[33] The Bill Status system provided details of the stage a bill had reached, and its progress up to that point, with any changes notified within twenty-four hours. The House of Commons of the Canadian Parliament was an international innovator. It had pursued 'the development of computer based information systems ... planned ... to integrate information retrieval and computerised printing'. With a programme for the replacement of traditional 'hot metal' printing methods that began in 1965, it had adopted computer-based techniques for the entirety of its published materials. Their contents therefore existed in machine-readable mode, awaiting appropriation for other purposes. The Canadian House of Commons sought deliberately to capitalise upon this resource, and by 1973 it had made some of this material available in database form.[34] We will return to the Canadian example below.

The European context was important. The UK had joined the European Communities on 1 January 1973. Though this decision was controversial, a UK-wide referendum held in June 1975 had supported continued participation by a substantial margin. The continuing – and possibly increasing – prominence of the continental integration project within the UK political system was, therefore, an underlying assumption at this time. That it would figure in a discussion of the computerisation of the UK Parliament was natural. The first intended function of the system that the House of Lords approved in 1976 was to perform an indexing task, enabling the identification of materials that could then be located in hard copy. They included a wide range of European documents.[35] The European Communities, the Informal Joint Committee noted, were in the process of initiating the 'Celex' computer

32 Parliamentary Informal Joint Committee on Computers, *Report of the Informal Joint Committee on Computers to the Leaders of Both Houses*, January 1977, p. 2.

33 'Bills before Parliament', available at: https://services.parliament.uk/Bills/2019–21.html, last accessed 24 September 2020.

34 Parliamentary Informal Joint Committee on Computers, *Report of the Informal Joint Committee on Computers to the Leaders of Both Houses*, January 1977, p. 6.

35 Ibid., p. 4.

system in Brussels for the recording of various European documents. The legislatures of two individual member states – Italy and (West) Germany – had introduced computers and similar plans were underway in France. Separate from the Communities, the Council of Europe was interested in promoting technical harmonisation in this area between the legislatures of its members.[36]

The impetus for change, then, was both diverse in nature and powerful. It led the Informal Joint Committee to anticipate 'that computers will be used extensively in Parliament within a reasonably short period of time'.[37] The implications were great. The Committee avowedly concentrated on contemporary issues, though acknowledged that future developments could lead to more fundamental changes in the way in which the system of representative democracy functioned. It explained that '[c]urrent advances in computer technology open up prospects of parliamentary aids becoming available on a scale well beyond our immediate concerns'. The Committee judged it possible that such 'mechanical aids' might be introduced 'to an extent that may change the character of Parliament and the work and duties of Members'.[38]

The report was correct in its assessment that Parliament was on the brink of considerable change. The way in which the institution recorded, accessed, processed, and presented information would alter. At first, such developments were not as noticeable externally as they would later become, since the basic external outputs of Parliament – public debates in the two Chambers (which were not yet being regularly broadcast in any form) and printed papers (albeit set by computers) – remained as they were. Initially, transformation was internal to the institution. But changes being somewhat tentatively embarked upon in this early era would eventually make possible new ways of conducting external relations, via the Internet. Further possibilities would become increasingly apparent in the years that followed the Informal Joint Committee report. Computers would impact upon the nature of the domestic business of Parliament, the manner in which it interacted with the outside, and the way in which it performed its basic constitutional functions. They also had implications for the staff it employed and the skills they needed, and could help perform tasks such as guaranteeing security through administration of the pass system.[39]

The Joint Informal Committee concluded that developments to come would 'merit careful consideration in the future'.[40] It had recognised a tendency that has been sustained up to the present: the difficulty in keeping pace with a

[36] Ibid., pp. 6–7.

[37] Ibid., p. 8.

[38] Ibid., p. 1.

[39] See A. R. W. Robinson, Central Computer Agency, CSD, Select Committee on House of Commons (Services), *Computer Applications for the House of Commons*, Seventh Report of Session 1977–78, HC 617–II (Stationery Office, London, 1978), Appendix 1.

[40] Parliamentary Informal Joint Committee on Computers, *Report of the Informal Joint Committee on Computers to the Leaders of Both Houses*, January 1977, p. 1.

continuously changing technology. As a long-established, complex institution required continuously to perform various functions of critical importance to the functioning of the UK polity, responding appropriately to a new technology was inevitably a considerable challenge, and one that could not be surmounted at any single point, because of its constantly morphing quality. The nature of Parliament and of the technology placed the former in a structural time-lag behind the latter. The Informal Joint Committee was correct in the assessment that ongoing review would be required. Its members could not have been expected to anticipate the scale, duration, or precise form of that which awaited.

The report, therefore, suggested the existence within Parliament of some wariness about difficult-to-foresee but potentially great implications of engaging with a fast-developing technological field. Such a perception was probably a source of some reluctance to embrace computing. A further obstacle was the financial implications. In 1974, CCA had produced a report on potential uses of computers in Parliament. It recommended the commissioning of consultants to carry out a more extensive investigation. The likely charge – about £20,000 in 1977 prices – seems to have been a disincentive to the conduct of this exercise.[41] (Computing costs at this time were split between the CCA, which financed equipment, and Parliament, which paid for staffing).[42] A further obvious problem was lack of expertise among potential users. The Informal Joint Committee reflected this concern with its insistence that 'applications should be easy to use by someone unskilled in the use of computers'. It was also exercised about malfunctions and the need to provide 'backup facilities which will ensure the minimum possible interruptions of service'.[43] Fear of more fundamental failure, and presumably the embarrassment and public criticism that might come with it, was an inhibitor with respect to fuller and more radical adoption of the technology. In its discussion of the practices in the Canadian House of Commons, the Informal Joint Committee dwelt on difficulties experienced. The report described how:

> The first attempt to introduce computer facilities into the offices of the House [in 1968] ... proved disastrous due to insufficient planning and the failure to explain the long-term advantages to those using the facilities. This failure set back some uses of computing by the House for several years, and provides a salutary lesson in the need for careful planning and equally careful implementation of computer developments of whatever kind.[44]

41 Ibid., p. 3.

42 Ibid., p. 5. For the financial arrangements, see TNA T 583/18, Repayments by Parliament to the Central Computer and Telecommunications Agency (CCTA) and HM Stationery Office (HMSO), 1982.

43 Parliamentary Informal Joint Committee on Computers, *Report of the Informal Joint Committee on Computers to the Leaders of Both Houses*, January 1977, p. 6.

44 Ibid.

This passage appeared in the context of a discussion of what was ultimately a successful programme of innovation in Canada – and one that, from the perspective of subsequent developments, seems to have anticipated much that followed. A possible interpretation that the Joint Informal Committee might have placed on the early difficulties experienced was that they were part of a learning process and were a component of later positive achievements. But the tone employed in this account – though it made a reasonable point – suggested an inclination to prioritise the avoidance of failure. While the Joint Informal Committee was firm in its support for the systematic introduction of computers to Parliament, it proposed a 'phased implementation' of computers 'over several years'. This approach, the Committee hoped, would avoid setbacks of the Canadian variety, brought about through a misguided effort 'to implement complex systems all at once'. It would also facilitate, the report suggested, 'flexibility in development', with 'a step-by-step' technique that could 'ensure the integrated and coherent implementation of each new application'.[45]

In this sense, the Informal Joint Committee reconciled the desire for a single strategy with the piecemeal development that Parliament, as an internally differentiated entity, was already following. Supporting an approach that was 'phased' in nature enabled it to endorse 'the projects begun in the Parliament Office and the House of Commons Library' as 'a start in this direction'.[46] At the same time, there was a need, the report judged, to establish a single service supporting both Houses of Parliament and all offices within it.[47] Furthermore, given a gradual approach, the Informal Joint Committee insisted that particular decisions about the use of particular technologies should not 'pre-empt future developments' and needed to be 'independent of any particular manufacturer', avoiding the restrictions that might come about from this kind of reliance.[48]

Parliament and Networked Computers

The report made no express reference to the embryonic internet. But it showed a broader awareness of potential for the use of computers within communication networks of some kind. Indeed, such functions emerge in the text as integral to the purpose of this technology. The committee described how (early difficulties notwithstanding) the Canadian House of Commons, capitalising on the availability of machine-readable texts of parliamentary publications arising from the shift to computerised printing processes, had developed:

[45] Ibid., p. 8.
[46] Ibid., p. 12.
[47] Ibid.
[48] Ibid., p. 8.

> six experimental databases containing the text of all oral questions since 1973 in both English and French, the text of all written questions in both languages and the Standing Orders of the House in both languages. The system has also enabled the House to have access to a variety of outside databases, and to provide links to users in other cities (e.g. Toronto, Vancouver) … It is expected that if the experimental use of the information retrieval side of the system continues on its present course, it will be possible to provide all current parliamentary proceedings on an information retrieval network throughout the country at nominal cost to the user. At present, all the data-bases are operated on computer facilities at Ottawa University. The charge to outside users is $1.00 to sign on to any database and $1.00 for each search within the database.[49]

The report also depicted networking as playing a part in the previously discussed European dimension to the parliamentary employment of computers. The Committee noted that the European Communities were planning to co-operate with the telecommunications agencies of member states on the formation of the so-called 'Euronet' system. Then in an early stage of development, Euronet was envisaged as 'an international public network for data transmission'. It was intended to provide, when introduced, 'scientific, technical, economic, social and legal information'.[50] The European Communities would integrate Euronet with their own 'Celex' service, to which the French Senate had decided to establish a link by 1977. The Council of Europe programme to encourage compatibility between the computer systems of different legislatures was motivated by a desire to ensure 'that national Parliaments do not exclude themselves from the benefits of access to computerised European information networks'.[51]

What then were the possibilities for the UK Parliament? The Informal Joint Committee noted that the system intended for introduction after the House of Lords authorisation of 1976 was intended to be connected to a computer in the possession of the Greater London Council (GLC).[52] When the CCA provided the Informal Joint Committee with a list of possible uses of computers, one of the items was 'Message switching', within which category '[c]omputers are used to pass, display or broadcast information to selected points or individuals'.[53] The report demonstrated awareness of this kind of function, though in keeping with its relatively cautious tone, presented it more as a consideration for the future than an immediate priority. For instance, it drew attention to:

> developments being undertaken which will enable access to databanks and modelling systems, whether in or outside government … An increasing number of reference databases are now accessible for on-line consultation over the

[49] Ibid., p. 6.
[50] Ibid., pp. 6–7.
[51] Ibid.
[52] Ibid., p. 4.
[53] Ibid., pp. 17–20.

> telephone network. These cover a wide range of subjects and sources both from the United Kingdom and abroad. All that is needed to make access to any of the services possible is the installation of a single terminal.[54]

The Committee was concerned that to facilitate such access, 'systems developed in Parliament should, whenever possible, follow generally accepted design practices'. As well as anticipating that users within Parliament might wish to communicate with computers on the outside, the report judged that there might be traffic in the opposite direction. It proposed that '[d]evelopment should take into account the possibility of public access to some parliamentary databases in return for payment, without prejudice to use by either House'.[55] At the time of writing, a little over four decades later, Parliament enthusiastically promotes itself to the outside world, using its own website and across multiple platforms, maximising the availability of its content without charge to users, with take-up by millions around the UK and the world. It uses the technology actively to incorporate the public into its work and for direct, two-way communications with individuals and groups. This proposal from January 1977 represents an early, far-from-enthusiastic, recognition of potential in this area.

Though the 1977 report did not refer specifically to the technology, the existence of what became the Internet had been brought to the attention of Parliament early in that decade. In 1970 sub-committee D of the House of Commons Select Committee on Science and Technology began work. Its terms of reference required it to consider '[t]he prospects for the United Kingdom computer industry in the 1970s, including the possibilities of international collaboration and the functions of Government in this field both as policy maker and user'. The full committee and its sub-bodies ceased to exist with the dissolution of Parliament at the June 1970 General Election. A new committee and sub-committee, A, were formed after some delay. As the committee subsequently commented: 'Nine months in the computer business is a very long time.'[56] Parallel developments in the realm of networked systems confirmed this point. The first oral evidence session of the sub-committee took place on 4 February 1970. At this point, the precursor to the Internet, the ARPANET, had existed as a functioning entity for a little over three months, beginning with a connection between computers in the University of California, Los Angeles and in the Stanford Research Institute at about 10.30 p.m. on 29 October (Pacific Standard Time). By early December there were four participants in the network, with the University of California, Santa

[54] Ibid., p. 9.

[55] Ibid., p. 8.

[56] House of Commons Select Committee on Science and Technology, Fourth Report 1970–1971, Volume 1, Report, *The Prospects for the United Kingdom Computer Industry in the 1970s*, HC 621–I (Stationery Office, London, 1971), p. vii.

Barbara and the University of Utah joining the original two. As the sub-committee sat, expansion and development continued.[57]

Though it remained an obscure scientific project, evidence to the sub-committee contained some reference to this technology. On 24 March 1970, it held an oral session with I. M. Barron, T. A. Margerison, and John Woods of Computer Technology Ltd. When questioned on their support for the establishment of 'a separate network for computers quite apart from the telephone system', one of them – seemingly Barron – sought to emphasise the viability of this proposition by noting that 'there has been such an experimental network set up in America. The decision to establish this experimental network was, I believe, taken at the beginning of 1969 and a number of nodes were operational at the end of the year.'[58] Though not specifying it, the witness presumably had the ARPANET in mind.

Even clearer reference to the embryonic internet came in sub-committee proceedings the following year. On 27 April 1971, Herbert R. J. Grosch, Research Fellow at the US National Bureau of Standards gave oral evidence. The general themes of the session were standardisation and compatibility of systems. Questioning turned to the subject of 'data communications in the US'. The Conservative MP Ian Lloyd (whose contribution is discussed further elsewhere) remarked that he had 'learned this morning that there is a system connecting 20 of the largest computers in the United States being studied at the Stanford Research Institute where they are doing a lot of research in this area ... Would this be a private system, or using the Federal communications system?'

Grosch replied that:

> This was funded by the Advanced Research Projects Agency of the Department of Defense, so in that sense it is Government funded, but it is a university type enterprise. [the Conservative MP and Secretary of State for Trade and Industry] Mr. [John] Davies and someone from the Post Office to the ... co-ordinator of this project on their last visit to the United States. While I think it is a very valuable experiment it seems to me artificial in the sense they have intentionally hooked together such extremely disparate computers, moreover, computers so powerful that they do not really need to ask each other for help. To link an 1108 in one part of the country to an IBM 360/65 in another part seems to be essentially unnecessary, particularly if all you are doing with either party is trivial or academic work. Nevertheless, for what it is worth they have determined what sort of hardware interfaces would be needed to help this compatibility. It turns out they are rather expensive. You might say they are now ready

57 Katie Hafner and Matthew Lyon, *Where Wizards Stay Up Late: The Origins of the Internet* (Simon and Schuster, New York, 1996), p. 166.

58 House of Commons Select Committee on Science and Technology, Session 1969–70, *UK Computer Industry*, Volume I, Minutes of Evidence, 24 March 1970 (Stationery Office, London, 1970), Q. 1055, p. 189.

> to do something with the bio-medical information network. Repayment of drug bills under an advanced form of Medi-care might be a requirement for this. So they do have some experience ready to go if this is required.[59]

This 'project' – 'very valuable' as an 'experiment' but 'artificial', linking devices that had no need for each other, 'essentially unnecessary' – would, within a few decades, become a primary means of global communication in the broadest sense. Some of the purposes for which it was employed were indeed – as Grosch suggested – 'trivial' and 'academic'; but it had many other functions also. A lesson to be drawn from these remarks is not that we should single out Grosch individually or as part of a collective that failed to predict this outcome. It is that successful anticipation of the future course of technological development, the use made of it, and the impact it will have, is difficult (though the reference made in the session with representatives of Computer Technology Ltd. was suggestive of greater significance than Grosch allowed for). By extension, it is understandable that, at this stage, the sub-committee, working with the evidence presented to it, did not discern the full potential of this system. Nonetheless, it did have a more general perception of computers as devices that might be incorporated into communications networks. This perspective is suggested by the glossary of terms provided in the report. It included the following entries:

> **Communication Terminals**
> Communication terminals are devices for the inputting and outputting of information, which are linked to computers by automatic data transmission links such as telephone lines. Communication terminals include devices such as teletypes, cathode ray tube display units, batch readers etc.
>
> **Data Communications**
> Data communications refers to the use of automatic data transmission methods for the transmission of data or information to and from a computer over distances. Data communications can be achieved by means of telephone lines, micro-wave circuits, earth satellite transmissions etc.
>
> **Remote Access Terminals**
> Remote Access terminals are terminals linked to a computer by data transmission lines.
>
> **Remote Job Entry**
> Remote job entry refers to the entry of jobs into a computer from a terminal or station which is not on the computer site itself and may be any distance from the computer itself . . .

[59] Fourth Report from the Select Committee on Science and Technology, Session 1970–71, *The Prospects for the United Kingdom Computer Industry in the 1970s*, Volume II, HC 621–II, Minutes of Evidence (Stationery Office, London 1971), Q. 1359, p. 247.

On-line
On-line refers to a process which is directly linked to the computer. . .

Satellite computers
Satellite computers are generally small computers linked to larger computers and used to carry out specific limited tasks, such as, for example, editing data which is to be processed by the larger computers.

Data utilities, Computer utilities
Data utilities are generally large computers which can be accessed by a large number of users to provide computing powers in rather the same way as electricity power stations can be drawn upon by a large number of users of electricity.

Computer networks
Computer networks are a number of computers linked together by data transmission links and capable of working in a coordinated fashion, so that, for example, it is possible for one computer in the network to switch work to another computer in the network if it is overloaded or requires maintenance.[60]

The sub-committee approach to computers, then, was that they were more than free-standing units, and that that they take part in the rapid transfer of information from one place to another and the remote utilisation of services. It received a wide range of evidence on these themes. For example, F. E. Warner of the firm Urwick Orr & Partners, described twin developments in a written submission. First was that of '[v]ery large time-sharing systems serving a number of users each with their own input and output equipment connected to a central processor by Post Office data links'. Second would be the advent of '[v]ery small desk-top size computers' that might 'also become more significant as a result of current technological development . . . they may develop the power to enable small users to afford individual, independent facilities without having to rely so much on bureau facilities or time-sharing with attendant transmission costs'. While he had identified 'two extremes of development' they were 'not entirely opposing because the very small computer' might become part of a network involving a more powerful device.[61]

The sub-committee noted that it had received evidence from one company, Scientific Control Systems (Scion) that by 1973 'there would be 50,000 remote access terminals in the United Kingdom'. However, Scion also held that while 'some larger organisations would link systems during this period

[60] House of Commons Select Committee on Science and Technology, Fourth Report 1970–1971, Volume 1, Report, *The Prospects for the United Kingdom Computer Industry in the 1970s* (Stationery Office, London, 1971), pp. lxviii–lxix.

[61] 'Memorandum by Mr. F. E. Warner, of Urwick Orr & Partners Limited', Appendix 31, Select Committee on Science and Technology, Session 1969–70, *UK Computer Industry*, Volume II, Appendices (Stationery Office, London 1970), pp. 119–20.

[the subsequent half decade] it was unlikely that large quantities of data would be transmitted from place to place on any scale.' The sub-committee went on to note that an organisation called the 'Real Time Club' was less 'cautious' in its outlook. One of its predictions was 'that in due course there would probably be no free-standing computers of any sort whatever and that every computing system would eventually be linked up to every other'.[62]

The Real Time Club formed in 1967 (and continues to function today).[63] It had a limited membership, with recruitment through invitation. The participants were people working in the computing sector. Specifically, they were those with an interest in, as the name suggested, 'Real Time' technology, broadly a reference to mechanisms for the provision of remote access from multiple points to large computers to ensure their capacity was utilised to the maximum. The club had no permanent staff and convened through monthly dinners at which discussions took place. In pursuit of its ends, it lobbied various public bodies, such as the Post Office, then responsible for telecommunications in the UK, and sought public attention for its agenda, holding an event at the Royal Festival Hall on 3 July 1968.[64] The March 1970 reference to what was seemingly the ARPANET, when Computer Technology Ltd gave evidence to the sub-committee, was in the context of a discussion of Real Time Club proposals.[65]

In a memorandum to the sub-committee published in 1970, the club argued that:

> the developments of the last few years, namely the use of a central computer by a number of different people from remote locations using terminals connected to a central computer by means of Post Office circuits, signifies a revolution in computer usage which at the moment is barely apparent, but which, within the coming few years, will drastically change the structure of computing as we know it today.

It was 'only a matter of time before it becomes customary for every computer in the country, whether operated privately or as a public bureau, to be linked

[62] House of Commons Select Committee on Science and Technology, Fourth Report 1970–1971, Volume 1, Report, *The Prospects for the United Kingdom Computer Industry in the 1970s* (Stationery Office, London, 1971), p. xi.

[63] See https://realtimeclub.co.uk, last accessed 14 June 2020. For an in-house history of the Real Time Club, see Shirley F. Redpath, *A History of the Real Time Club* (Real Time Club, 2007/2013), available at: http://realtimeclub.co.uk/wp-content/uploads/With-All-Due-Respect.pdf, last accessed 24 January 2021.

[64] 'Memorandum by Real Time Club', 21 April 1971, House of Commons Select Committee on Science and Technology, *The Prospects for the United Kingdom Computer Industry in the 1970s*, Fourth Report, Session 1970–71, HC 621–II, Volume II, Minutes of Evidence (Stationery Office, London, 1971), p. 254; 'Memorandum by The Real Time Club of Great Britain', Appendix 88, Select Committee on Science and Technology, Session 1969–70, *UK Computer Industry*, Volume II, Appendices (Stationery Office, London 1970), p. 289.

[65] House of Commons Select Committee on Science and Technology, Session 1969–1970, *UK Computer Industry*, Volume I, Minutes of Evidence, 24 March 1970 (Stationery Office, London, 1970), Qs. 1048–57, p. 189.

to other computers performing associated operations or controlling data banks provided either by Government bodies or by commercial companies'.[66] During the 1970s, commercial, industrial, and educational activities, alongside those of government, would rest on 'multiple real-time systems which will be the first phases of a sophisticated national computing network'. It would comprise 'as vital a component in the social infra-structure as the road system, the electricity grid, or the present voice telephone system. It could be described as the future "nervous system" of our society. As such it will play a very significant part in determining the position of this nation in world markets.' The submission therefore advocated urgent action by the Post Office to commence the establishment of a 'data communication network', that was 'a matter of the greatest concern to the whole nation, affecting every area of business and industry'.[67] In a further memorandum from April 1971, the Club reiterated its case. It held that 'the most urgent and important matter demanding public attention at the present time is the provision of a data transmission network'. It regretted that Post Office proposals for the development 'of a data network' were tentative, with references to the *possibility* of 'initial elements' being available by 1977. The memorandum closed by urging the sub-committee to recommend that 'necessary finance' be made available.[68]

When the sub-committee took evidence from Real Time Club members in April 1971, C. T. Ross of the club expressed the view cited in the ultimate sub-committee report that:

> in due course there will probably be no free-standing computers of any sort whatsoever and that at a point in the future every computing system will be linked up in some way or other to every other. The problem is always the time scale. This is something which nobody could ever attempt to forecast, nor can the various attempts at market research ever clearly answer this because it might be five years, it might be ten years. But we can say without any doubt that in our opinion before the end of the century there will be as many terminals in this country as there are telephones today, or more, and that no computer will be unconnected to the network.[69]

One particular subject of interest on which the sub-committee pressed representatives of the Real Time Club was the lack of cost–benefit analysis in its proposal.[70] Ultimately the sub-committee was unpersuaded to adopt these ideas as recommendations to government. The final report subscribed in

[66] 'Memorandum by The Real Time Club of Great Britain', Appendix 88, Select Committee on Science and Technology, Session 1969–70, *UK Computer Industry*, Volume II, Appendices (Stationery Office, London, 1970), p. 287.

[67] Ibid., p. 288.

[68] 'Memorandum by Real Time Club', 21 April 1971, House of Commons Select Committee on Science and Technology, *The Prospects for the United Kingdom Computer Industry in the 1970s*, Fourth Report, Session 1970–71, HC 621–II, Volume II, Minutes of Evidence, pp. 254–5.

[69] Ibid., Q. 1404, p. 257.

[70] Ibid., Q. 1405, p. 258.

general to the idea of the growing significance of computers.[71] However, it explained that it would not address 'future data communications needs', though acknowledging that they were 'of crucial importance'.[72] Following its initial terms of reference, it concentrated on commercial matters and the opportunities for the UK in this regard. Moreover, of further significance from the point of view of the present work, it did not give direct consideration to the implications of computers for the functioning of the political system. In as far as it discussed matters such as central and local government, as well as other parts of the public sector, it did so from the perspective that they were major consumers of the technology, and considered the effect that decisions about procurement and regulation might have (as discussed above, one of its recommendations led to the formation of the CCA).[73] Nor did it discuss the implications for Parliament itself. While interest in the possibilities was already developing among some parliamentary staff, fuller consideration had to wait until later in the decade, and the Informal Joint Committee inquiry.

In the years following the 1977 Informal Joint Committee report, there was steady pressure in support of computerisation. The House of Commons Library continued to be a significant force. In the first instance, it sought the means to use the technology for the purposes of indexing its material.[74] The existing hardcopy system had been established in 1955 and the task involved was, according to the Librarian, D. Menhennet, now 'much bigger and a much more complicated process than it was when first introduced'.[75] In a memorandum discussed in Chapter 5, the Library referred in support of their case to a series of constitutionally derived pressures that created a need for computer-based indexing.[76] By mid-1978, the House of Lords counterpart to the House of Commons Library, using the system already available to it, had made practical progress in this regard, creating an index of around 5,000 items. It expected to add 2,000–3,000 further entries each year.[77]

[71] House of Commons Select Committee on Science and Technology, Fourth Report 1970–1971, Volume 1, Report, *The Prospects for the United Kingdom Computer Industry in the 1970s*, HC 621–I (Stationery Office, London), p. viii.

[72] Ibid., p. vii.

[73] Ibid., p. xl.

[74] Menhennet and Englefield, 'Outline History of the Library's Experiments with Computer Applications', p. 50.

[75] Select Committee on House of Commons (Services), *Computer-Based Indexing for the Library*, Fifth Report of Session 1976–77, HC 377, Minutes of Evidence, 5 April 1977 (Stationery Office, London, 1977), Q. 35, p. 21.

[76] 'The Library's Proposals for Computer-Based Indexing', Memorandum by the Librarian and Deputy Librarian, Select Committee on House of Commons (Services), *Computer-Based Indexing for the Library*, Fifth Report of Session 1976–77, HC 377, Minutes of Evidence, 5 April 1977 (Stationery Office, London, 1977), Q. 35, p. 21.

[77] A. R. W. Robinson, Central Computer Agency, CSD, Select Committee on House of Commons (Services), *Computer Applications for the House of Commons*, Seventh Report of Session 1977–78, HC 617–II (Stationery Office, London, 1978), Appendix 1, p. 31.

Committees in the Commons and Lords continued to consider the prospects for the use of computers, sometimes meeting together in single sessions, in fulfilment of a recommendation in the 1977 Informal Joint Committee report in favour of such a practice.[78] In July 1978, agreeing with a submission from the CCA, the Select Committee on House of Commons (Services) stated that 'the time has now come for a Computer Officer to be appointed at a fairly senior level to advise on and to oversee future planning and developments'. The individual concerned could work for the House of Lords as well as the Commons, if the Lords was content.[79] Such a postholder could promote a unified parliamentary approach. The Services Committee placed a premium upon this quality, writing that 'the fact that the overall use of computers in Parliament has so far evolved in an unplanned, piece-meal fashion means a danger of different applications being implemented as a series of mutually-incompatible small systems'.[80] A Computer Development Officer was appointed in 1979.[81]

While there is evidence of a desire to utilise computers on the part of some staff within the institution, other colleagues were less enthusiastic. One clerk (who nonetheless supported further exploration of the possibilities) argued to the Informal Joint Committee in June 1976 that '[t]here is no aspect of the work of the [House of Commons Clerk's] Department which is at present thought to be positively disadvantaged by the absence of computer facilities'.[82] When A. R. W. Robinson of the CCA appeared before the Computer Sub-Committee of the House of Commons (Services) Committee in 1978 to discuss a report he had produced on potential applications of the technology in Parliament, in a discussion of the level of interest in the use of word processing, he described:

> a general feeling from various people, that people would not like to use it. It is an approach I have come across before, not just within the two Houses but elsewhere – most people are quite often unwilling to admit directly that they are unhappy about it, so they may say they have a friend who doesn't like it. It is a fairly common resistance that I have found, where Word Processing has been introduced.[83]

[78] Select Committee on House of Commons (Services), *Computer Applications for the House of Commons*, Seventh Report of Session 1977–78, HC 617–I (Stationery Office, London, 1978), p. v.

[79] Ibid., p. vi.

[80] Ibid., p. vii.

[81] Select Committee on House of Commons (Services), *Computer Services for Members*, Fourth Report of Session 1989–90, HC 614 (Stationery Office, London, 1990), p. viii.

[82] Cited by Richard Barlas, Clerk of the House of Commons, 'The Application of Computers to the Work of the Clerks' Department', p. 54.

[83] Select Committee on House of Commons (Services), *Computer Applications for the House of Commons*, Seventh Report of Session 1977–78, HC 617–II, Minutes of Evidence, 7 June 1978 (Stationery Office, London, 1978), Q. 4, p. 2.

When a service became available within Parliament, take-up might prove slow. Such proved to be the case with the computerised House of Lords Library index. In 1978 Robinson expressed puzzlement about low levels of interest in this service, speculating that the cause 'could be a lack of knowledge of the facilities available, a reluctance to use computers, or continuing reliance on familiar manuscript indexes'.[84] A source of concern within Parliament about the use of computers was that it might generate a need for new protocols around the storage of confidential materials. The Clerk of the House of Commons, Richard Barlas, raised this issue in relation to select committee employment of computers in a February 1978 memorandum:

> One note of caution must be sounded. Select Committees often hear oral evidence in private, and all such information must be treated as confidential until reported to the House. In addition committees often receive classified or otherwise confidential evidence – both orally and in memoranda – which they do not publish. If any such data were stored on a computer, it would be essential to ensure that access to that data was strictly limited to Members of the Committee and the Committee staff. Similar problems could arise with Committees' working papers, such as Chairman's Notes and draft Reports, which are, of their nature, confidential documents.[85]

Sometimes the desire to ensure that Parliament took a concerted approach, adopting technically compatible systems and acting in accordance with a comprehensive strategy, could seem a blockage from the point of view of more specific initiatives within Parliament. In the late 1970s, for instance, a view existed within the House of Commons Library that an insistence on developing an approach for the whole of Parliament before progressing, as the CCA encouraged, might delay the proposed indexing programme.[86] Another blockage on change could be that while technology could in theory deliver a particular service, it had not yet reached the point of development required to perform it to a satisfactory level.[87]

Within this wider debate and pattern of development around the parliamentary employment of computers, their use as part of communications networks continued to be a subset. The report Robinson of the CCA produced in 1978 discussed subjects including 'Word Processing', 'Full Text Retrieval', and 'Indexing'. A further topic was 'Access to External Databases

[84] A. R. W. Robinson, Central Computer Agency, CSD, Select Committee on House of Commons (Services), *Computer Applications for the House of Commons*, Seventh Report of Session 1977–78, HC 617–II (Stationery Office, London, 1978), Appendix 1, p. 31.

[85] Richard Barlas, Clerk of the House of Commons, 'The Application of Computers to the Work of the Clerks' Department', p. 56.

[86] Select Committee on House of Commons (Services), *Computer Applications for the House of Commons*, Seventh Report of Session 1977–78, HC 617–II, Minutes of Evidence, 12 July 1978 (Stationery Office, London, 1978), Q. 67, p. 17.

[87] Menhennet and Englefield, 'Outline History of the Library's Experiments with Computer Applications', p. 50.

Files and Systems', in which it discussed the present and potential use of computers in the libraries of both Houses to acquire information from outside in support of their research.[88]

1983: Parties and MPs

A renewed effort to advance the parliamentary use of computers occurred in 1983. In this year, the Select Committee on House of Commons (Services) Computer Sub-Committee commissioned a consultancy, the Economist Intelligence Unit, to conduct a survey of MPs and their staff, to ascertain their requirements for information technology – a category within which computers were treated as the most prominent item, but which also included telephonic devices.[89] Around this time both computers and electronic communications technology had a reasonable degree of political salience. In the same year that the research was carried out, a General Election took place (the survey was of MPs in office before the contest). Party manifestos contained content related to these fields.[90] The governing Conservative Party (which comfortably won the contest) proclaimed that:

> Britain has more micro-computers in relation to its population than any other country. We have speeded this progress by supporting research and spreading knowledge of the technologies of tomorrow; and by increasing government support for the new technologies.

The Conservative text committed to supporting, with the private sector, 'the Alvey programme for research into advanced information technology'; to encourage the swifter commercial application of scientific advances; to assist companies in introducing 'new products'; to continue to support the use of computers in schools and for younger people; and to 'sanction the launch of new cable networks to bring wider choice to consumers, not just for entertainment, but for the whole new world of tele-shopping and tele-banking'. The Conservatives noted that the Data Protection Bill it had introduced would 'meet public concern that computers pose a particular threat to privacy'. It would enable the UK to 'ratify the European Convention on Data Protection'.

Labour did not make specific reference to computers. But it advocated the use of technologies, including for democratic ends, in a fashion similar to that considered in earlier chapters. In some ways it echoed the views Benn first advocated in 1968 and for a while afterwards. This similarly was apt given his

[88] A. R. W. Robinson, Central Computer Agency, CSD, Select Committee on House of Commons (Services), *Computer Applications for the House of Commons*, Seventh Report of Session 1977–78, HC 617–II (Stationery Office, London, 1978), Appendix 1, pp. 34–5.

[89] Select Committee on House of Commons (Services) Computer Sub-Committee, Session 1983–84, HC 109–I, Minutes of Evidence, 8 November 1983 (Stationery Office, London 1983).

[90] For the texts of manifestos, see F. W. S. Craig (ed.), *British General Election Manifestos: 1959-1987* (Aldershot, Dartmouth, 1990).

leading role at the time on the radical Left wing of Labour that had achieved prominence within the party. Generally, the Labour text expressed the view that '[s]cience and technology are essential to Britain's economic and social regeneration. The Tories have undermined research and development in the science-based research industries of the future.' While under the Conservatives 'new technology has brought major job losses in some sectors', Labour would 'plan new technology to meet our commitment to full employment'. If it came to power a priority would be to '[e]nsure that research and development are directed towards society's needs, with a reduction in the present high proportion of defence research'. It stressed the importance of education and training, on a basis of gender equality. To these ends, Labour would '[i]ncrease technological literacy in schools and give boys and girls equal opportunities to study science and technology'. It would also '[p]romote the supply of engineers and technicians, including women, to meet the needs of industry and the community'.

Under the heading 'Telecommunications', it stated that:

> A national cable system will make possible a wide range of new telecommunications services, greater variety in the provision of television, and a major stimulus to British technology and industry. But it must be under firm public control. A publicly-owned British Telecommunications will thus be given the sole responsibility to create a national, broadband network (including Mercury, the new privately-owned telecommunications system for business), which integrates telecommunications and broadcasting.

Labour would, moreover: '[p]romote the development and use of new information and communication services to support a wider democracy'.

The ideological distance between the parties was on display in these passages. The Conservatives presented technology in consumerist terms and as means of making people economically active. Labour emphasised the public sector and the pursuit of equality and common good. In the consideration of matters of a democratic nature, the Conservative concern was negative: protecting against the infringement of individual rights; while for Labour the objective was the positive attainment of democratic empowerment.

The third force at the 1983 General Election, the centrist Liberal–Social Democratic Party (SDP) Alliance, addressed some of the same issues. Generally, it wanted to 'invest resources in the high-technology industries of the future'. Moreover, it noted that 'the expansion of television technology through cable, video cassettes and satellite offers great opportunities in the creation of a better informed society and provides new opportunities for the Arts'. But, it went on, 'these technologies also carry dangers to our society if they become vehicles for pornography and violence. This must not be allowed to happen, and the State must have particular regard to its responsibilities for the young.' A further example of caution on the part of the Alliance came with the remark that '[c]hanges in the power of the State, the media and in technology require specific protection of rights by statute'.

This manifesto content showed that the matters considered in this book – technology, including communications and computers, and their social and political implications – could figure in political debate at this time. There were other items higher on the agenda. For instance, at this election, matters such as defence, the economy, and membership of the European Communities received far more attention. Moreover, while these earlier discussions in many ways prefigured debates about the Internet, issues connected to this digital network would become more salient still than they were in the 1980s; for instance, at the time of the 2019 General Election, as we will see. Nonetheless, it is significant that parties should have addressed these questions.

Whatever positions their parties might take on the subject of technology at the 1983 election, the findings of the Economist Intelligence Unit suggested that, as a group, MPs making up the House of Commons at the point when Parliament was dissolved for this contest were not the most active utilisers of computers and related devices. Its report, notably stressing the idea of communication as a purpose of information technology, made the following observation:

> Although 'communication' lies at the core of a Member's work, there has been very little adoption of Information Technology by Members. Some computerisation of central services has occurred within the House (eg Library, Fees Office, Serjeant at Arms department [responsible for security]) but Members themselves have not widely adopted the new technology to assist them in their work. In part this is due to the lack of a source of finance for such Information Technology support.[91]

The Economist Intelligence Unit survey took place at the close of the 1979–83 Parliament.[92] It produced a source that could be valuable to any historian seeking an account from an outside observer of Parliament as it operated in the early to mid-1980s. It locates the prospects for the dissemination of technology in a wider institutional context. Any effort to promote adoption of computers would need to contend with a peculiar cultural environment. The report noted that '[a]lthough the House of Commons can be classified as an organisation . . . there is wide variation in individual Members' perceptions of that purpose. Each Member plays a highly individualistic role within the organisation, in line with his own perceptions.' Consequently, the Commons 'must be considered as the sum of the 650 (now) elected representatives within it – a good analogy being an amalgam of 650 small business owners, each operating in line with his own perception of his "business", and how it should be organised, administered and staffed'. The House had 'a hierarchical management structure', with the closest equivalent to a source of authority being

[91] Ibid.

[92] Select Committee on House of Commons (Services), *Information Technology: Members' Requirements*, First Report of Session 1983–84, HC 97-I (Stationery Office, London, 1983), p. v.

'the Whips'. As a consequence, MPs made their own decision not only about staffing but also equipment, which financial allowances did not properly cover. The report noted that 'in some cases the secretaries have to provide their own typewriter (often manual), but in other cases Members are prepared to purchase expensive electronic typewriters for their secretaries' use'. The bulk of MPs, the Economist Intelligence Unit found, 'cherish ... this slightly egocentric spirit of independence'. Awareness of this characteristic had to inform any assessment of 'the selection, funding, organisation and support of any proposed investment in Information Technology'.

The report remarked further upon 'the importance of the "traditions" of the House ... On first impressions some of the systems and protocol in the House appear to be "unacceptable" in terms of more commercially orientated criteria.' Yet it was 'clear that many of the "traditional ways of doing things" are surprisingly unquestioned by Members and are considered to be integral to the "character" of the House'. The authors detected a generational shift, however, with MPs joining from 1979 and thereafter less interested in 'preserving "custom and practice"' (while at the same time having 'become almost complacent about' amateurish practices). These newer entrants tended to anticipate that changes were coming.[93]

In parts the report resembles a survey of an underprivileged neighbourhood by a would-be social reformer, as in the following account of the practical restrictions upon computerisation:

> **The Physical Layout of the Organisation**
> 2.6 Many of the interviews were carried out (where appropriate) within the office of the respondent. All the major accommodation areas were visited, and the varying standards of accommodation were noted. The dispersed nature of the office accommodation, and the methods of allocation clearly exacerbate the integration and communication problems of the organisation. On the whole we were surprised by the poor standard of accommodation, particularly the extent to which Members have to share what is, in many cases, very cramped accommodation.[94]

The fuller use of computing would require various refurbishments. For instance, establishing an internal Local Area Network linking devices to a single central system would necessitate laying of cables across the estate, which some sceptics seem to have held was a prohibitively difficult challenge.[95]

The Unit noted the methodological difficulties it faced. Its sample was self-selecting, and therefore – the Unit judged – it leant towards positive attitudes

[93] Select Committee on House of Commons (Services) Computer Sub-Committee, Session 1983–84, HC 109–I, Minutes of Evidence, 8 November 1983 (Stationery Office, London 1983), p. 4.

[94] Ibid., pp. 4–5.

[95] Select Committee on House of Commons (Services) Computer Sub-Committee, Session 1983–84, HC 109–IV, Minutes of Evidence, 13 December 1983 (Stationery Office, London, 1983), Q. 207, p. 110.

regarding the technologies concerned.[96] Yet even given this distortion, the results might not have suggested that the chances for rapid take-up of computers were great. For instance, as few as 10 per cent of respondents judged it to be 'at all advantageous for Members to be able to collaborate more through some kind of formal communications system'. Close to a fifth 'expressed very strong views against any kind of system linking Members, and an additional 44 per cent felt that it would not be at all advantageous'. While a substantial number believed that IT would be useful to them, they 'seemed daunted by the practical stages needed to adopt the technology'.[97] The individualism of MPs was a factor in such responses.[98] Moreover, 'only two Members said that they wanted to be able to (directly) access constituency information held on a proposed computer database maintained by the secretary'.[99] More than a fifth reported that 'they had little or no experience with word processors, personal computers or other types of office automation'. Furthermore, 'the 23 per cent who made no specific comments are also likely to include many who have had no experience of these systems'.[100]

Pressure and Frustration

The 1983 survey was part of a wider investigation by the Computer Sub-Committee into the prospects for parliamentary use of the technology. A consideration of its work provides insight into not only the issues and challenges that arose, but also who among parliamentarians the advocates of adoption were, and how they went about promoting their objectives. One prominent campaigner was a member of the sub-committee, the Conservative MP Ian Lloyd. We have already seen how, as a participant in the House of Commons Select Committee on Science and Technology sub-committee on computers, he had raised the subject of the embryonic Internet as early as 1971. Still looking across the Atlantic for inspiration, Lloyd continued to draw attention to developments in similar areas as a member of the Computer Sub-Committee. For instance, on 10 November 1983, when taking evidence from Richard Morgan, the Commons Computer Development Officer, Lloyd referred to 'some of the things which apparently are now available to a Member of Congress'. He remarked that 'all one hundred Members of the Senate now have an installed video computer system in their offices … with access to a wide variety of databases'. Moreover, Lloyd believed that 'each Senator is now entitled to four communicating screens in his own territory, so that his local staff can communicate

96 Select Committee on House of Commons (Services) Computer Sub-Committee, Session 1983–84, HC 109–I, Minutes of Evidence, 8 November 1983 (Stationery Office, London 1983), p. 3.

97 Ibid., p. 20.

98 Ibid., p. 24.

99 Ibid.

100 Ibid, p. 26.

with him at his office in Washington'.[101] Lloyd went on to note that 'the US Congress is now spending more on information technology than the total cost of the Palace of Westminster, including the pay of every single Member of Parliament'.[102]

Lloyd was one of a number of parliamentarians of similar outlook to his own. A significant convening body in this field was the Parliamentary Information Technology Committee (PITCOM), of which he was chair from its formation in 1981 until 1987. An Associate Parliamentary Group rather than a committee of Parliament, it was in effect an all-party pressure group for those with an interest in promoting computing within the political environment. Created out of a merger of the Parliamentary Computer Forum and the All-Party IT Committee, it continued enthusiastic advocacy for its cause until 2011 when it combined with the All-Party Group on the Digital Economy to become the Parliamentary ICT Forum (PICTFOR).[103] During the course of its existence, PITCOM took an interest both in general computer-related policy and in encouraging parliamentary use of the technology.[104]

Attached to different parties, those MPs who advocated the use of computers in Parliament often came from professional backgrounds in the field. The Labour MP, Stuart Randall, was previously an electrical engineer whose employers included corporations such as English Electrical Computers.[105] A memorandum he submitted to the Computer Sub-Committee in 1983 complained that '[t]he usage of information technology (IT) by Members is very low indeed'. Nonetheless he held that there was 'immense scope for using IT'. In his account of difficulties, solutions, and prospects, Randall referred to the possibility for MPs 'of linking various terminal devices . . . to a whole network of other computers and terminals which could be linked to the existing telephone network'. He posited a scenario in which 'it would be possible to send a text message to a Minister whose Departmental switch would be external to the House of Commons, suggesting dates for a meeting'.[106]

[101] Select Committee on House of Commons (Services) Computer Sub-Committee, Session 1983–84, HC 109–II, Minutes of Evidence, 10 November 1983 (Stationery Office, London, 1983), Q. 46, p. 64.

[102] Ibid.

[103] 'PITCOM History', available at: www.pitcom.org.uk/pitcom-history.html, last accessed 24 September 2020.

[104] Ross Ferguson and Laura Miller, *Parliament for the Future: Forecasting the Form of a Digitally-Enabled Parliament* (Hansard Society, London, 2007), pp. 6–7.

[105] Tam Dalyell, 'Lord Randall of St Budeaux: MP Who Put His Industrial Experience to Good Use', *The Independent*, 5 September 2012, available at: www.independent.co.uk/news/obituaries/lord-randall-of-st-budeaux-mp-who-put-his-industrial-experience-to-good-use-8104876.html, last accessed 18 June 2020.

[106] 'Information Technology and Members', Memorandum submitted by Stuart Randall MP, Select Committee on House of Commons (Services) Computer Sub-Committee, Session 1983–84, HC 109–IV, Minutes of Evidence, 13 December 1983 (Stationery Office, London, 1983), pp. 95–6.

Not all advocates of parliamentary use of computers were technical experts. Paddy Ashdown, then a newly elected Liberal MP who would later become leader of the Liberal Democrats (after the Liberals merged with the Social Democratic Party), was an example of an MP with a non-specialist standpoint who nonetheless chose to give evidence in support of their promotion within Parliament to the Computer Sub-Committee inquiry in 1983. As he put it to the Committee: 'I know absolutely nothing about what goes on inside a computer or about computer programming.'[107] Ashdown seems to have rested on the support of a Mrs G. Gunner, a computer programmer, who attended the committee session with him. One of the basic functions of computers he identified was to obtain 'access to information and the capacity to be able to tap in effectively and efficiently to information systems'.[108]

As the views of Randall and Ashdown show, the idea of using computers for communications as well as for the storage and processing of information was clearly recognised among advocates of the technology, and presented in evidence to the Computer Sub-Committee. One expert witness, P. Benton, told the inquiry that 'Britain and, I feel sure, Europe, is moving towards an enhanced network at two levels: a universally available, certainly in Britain, Integrated Services Digital Network (ISDN) based on switched 64 kilobit paths and a 2 megabit switched network, linking the major commercial areas.' Benton judged '[i]t would be strange if Members of Parliament were not to have the benefit of such networks in their own activities'. They included 'fast data retrieval, which gives the effect of flicking through pages of a book, facsimile in 3–4 seconds for a page of A4 and picture Prestel for a full screen colour photograph in nine seconds, as against eight minutes it requires to give you similar information on the present system'. The system would provide 'high quality graphics and voice combined, with improved communications between individuals plus slow scan TV'. It would 'enhance Members' briefing in terms both of the range of information available and the speed with which this information can be obtained without Members having to move physically around the House or other places elsewhere in London and abroad'. The benefits would include 'video conferencing'.[109]

In keeping with such evidence, the resulting 1984 report from the Committee on House of Commons (Services) to the Speaker of the House of Commons was clear in its view that computers were, in part, communications devices. It presented the argument that:

[107] Select Committee on House of Commons (Services) Computer Sub-Committee, Session 1983–84, HC 109–III, Minutes of Evidence, 7 December 1983 (Stationery Office, London 1983), Q. 123, p. 84.

[108] Ibid.

[109] Mr P. Benton. Select Committee on House of Commons (Services) Computer Sub-Committee, Session 1983–84, HC 109–VIII, Minutes of Evidence, 7 March 1984 (Stationery Office, London 1984), p. 158.

> as institutions outside the House are busily embracing this technology as a business standard, the House will need to keep up with such advances if it is to play its full political role. The growth of statistical data available and the mass of other information with which all Members must deal makes the speedy introduction of an effective information technology system of vital importance.[110]

Alongside perceived developments in the business sector and in the availability of data, the Committee drew motivation from practices in other governmental institutions, both in the UK and abroad. They included the Greater London Council and the Strathclyde Regional Council. A project underway in the US Senate sought to supply the office of every member with between twenty-five and forty-five 'work-stations'. Equipment was also available to members of the US Congress, and of the House of Commons in Canada.[111] Electronic mail, the Committee learned, was available in these North American institutions, as well as the French National Assembly.[112] The Committee also discussed teletext. In the UK two services of this type, CEEFAX and ORACLE, provided a variety of information via television sets; and the Committee envisaged that they might be incorporated into a parliamentary network.[113] A more advanced technology was viewdata, which allowed users to search for information. The Post Office had established a system of this type, called Prestel, in 1979. It subsequently came under the control of Telecom.[114] The need for electronic access to large sources of data had received recognition but the precise means of obtaining it were not yet clear. The Committee set out a plan, over a period of twenty-one months, for providing Members with computer services among which were 'electronic mail', '[a]cess to POLIS' (the internal parliamentary electronic information system), and '[a]ccess to commercial databases'. It would involve laying cable to provide for a Local Area Network. The total estimated cost would be slightly over £5 million.[115]

A debate of the report took place in the Commons on 12 July 1985. But the proposals contained in it went unimplemented. Though the technology had supporters, their enthusiasm must not have not have been matched widely enough across the institution (or within government). Factors previously identified, including wariness of the costs and complications involved, presumably played a part. After half a decade of barely perceptible progress – one of the most notable features of which was a limited trial during the first half of 1987 of the British Telecom 'Telecom Gold' electronic mail service – the

[110] Select Committee on House of Commons (Services), *Information Technology: Members' Requirements*, First Report of Session 1984–85, HC 97–I, pp. v–vi.
[111] Ibid., pp. ix–x.
[112] Ibid., pp. xi–xii.
[113] Ibid., p. xiii.
[114] Ibid., p. xiv.
[115] Ibid., pp. vi–ix.

Committee issued another report in 1990.[116] It noted two issues involving the parliamentary estate as bearing upon the subject. The first was the existing annunciator system, an electronic network providing basic information about parliamentary proceedings. Installed in the late 1960s, it was becoming obsolete. When a replacement became necessary, an appropriate point might arise for the laying of cables. But by the late 1980s the government had become reluctant to concede that the annunciator system was near the end of its life cycle.[117] The second factor was the plan to build the 'New Parliamentary Building'. This project was ultimately realised as Portcullis House. Its purpose was to create much-needed office space and it was anticipated it would provide more modern facilities than those available in the main Palace accommodation, or other spaces on the estate. This prospect therefore encouraged consideration of the equipment and services that should be available to MPs and their staff.[118]

Usage of computers among MPs had increased substantially since 1985. In this year, the Computer Sub-Committee had carried out a survey, to which 321 MPs replied, 94 of whom had computer-related equipment, with another 49 at least considering obtaining it.[119] A follow-up exercise came in 1990. Of 355 respondents, 293 were employing the technology, and 21 planned to. Among them, many were interested in having access to services such as POLIS and electronic mail.[120] Foreign examples of a more proactive approach had proliferated since the mid-1980s. Considering specific examples from West Germany, Norway, France, Italy, Sweden, the United States, and Canada, and assessing a study of thirty-four states,[121] the Committee concluded that Parliament was 'clearly out of step with the parliaments of many other countries', both because it left 'the acquisition of IT equipment entirely to individual discretion and to the individual choice of Members' and because it failed to offer 'a range of mutually compatible computerised information services, together with some form of general technical support services for the use of all Members'.[122] The Committee therefore recommended the introduction of a 'long-term policy' to provide 'the best available information technology services for Members from central funds', combined with the retention of 'a reasonable degree of individual discretion in the choice of systems for use by Members and their staffs'.[123]

[116] Select Committee on House of Commons (Services), *Computer Services for Members*, Fourth Report of Session 1989–90, HC 614 (Stationery Office, London, 1990), p. v.

[117] Ibid., p. vi.

[118] Ibid., p. vi.

[119] Ibid., p. v.

[120] Ibid., p. vii.

[121] Ibid., p., x.

[122] Ibid., p. xi.

[123] Ibid.

Within the system it proposed:

> at an early date that all Members with suitable computers would be able to access the Library's Parliamentary On-Line Information System (POLIS), including not only the system's indexes of current and previous parliamentary proceedings, but also the relatively new databases of Early Day Motions, Government press releases etc. Similarly, the cable network from an early stage would be developed to handle electronic mail and messaging services, facsimile transmission (fax), and communications between Members' offices in Westminster and their constituency or home offices . . . Subsequently, we would expect the network to expand to offer access to external databases in the public sector and to other commercially provided services.[124]

The Rise of the Internet

During the decade that followed, a linking together of systems into a network of networks became possible with the rise of the Internet. As discussed previously, this system gained increased attention during the first half of the 1990s. In 1994, the term began to appear in parliamentary debates, sometimes in passing, at other times as the focus of discussion (it could be treated as interchangeable with 'information super-highway' and 'world wide web' at this time). Just as enthusiasm for computers cut across party divisions, so did internet advocacy. On 7 March 1995, Graham Allen, a Labour MP[125] spoke in the Commons on the subject of the 'Information Super-Highway'. He presented the view that '[s]eizing the advantages of the super-highway is possibly the most important issue facing our nation'. Allen was influenced by debates on the subject taking place in the United States. He noted that '[t]he Government have a role in providing leadership and vision. Al Gore has provided that in the United States, and even Newt Gingrich had his say.'[126] As the reference to 'Government . . . leadership' suggested, Allen saw a need for public authorities to take responsibility for ensuring that the technology was made widely available and used in beneficial ways. In this sense, his approach had a Left dimension to it, and he was critical of a supposed lack of action under the then present Conservative government. Allen suggested that:

> We could do worse than use Parliament as our first model, symbolically to show that we in this place are committed to the information super-highway. Every Member of Parliament should be provided with access to the Internet, if they so wish, and facilities for sending e-mail just as they now send letters or use the telephone.[127]

[124] Ibid., p. xiv.
[125] The present author worked in the office of Graham Allen MP from July 2002 to July 2004.
[126] Hansard, HC Debates, 7 March 1995, col. 241.
[127] Ibid., col. 243.

The specific emphasis was on representative democracy. Allen argued that there was a need to be 'wary of looking at snap referendums through electronic means'. He preferred considering 'the possibility of allowing interaction between a Member of Parliament and his or her constituents, or direct e-mailing on certain occasions'. While he suspected that '[t]he ingenuity of Members of Parliament could be tested', Allen was 'sure that they would come up with some excellent ideas'.[128] In promoting this approach, he diverged from a particular variant of electronic participation stretching back to Benn and, before him, Fuller and Birkenhead. On more general policy, Allen predicted that a future Labour government would 'construct a truly nationwide network', ensuring that social goods as well as commercial needs were supported.[129] He was impressed by a variety of local initiatives to encourage Internet use, including among socially more excluded groups. While generally positive about the technology, he anticipated one particular complication that remains a subject of considerable controversy. Allen warned of a need 'to address the difficult question of regulation of content'. He sensed that '[e]xisting regulatory frameworks may suffice for services and conventional cabling, but the Internet throws up particular problems'. In his view, '[a]n incoming [Labour] Government, particularly a Government committed to reinventing democracy in the United Kingdom' should oppose online censorship. But 'crimes such as racial hatred, pornography and defamation can never be tolerated in any section of society'. He called for 'a broad review of the relevant legislation to ensure that there are no loopholes or inconsistencies'.[130] Parliament was still struggling to resolve this issue a quarter of a century later.

In the early hours of 15 December 1995, the Conservative MP David Shaw spoke on this subject. Shaw believed he was 'the first Member of Parliament to subscribe to Internet, in April this year'. He viewed the technology as a driver of far-reaching social transformation, arguing that 'an enormous change in our lives will result from the Internet and the information super-highway'. Seeing specific potential for Parliament, Shaw noted that he hoped 'to be able to place a copy of this debate on the Internet in the next fortnight. I hope that it will be seen and read by as many as 30 million people, instead of the small number of hon. Members in the Chamber now, at 3.15 am.'[131] Official online publication of Hansard would commence the following year. In planning to make the text available, Shaw anticipated this practice. He also presented a view of the technology that would become increasingly prominent: that it offered dramatic opportunities for large-scale communication with the public.

Like Allen, while Shaw perceived radical potential in the Internet, he hoped it could be harnessed to support Parliament and the wider system of which

[128] Ibid.
[129] Ibid., cols. 245–6.
[130] Ibid.
[131] Ibid., 15 December 1994, col. 1242.

this institution was a part, rather than supplanting them. He turned to the subject of '[p]eople who get carried away with Internet and become over-endowed with excitement'. They were 'known as techies or techno nerds'. Shaw considered their idea that 'Internet will make politicians obsolete.' He hoped 'that will not happen. I do not subscribe to their vision of the future, which is that 40 million people or more will vote by electronic means, on television. We are a long way from that.' Having asserted the value of representative democracy as against the possible threat of online referendums, Shaw nonetheless noted 'there will be enormous changes, and opportunities for people to express opinions and views. The Government's world wide web server on the Internet allows the public to convey views and comments to the Government and Ministers.'[132] In favouring the enhancement of existing forms of democracy over the adoption of different models, Shaw shared ground with Allen. In this sense, two supporters of what they regarded as a dynamic technology, from different parties, were united around a distinctive approach that advanced the interests of their institution, Parliament. However, also like Allen, in his speech Shaw included some of his own party-political perspective. In particular, he referred to the possibilities 'for many Government services to be privatised using the information super-highway'.[133]

Interest also came from the Second Chamber. The House of Lords Information Committee agreed a report in July 1996 entitled *Information Society: Agenda for Action in the UK*. The recommendations it made regarding parliamentary use of the Internet are discussed in Chapter 2. It found that '[t]he world is undergoing a technological revolution and entering the age of the Information Society'.[134] It depicted the Internet as '[t]he most public face of the information superhighway'. It was 'a global network of computers linked mainly via the telephone system and the academic, research and commercial computing networks'. Yet the Committee, even by this point, perceived the Internet as limited to being a transitional technology. It was 'not a genuine superhighway because it does not offer the basic capability of two-way realtime video transmission and interactivity'. Nonetheless it offered 'a useful prototype from which a full information superhighway might evolve'. The Committee, moreover, was impressed by the expansion in 'the number of computer hosts connected to the Internet . . . a few tens of thousands of hosts in the late 1980s, one million hosts by 1992, three million by 1994, during 1995 the five million host mark was passed and in January 1996 the world total was 9,472,224'.[135] Growth of take-up would continue, and the Internet would

132 Ibid.

133 Ibid., col. 1243.

134 House of Lords Select Committee on Science and Technology, *Information Society: Agenda for Action in the UK*, Fifth Report of Session 1995–96, HL 77, para. 1.1, available at: https://publications.parliament.uk/pa/ld199596/ldselect/inforsoc/inforsoc.htm, last accessed 15 April 2020.

135 Ibid., para. 1.8.

in time develop some of the capabilities that the Committee suggested were needed. The Internet would outlast the 'information superhighway' term.

In a debate on the Committee report, Baroness Hogg, a Conservative, described on 25 October 1996 the ease with which it was possible 'to be intoxicated by the potential of digitisation'. She noted that the potential 'to transform all forms of information – data, text, picture, sound, even to replicate the sensations of touch – into a digital stream, and to transmit massive quantities of information worldwide virtually instantaneously' amounted to 'an extraordinary power which has been associated with the notion of a second Industrial Revolution'. Hogg regarded '[t]he exponential growth of the Internet – driven by the market, not by some government plan' as 'evidence of the potential speed of development in this area'. It posed a 'challenge' to 'notions of national regulation and sovereignty; there are, as has been said, no Customs posts in cyberspace'. There were both risk and benefits on offer, though 'it is important to keep at least one toe on the ground'.[136]

Some within Parliament were openly sceptical about the technology. Dr Lewis Moonie, Labour MP for Kirkcaldy told the Commons on 15 March 1995:

> I have a confession to make. I am not on the Internet, and I have no intention of going on the Internet. None of my constituents appears to be on the Internet, because none of them seeks to send me any electronic mail. As the political speeches made in this place are so boring, the idea of reading speeches from other parts of the world frankly fills me with horror.[137]

Nonetheless, by 1996, Parliament had introduced its own website. This development was the outcome of the usual tendencies that had driven computerisation itself: supporters within the institution, increased usage across various sectors within the UK and internationally, and practices in other political institutions including legislatures. There was also pressure from specific groups, such as the Campaign for Freedom of Information, that argued in favour of making parliamentary material available on the Internet from the point of view of public openness and accountability.[138]

On 27 March 1996, the House of Commons Information Committee, chaired by the Conservative MP Gary Waller, sent a report to the printers entitled *Electronic Publication of House of Commons Documents*. It is notable that, as this title suggests, the introduction of a website was perceived as a means of disseminating material to the public, rather than of two-way interaction. The Committee publication was a response to a report it had received from the Electronic Publishing Group (EPG), a body comprising House of

[136] Hansard, HL Debates, 25 October 1996, col. 65.

[137] Hansard, HC Debates, 15 March 1995, col. 943.

[138] Stephen Coleman, 'Westminster in the Information Age' in Stephen Coleman, John Taylor, and Wim van de Donk (eds.), *Parliament in the Age of the Internet* (Oxford University Press, 1999), pp. 9–25, 14.

Commons officials, chaired by Ian Church, the editor of the Official Report.[139] The central purpose of the EPG had been '[t]o examine the considerations arising from the distribution in electronic form to consumers outside the House of parliamentary publications or material derived from them, to seek to determine who might want such material and for what purpose'.[140]

Any external publication would be building on previous internal developments. As the EPG put it:

> Parliament is, by nature, a conservative institution. However, in recent years it has made a start in introducing new technology in the production of its papers and new production methods have revolutionised their printing and publication. The development of first POLIS and subsequently the PDVN [the Parliamentary Data and Video Network] have brought the benefits of IT to the working of the House. The House of Commons *Official Report* is now available electronically over the PDVN, and it is to be expected that in the next few years in-house electronic distribution of House documents will be extended. This is not to say that there will no longer be a demand for printed documents – Members will continue also to require printed versions to do their jobs – but there is a clear demand inside Parliament for more electronic availability of material, in addition to the frequently voiced demand from external users.[141]

Furthermore, late in 1995, an experiment had begun with placing parliamentary Public Information Office materials on the Internet.[142] In its inquiries, the EPG found that in various countries worldwide ('Australia, Canada, New Zealand and the United States') there was 'extensive free availability of certain parliamentary documents'. It noted that '[t]he means of distribution is the Internet'.[143] This latter point was significant because it showed that, at this time, the Internet was attaining hegemony as a form of digital communications. Yet this dominance had not seemed inevitable and, like the House of Lords Information Committee, the EPG did not assume that it was guaranteed forever. There were other means of electronic dissemination, the EPG noted, but the Internet was the most convenient and effective on offer. Its report left open the possibility that this position might change and some other system might supplant the Internet. Within the UK there was momentum to follow this developing international tendency. As the EPG put it:

> In the United Kingdom there has been sustained pressure from interest groups and potential users for our Parliament to follow suit. Within Parliament, Members have pressed for the same objective on the ground that the price and the difficulties of obtaining paper documents are barriers to legitimate

139 House of Commons Information Committee, *Electronic Publication of House of Commons Documents*, First Report of Session 1995–96, HC 328 (Stationery Office, London, 1996).

140 Ibid., p. v.

141 Report of the Electronic Publishing Group, House of Commons Information Committee, *Electronic Publication of House of Commons Documents*, First Report of Session 1995–96, HC 328 (Stationery Office, London, 1996), Annex, p. viii.

142 Ibid., p. vi and Annex, p. viii.

143 Ibid., Annex, p. vii.

> public and wider readership. Government departments are using the Internet to distribute electronic versions of their material.[144]

The Group was persuaded:

> that Parliament as well as the public has a substantial interest in making its papers available in electronic form. As a law-making body, Parliament needs to ensure that those subject to its laws have easy access to them and the law-making process, and the group believes that there is a clear public right to unfettered access to this material. From the group's external contacts it is clear that there is widespread support from all interested sectors for making parliamentary papers available in electronic form. The academic and public interest groups argued that there should be no charge, and two of the three commercial organisations which were invited to comment favoured some form of free distribution. The Cabinet Office supported the idea even if that meant a cost to the Exchequer.[145]

An environment conducive to this move had come about; and the EPG envisaged 'a Parliament home page ... describing the complete set of parliamentary information that was available over the Internet'. It would draw on 'a central electronic source of parliamentary copyright material'.[146]

The Group recognised there were concerns involving the financial implications and copyright issues.[147] The likely expense seems to have been a reason for its proposal that parliamentary internet and intranet functions be made distinct. The Group also regarded the two tasks as qualitatively different in nature, therefore requiring of discreet treatment. It stated:

> Some additional costs will arise from the group's proposals, and there will be implications for the PDVN. In view of our recommendation that all parliamentary documents should be made available in electronic form, the group believes that it would be undesirable, and indeed beyond any reasonable deployment of internal resources, for this electronic publishing task to be carried out in-house. It is a distinct task, separate from the provision and management of internal Internet servers.[148]

This differentiation, as we have seen, would later be a subject of criticism, and was reversed. Where copyright was concerned, the Group recognised that 'once the material has been accessed, there is no certain method of preventing any user from downloading the material and making further use of it'.[149] Consequently it held that:

[144] Ibid.
[145] Ibid.
[146] Ibid., Annex, p. x.
[147] Ibid., Annex, p. viii.
[148] Ibid., Annex, p. x.
[149] Ibid., Annex, p. ix.

> Free publication on the Internet does not preclude commercial organisations reselling the material that they have processed. There is a market for value-added services. The group recommends that external bodies wishing to make use of parliamentary copyright electronic material with a view to added-value processing and selling on, or combining with other electronic information, should be allowed to do so under licence agreements made with each House. The licensing arrangements should encourage the widest possible dissemination of parliamentary material.[150]

The adding of value, as EPG saw it, was for others. Staff within Parliament would not engage in creating content for online consumption. It was 'a matter of principle' that 'parliamentary documents published electronically should, like the printed versions, be made available by Parliament only in full'. Furthermore, 'departments of both Houses should not be permitted to engage in value-added processing of their own material for electronic distribution beyond their responsibilities for meeting the needs of their House'. (An exception to this rule would 'apply to the Public Information Office'.)[151] One motive for this stipulation was probably an instinct to preserve the basic features of the publications, even in a different, electronic, format. Alterations, moreover, would have implications for staff time, and would bring with them various complications – such as discussions or even controversy about what was an appropriate way of processing the material.

The Commons Information Committee, on considering the report from the EPG, took the view that the proposals it made, were they put into force, would represent a beneficial expansion in the means of dissemination of Commons publications.[152] In particular it regarded the recommendation 'to make documents of the House available via the Internet free of charge' as of great potential value 'since it would, in the Committee's view, encourage wider public interest in, and knowledge of, the business of the House'.[153] While noting that there would be cost implications requiring attention, and addressing complications that might arise from the intended privatisation of the Stationery Office, the Committee 'commends the EPG report to the House and hopes that the recommendations can be effectively and speedily implemented'.[154] The development of the parliamentary website beyond its embryonic state, as discussed in Chapter 2, followed from this proposal.

The appearance of this external electronic profile accompanied continued growth in the usage of computers by Members and their staff through the 1990s. By 1993, a questionnaire showed that IT was in use in 76 per cent of constituency offices and in the same proportion of MPs' offices in

150 Ibid., Annex, pp. ix–x.
151 Ibid., Annex, pp. viii–ix.
152 House of Commons Information Committee, *Electronic Publication of House of Commons Documents*, First Report of Session 1995–96, HC 328 (Stationery Office, London, 1996), p. v.
153 Ibid., p. v.
154 Ibid., p. vi.

Westminster.[155] To look slightly beyond the strict time limits of this chapter, a mid-2000 survey showed that computers were in use in 92 per cent of constituency offices and 89 per cent of offices in Westminster.[156] Nonetheless, by the end of the 1990s, a concerted parliamentary approach to computing was in some senses still lacking. On 30 June 1994, the Commons had agreed with the view of the House of Commons Information Committee in its rejection of the idea of central provision of Information Technology (IT) – that is, the supply of standard equipment that belonged to the institution, not the MPs using it. At this point, MPs remained responsible for making their own arrangements for computer equipment, paid for from their parliamentary allowance or by other means, and choosing products for themselves. One who captured the argument in favour of this established approach among those who supported technological advance was the Labour MP Jeremy Bray. He argued in the Commons on 30 June 1994 that '[i]t is right to leave the provision of equipment to the individual responsibility of Members, to finance under their own office costs allowance'. Bray regarded '[i]ndividual procurement' as having facilitated 'in recent years, a far faster rate of penetration of new techniques in the House than it would have done if there had been a centrally provided House of Commons service on the pattern of some past proposals that have been put to the House'.[157]

But the latitude Bray valued was a problem from the point of view of the development of a coherent whole. In 1996, in tandem with the introduction of the external facing website, a new internal electronic system for MPs and their staff in Westminster and constituency offices, the Parliamentary Data and Video Network (PDVN), launched. Cabling of the estate was underway, and it was intended that this task would be complete by 2001–2, providing superior access to PDVN for office computers. Pending this completion, connections were also available through telephone lines. However, the potential effectiveness of the system and the prospects for developing it further in future were limited by the fact that not all equipment in use by MPs was fully compatible with the PDVN.[158]

The results of the 2000 questionnaire showed that 73 per cent of MPs who responded favoured moving to some kind of centrally co-ordinated system for the supply of IT. In this year the House of Commons Information Committee, which had conducted the survey, considered the options for standardisation, combined with cost savings. It drew a distinction between two possible approaches that could meet these requirements. They were

155 House of Commons Information Committee, *The Supply of Members' Information Technology Equipment, Software and Associated Services*, Second Report of Session 1999–2000, HC 758 (Stationery Office, London, 2000), p. viii.

156 Ibid.

157 Hansard, HC Debates, 30 June 1994, col. 943.

158 House of Commons Information Committee, *The Supply of Members' Information Technology Equipment, Software and Associated Services*, p. xi.

'central provision' and 'central procurement'. The former entailed (as noted above) Members having the use of specific equipment owned by the House.[159] The second, more flexible, arrangement would involve allowing Members to obtain equipment of their choice, provided it was compatible with the PDVN. Of the two basic approaches, the second would provide more discretion to Members to choose the devices they wanted than the first.[160] Either would be a means of ensuring that MPs could make full use of the PDVN, which at present was not guaranteed.[161] In other words, they would incorporate MPs into a single parliamentary computer network, fulfilling what the Committee referred to as 'PDVN convergence strategy'.[162] A consideration for the Information Committee was balancing the gains against a possible desire on the part of MPs for flexibility in making decisions about how to equip their offices.[163] It therefore recommended a central procurement model, providing MPs with '[t]he choice of a range of IT equipment and software together with associated maintenance, support and training, which could be supplied and installed by the House and claimed against the Office Cost Allowance'.[164] This proposal eventually provided the basis on which the House of Commons moved forwards.

The overall picture that emerges from this chapter is one of an institution that, for good or ill, lacked centralised force for the adoption of computer technology and, by extension, the use of digital networks, including the Internet. Innovation tended to come from specific offices and on the initiative of particular MPs, acting alone or in groups. This pattern reflected the dispersed nature of Parliament – in its bicameralism, in its organisational make-up, and in the individualism of the representatives who sat within it. Attempts to impose more consistent action were likely to meet with resistance and might contain within them the potential of retarding such progress as was being made. When it came, the introduction of a website, as shown in Chapter 2, took place in a manner lacking in co-ordination between the Commons and Lords.

This uneven quality perhaps made overall change more gradual than it might have been were there a more comprehensive approach. There is some evidence of the UK Parliament at times lagging behind comparable legislatures. Any claims about UK peculiarity in this regard, however, would require a systematic comparative study. It would need to take into account various factors, including, for instance, that internal differentiation connected to bicameralism could occur in other legislatures, as case of the US Congress demonstrates. Such an analytical task would have value. But the purpose of

159 Ibid., p. vi.
160 Ibid.
161 Ibid., p. vii.
162 Ibid., p. xi.
163 Ibid.
164 Ibid.

this work is to consider historic adoption of the Internet by one particular Parliament. It occurred within the diverse framework and in the piecemeal fashion suggested here. This context itself had implications for the process of change, which was also subject to further motivating and limiting tendencies. The drivers of the incorporation of computers, including their networking capacity, included patterns in wider society, international observations, and generational change among MPs. Some hoped to enhance the effectiveness of Parliament, protecting its position and preserving its relevance in the face of various perceived constitutional pressures. These forces had to overcome resistance arising from characteristics such as aversion to failure and concerns about matters including technological complications, cost, and whether the demand existed within Parliament. It was always difficult to know what applications would prove to be effective and lasting in nature.

But by 1996, a transition had occurred: computers were an accepted part of the work of Parliament and becoming more so, and it had a website (in experimental form from late 1995). It was only relatively late on in the period discussed in this chapter that the Internet, brought to the attention of Parliament in its embryonic form in 1970, began to achieve hegemony among digital communications systems. Interest in this technology began to increase in both Houses. Some parliamentarians sensed opportunities to enhance the effectiveness and legitimacy of their institution through the Internet, and perhaps to resist the possible threat of direct democracy. We have already seen an outline of what followed for Parliament in its use of this network from 1996. In the following two chapters we consider, first, how and why certain practices developed (or did not). Then, secondly, we look beyond the way in which Parliament employed the Internet for its own immediate purposes, and consider the approach it took towards this technology in its wider social context.

7

Pressures, Resistance, and Possibilities in Parliament since 1996

In June 2002, the House of Commons Information Committee received a memorandum entitled 'The Future? – A Day in the Life of an MP in 2012'. The author was Stuart Hill, director of Stepchange, a British Telecom 'initiative established to help government meet the challenge of creating a modern, integrated public sector and transform the delivery of public services'.[1] One of the interests of the committee, which was in the process of considering the use of computer technology and how it could support Parliament in preforming its functions, was 'to look ahead and to try to anticipate the kind the information and communication environment that will prevail ten years from now'.[2] As the title of his evidence suggested, Hill had offered his perspective on this subject. The narrative began:

> As you leave your house in the morning you put on your ACTIVE LENS (like a contact lens) and then using VOICE ACTIVATION you can view your diary for the day, your personalised newspaper and even read your briefing papers.
>
> The technology that allows this to happen is in the fabric of your clothes (WEARABLE COMPUTING) and the power is drawn from a combination of new, more powerful types of batteries (ENERGY CELLS) and PARASITIC POWER HARVESTING.
>
> On the way to the House you complete the mundane tasks of the day such as agreeing the flight and hotel details that your PERSONAL INTELLIGENT AGENT has suggested, before it goes and completes the arrangements ...
>
> Once you arrive at the House of Commons ... you select the first free desk in the COMMUNAL OFFICE AREA ... From this desk you carry out a constituency surgery and through the use of AVATAR technology and HOLOGRAPHIC projections both you and your constituent appear and can interact as if you are in the same room even though you are hundreds of miles apart.

[1] House of Commons Information Committee, *Digital Technology: Working for Parliament and the Public*, First Report of Session 2001–02, HC 1065 (Stationery Office, London, 2002), p. 7 and fn. 9.

[2] Ibid., p. 7.

> In the afternoon you attend a session in the Chamber. Your opposite number is speaking and quoting some figures – your support team are also watching the debate and are therefore able to send you a message onto your screen highlighting that the figures are grossly inaccurate so that when you respond you can inform the Chamber what the real figures are …
>
> As it is a Thursday afternoon it is time to complete your weekly WEBCAST to update your constituency of the week's activities … Through the use of technology you are able to receive feedback on how the WEBCAST was received and what areas people were interested in.
>
> One of your pet topics over the last 10 years has been COLLABORATIVE DEMOCRACY and you are still surprised that it has not been fully adopted, which you believe is due, in part, to the slow process of Parliament and a surprisingly slow uptake by citizens, although participation in democracy has steadily improved …

The submission goes on in similar vein. After the MP returns to their residence, it closes by describing how:

> As you lie in your bed you try to recall how you managed 10 years ago – the long hours travelling, the inefficient ways of communicating with your office, colleagues and constituents, and the difficulties in trawling for information. Although you initially found it difficult to adopt the new ways of working that the technology allowed, the reasons moved from being convincing then compelling before it was almost compulsory in order to stay on top of things and complete your job. And now, you couldn't do without it – how things have changed!![3]

The year 2012 – like 1984 and 2000 – proved, presumably coincidentally, a popular setting for speculation about the future (and even for some form of apocalypse). William Morris, for instance, chose it for *News from Nowhere* (depicting a markedly different outcome to that conveyed by Hill). Like other such scenarios with specific dates attached to them, they were destined to prove at least partially false. While he captured some of the uses for which MPs would increasingly employ the Internet – including virtual participation in meetings and online public updates – Hill overestimated the useable technology that would be available within ten years (or indeed by 2021): holograms, eye inserts, computerised clothing, and so on. An entirely fluid, communal system of parliamentary office provision had not come about and there was resistance, as we will see, to the idea of remote briefing teams supporting MPs while participating in debates. The evidence submission contained deterministic elements – suggesting that MPs, whatever their initial misgivings, would come to use and be reliant upon the technology he described. Indeed, partly because of this tone of

[3] Memorandum by Mr Stuart Hill, Director of the BT Stepchange Programme, House of Commons Information Committee, *Digital Technology: Working for Parliament and the Public*, First Report of Session 2001–02, HC 1065 (Stationery Office, London, 2002), Appendix 1, pp. 36–7.

inevitability, the vision Hill presented could as readily be reimagined as the horrifying vision of a Forster, Zamyatin, or Orwell. This alternative narrative could depict humans – communications devices implanted into their bodies and garments – as forced into an unhealthy dependency upon machines, subject to incessant electronic propaganda, their privacy and free will compromised. The experience of the pandemic could add a further unpleasant quality to such an account: that people were forced increasingly into this position by a global health emergency, during which they came ruefully to recall the in-person interactions of the past (though an updated version of the more optimistic Hill account might depict the technology as redeemer, making it possible for MPs to adhere to coronavirus protocols while continuing to perform their democratic functions).

Another notable quality of the Hill text was the reference to 'collaborative democracy' being retarded partly by 'the slow process of Parliament'. It suggests a view that the Internet was suited to forms of public engagement which might come into conflict with more traditional versions of representative democracy: a key theme of discourse around this technology. Yet the parliamentary body in receipt of this paper was relatively positive about its message.

In commenting on the Hill submission, the Information Committee observed that:

> Some features of this vision might seem over-imaginative and fantastical now, although that does not mean it should be dismissed. Ultimately, we cannot pretend to have any clear idea either of what will be possible technologically in ten years' time, or of the extent to which the public will take up such technologies. However, it remains important that the United Kingdom and its Parliament are comfortable in maximising use of changing technologies.[4]

The Committee concluded that: 'Information and Communications Technologies (ICT) . . . cannot be ignored.'[5]

This chapter explores the dynamics at play in the process of parliamentary adoption of the Internet in the period from 1996 onwards. It focuses in particular on the perspective from within Parliament itself, considering what forces drove it to utilise the technology; who and what drove this usage; the resistance encountered; and the significance of the different options considered, and what they were supposed to achieve. To illustrate some of these themes it includes more detailed studies of the rules applied to use of hand-held devices, the impact of e-tabling of questions, and the relationship between Parliament and the executive, in particular with respect to the introduction of e-petitioning to the House of Commons.

Motives for Adoption

Some within Parliament emphasised the idea of the Internet as possessing exceptional qualities, with important consequences for the functioning of

[4] House of Commons Information Committee, *Digital Technology*, p. 7.
[5] Ibid., p. 5.

society. In 2004 the Select Committee on the Modernisation of the House of Commons presented the Internet as different to other technologies, and suggested that its exceptional qualities had important consequences for the operation of the political system:

> Digital media have a number of characteristics which determine the way in which they can be used. They are 'deep media', containing many layers and types of information, which users can store, retrieve or search for at the level of their choice. Digital media are capable of reaching a small, target audience; they are interactive, capable of conveying users' feedback; and they do not embody clear boundaries between different types of media, such as television, the press, radio and photography.[6]

This distinctiveness had important implications for the way in which Parliament might seek to use the technology. The Committee recorded being told by Stephen Coleman 'that it was important to recognise the distinction between connecting with the public as spectators and connecting with them as participants; treating the Internet simply as "television for small audiences" was a mistake'.[7]

Adoption of this exceptional mechanism was more than a one-off exercise. An influence on parliamentary employment of the Internet was the idea of a technology in a continual condition of development, accompanied by changing patterns of usage. Parliament, it was argued, had fully to engage with this process or risk appearing anachronistic. In 2002 the House of Commons Information Committee held that '[t]he arrival of the Internet as a mass public network is already having a profound effect on the work of Members. Technologies are developing constantly.' This shift would 'increasingly lead people to shop, bank, learn and communicate with one another online'. As a consequence, MPs should be ready for 'the nature of their work to change significantly over the coming years'. Given proper support, they might achieve gains. But it was 'important that these opportunities are grasped ... otherwise Parliament will be open to criticism that it is falling behind'.[8] As these remarks suggest, a sustained motivating factor for Parliament, urged on it by organisations such as the Hansard Society, was to avoid the perception that it was eschewing the opportunities of the Internet as they unfolded, and was generally slow to adapt as an institution.[9]

Change continued. With the rise of interactive features during the first decade of the twenty-first century (and the advent of what was labelled 'Web 2.0') came pressure upon Parliament to adjust its provision accordingly, or

[6] House of Commons Select Committee on Modernisation of the House of Commons, *Connecting Parliament with the Public*, First Report of Session 2003–04, HC 368 (London, Stationery Office, 2004), p. 25.

[7] Ibid.

[8] House of Commons Information Committee, *Digital Technology*, p. 6.

[9] House of Commons Procedure Committee, *e-Petitions*, First Report of Session 2007–08, HC 136 (London: Stationery Office, 2008), p. 9.

face irrelevance. In 2009, the House of Lords Communication Committee described being informed by the Hansard Society about the emergence in recent years of 'a different approach to the internet, one which stresses an architecture of participation, whereby users expect to have opportunities for their voice to be heard'. A communications consultancy firm, Rufus Leonard, warned the Committee that:

> [l]ike it or not Parliament and members of both Houses need to move towards two-way communication with the general public and with the specific interest groups who lobby and push for change in key areas of interest. Some of these discussions will still happen face-to-face, but online channels are uniquely well-placed to make these communications prompt, cost-effective and scalable. If you do not embrace this opportunity, then the discussion on key topics will simply take place elsewhere and Parliament will appear marginalized and out of touch.[10]

Developments in the dissemination of particular forms of hardware required responses. In 2011, when discussing the proper approach to regulating the use of hand-held devices in the Chamber or in Committees, the Commons Procedure Committee remarked:

> it has to be acknowledged that electronic devices are ubiquitous now in a way that even four years ago was not the case. Banning them from the Chamber might make the House appear out of touch with modern life and would mean that those in the Chamber would be the last to know of breaking news widely available on the internet.[11]

Similar recognition of the constantly changing picture came in the review mySociety conducted for Parliament of its online services, published in 2014. It found that:

> [e]xpectations of what is normal on the internet change very fast. What would have counted as an elegant, usable, interesting webpage just five years ago will now come across as clunky, unhelpful and perhaps hard or impossible to read on a smartphone or tablet (devices that did not exist until recently).[12]

Furthermore, mySociety found: 'The pace of change on the internet in the next five years is almost certain to continue at great speed. It will take major efforts simply to keep up with what is seen as normal.'[13]

[10] House of Lords Information Committee, *Are the Lords Listening? Creating Connections between People and Parliament*, vol. I: *Report* (London: Stationery Office, 2009), HL 138–I, First Report of Session 2008–09, pp. 18–19.

[11] House of Commons Procedure Committee, *Use of Hand-Held Electronic Devices in the Chamber and Committees*, Third Report of Session 2010–11, HC 889 (Stationery Office, London, 2011), p. 8.

[12] mySociety, *Review of Parliament's Online Services: A Strategic Review containing Strengths, Weaknesses and Recommendations*, undated, published online 17 March 2014, p. 17, available at: www.parliament.uk/documents/news/2014/mysociety-report-on-online-services.pdf, last accessed 4 April 2020.

[13] Ibid., p. 21.

Aside from the qualities of the Internet itself – and their developing nature – the simple fact of large and growing numbers of people being users of this system was a central motivation for parliamentary attraction to it. In October 1996, the chair of the Commons Information Committee, Gary Waller MP, explained the decision to make Hansard available online in the following terms:

> Direct access to the Official Report of the House of Commons has been limited in recent times to relatively few people. As an increasing proportion of the public is able to access the Internet, I hope that many will find it useful to be able to see Hansard and other documents for themselves. In my view, this can only benefit the democratic process, and Parliament must take advantage of modern communications technology to ensure that its work is widely known and understood.[14]

Advocates of innovations such as the introduction of e-petitioning held that to do so was a necessary acceptance of the increased permeation and public use of this communications medium, into which the legislature would benefit from integrating itself.[15] But such arguments tended to be carefully qualified. The Commons Information Committee noted in 2002 that:

> 38 per cent of households in the United Kingdom have Internet access, and 51 per cent of adults in the United Kingdom have accessed the Internet either at home, at work, or from a public access point.[16]

But, as the Committee noted, there were differentials in popular take-up which any parliamentary engagement strategy must take into account. Identifying – in the terminology of the time – a 'digital divide'[17] – it described how research conducted 'in July 2001 found that 35 per cent of the survey sample . . . would be "very unlikely" to use the Internet during the next year'. Furthermore, 'whereas approximately 70 per cent of households in the highest income decile have home access to the Internet, fewer than 10 per cent of households in the lowest two deciles have such access'.[18] There were also inequalities involving age: at one end of the scale, 89 per cent of 16–24 year olds had used the Internet; while at the other end, for those aged 65 and upwards, the figure was only 12 per cent.[19] Nonetheless, the Information Committee presented the Internet and related devices as a means by which the Commons could:

[14] For an announcement specifically referring to the Commons text, see 'Hansard on the Internet', Information Committee Press Notice No. 1 of Session 1996–97, Philip Moon, Clerk of the House of Commons Information Committee, 23 October 1996, captured 23 February 1997, available at: https://web.archive.org/web/19970223114954/http://www.parliament.uk/commons/selcom/INFOPN1.HTM, last accessed 14 April 2020.

[15] House of Commons Procedure Committee, *e-Petitions*, pp. 14–15.

[16] House of Commons Information Committee, *Digital Technology*, p. 5.

[17] Ibid., p. 7.

[18] Ibid., p. 6.

[19] Ibid., p. 7.

> increase public participation in its work, enabling it to draw on the widest possible pool of experience, including particularly those who have traditionally been excluded from the political and parliamentary process.[20]

The Speaker's Commission on Digital Democracy recognised similar challenges in 2015, remarking that:

> In the past decade there has been a rapid move to delivering commercial and Government services online. For some people, this has made it easier to access information and services, but those who are not online will have benefited less ... Around a fifth of UK adults lack basic digital skills and 16% are not online.

The Commission found it 'promising to see that the proportion of people who are using the internet has been increasing steadily in recent years. But certain groups are more likely to be "digitally disengaged", including older people, those with disabilities, and people without qualifications.' While the Commission supported measures to make 'Parliament ... more accessible and open', there was a need to accompany them with 'a strategy for ensuring that the digitally disengaged are not excluded from understanding or engaging with its work'.[21]

The comparative perspective was significant.[22] The Commons Information Committee in 2002 referred to the importance of keeping pace with 'Parliaments worldwide (and devolved parliamentary bodies closer to home)'.[23] It hoped to 'share good practice' with these and other outside entities.[24] The Canadian House of Commons continued to provide models from which some sought to learn,[25] as did the Scottish Parliament[26] and the National Assembly for Wales (then both elected for the first time in 1999). A variety of other legislatures – Australian, German, Portuguese, and the European Parliament – were sources of influence, upon which various parliamentary assessments drew.[27] Advocacy of more sophisticated parliamentary employment of the Internet could refer to global adoption of the Internet as a significant trend to take into account. Using words which might affect the reader differently since the ascendancy (and subsequent fall) of Donald Trump, the mySociety review published in 2014 noted that: 'Social networks are now used to share large amounts of serious information, as well as large

[20] Ibid., p. 8.
[21] Digital Democracy Commission, *Open Up! Report of the Speaker's Commission on Digital Democracy* (Speaker's Commission on Digital Democracy, London, 2015), p. 52.
[22] Jens Hoff, Stephen Coleman, Peter Filzmaier, and Gustavo Cardoso, 'Use of ICT by Members of Parliament', *Information Polity* 9(1–2) (2004): 1–4, 1.
[23] House of Commons Information Committee, *Digital Technology*, p. 5.
[24] Ibid., p. 8.
[25] e.g. ibid., p. 10.
[26] Ibid., p. 11.
[27] e.g. House of Commons Procedure Committee, *e-Petitions*, para. 12–14, p. 8; House of Commons Procedure Committee, Use of Hand-Held Electronic Devices in the Chamber and Committees, p. 6.

amounts of entertainment and trivia. Around 80% of world leaders are now on Twitter, for example.'[28]

An example of perceived domestic and international trends combining to produce an urge to act can be found in the fourth chapter of the 2009 report by the House of Lords Information Committee, *Are the Lords Listening? Creating connections between people and Parliament.* The title was 'Setting Parliamentary Data Free'. The Committee described how it had:

> heard a powerful case that Parliament should make its data more easily available online. Ben Hammersley, Associate Editor of *Wired* magazine, argued that it was 'morally and ethically wrong' for Parliament not to make its data available in a form which could be re-used and analysed by others.[29]

The Committee discerned a zeitgeist, abroad and at home, with which it concluded it should conform. It referred to 'a general drive to make public data available online for re-use'. At the very outset of his presidency, Barack Obama had 'issued a "Memorandum on Transparency and Open Government"'. It referred to the need to utilise 'new technologies to put information about ... operations and decisions online and readily available to the public'.[30] In June 2009, the UK Prime Minister, Gordon Brown 'had asked Sir Tim Berners-Lee, who is credited with inventing the worldwide web, to help the Government "to drive the opening up of access to Government data on the web over the coming months"'. The then-Leader of the Opposition, David Cameron, had pledged to pursue openness in this area, should he form a government.[31] The Committee therefore concluded that:

> Parliament must not be left behind as others set new standards for online publication and engagement with the public. We recommend that information and documentation related to the core work of the House of Lords (including Bills, Hansard, transcripts of public committee meetings, evidence submitted to committees, committee reports, records of divisions, expenses and the register of Lords' interests) should be produced and made available online in an open standardised electronic format that enables people outside Parliament to analyse and re-use the data.[32]

A background perception encouraging internet usage was one of supposedly declining public confidence in the political system in general and Parliament in particular. The Internet, according to such narratives, could help Parliament to address this problem, and was perhaps even essential to its efforts to do so. As the House of Commons Information Committee put it in 2002:

[28] mySociety, *Review of Parliament's Online Services*, p. 20.
[29] House of Lords Information Committee, *Are the Lords Listening*?, vol. I: *Report*, p. 22.
[30] Ibid.
[31] Ibid., p. 23.
[32] Ibid., pp. 23–4, para. 66.

> There is concern amongst the public – and indeed amongst Members – that the House appears remote, that it does not respond as well as it might to the public, and that it could do more to hold the executive to account. Public perceptions and expectations of Parliament appear to be changing and there is authoritative evidence to indicate that public participation in the political process appears to be in decline. When the public does engage with Parliament, its perception of it is most commonly formed from a distance, via correspondence and reports of proceedings.[33]

The Committee proposed that 'Information and Communications Technologies (ICT) can play an important role in influencing perceptions and helping to meet public expectations'.[34] They were, it judged, a means by which 'the role and reputation of Parliament can be enhanced'.[35]

In 2004, the Select Committee on the Modernisation of the House of Commons, in a report which, among other measures, called for innovative digital engagement with the public, referred to a 'decline in political participation and engagement in recent years, as well as in levels of trust in politicians, political parties and the institutions of State'. A key indicator to which the Committee referred was evidence of 'fewer and fewer people trusting politicians. Lower levels of trust are translating into a disconnection from the institutions of democracy. The fall in election turnout from a post-war high of 84 per cent in 1950 to 59 per cent in 2001 is the most obvious indicator of this decline. Turnout at elections in the UK is lower than most other European countries.' This general trend of deterioration, the Committee went on 'should be of concern to every citizen. But it should be of particular concern to the House of Commons.' The Committee reasoned that '[i]t is here that our laws are made and it is from its Members that governments are formed. The sovereignty of Parliament is the fundamental expression of the sovereignty of the people. It is the apex of our democratic system.'[36] One of the questions the Committee had posed as part of its own 'on-line consultation' was 'does Parliament adequately reflect the concerns of ordinary people?' The Committee concluded that 'the overall impression was that it did not'.[37] With such concerns in mind, the Committee described 'the purpose of this Report' as being 'to make recommendations which will better reconcile the necessary purpose of Parliament with the reasonable expectation of the people to have access to the processes by which we govern ourselves'.[38] The Committee judged that '[g]etting the

[33] House of Commons Information Committee, *Digital Technology*, p. 5.
[34] Ibid.
[35] Ibid.
[36] House of Commons Select Committee on Modernisation of the House of Commons, *Connecting Parliament with the Public*, pp. 10–11.
[37] Ibid., paras. 53–9, p. 21.
[38] Ibid., pp. 10–11.

website right is ... probably the single most important thing that Parliament needs to do in this area'.[39]

One hope attached to the Internet was that it might provide access to a particular social group that tended to be less involved in politics. The Select Committee on Modernisation of the House of Commons put forward proposals the objectives of which included, 'to make greater efforts to engage young people' and 'to encourage better use of information and communication technology'.[40] A House of Commons Commission review in 2007 proposed 'that the Parliamentary website and the internet generally should be regarded as a key element in fostering close connections between Parliament and the public, and crucially the younger generation, and should be developed and funded accordingly as a priority'.[41] In 2008 the House of Commons Procedure Committee referred specifically back to the two Modernisation Committee goals when supporting the introduction of e-petitioning to the House of Commons, arguing that it would help attain both. In particular, the Committee saw high relative levels of internet usage among the young as creating an opportunity for attracting a group among which the rate of political participation was low. More generally, it felt that mechanisms such as e-petitioning could be an entry point into Parliament and its various activities, raising public awareness, interest, and involvement. The Committee quoted the then-Conservative MP, Douglas Carswell, as arguing that a suitably designed e-petitioning system could mean that 'a lot of people who are otherwise disaffected and disillusioned with the political process – 40 per cent do not vote, people under the age of 30 not only do not vote but have never formed the habit of doing so – would take a greater interest in politics through Parliament'.[42]

The parliamentary expenses scandal of the following year created reputational problems for the Commons and the Lords. It added impetus to claims that Parliament needed to pursue better relations with the public, and that the Internet offered means by which it could do so. In 2009, the House of Lords Information Committee issued a report entitled *Digital Technology: Working for Parliament and the Public*, in which it held that:

> Parliament's public reputation is at a low point. Media coverage about Peers' allowances and MPs' expenses and the suspension of two members of the House of Lords have had a negative impact on people's perception of Parliament. There has been a lot of consequent talk about constitutional reform, but many of the changes under discussion bear little direct relation to the problems that have been revealed. What is needed are reforms within Parliament. The need for

[39] Ibid., p. 16.

[40] Ibid., pp. 10–11.

[41] Sir Kevin Tebbit, *Review of Management and Services of the House of Commons*, House of Commons Commission (Stationery Office, London, 2007), p. 52.

[42] House of Commons Procedure Committee, *e-Petitions*, p. 16.

> Parliament to be open and transparent was apparent before the recent revelations and the need will remain.[43]

The Committee had commenced its inquiry before the advent of the scandal. But the recommendations it made for enhanced use of digital engagement by the Lords were, it judged, relevant to this episode and its consequences. The publication was intended to 'contribute to making the House of Lords more open and transparent. We want to see better public appreciation of the role and work of the House of Lords. In our view, that can only be achieved once the House has taken further steps to increase public understanding of, and engagement with, the House.'[44]

This contribution suggests that the transformative potential of the Internet was – in relative terms – even greater for the Lords than the Commons. As an unelected chamber, the Lords did not have the same pre-existing systemic link with the public as the Commons. Direct interaction with the population, both mass and targeted, could therefore offer especially significant gains from the point of view of the Second Chamber. The Lords was already developing in significant ways. In 1999, all but ninety-two hereditary Peers were removed. The Second Chamber subsequently took on an increasingly professional and less anachronistic aura. Members of the Lords began increasingly to behave as though, with the ejection of most of the aristocratic component, their institution had become more legitimate, and could resist proposals emanating from the executive and agreed to by the Commons. Yet still the Lords lacked the authority that might come from public elections. Underlying doubts continued about its long-term future and how far it was appropriate for it to exercise its full legal powers. In this context, the attraction of a technology that might add to the progress already made and cultivate public relations is understandable. This general outlook is detectable in this passage from the 2009 House of Lords Information Committee report:

> We consider the House of Lords to be an effective, value-for-money second chamber. It makes a substantial contribution to the law-making process; its members' expertise adds value to the process; and it complements the work of the House of Commons. However, it is not enough for the House to perform these functions. People must be able to see that the House performs this role, and our recommendations should help to achieve this end.[45]

As part of this programme, the Committee proposed a series of changes for the Lords involving the use of the Internet. They included YouTube broadcasting of proceedings, electronic alerts services for the public, making published materials accessible for people with disabilities, and enabling members of the public to 'participate in an online debate in parallel to a debate in the Lords

[43] House of Lords Information Committee, *Are the Lords Listening*?, vol. I: *Report*, p. 7.
[44] Ibid.
[45] Ibid., p. 8.

Chamber'.[46] These recommendations demonstrated the degree of enthusiasm for deployment of the Internet that could emanate from within the Lords. It was the same institution that, at times, had taken a lead over the adoption of computers and the analogue broadcasting of proceedings. As the Committee recalled when supporting expansion in the use of webcasting: '[t]he House of Lords has always taken a more relaxed view of cameras in the Chamber than the House of Commons, and in 1985 the Lords was the first Chamber to begin a televising experiment'.[47] In 2015 the Speaker's Commission on Digital Democracy acknowledged the Lords openness to change, in writing that:

> Parliament is made up of two independent bodies, the House of Commons and the House of Lords. Although our recommendations are addressed mainly to the House of Commons, we hope that they will also be of interest to the Lords, and we know that many members of the House of Lords follow digital developments closely.[48]

Advocates of Use

A range of groups and individuals actively advocated enhanced parliamentary employment of the Internet. Some came from the commercial technology sector, such as Stuart Hill and his British Telecom Stepchange programme, cited at the head of this chapter. Others outside Parliament seemed to have an interest in the Internet as a tool for the exertion of political pressure. For them, parliamentary adoption of mechanisms such as e-petitioning could create new means of influencing parliamentarians and by extension government, and perhaps attracting public interest to given causes and objectives. In its 2008 report on the prospects for introducing e-petitioning, the Commons Procedure Committee noted that the idea had support from groups including the Association of Political Consultants and Cancer Research.[49] Professional communications consultants might also impress upon Parliament the value of the digital medium.[50] Academic institutions could wield influence. For instance, during the first decade of the twenty-first century, the International Teledemocracy Centre, based at Edinburgh Napier University, encouraged consideration of 'how ICTs can enhance and support the democratic decision-making processes'.[51]

An important individual figure, bridging various ideas and groups, was Stephen Coleman. His connection to UK Citizens Online Democracy (UKCOD) – an organisation which itself links to earlier traditions of activism

[46] Ibid., pp. 8–9.
[47] Ibid., pp. 29, para. 82.
[48] Digital Democracy Commission, *Open Up*!, p. 16.
[49] *House of Commons Procedure Committee, e-Petitions*, p. 14–15.
[50] House of Lords Information Committee, *Are the Lords Listening*?, vol. I: *Report*, pp. 18–19, paras. 46–51.
[51] International Teledemocracy Centre (P13), House of Commons Procedure Committee, *e-Petitions*, First Report of Session 2007–08, HC136 (London: Stationery Office, 2008), Ev. 31.

and US-derived, counterculturally infused attitudes towards the Internet – has already been discussed. During the course of his career, Coleman has worked in universities and in a role at the Hansard Society for Parliamentary Government. He made an early contribution to the sustained efforts of the latter organisation in promoting innovative parliamentary use of the Internet.[52] It ran a series of experiments in online consultations by parliamentary committees in the late 1990s and early 2000s.[53] Coleman oversaw this programme, also serving as specialist adviser to the House of Commons Information Committee inquiry that produced the 2002 report cited in this chapter.[54]

Other than the Hansard Society and UKCOD, various other civil society organisations could wield influence. They included Involve, 'a non-governmental organisation specialising in public participation', which was, for instance, cited by the House of Lords Information Committee in its 2009 advocacy of parliamentary online engagement.[55] Projects such as FaxYourMP and TheyWorkForYou provided a means by which members of the public could engage with Parliament and created a stimulus for more enhanced use of the technology by Parliament itself.[56] As Richard Allan, the former Liberal Democrat MP, put it in 2006:

> These external pressures can cause initial resistance but where the ideas are patently good and driven by a genuine desire to enhance democracy they are politically unstoppable. The response over time is more likely to be one of co-option rather than resistance.[57]

TheyWorkForYou was from 2006 incorporated into mySociety (the parent entity of which was, in turn, a resuscitated UKCOD.[58]) The central figure in the establishment and operation of mySociety was Tom Steinberg. During his tenure, the organisation attained a considerable degree of influence within Parliament and government; and Steinberg himself became an accepted authority on uses of the Internet for political engagement purposes.[59] A clear illustration of the status mySociety attained was that it was engaged

[52] House of Commons Public Administration Select Committee, *Innovations in Citizen Participation in Government*, Sixth Report of Session 2000–01, HC 373-I (Stationery Office, London, 2001), para. 55.

[53] House of Commons Information Committee, *Digital Technology*, p. 15.

[54] Ibid., p. 6.

[55] House of Lords Information Committee, *Are the Lords Listening*?, vol. I: *Report*, pp. 18–19, paras. 46–51.

[56] House of Commons Information Committee, *Digital Technology*, p. 10.

[57] Richard Allan, 'Parliament, Elected Representatives and Technology 1997–2005 – Good in Parts?', *Parliamentary Affairs* 59(2) (2006): 360–5, 363.

[58] Memorandum from mySociety (P 13), 'Online Petitions at No 10: A Submission to the Procedure Committee', Tom Steinberg, Director, January 2007, House of Commons Procedure Committee, *Public Petitions and Early Day Motions*, First Report of Session 2006–07, HC 513 (London, Stationery Office, 2007), Ev. 21.

[59] See e.g. House of Commons Procedure Committee, *e-Petitions*, pp. 16–17.

in 2006 to create the No. 10 online petitions platform,[60] the technical success and popularity of which helped bring about its transition into a system shared with the House of Commons. As previously discussed, mySociety also produced a report for Parliament on its utilisation of the Internet, published in 2014, that led to a reorganisation of services.

One mySociety initiative aimed directly at parliamentary practice was the 'Free Our Bills!' campaign of 2009. The announcement webpage complained that:

> the way in which Bills are currently published out [sic] is completely *incompatible with the Internet* era. As a consequence few people ever get to find out what a Bill says before it becomes law and binds us all. Bills are currently buried within the Parliamentary website, published in a hopelessly old fashioned way that makes them difficult to find, difficult to read and impossible to do anything clever with.[61]

The campaign called for various changes that would create transparency around the legislative process, including the impact of proposed amendments.[62] It generated political traction, and a widely supported Early Day Motion in the House (a device with little significance in its own right, but which can serve as an indicator of parliamentary opinion).[63] Parliament has subsequently taken steps to present the passage of Bills in a more coherent and informative fashion, though the full range of innovations mySociety envisaged has not yet been realised.

Support for fuller utilisation of the Internet came from within Parliament itself. An example of such an advocate was Allan, an MP between 1997 and 2005 and a member of the Information Committee (that produced the 2002 report *Digital Technology: Working for Parliament and the Public* analysed here). As Allan noted, MPs who were 'early' users of the Internet often had support from what he termed 'geeks with white hats'. They were 'individuals from the technical community 'who assisted particular MPs with 'websites, text messaging and blogging'. Often, Allan wrote, they came 'through party affiliation and are invaluable to MPs juggling limited resources'.[64] A later instance of an MP seeking to promote Internet usage came when John Bercow, as Speaker of the House of Commons, convened the Speaker's Commission on Digital Democracy late in 2013.[65]

Parliamentary committees as well as individual parliamentarians could promote the use of the Internet. One instance was the House of Commons

[60] Memorandum from mySociety (P 13), 'Online Petitions at No 10: A Submission to the Procedure Committee', Tom Steinberg, Director, Ev. 20–1.

[61] 'Free our Bills!', available at: www.theyworkforyou.com/freeourbills/, last accessed 3 July 2020.

[62] Ibid.

[63] See House of Lords Information Committee, *Are the Lords Listening?*, vol. I: *Report*, p. 22.

[64] Allan, 'Parliament, Elected Representatives and Technology 1997–2005 – Good in Parts?', p. 362.

[65] Digital Democracy Commission, *Open Up!*, p. 76.

Public Administration Select Committee (PASC) which, in its 2001 report *Innovations in Citizen Participation in Government*, insisted 'There are many ways in which the new technologies could be pressed into the service of parliamentary democracy.' There was, PASC noted, 'already evidence of this happening'. But:

> [i]n future we look to see a more integrated system with greater facilities for making links between one element and another. The new technologies have major potential implications for Parliament. It is important that they are explored to the full. This requires a long-term strategy for e-access to Parliament to be as easy, attractive and well-used as possible.[66]

When, in response to the various pressures to utilise the Internet, Parliament established internal structures and teams intended to serve this purpose, these entities themselves became forces for enhanced incorporation of the technology.[67] Impetus could also come from within the executive. Robin Cook, the Labour MP, was Leader of the House of Commons from 2001 to 2003. In this capacity he was chair of the Select Committee on Modernisation of the House of Commons, and was a promoter of enhanced use of new technologies as a means of engaging the public. For instance, the House of Commons Information Committee in 2002 cited his support for change as adding salience to its own recommendations.[68]

Models of Usage

What specific models of internet usage were offered? One was that it might be a means of attaining enhanced institutional performance. As the Speaker's Commission on Digital Democracy put it in 2015: 'Parliament has already begun to use digital to work more effectively, increase efficiency and reduce costs.' It cited examples such as 'publishing more documents online and reducing the number of paper copies printed'. But, the Commission argued:

> there is potential to use digital to bring further efficiency savings and better ways of working . . . For example, much parliamentary information is not created in a format that can be made available to the public as open data. It has to be converted into another format in order to do this, which is costly and time-consuming. These kinds of inefficient processes must be reformed so that information is handled more efficiently and a digital-first approach is taken.[69]

[66] House of Commons Public Administration Select Committee, *Innovations in Citizen Participation in Government*, para. 74.

[67] Dominic Tinley, 'The UK Parliament in the Digital Age: A Personal Perspective' in *Parliaments in the Digital Age*, Forum Discussion Report 13 (Oxford, Oxford Internet Institute, 2008), pp. 45–8, 45.

[68] House of Commons Information Committee, *Digital Technology*, p. 5.

[69] Digital Democracy Commission, *Open Up!*, p. 62.

As well as assisting Parliament as an institution, the Internet could be used by individual MPs 'in organising their work more efficiently', as the House of Commons Information Committee put it in 2002.[70] For instance, it could make communication more convenient. The possibility of using 'video-conferencing' in place of physical meetings was a subject of interest long before the 'virtual Parliament' initiative of 2020. In 2002 the Commons Information Committee presented this practice primarily as a means by which MPs – particularly those who were located far from London – could hold surgeries and other meetings remotely. Providing another (unwitting) echo of Forster, it concluded that:

> Although not a perfect substitute for face-to-face discussions within the same room, video conferencing is a valuable tool when time or the cost of travel inhibits contact in person. The House could do more to promote the use of video conferencing by Members. Regular investment may be needed to take account of developments in technology (including ISDN and broadband) which improve picture quality, overall reliability, and opportunities for simultaneous translation.[71]

The use of the Internet for surgeries points to an important aspect of its potential: as a means of interaction with members of the public, representing whom was the principal purpose of Parliament.[72] In 2002, PASC described evidence it took from the academic, Christine Bellamy, who described a range of possible functions, all of which involved facilitating relations with the outside, whether indirectly or directly. Bellamy had:

> provided an ascending scale of possibilities, starting with 'supporting internal business associated with representation and participation' through 'the dissemination of information about Government and Parliament' and the support of communication between MP, Government and individual citizens on matters of individual or consumer concern to supporting the participation of citizens in deliberation/consultation about matters of public (collective) concern.[73]

In 2002 the House of Commons Information Committee depicted the Internet as potentially helping MPs in 'maintaining better communications with constituents'; and 'in their efforts to improve contact between the public and their elected representatives'.[74] The Speaker's Commission on Digital Democracy held in 2015 that:

> if MPs were better supported in managing their digital communications, this would help them to respond more fully to their constituents. This in turn may

[70] House of Commons Information Committee, *Digital Technology*, p. 5.
[71] Ibid., p. 11.
[72] House of Commons Public Administration Select Committee, *Innovations in Citizen Participation in Government*, para. 74.
[73] Ibid.
[74] House of Commons Information Committee, *Digital Technology*, p. 5.

> help to ensure that constituents have a positive experience and are encouraged to engage with their MP or Parliament again.[75]

One aspect to this function was – as the Commons Information Committee put it in 2002 – 'openness', allowing 'the public to have access to its proceedings and papers'.[76] The idea that the Internet had value as a facilitator of 'transparency' was a recurring theme.[77] Parliamentary plans for the increased use of the technology could appear as part of wider agendas intended to increase the accessibility of the institution across a number of matrices. They might include such items as improving educational outreach, facilitating visits to the physical estate, and providing information to the public. The Speaker's Commission made a variety of recommendations for enhanced internet usage in 2015, one of the purposes of which was 'increasing public awareness of the role of Parliament and MP'. They included a better functioning website, the use of more visual images alongside text, simplified language, and more attention to the needs of 'people with disabilities and sensory impairments'.[78]

The drive to connect with a wider public through the Internet led to a perception that the parliament.uk site was not sufficient in itself, and that Parliament needed to utilise other online services to maximise its reach. As the House of Lords Information Committee put it in 2009:

> There is a limit to the level of public engagement Parliament can generate on its own website, because some people may not be drawn to interact directly with the parliamentary website. To counteract that fact, we recommend that the administration work in partnership with already established websites catering for interest groups.[79]

Social media became a particular focus for parliamentary efforts to extend its reach. The Speaker's Commission on Digital Democracy described in 2015 how during its evidence-gathering:

> [a] key message that came through in our discussions with people was that Parliament needed to get better at 'going to where people are' to engage with them, by connecting with people in the digital spaces where they spend their time and in the way they like to connect. For example, many people, especially younger people, asked for more video and social media, pointing out that social media platforms such as Facebook and Twitter are where people spend a lot of time.[80]

This observation leads to a question: who, precisely, was Parliament trying to interact with? We have already seen that one group of interest was the young,

[75] Digital Democracy Commission, *Open Up!*, p. 38.
[76] House of Commons Information Committee, *Digital Technology*, p. 5.
[77] House of Commons Procedure Committee, *e-Petitions*, p. 16.
[78] Digital Democracy Commission, *Open Up!*, p. 8.
[79] House of Lords Information Committee, *Are the Lords Listening?*, vol. I: *Report*, p. 18.
[80] Digital Democracy Commission, *Open Up!*, p. 27.

broadly viewed as both less likely to be politically active and more likely to be using the Internet. In May 2009, the bicameral internal body of officials, the Group on Information for the Public, described in evidence to the House of Lords Information Committee its 'Public Engagement Strategy', of which the use of digital technology was a central component.[81] The memorandum referred to a perceived need 'to reach five different, if overlapping, groups'. The first comprised MPs, Peers, and others working within Parliament. Beyond the institution, the strategy targeted people who were 'professionally engaged with the work of Parliament, including civil servants, NGOs, lobbyists, journalists and others'. Within this category were 'critical intermediaries who interpret what Parliament does to others and therefore condition the understanding that the wider public has of Parliament's work'. Next were those who were 'democratically active', who took part in elections and had 'an interest in politics, policy and current affairs'. Then came what the paper described as 'democratic outsiders'. This term was intended to apply to those who were 'not (yet) interested in politics, policy and current affairs and those who do not participate in the political process'. Lastly, the strategy aimed at 'young people, both within the formal education system and informally'.[82]

In its 2015 report, the Speaker's Commission on Digital Democracy emphasised the importance of focusing attention on the marginalised. It recommended that the House of Commons should:

> pilot and test new online activities, working with national and local partners, to target and engage specific groups who are not currently engaged in democratic processes. These target groups could include, for example: 18–25 year olds not at university, people with learning difficulties, homeless people and people living in communities with very low voter turnout.[83]

In its quest to reach people, the view developed within Parliament that to deploy the Internet only as a means of disseminating information to the outside world was an overly restrictive approach. We have already noted that an attraction of the Internet was that, for communications purposes, it was more sophisticated than other media. As the Select Committee on the Modernisation of the House of Commons put it in a 2004 passage that was reminiscent of the hopes Brecht once expressed for the radio: '[t]he internet is more than a medium for publishing documents and broadcasting proceedings in Parliament; it is an interactive medium that allows genuine two-way

[81] 'The Public Engagement Strategy in Parliament since 2006', Memorandum on behalf of the Group on Information for the Public, Elizabeth Hallam Smith, Director of Information Services and Librarian, House of Lords and John Pullinger, Chairman, Group on information for the Public and Librarian and Director General, Information Services, House of Commons, House of Lords Information Committee, *Are the Lords Listening? Creating Connections between People and Parliament*, vol. II: *Evidence* (London: Stationery Office, 2009), HL 138–II, First Report of Session 2008–09, pp. 117–18.

[82] Ibid.

[83] Digital Democracy Commission, *Open Up!*, p. 52.

communication between politicians and the people they represent'.[84] In such analysis, the technology could facilitate an interactive communication loop between Parliament and public. The former could transmit messages to the latter, which could in turn respond, and vice versa. Considering the possible value of the introduction of e-petitions in 2008, the Commons Procedure Committee argued that:

> it would create an opportunity for interaction. It could enable petitioners and signatories to receive emailed responses to their petitions. These might simply be information about the progress of the petition or other associated parliamentary proceedings. They might also include messages from the petitioner's constituency Member of Parliament.

The critical point made to the Committee in evidence was that the Internet was 'a conversation medium' as opposed to 'a broadcast medium or a post office'. It created the possibility of 'a meaningful dialogue with people'.[85] The following year, the House of Lords Information Committee reported being informed in its inquiries that parliament.uk was 'to a large degree, a traditional information delivery website'. Evidence-givers had urged 'that online communication should mean two-way communication and that Parliament should use the parliamentary website not just to provide information but also to listen to the public'. The Committee took the view that, '[w]hilst Parliament does well at using its website to inform people, it needs continually to develop the way in which it uses the internet actively to engage with people'.[86]

By this point, Parliament had in fact been exploring online interactivity for more than a decade, developing processes into which it could directly incorporate members of the public. As previously discussed, ideas in this area were a product of wider thinking about participatory mechanisms. Advocates of this school supported the use of techniques that enabled more developed democratic involvement, beyond practices such as voting. As PASC put it in 2001, 'the period since the middle 1990s has seen an explosion of interest in involving the public more frequently, more extensively, and in much more diverse ways in the conduct of decision-making within the public services'.[87]

This approach found an outlet via digital technology in the form of 'online consultations'.[88] Indeed, a number of parliamentary inquiries into possible uses of digital technology cited in this chapter made use of such processes. They were, therefore, experimenting in the very area they were examining,

[84] House of Lords Select Committee on Modernisation of the House of Commons, *Connecting Parliament with the Public*, paras. 53–9, p. 21.

[85] House of Commons Procedure Committee, *e-Petitions*, paras. 33–42, p. 16.

[86] House of Lords Information Committee, *Are the Lords Listening*?, vol. I: *Report*, pp. 18–19, paras. 46–51.

[87] House of Commons Public Administration Select Committee, *Innovations in Citizen Participation in Government*, para. 75.

[88] House of Commons Information Committee, *Digital Technology*, p. 6.

using methods they would advocate. Innovative use of the Internet was legitimising and helping facilitate more of the same. The PASC inquiry held 'an on-line discussion forum on the participatory possibilities offered by the new electronic technologies'. Facilitated by the Hansard Society, it was a 'new departure for a House of Commons Select Committee'.[89] Following on from PASC, the Commons Information Committee ran an 'online forum' as part of evidence-gathering leading to its 2002 report.[90] The 2004 Select Committee on the Modernisation of the House of Commons report described how:

> [w]e conducted our own on-line consultation as part of this inquiry, both to canvass public opinion on the issues we were examining and to explore the consultation process itself. We devised the list of key questions that we wanted participants to address and the Hansard Society designed, maintained and moderated the site. The exercise generated a total of 152 responses from a wide range of people ranging from those with a long-standing interest in or connection with Parliament to those with no special interest in Parliament at all. It is highly unlikely that we would have received such a volume and range of responses to a traditional 'call for evidence' inviting interested parties to submit memoranda in writing to the Clerk.[91]

The House of Lords Information Committee 2009 report referred to a 'web forum' it had run.[92]

The Commons Information Committee suggested in 2002 that these mechanisms were a means by which Parliament could make 'full use of the insights to be gained from public experience and expertise, with no sector or social group being ignored'.[93] It also suggested that other material on the parliamentary website, such as the electronic version of Hansard, could include a feature allowing members of the public to make remarks on specific content which would then be forwarded on to relevant people and offices.[94] Influenced by its specialist adviser, Coleman, the Committee stressed that such techniques had potential value provided they were approached with certain principles in mind. There was a need for clarity from the beginning about the objectives and parameters of the exercise. Those taking part had to be made aware that, while they could contribute to decisions, they could not actually make them. It was necessary to incorporate people or groups with actual 'experience and expertise' to contribute. A neutral intermediary should distil the inputs to the consultation. Processes should be evaluated to ensure that they were beneficial both to participants and those who

[89] House of Commons Public Administration Select Committee, *Innovations in Citizen Participation in Government*, para. 3.
[90] House of Commons Information Committee, *Digital Technology*, p. 6.
[91] House of Lords Select Committee on Modernisation of the House of Commons, *Connecting Parliament with the Public*, p. 21.
[92] House of Lords Information Committee, *Are the Lords Listening*?, vol. I: *Report*, p. 11.
[93] House of Commons Information Committee, *Digital Technology*, p. 14.
[94] Ibid., pp. 15–16.

instigated them; and there should be 'feedback' to those who took part on the results of the exercise. Crucially, there needed to be regard for the so-called 'digital divide'. Careful attention should be given to soliciting the inputs of people without internet access, lacking skills in using the technology, and who did not have organisations to represent them.[95]

In 2004, the Select Committee on Modernisation of the House of Commons endorsed these stipulations, and the general idea of online consultation. It referred to evidence from Coleman stating that:

> On-line policy consultations are something that you have in fact pioneered, and have done better than any other parliament in the world. There is quite a lot of data suggesting that these consultations have had an effect on the fairly small minority of people who have engaged in them – because they have been deliberative, because they have been expansive over a period of a month, and because you have taken people seriously.[96]

The Committee concluded that 'greater use of on-line consultation is a good way for Parliament to take account of the views of the wider public'. Such exercises, it held, had 'generally been successful and have proved effective as a way of engaging members of the public in the work that we do and of giving a voice to those who would otherwise be excluded'. The Committee urged 'select committees and joint committees considering draft legislation to make on-line consultation a more regular aspect of their work'.[97] The employment of internet forums to scrutinise draft legislation in particular received further support from the House of Lords Information Committee five years later. It held that this application was particularly appropriate, more so than using it to consider a bill proper that was passing through Parliament. The Lords Information Committee noted that: 'bills are considered by the House; draft bills are considered by a committee. This distinction is important, because a committee can more easily put in place a transparent process for dealing with the comments it receives.' (Indeed, such an exercise had already been carried out, by the Joint Committee on the Draft Communications Bill in 2002.)[98] Yet a more regular use of such consultations on draft bills did not come about. This is a subject to which we will return.

Resistance and Complications

Adoption of the Internet often benefited from support outside and goodwill within Parliament, attached to specific ideas about how it should be put into practice. But there was also resistance of various forms. Change was not

[95] Ibid.
[96] House of Lords Select Committee on Modernisation of the House of Commons, *Connecting Parliament with the Public*, paras. 53–9, pp. 20–1.
[97] Ibid., paras. 53–9, p. 21.
[98] House of Lords Information Committee, *Are the Lords Listening?*, vol. I: *Report*, p. 21.

necessarily easy to bring about in an institution that in some senses dated back to the medieval period. Various potentially obstructive customs and rules existed. For instance, understandings of what were the proper roles and privileges of Members – and the tendency for them to be highly protective of what they believed them to be – could create a barrier.[99] It was natural that the prospect of their disturbance might be approached with some caution, entail complications, and generate objections. A 2008 Commons Procedure Committee report on e-petitioning revealed complicating factors of this type. Under the traditional method of hardcopy petitioning, individual Members accepted petitions and presented them to the House. The Committee anticipated that it would apply this principle to an electronic system. This approach might appear archaic. On the surface it would seem to make more sense simply to make the Commons or Parliament as a whole the direct recipient. But such a procedure, the Committee suspected, would inflame sensitivity about the bypassing of Members.[100] This concern was eventually overcome, but that it was deemed to require such careful handling was revealing regarding the nature of the environment within which change took place.

Entrenched rules could be a constraint upon the employment of the Internet. Early on, for instance, the prospect of online publication of parliamentary materials raised issues about copyright and licensing that needed to be addressed.[101] Later, in 2015, the Speaker's Commission on Digital Democracy discussed means of bringing about greater public involvement in the legislative process, in the broader context of digital engagement. It considered whether it would be possible to:

> change the way that amendments are written and debated. They could be written in plain English, and this would enable MPs to focus on the effect of the amendment rather than on technical drafting. Amendments could be voted on in the usual way, with technical drafting then being provided by legal experts.

While the Commission was 'attracted by this suggestion ... we also recognise that it would be a radical departure from the current system. Careful consideration and piloting would be required before it could be taken forward.'[102]

The Commission found customs and tradition a limitation on the potential exploitation of internet technology in another area. When considering the possibility of electronic voting by MPs, it stressed that 'Members value the chance to meet Government Ministers and other MPs during votes, as this

[99] See e.g. Allan, 'Parliament, Elected Representatives and Technology 1997–2005 – Good in Parts?', p. 361.

[100] House of Commons Procedure Committee, *e-Petitions*, pp. 9, 11–12.

[101] House of Lords Select Committee on Science and Technology, *Information Society: Agenda for Action in the UK*, Fifth Report of Session 1995–96, HL 77, paras. 3.53–4, available at: https://publications.parliament.uk/pa/ld199596/ldselect/inforsoc/ch3.htm#3.48, last accessed 14 April 2020.

[102] Digital Democracy Commission, *Open Up!*, p. 22.

gives them an opportunity to raise important issues with one another.'[103] But in sufficiently urgent circumstances, major modification of established principles was possible: specifically, in response to the coronavirus emergency in 2020. Under the arrangements introduced at this time, Members were able – using internet technology – to take part in proceedings without physically being present. On 20 April of this year, the Procedure Committee conveyed the historic importance of the measures that were taken (albeit temporarily), in its report entitled *Procedure under Coronavirus Restrictions: Proposals for Remote Participation*. It explained:

> [a] basic principle of the House's procedure and practice is that a Member is required to be present in the Chamber in order to participate in any proceeding of the House. The right of Members to attend the House without obstruction, in order to participate in its proceedings, is an ancient and unchallenged privilege of the House. While some ancillary elements of participation, such as the tabling of questions and motions or of amendments to bills, have long taken place outside the Chamber for administrative convenience, a Member has to be present in the Chamber to present a bill, to put an oral question to a Minister and to participate in a debate. Only very recently has the House consented to a pilot scheme whereby new parents are able to vote by proxy in divisions.[104]

The temporary introduction of remote participation in 2020 provided a bald illustration of a potential source of reluctance regarding the employment of the Internet. Not all parliamentarians were as willing to adapt swiftly to change as others, and uses of the technology could, for some, conflict with their perceptions of their constitutional role. The Commons Procedure Committee conveyed the divergence that had appeared, explaining that:

> [m]any colleagues ... have no choice but to be absent from Westminster while restrictions continue. Of those who do have the choice, many believe they ought to undertake their duties to the best of their abilities while following the restrictions which are being applied across the country, since to do other than to observe the restrictions imposed on the general public could have a negative impact on the reputation of the House and might undermine attempts to promote 'stay at home' and social distancing messages ... Others consider that they ought to be seen to be present in the Chamber, thereby demonstrating to their constituents that the work of the House on their behalf and on behalf of the nation continues despite the extraordinary conditions which all are experiencing.[105]

This new use of the Internet in 2020 raised questions of principle, with testing procedural implications. They included the need for a hybrid of remote and physical participation to be reconciled with the principle of 'parity of

[103] Ibid., p. 64.

[104] House of Commons Procedure Committee, *Procedure under Coronavirus Restrictions: Proposals for Remote Participation*, First Report of Session 2019–21, HC 300 (House of Commons, London, 2020), p. 5.

[105] Ibid.

treatment'.[106] Achieving this goal meant in practice a levelling down: all MPs – whether taking part in Westminster or digitally – had to be subject to more restrictions on their participation than they would otherwise. The purpose was to ensure that MPs present in the Chamber (limited to fifty) were not at an advantage over those who were not there. Rules were applied to the effect that 'spontaneous supplementary questions were disallowed, interventions on all contributions were not permitted, all requests to speak on any urgent question or statement and in any debate had to be submitted in advance, and no points of order could be accepted unless by prior arrangement'. Naturally, a number of Members felt that there was deterioration in the overall standard of proceedings as a consequence.[107] Complaints included that:

> Assertions made during debate and in response to questions have been allowed to pass unchallenged; Members have been unable to follow up swiftly on matters of concern to them; and debates have become recitals of prepared texts rather than lively exchanges of view.[108]

A more general objection connected to online debates was that they did not make it possible in a traditional sense to 'take the sense of the House' or to 'read the room'.[109]

A further challenge from the point of view of full exploitation of the Internet was connected to the bicameral nature of Parliament. The mySociety review of 2014 found a 'degree of tension between the Houses over the issue of how online services are delivered'. Staff working in the Lords told those conducting the review that the existing system did not properly provide for the needs of their House. The problem, mySociety judged, was the lack of a clear single strategy that protected digital activities from day-to-day interference, skewing the work of staff towards the needs of one House over the other.[110]

Employing the Internet could create practical difficulties that in turn had further problematic consequences. In 2001, PASC noted that '[w]hether or not e-mail is a qualitatively different form of communication from letter-writing, it certainly encourages voluminous correspondence'. It had taken evidence from the academic Helen Margetts 'that UK Members of Parliament are not currently equipped to deal with the quantity of representations they may now expect'.[111] Dealing with the same subject, the Information Committee argued in 2002 that:

[106] See further Allan, 'Parliament, Elected Representatives and Technology 1997–2005 – Good in Parts?', p. 361.

[107] See House of Commons Procedure Committee, *Procedure under Coronavirus Restrictions: The Government's Proposal to Discontinue Remote Participation*, Third Report of Session 2019–21, HC 392 (House of Commons, London 2020), p. 12.

[108] See ibid., p. 13.

[109] See ibid., p. 15.

[110] mySociety, *Review of Parliament's Online Services*, p. 27.

[111] House of Commons Public Administration Select Committee, *Innovations in Citizen Participation in Government*, para. 71.

> [t]he ease with which constituents and others can send e-mail is seen by Members as both an opportunity (in that databases of constituents and correspondence can be created and maintained with comparatively little effort) and as a threat, in that it could generate a demand that Members cannot meet with existing structures and resources . . . One issue of concern to Members is the use of e-mail by pressure groups for mass campaigns. Publicising an e-mail address to the full membership of an organisation can prompt mass posting of a standard e-mail to any one Member. The Member and his or her staff will then have to deal with each e-mail. A Member may decide to delete each one without reading it first; but care will need to be taken to identify and preserve mail from constituents.[112]

The 2014 mySociety report suggested the existence of various internal barriers to the more effective employment of the Internet by Parliament. It described how staff seeking updates to content on parliament.uk relied on a Web and Intranet Services team the performance of which was poor. The review stated that '[n]umerous people we spoke to expressed the view that if they were to lodge a request with WIS, then there is a high probability that they would not see their project delivered in a timely fashion, or indeed at all'. Some staff told the reviewers that, as a consequence of previous unsatisfactory experiences, they avoided engaging with WIS at all if possible.[113] The mySociety paper found that one reason for this weakness was a lack of 'access to enough appropriately skilled computer programmers to meet the online service needs of Members, the public or staff'. It noted that while Parliament had an allocation of six, mySociety itself – 'a small social enterprise' – had twelve. Noting – as an illustration of larger difficulties – two specific shortcomings in the way users were able to access information on the website (discussed in Chapter 2), the review held that:

> The question to consider is not . . . 'How do we resolve these two problems?' Instead it is 'Why were these problems not resolved some time ago?' Neither of them is technically insuperable. There is no strong mitigating circumstance that explains why an institution of Parliament's size and resources would be operating services with these issues.[114]

To address such concerns, the key mySociety recommendation – adopted by Parliament – was for the formation of a single Digital Office under a Head of Digital.[115]

In 2008 the Commons Procedure Committee, in a discussion of the merits of an e-petitioning system, advanced a series of possible problems it might bring, some of which had wider applicability. One was the prospect that it might lead to Parliament receiving such a quantity of submissions as to be

[112] House of Commons Information Committee, *Digital Technology*, p. 9.
[113] mySociety, *Review of Parliament's Online Services*, p. 9.
[114] Ibid., p. 17.
[115] Ibid., p. 22.

difficult to manage. Furthermore, it would absorb scarce financial resources – the exact extent of which might be difficult to predict – that could otherwise be employed for other engagement purposes.[116] The Select Committee on the Modernisation of the House of Commons had made a similar point four years previously. It had complained that:

> [u]nlike some other organisations, the House cannot easily make savings in other areas to pay for web development. Web publication does not replace the need to provide printed documents for internal and external use (in particular, for libraries); nor does the development of the Explore Parliament website replace expenditure on the school visits programme; nor webcasting replace televised broadcasting; nor on-line consultation replace conventional consultation by committees. The House authorities have had to consider plans to expand and enhance the website alongside a range of other pressures on the administration budget.[117]

This point is a reminder that, however rapid and extensive the penetration of the Internet was, it did not replace other forms of communication, and they required continued parliamentary attention. The prospect of e-petitioning generated further apprehensions. The Procedure Committee expressed in 2008 the fear that such a system might raise unrealistic public expectations regarding the potential to wield influence and be taken seriously by political authorities. Damaging disappointment might follow. An exercise intended to enhance engagement with Parliament would have had the opposite effect.[118]

Mistakes and malfunctions were another significant concern. The Commons Procedure Committee feared that, because of human error, personal details of signatories of petitions were likely to leak at some point.[119] Technical issues generated unease. The Committee found that:

> there are relatively few e-petitions systems currently established, and none, as far as we are aware, with the features we might be looking for. If the House introduced a system which then went wrong, it could do significant reputational damage. Our witnesses agreed that failures in the ICT systems, so that the public could not access or submit e-petitions, would undermine public confidence in the system as a whole.

As these remarks suggested, an underlying apprehension arose from the very possibility of failure and what it might mean. Not all MPs would want to take part, the Committee judged. They might regard the process as a distraction, and – depending on the volume of submissions generated – an excessive burden. If a significant number of MPs declined to participate, the whole

[116] House of Commons Procedure Committee, *e-Petitions*, pp. 9, 11–12.

[117] House of Commons Select Committee on Modernisation of the House of Commons, *Connecting Parliament with the Public*, p. 18.

[118] House of Commons Procedure Committee, *e-Petitions*, pp. 10–11.

[119] Ibid., pp. 12–13.

initiative might be doomed.[120] Furthermore, proper public involvement was not guaranteed. As the Procedure Committee put it:

> If we cannot be confident that we can establish an e-petitions scheme which Members and the public find easy to understand and straightforward to use, which is responsive and meets their reasonable expectations and which is reliable and technologically robust, we might be better not proceeding with a scheme at all.[121]

As we have seen, alongside petitions, another potential tool for parliamentary engagement was the use of online forums. From the late 1990s onward, there were a variety of these exercises and a significant degree of support for their use in interested circles. However, some doubts and questions were also raised, as revealed by the House of Lords Information Committee in its 2009 report. The Committee noted that – alongside the advocates – 'a number of people were sceptical about the potential for Parliament's website to host constructive public policy debate'.[122] One concern raised was that participation levels in previous parliamentary initiatives of this type had been relatively low. A further issue involved resource-effectiveness. The Committee recalled being informed by the Labour MP Tom Watson, who at the time he gave his evidence was Minister for Digital Engagement, that:

> [w]hen you have any conversation it has to be moderated, so if Parliament took the decision to have a kind of giant conversation with the nation there would be a very large resource issue there because if you are going to do it at scale you need people who will moderate the conversation and stop people doing the sorts of things they can get up to online. So the decision really would be a cost-benefit analysis and the truth is I do not know the answer about whether we would gain, as parliamentarians, great wisdom through that route.[123]

In 2015, the Speaker's Commission on Digital Democracy expressed similar concerns regarding digital forums and suggested a further factor that could act as a brake upon parliamentary exploitation of the Internet: a sense that the technology had not yet reached the necessary level of sophistication required of it to execute a particular task satisfactorily. The Commission described how it had received evidence about 'online forums' to the effect that they were not easy to use with large-scale public consultations. It recounted the view of 'some experts . . . that although technology is "excellent at gathering information", it is still not very good at large-scale deliberation. One person said that public forums "can be a mess".' A means of circumventing this problem was 'to factor in "substantial human activity" to

[120] Ibid., pp. 9, 12–13.
[121] Ibid., p. 13.
[122] House of Lords Information Committee, *Are the Lords Listening?*, vol. I: *Report*, pp. 18–19, paras. 46–51.
[123] Ibid.

support the process, for example by moderating online discussions and analysing the contributions received'. However, 'the resource implications of this would place a limit on how many large-scale forums could be offered'. A further option was 'to enable those who take part to manage the process themselves, debating ideas and voting on or rating the best ones, so that the most popular are given greater prominence'. While the Commission was 'confident that online participation by the public in the work of Parliament will be increasingly important', it 'deliberately set out a cautious approach to this, at least initially, to avoid early experiments being crushed by the weight of expectations'. Yet the Commission anticipated 'a need in the relatively near future for Parliament to build or better still adapt existing tools to support large-scale online participation'.[124]

The reference Watson made in evidence to the Lords Information Committee to the requirement to 'stop people doing the sort of things they can get up to online'[125] touched upon a dilemma more fundamental than issues around resource allocation, important though they were. Opening up Parliament to participation from outside carried with it a risk. Those taking advantage of the opportunity to participate might behave in ways that went beyond what was, from the point of view of the institution, acceptable. Online consultations or forums were considered vulnerable in this way, including by their advocates. For instance, in 2004, the Select Committee on Modernisation of the House of Commons acknowledged this concern, albeit while asserting that it need not be a serious problem for Parliament:

> Professor Coleman told us that these consultations had generally been successful, drawing on public expertise, treating the public with respect and encouraging a respectful attitude. It was notable that Parliamentary consultations did not attract the actionable or offensive contributions which accounted for 20–25% of those submitted to Government departments' on-line forums.[126]

Comparable concerns arose in relation to petitioning. In 2008, the Commons Procedure Committee had noted that petitions might be designed as jokes rather than as attempts seriously to engage with policy issues. Drawing on the experience of the No. 10 platform, the Committee recalled that: '[o]ne of the five most signed petitions in the first part of 2008 was a petition to make TV presenter Jeremy Clarkson Prime Minister'. It was difficult to devise satisfactory ways of preventing such activity. As the Committee remarked:

> What appears trivial to one group of people may be very important to another and a rule which in the end depends for its implementation on largely subjective

124 Digital Democracy Commission, *Open Up!*, p. 49.

125 House of Lords Information Committee, *Are the Lords Listening?*, vol. I: *Report*, pp. 18–19, paras. 46–51.

126 House of Lords Select Committee on Modernisation of the House of Commons, *Connecting Parliament with the Public*, p. 21.

judgements can easily become not only discredited but grounds for suspicion of a deliberate campaign to exclude particular groups or issues.[127]

Technological development, in this instance in the form of the Internet, had once again helped raise a dilemma, recurring in different forms, involving free expression and its consequences. On this occasion the Committee expressed fear regarding the possibility of efforts at control raising more difficulties than they resolved. Yet – like Milton – even though it generally opposed such regulation, it held that there needed to be some limits. The Committee noted that:

> Alongside the relatively frivolous and the mischievous, however, there may also be e-petitions with a more mischievous or even sinister purpose. There is a risk that people may attempt to use e-petitions to demonstrate support for offensive or even illegal causes.[128]

The Committee took the view that '[i]n principle . . . such petitions should not be allowed'. It held that it would be possible to take preventative measures, while acknowledging 'a risk that, despite the best efforts of all concerned, not every such e-petition would be spotted and rejected'.[129]

Accompanying concern that people might abuse the opportunities that online engagement created was another reservation: that they might lack the motivation to take part at all. The Committee on Reform of the House of Commons formed in 2009 with the Labour MP, Tony Wright, in the chair. The tone of its report, *Rebuilding the House*, was sceptical regarding the need for further online initiatives (though it was not entirely dismissive and held they could have value.) It argued that: 'Members of the public . . . participate in proceedings in the House as witnesses in select committee and public bill committee hearings. Furthermore, online forums are now frequently used by select committees to garner experience directly from the public on specific topics.'[130] But it observed that '[t]here are varying views about the prospects for greater public participation. Recent research from the Hansard Society conveyed in its submission to us warns that the level of public desire for direct involvement may be low and falling.'[131]

Around this time, others were also recommending caution. Nigel Jackson, an academic specialising in communications, referred to potential shortcomings in parliamentary use of the Internet in evidence to the House of Lords Information Committee. This Committee referred in 2009 to his warning regarding possible failure to establish 'a clear, defined and measurable purpose

127 House of Commons Procedure Committee, *e-Petitions*, p. 10.
128 Ibid., p. 10.
129 Ibid.
130 House of Commons Reform Committee, *Rebuilding the House*, First Report of Session 2008–9, HC 1117 (Stationery Office, London, 2009), p. 66.
131 Ibid., p. 67.

for adopting the internet'. He took the view that any efforts at providing information and interacting with the public should be directed towards assisting the legislative process and with oversight of the executive. Jackson held that online initiatives that did not serve these purposes would be 'window dressing. It will not help the House of Lords, or individual Peers, function better and more importantly online users will come to recognise this and disengage.' He was wary of unthinking efforts to embrace Web 2.0, warning that '[j]ust because new technologies, such as social networking sites, exist is a poor reason alone for adopting them'.[132] Along similar lines, in 2015, the Speaker's Commission on Digital Democracy referred to the 'perceptive' advice it had received from Involve. The organisation had told it to:

> [l]et the purpose, not the tools, be the driver. As with any effort to improve citizen engagement (whether digital or offline) it is critical to clarify the purpose first and then find the right tools to achieve it ... the essential first step is to determine *why* citizen voice is desired within a particular process, and what citizens add that actors already in the process don't already bring.[133]

Day-to-day Work Routines: Hand-Held Devices and e-Tabling

Some challenges and controversies involved the incorporation of internet-related technology into the regular work of MPs and Peers within Parliament. A consideration of a House of Lords Administration and Works Committee report from late January 2011, *Use of Electronic Devices in the House*, gives an idea of the complex concerns that could require resolution. In defining terms, the Committee held that 'it is important to avoid too much detail because the rules would rapidly be overtaken by new technology – as has happened with the current rules'. It stated that '[i]t has become clear that the rules regulating the use of mobile telephones and other electronic devices ... in the House are incomplete, outdated and contradictory'. The existing position, established by the Committee itself four years previously, was that '[m]obile telephones must be silent in the Chamber, Prince's Chamber, Peers' Lobby, division lobbies during divisions, the Moses Room and committee rooms during committee meetings'. This rule also applied to 'the Library, the Salisbury Room, the Writing Room, and all bars and restaurants. Elsewhere they may be used with discretion.' Meanwhile, '[i]n the Chamber and in committee rooms, pagers or other electronic devices must not be used to transmit messages to members of the House for use in proceedings'.[134]

132 House of Lords Information Committee, *Are the Lords Listening?*, vol. I: *Report*, pp. 18–19, paras. 46–51.

133 Digital Democracy Commission, *Open Up!*, p. 49.

134 House of Lords Administration and Works Committee, *Use of Electronic Devices in the House*, HL 92 (London, Stationery Office, 2010–11), pp. 3–5.

The Committee found fault with its own regulations, both because they contained internal tensions and because they were anachronistic. Requiring mobile telephones to be 'silent' suggested that it was permissible to use them 'in silent mode to send text messages or check emails and the internet'. Yet at the same time the stipulation about their use in other places 'with discretion' implied 'that they may not be used at all (even in silent mode) in the restricted areas'. Furthermore, 'the reference to pagers is outdated' and there was no consideration of 'other devices such as iPads and laptops' except in as far as there was a prohibition on 'transmitting messages for use in proceedings'.[135]

The central concern of the report was whether and, if so, how Members could 'use electronic devices while in the Chamber or Grand Committee'. On the subject of 'the use of electronic devices to send or receive messages for use in proceedings', it noted the different sides of the argument. There was not a ban on 'officials sending handwritten notes to Members (generally front-benchers)' while in the Chamber or Grand Committee. On this basis it might be held that electronic devices could be deployed for the same purposes. However, the Committee argued that 'there is a profound difference of scale'. A question already raised in this book had asserted itself. Might the technology merely make it possible to carry out existing practices with greater ease, or was a qualitative change in prospect (in this case because of the volume of activity that might come about)? The Committee leant towards the latter interpretation. It concluded that it might be detrimental 'to good debate to allow Members to send or receive streams of messages to and from researchers or advisers outside the Chamber or Moses Room'. On these grounds the Committee advocated maintaining the existing prohibition on the use of electronic devices 'to send or receive messages for use in proceedings'.[136] The Committee had considered an important question. Did the use of a device connected to the Internet for a pre-existing activity alter that activity to such an extent that it changed in its nature? In this instance, the issue was whether an increase in the quantity of messages on the scale anticipated, were the ban lifted, would entail a qualitative alteration in the way a key feature of the business of Parliament operated. The Committee decided that it would, and that the transformation itself would be undesirable.

The report demonstrated more sympathy for the idea that members might use electronic devices to 'access ... documents relevant to the business before the House'. These texts might include 'the Order Paper, Hansard, texts of bills or explanatory notes, white papers or other Government publications, and reports by external bodies'. The dependence on hard copies would thereby be reduced. However, the Committee was concerned regarding the possibility that 'internet access could be abused'. For example, it opposed the idea 'that Members participating in proceedings should be permitted to use electronic

[135] Ibid., p. 3.
[136] Ibid., pp. 3–4.

devices to search the Web speculatively in the hope of finding information for use in debate which is not generally available to other participants'. Ultimately, it would be difficult to prevent or even precisely to define in advance inappropriate activity. 'Policing the use of the internet, and in particular distinguishing between appropriate and inappropriate use, would be difficult.' There would be a need to rely heavily upon 'self-regulation, and on the common sense and self restraint of individual Members'. Nonetheless the Committee advocated 'a one-year trial period' in which Members taking part in debates could use electronic devices in the way it had already suggested was appropriate. The recommendation, however, applied only to 'hand-held devices' and not 'conventional laptops'.[137]

The Committee further proposed that, while they were not speaking, Members should also be able to employ devices 'in silent mode, for any purpose not related to the proceedings before the House or Grand Committee, provided they do not distract other Members'. Nonetheless, 'as a courtesy to other Members', the Committee opposed 'repeated use of such devices'. The report noted further that Members were using electronic devices 'in place of paper notes' when making speeches. 'At least one Member has made a speech in the Chamber using his iPad in recent weeks.' The Committee found no problem with this practice, though it was at the time forbidden in the House of Commons. There was 'no qualitative difference between using a pad of paper for speaking notes and using an iPad or other device'. The existing ban on 'reading speeches', however, would remain in place. The Committee at this point proposed a further, associated, innovation. The Editor of Hansard had agreed to receive speaking notes via email, if they were stored on electronic devices, a change of practice that the report supported. The Committee acknowledged that the same standards did not apply to meetings of select committees, which were 'different in atmosphere from proceedings in the Chamber'. It proposed no limitations on electronic devices, even laptops, in these forums, except that they should be silent and their employment or otherwise should be subject to the 'discretion of the Chairman'.[138]

Once again, the Lords proved to be a parliamentary pathbreaker in its handling of technology. The House of Commons Procedure Committee issued its own report on the use of hand-held devices shortly after the Lords, in March 2011. The existing Commons rule, dating from October 2007, was that MPs could use such technology in the Chamber 'to keep up to date with emails . . . provided that it causes no disturbance'. They could not, however, use it as a 'prompt' when taking part in proceedings or speaking.[139]

[137] Ibid., pp. 4–5.
[138] Ibid.
[139] House of Commons Procedure Committee, *Use of Hand-Held Electronic Devices in the Chamber and Committees*, p. 5.

Technological change and social patterns in usage in the period since 2007 had created the need for reassessment. As the Committee put it:

> the availability of new technology and the use of that technology both within and outside Parliament have increased dramatically. There are many new devices, including portable 'tablet' computers such as iPads or smartphones, which were not known to the Modernisation Committee which drew up the report which led to the House's resolution [providing the basis for the existing rule]. There are also new uses of technology, for example Twitter, which were similarly unknown but on which the Speaker and the Chair of any committee may be expected to rule.[140]

The issue was divisive, in a cross-party fashion, and became more so. As the Committee noted, 'around 225 Members . . . tweet, coming from all parties in the House'. Tweeting, then, created particular challenges:

> As an example of a practice which could not have been predicted by the Modernisation Committee in 2007, tweeting could hardly be bettered. The use of Twitter by Members is very popular and its use in the Chamber or Westminster Hall has caused comment from Members themselves and from the public. Many different views have been expressed, from those who believe that it is a threat to the dignity of parliamentary proceedings to those who argue that it brings Parliament to a whole new audience.[141]

The Committee identified some of the main objections present within the Commons to the use of electronic devices. They were that Members should be focused on taking part in proceedings, not on their device, and that they should not 'distract others' in the process. Some members of the public had expressed objections when noticing MPs using such technology. A fundamental constitutional point was 'that transmitting messages in and out of the Chamber might allow others to influence the course of a debate which could constitute interference in parliamentary proceedings'.[142] The Committee depicted a worst-case outcome that was similar to a scenario that Stuart Hill (in his evidence to the House of Commons Information Committee in 2002 quoted at the head of this chapter) had predicted would come about within ten years. It involved:

> Prime Minister's Question Time being conducted by instant rebuttal teams briefing the principals on what they should say, whilst all other Members were bombarded with messages from the public and others commenting on and attempting to offer contributions to the debate.[143]

140 Ibid.
141 Ibid., p. 11.
142 Ibid., pp. 7–8.
143 Ibid., p. 9.

The Committee was aware of the difficulties of regulation in this area, since in such a fast-developing context they would be likely soon to become dated.[144] Ultimately it proposed:

> [t]hat hand-held electronic devices (not laptops) may be used in the Chamber, provided that they are silent, and used in a way that does not impair decorum; that Members making speeches in the Chamber or in committee may refer to electronic devices in place of paper speaking notes; and that electronic devices, including laptops, may be used silently in committee meetings, including select committees.[145]

Other internal uses of digital communications technology gave rise to concerns and complications. In 2002, a mechanism whereby MPs could electronically submit questions for written responses became operational. It made the task easier, since MPs were otherwise required to fill out a physical form and submit it in person to Table Office. In this sense, digital network technology was enabling MPs to perform more efficiently in contributing to executive accountability to Parliament. However, the e-tabling system came to cause concerns. They were connected partly to its association with a rise in the total volume of written questions, which by 2011 had reached record levels. One objection was resource-related. As of 2011, each written question cost the Commons £80 and the government £154. A further issue was that the more questions were asked, the less likely it was that MPs rather than their staff were closely involved in their drafting. As the House of Commons Procedure Committee put it in 2011:

> there is a perception that some questions, especially those submitted electronically, are devised and tabled by Members' staff without always the explicit approval of Members which in itself reduces the significance of the process.[146]

Moreover, a rise in the overall number, some felt, might have the effect of engulfing better-devised questions in their mediocre equivalents. In the words of the Commons Procedure Committee: '[f]or Members, the danger is that good sharp questions may get swamped by the sheer volume of questions published'.[147] Finally, if MPs were not present in the Table Office to submit them, there was a greater likelihood that there would be problems with the wording or content of questions that they might then need to resolve in person. However, the introduction in 2011 of a cap on the number of e-tabled questions to five per day for each MP was not successful in reducing the

[144] Ibid.

[145] Ibid., p. 10.

[146] House of Commons Procedure Committee, *Improving the Effectiveness of Parliamentary Scrutiny*, Second Report of Session 2010–11, HC 800 (Stationery Office, London, 2011), p. 16.

[147] Ibid., p. 17.

total number submitted, with MPs proving willing to attend the Table Office in person rather than reduce their frequency.[148]

This episode demonstrates the difficulty – when analysing the impact of networked computing on Parliament – of establishing causality. e-Tabling was certainly helpful to MPs wanting to submit questions. Yet they proved able and willing to use more traditional means if need be. Perhaps the availability of digital facilities had encouraged them to table more questions in the first place. But if it did, it led to their acquiring a habit that was self-sustaining, irrespective of their having the same level of access to the technology that had first stimulated it. Ultimately, we are in the realm of speculation. But what is certain is that the Internet and associated internal communications systems had forced Parliament to change, scrutinise, contemplate, and revise the way in which it went about one of its fundamental activities: posing questions to the executive in order to hold it to account.

The concern about the impact of e-tabling upon the nature of the overall system highlighted a further important concept already discussed above in relation to the employment of hand-held devices inside Parliament. The use of a technology for the purposes of carrying out an established activity more efficiently, rather than to facilitate a new practice, might nonetheless have had (possibly unforeseen) transformative effects. A quantitative increase in questions for written answer could – so the concerns raised suggested – have qualitative consequences, by lessening the direct involvement of MPs in drafting, and smothering contributions of higher calibre. Whether or not one accepts that such effects were actually taking place and, if so, that they were attributable to the use of a given technology, such concerns were present as theoretical possibilities. Some within Parliament took them seriously and this credence influenced their attitude towards the use of digital communications.

Government–Parliament Relations

The relationship between the executive and legislative branches of the constitution is complex, and a consideration of parliamentary usage of the Internet reflects this quality. On the one hand, a purpose of the Internet could be to enable representatives in the Commons and the Lords better to hold government to account.[149] The Commons Procedure Committee described in 2008 being told by Carswell that 'if we were bold about it and we were really willing to allow the Internet to change our political system for the better, we

[148] See ibid.; House of Commons Procedure Committee, *e-Tabling of Parliamentary Questions for Written Answer*, Eighth Report of Session 2010–12, HC 1823 (Stationery Office, London, 2012); House of Commons Procedure Committee, *e-Tabling of Written Questions*, Third Report of Session 2012–13, HC 775 (Stationery Office, London, 2012).

[149] House of Commons Information Committee, *Digital Technology*, p. 5.

could allow it to help Parliament to hold the Executive to account'.[150] The following year, the Lords Information Committee described a core objective of online activity by Parliament as being to support it in 'scrutinising the Government'.[151] On the other hand, significant changes in Parliament in practice generally require the support of the executive. For instance, as discussed above, Robin Cook, as Leader of the House of Commons, provided motivation for change. In 2002 the Commons Information Committee cited Cook's statement from December the previous year in a memorandum to the Modernisation Committee that the Commons had 'opportunities' to:

> harness the new technologies to connect with the wider electorate and with civil society. The Internet, for example, gives opportunities for two-way communication and could be used more systematically for consultation with the public by Select Committees.[152]

In 2009, after setting out a proposed open data programme, the House of Lords Information Committee noted that:

> The vision we have outlined ... cannot be achieved without Government collaboration. The Government needs to share our commitment to use fully open standards for data. The Government should work with Parliament to implement common standards for the categories of information we mention in this paragraph, so as to improve the flow of information between Government and Parliament and to enhance the public's ability to re-use that information.[153]

In 2020, the ability of Parliament to introduce and then sustain remote working procedures during the coronavirus pandemic were, in effect, reliant on executive co-operation. Tension developed between the two constitutional branches at this time, most notably after the government, when introducing a recovery strategy on 11 May, exhorted Parliament to 'set a national example of how business can continue in this new normal ... it must move, in step with public health guidance, to get back to business as part of this next step, including a move towards further physical proceedings in the House of Commons'.[154]

The process by which e-petitioning came into use, the form it took, and the use made of it, help to illustrate the nature of the relationship between Parliament and executive. It exhibits its conflicting aspects, and the part that the Internet could play within them. A major change such as a shift to an e-petitioning system would be dependent upon the executive, given its numerical strength in the Commons and control over its agenda. For this

[150] House of Commons Procedure Committee, *e-Petitions*, p. 15.

[151] House of Lords Information Committee, *Are the Lords Listening?*, vol. I: *Report*, pp. 18–19, paras. 46–51.

[152] Cited in House of Commons Information Committee, *Digital Technology*, p. 14.

[153] House of Lords Information Committee, Are the Lords Listening?, vol. I: *Report*, pp. 26–7.

[154] See House of Commons Procedure Committee, Procedure under Coronavirus Restrictions: The Government's Proposal to Discontinue Remote Participation, pp. 9–10 and generally.

reason, the emergence of the system was protracted and took place in a form that failed fully to accord with the model favoured by many of its proponents.

Responding to a recommendation from its Procedure Committee, the Commons first approved in principle the idea of an e-petitioning mechanism on 25 October 2007.[155] A full system with a specific Petitions Committee to support it appeared nearly eight years later, at the outset of the 2015 Parliament. Along the way compromise had been judged necessary to achieve this outcome. The process was one of difference and occasional coincidence of interest between Parliament and government. An initial tension came about because the Prime Minister's Office acquired its own e-petitions system before Parliament, in 2006. This initiative represented a threat to the status of Parliament as the principal representative of the public. Being the repository of petitions was among its oldest functions. The executive was seemingly employing a new technology to operate a system that circumvented the legislature in the performance of its core role.[156] This development could be held to imply a downgrading of the system of parliamentary democracy itself. The Internet was therefore associated with constitutional destabilisation, with unfavourable connotations for Parliament. From the point of view of those who favoured the introduction of e-petitioning to the Commons, this same technological application might reverse a tendency they judged unwelcome. It could, they argued, utilise the growing popularity of the Internet to strengthen the operation of traditional parliamentary mechanisms.[157]

Subsequently, impetus came from the UK government to establish a system in the Commons. When Gordon Brown succeeded Tony Blair as Labour Prime Minister in mid-2007, he presented constitutional reform as the central part of his agenda. Unveiling a programme with the general title 'The Governance of Britain', it proposed a range of changes, including that the Commons needed to adopt 'up-to-date procedures for considering petitions' (it had similar plans for local government level as well). Making reference to the petitioning feature on the Prime Minister's Office website, the UK government held that 'people should be able to petition the House of Commons with as much ease as they are currently able to petition the Prime Minister'. Government support for a Commons e-petitioning system therefore appeared firm, even to the point of urging swift progress.[158]

In April 2008, the Commons Procedure Committee recommended that the Commons introduce an e-petitioning system, setting out a model for how it could work. The Labour administration responded positively the following July. But by the end of the same year, it became less enthusiastic and stalled implementation of the project. The main issue the government raised – in a

[155] House of Commons Procedure Committee, *e-Petitions*, p. 9.
[156] Ibid., p. 14.
[157] Ibid., p. 9.
[158] Ibid.

time of international economic downturn – involved the costs it had projected for the system the Procedure Committee envisaged. It believed that the initial outlay would be £500,000, and £840,000 per year thereafter. The Committee held that accurate predictions of this type were difficult, because there was no other project it could identify internationally 'of comparable scale and ambition'. It nonetheless acknowledged that substantial outlay at some level would be involved both in guaranteeing security and ensuring that the system functioned satisfactorily from the outset. However, it denied the validity of comparisons to the cost of the No. 10 system, which seems to have been substantially lower (though there were problems with establishing precise figures). Unlike this established version of e-petitioning, the mechanism the Committee envisaged for the Commons would be fully integrated into parliamentary proceedings, and provide a role for individual Members. These intentions brought with them resource implications. On this analysis, to function appropriately in a parliamentary context, e-petitioning would of necessity cost more than the No. 10 system. The Procedure Committee urged 'the Government to think again'.[159] The House of Commons Reform Committee then considered e-petitions as part of its remit. But in its 2009 report it made no firm recommendation in this area other than calling for discussions within the Commons to secure clear consensus around a way forward.[160] This goal was not achieved; and no progress was made in advance of the 2010 General Election and the changeover from a Labour to a Conservative–Liberal Democrat coalition.

The coalition agreement had contained a commitment to make petitions with 100,000 or more signatories 'eligible for formal debate in Parliament'. In July 2011, the government relaunched its system, moving it from No. 10 to the remit of the Leader of the House of Commons. Petitions reaching the 100,000 figure could be submitted (via individual MPs) to the House of Commons Backbench Business Committee (an entity formed in 2010 – in response to the findings of the House of Commons Reform Committee – that was responsible for allocating non-government time in the Commons), with a request that it try to create space for a debate.

The executive had unilaterally imposed an arrangement upon Parliament, whereby the latter in effect became responsible for petitions directed to the former. In this sense, through employment of the Internet, it was encroaching upon an activity that had been part of the business of Parliament since medieval times. Seeking to reassert what the Procedure Committee described as 'the House's historic role as the principal recipient of public petitions',[161] in May 2014 the Commons passed without division a motion stating that:

[159] House of Commons Procedure Committee, *e-Petitions: Call for Government Action*, Second Report of Session 2008–09, HC 493 (London, Stationery Office, 2009), pp. 3, 6.

[160] House of Commons Reform Committee, *Rebuilding the House*, p. 73.

[161] House of Commons Procedure Committee, *e-Petitions: A Collaborative System?*, Third Report of Session 2014–15, HC 235 (London, Stationery Office, 2014), para. 16, pp. 8–9.

> this House supports the establishment, at the start of the next Parliament, of a collaborative e-petitions system, which enables members of the public to petition the House of Commons and press for action from Government; and calls on the Procedure Committee to work with the Government and other interested parties on the development of detailed proposals.

Eventually, after the 2015 General Election, this proposal was put into practice, with a specific Petitions Committee formed to oversee the system. (It was at this point that there was a move to petitioning the Commons directly, rather than via individual MPs.) However, while the Commons had managed to achieve an arrangement more in line with its objectives than had previously been the case, this sequence of events also illustrated some of its weaknesses with respect to the executive. An effort at innovation had been delayed by some years. Change, when it did occur, was initially forced upon Parliament by the government. Furthermore, even the system as it operated from 2015 was a source of controversy among many advocates of parliamentary e-petitioning. Ideally, they would have liked a specific parliamentary mechanism, rather than one that was shared with the government. There was dissent among them about whether it was worth conceding this point in order to avoid the public confusion that might arise from the simultaneous existence of two different e-petition sites.[162]

A consideration of e-petitioning also makes possible some more general observations about parliamentary adoption of the Internet, and the constitutional consequences of this process. When the introduction of such a system was under consideration, views differed about the extent to which it would be compatible with the position of Parliament within a representative democracy. Carswell submitted evidence to the Commons Procedure Committee in November 2007 arguing in favour of a mechanism by which, if a defined number of members of the public supported it, a legislative proposal could receive a parliamentary Second Reading, at which MPs (assuming the vote was taking place in the Commons) would be given the opportunity to approve or reject the measure in principle. This idea went beyond the mechanism that was ultimately introduced, in that it entailed a firm procedure by which petitions would feed into legislative processes. But despite the power it would grant to external forces, Carswell held that '[g]iving people the power to e-petition and initiate Parliamentary debates online would not diminish the role of elected MPs. On the contrary, it would ensure that more people took a greater interest in what happened in the House of Commons.' He argued that it would stimulate responsible political engagement, and judged that – on a basis of international evidence – it would not necessarily lead to illiberal proposals such as restoration of the death penalty.[163]

162 For a narrative of these events, see ibid.

163 Mr Douglas Carswell MP (P10), 'e-Petitions and Initiative: Open Politics in the Age of YouTube', House of Commons Procedure Committee, *e-Petitions*, First Report of Session

In contrast, the Labour MP Graham Allen – whose early advocacy of internet-related technology we encountered in Chapter 6 – submitted evidence to the Commons Procedure Committee in January 2008 raising concerns about e-petitioning. Allen described the system as coming within 'the referendum/populist category of e-democracy', and suggested the Committee give consideration to a process of online participation in pre-legislative scrutiny 'which invites people into the world of representative democracy' in a considered and informative fashion. As a representative of a constituency that had the lowest level of educational attainment in the UK, he suspected that the practice would 'inevitably be skewed away from my constituents who have lower PC use, are less literate and include a high percentage of the elderly'. Furthermore, Allen's experience of email was that it was 'often more reactive and less considered than the comments and problems which I receive in letters'. Such a tendency would spill over into e-petitioning. The system would be open to manipulation by 'the 24/7 media', that would have 'no compunction in launching media e-campaigns'. All forms of petitioning, he recognised, were vulnerable to abuse. But the rapid potential reach of the Internet accentuated the risks. Furthermore, Allen doubted whether e-petitions would generate meaningful responses from the government.[164]

These divergent perspectives illustrate some of the complexities involved in the wider subject. Carswell and Allen were both firm supporters of the parliamentary use of the Internet as a means of democratic engagement. But they held conflicting views of the form it should take. That which the former regarded as a means of strengthening Parliament through public involvement, the latter perceived as a manipulative threat. Adoption of the technology was the beginning, not the end, of a debate. The Internet had prompted much parliamentary self-reflection and reorientation by the institution. It had encouraged examination of fundamental questions about the legislature and its external relationships, especially with the people it represented and the government that was both formed out of it and which it held to account. Both Houses were involved. Long-established principles of operation were challenged. New practices were developed and old ones revived in adjusted form.

A powerful force for change was a sense of democratic deterioration, supposedly with especially grave consequences for Parliament, that the Internet might assist in correcting. Belief in this tendency provided particular motivation for innovations such as online consultations and e-petitions. Yet, as we have seen, ideas about decline had precursors, as did the suggestion that a communications medium – such as television – might help address it. Enthusiasts for parliamentary use of the Internet often failed, it seems, to

2007–08, HC 136 (London: Stationery Office, 2008), Ev. 12–14, submitted for committee oral evidence session held on 28 November 2007.

164 Mr Graham Allen MP (P21), House of Commons Procedure Committee, *e-Petitions*, First Report of Session 2007–08, HC 136 (London: Stationery Office, 2008), Ev. 60–1.

recognise this point. As noted above, Robin Cook, in his role as Leader of the House of Commons, generated impetus for more extensive use of the technology early in the twenty-first century. In a diary entry for 17 July 2001, he discussed what he regarded as the need for parliamentary reform or 'modernisation'. Cook depicted Parliament as appearing anachronistic to the public 'in the age of the world wide web'. Increasing numbers of people, he held, lacked a feeling of 'ownership of their parliamentary democracy'.[165] For Cook, television (or at least the particular way it had been utilised) was part of the problem. He wrote:

> Two hundred years ago, Byron complained that MPs were more formidable as an audience than they were as speakers. But now we are on television. Or, more precisely, our most vituperative, bad-tempered exchanges make it on to television. Broadcasting loves the party political mud-wrestling of contests such as Prime Minister's Questions because for entertainment value it rivals any theatre. However, the kind of drama that gets the Commons air time with the broadcasters also gets it a bad name with the public.[166]

The 'widening gulf' between Parliament and public that Cook identified seemed, in his account, to be a relatively recent problem, at least in intense form.[167] But it appears remarkably similar to the phenomenon that Aneurin Bevan – as described in Chapter 5 – had discerned four decades previously. Bevan referred in 1959 to 'a considerable gulf growing between this House and the nation'. Like Cook, Bevan saw communications technology (then, newspapers and broadcasting) as part of the problem, but also of the potential solution, if deployed differently. He called for a specialised parliamentary channel as a means of 're-establishing intelligent communication between the House of Commons and the electorate as a whole'. Admittedly, Bevan disliked the idea of the edited highlights incorporated into more general coverage to which Cook specifically objected. In this sense it was a particular use of a device rather than the mechanism itself that was at issue. But it is notable that the programme for parliamentary use of the Internet that Cook supported would attach some of the same expectations to this newer technology that earlier reformers such as Bevan had once invested in the very practice, broadcasting, that Cook saw as contributing to the difficulties it was hoped networked computers could help address.

Some kind of adoption of the Internet would presumably have taken place with or without this particular motivation. Moreover, that there was concern among parliamentarians about trends in electoral turnout, and that they might consider ways of responding to them, is entirely understandable. But it is notable that transition to a technology encompassing many of the internal and

[165] Robin Cook, *The Point of Departure: Diaries from the Front Bench* (Pocket Books, London, 2004), diary entry for Tuesday 17 July 2001, p. 25.

[166] Ibid., p. 26.

[167] Ibid., p. 25.

external functions of Parliament occurred partly on the basis of premises about decline and the potential of communications devices, the veracity of which was open to debate, but that did not seem to receive the degree of scrutiny they merited, especially from an historical standpoint. Questions that might have been asked included: how do the supposed problems of today differ from those that came before; how effective were previous responses to them; and what are the implications for the likely success of present proposals?

Not only were the grounds on which the institution embraced the technology to some extent questionable. As the interventions of Carswell and Allen show, those who were firm supporters of the Internet as a means of democratic enhancement could disagree seriously about the precise uses to which it should be put and the likely consequences of decisions made. Indeed, uncertainty was considerable. The concerns about possible abuse of online forums, for instance, demonstrated that embracing particular uses of this communications technology entailed acceptance on the part of Parliament that it could not exercise complete control over the outcome. There might be consequences for its reputation with which it was not wholly comfortable. It had faced similar dilemmas previously: notably with printing, radio, and television. In each case it eventually came to accept that a trade-off was, to some extent, necessary or even worthwhile. The Commons Procedure Committee made such a calculation in its deliberations about the suitability of Commons e-petitions in 2008. It had reservations about them. But it also sensed the possibility of significant gains, in particular the potential for meaningful and wide public engagement. The Committee concluded: 'introducing e-petitioning is something of a gamble, possibly an expensive gamble, but a gamble which in our opinion is worth taking'.[168] Parliament has sometimes been depicted – including by those working within it – as an institution within which conservative inclinations predominate. But the technological and political context enabled such instincts to be overcome. The next chapter considers the outward-looking aspects, including parliamentary perceptions of the social impact of the technology, and the policy recommendations it promoted.

[168] House of Commons Procedure Committee, *e-Petitions*, p. 49.

8

Promotion and Regulation

Parliamentary Responses to the Internet since 1996

On 29 June 2020, the House of Lords Select Committee on Democracy and Digital Technologies reported. This ad hoc 'special inquiry' commissioned by the House of Lords Liaison Committee named its publication *Digital Technology and the Resurrection of Trust*. It was suggestive of an intensifying tone of parliamentary pessimism regarding the Internet. The previous chapter has shown how a succession of committee reports tended to depict this technology as creating opportunities for their institution to enhance its democratic legitimacy. One of the main threats they depicted was that Parliament might fail to keep abreast of developments in this field and that it would as a consequence appear increasingly irrelevant. But by 2020 negative perceptions regarding the social role of the Internet had developed and hardened. The chair of the Committee, Lord Puttnam – a Labour Peer from a background as an internationally distinguished filmmaker – had previously engaged with this subject matter, both as practitioner and advocate. In the first decade of the twenty-first century, he had chaired the Hansard Society Commission on the Communication of Parliamentary Democracy. In its 2005 report, it presented the Internet as an opportunity to be embraced, stating – among other findings – that '[i]nteractive, digital technologies provide a timely and fast-developing opportunity to expand and enrich public participation in Parliament's work'.[1] But now Puttnam and his Committee took the view that, for all their potential in this regard, digital technologies were having a negative impact upon democracy. In so doing, they specifically endorsed the radical thesis advanced by Shoshana Zuboff in her work *The Age of Surveillance Capitalism*, discussed in Chapter 1.[2]

In his foreword to the report, Puttnam noted that the publication was appearing in the midst of a global pandemic, but that it 'focuses on a different form of crisis, one with roots that extend far deeper, and are likely

[1] Hansard Society Commission on the Communication of Parliamentary Democracy, *Members Only? Parliament in the Public Eye?* (Hansard Society, London, 2005), p. 51.

[2] House of Lords Select Committee on Democracy and Digital Technologies, *Digital Technology and the Resurrection of Trust*, Report of Session 2019–21, HL 77 (House of Lords, London, 2020), p. 5.

to last far longer than COVID-19'. He identified 'a virus that affects all of us in the UK – a pandemic of "misinformation" and "disinformation"'. Were it 'allowed to flourish these counterfeit truths will result in the collapse of public trust, and without trust democracy as we know it will simply decline into irrelevance'.[3] Puttnam followed in the tradition of presenting the Internet as an environment in its own right, referring to 'the digital world'. It was, for him, a nightmare. Within it 'our belief in what we see, hear and read is being distorted to the point at which we no longer know who or what to trust'. The implications, in this scenario, were grave. Puttnam held that '[t]he prospects for building a harmonious and sustainable society on that basis are, to all intents and purposes, non-existent'.[4]

The main report presented democracy as a sophisticated, continually functioning and morphing set of processes, rules, relationships, 'institutions and shared values' upon which technological change could have an impact. Dependent upon support from a variety of sources in society, within and beyond public bodies, it was always vulnerable. Within this context the Internet – despite potentially offering so much – had become part of a problem. The Committee conveyed a sense of pronounced disappointment at a perverse outcome of historic significance. In a passage that merits reproduction, it wrote that digital technologies:

> are reshaping not only our private lives but also our public life and our democracy. People now have a printing press, a broadcast station and a place of assembly in their pockets. This gives them the opportunity to express themselves and challenge ideas in a way that was not possible even a decade ago. This has encroached on existing power structures in increasingly evident ways. Social media allows [sic] people to take part through tiny acts of participation that were never before possible. Previously, taking part in politics was the preserve of an active few who had the resources of time or money to lobby, join a political party or knock on doors during an election. Now more of the public can take part simply by liking a post, following a campaigner or sharing a video of a news item. More people now encounter political debate through social media than would have done so in the past. People who would not have previously engaged in the everyday discussion of democracy are now taking an active part. This increased participation, although it has empowered many, has, paradoxically, shifted power toward a very small group of new gatekeepers; the individuals who determine the ways in which the technology platforms operate. These individuals can, purposefully or not, change whose voice is heard. It has also introduced new opportunities for individuals and organisations with malign intentions to manipulate the flow of political debate.[5]

[3] Ibid., p. 4.
[4] Ibid.
[5] Ibid., p. 9.

The report noted that the 'digital and social media landscape' was 'dominated by two behemoths – Facebook and Google'. These entities were able broadly to 'pass under the radar, operating outside the rules that govern electoral politics'. The problem had become 'acutely obvious in the current COVID-19 pandemic', during which 'online misinformation poses not only a real and present danger to our democracy but also to our lives'. The pattern of a technology being welcomed (as in the 2005 Hansard Society report) then its impact being condemned (as in the 2020 publication) was familiar. More repetition came when the Committee advocated that intervention and new forms of usage could ensure that scientific advance served the interests of society. The report expressed the 'profound belief . . . that this can change. Technology is not a force of nature. Online platforms are not inherently ungovernable. They can and should be bound by the same restraints that we apply to the rest of society.' The Committee hoped that 'technology can become a servant of democracy rather than its enemy'.[6] It sought to explain how to bring about a scenario in which 'digital technology is no longer in danger of undermining democracy but rather where the wonders of technology can support democracy and restore public trust'.[7]

The report advocated a variety of reforms to achieve this end. Underpinning them was the effort to make the use of technology conform to pre-existing constitutional values, as encompassed in the 'Nolan Principles on Public Life'.[8] The government, it held, should press on with proposed 'Online Harms' legislation intended to address these issues,[9] and not allow itself to be dissuaded by lobbying from within the sector. The Committee called for the establishment of an 'ombudsman' charged with protecting users. It advocated transparency regarding the decision-making algorithms employed by those platforms for content moderation purposes, to help avoid problems such as discriminatory outcomes. Firm public regulation was required in this area, the report held. The rationale upon which platforms removed content, it went on, should be clear, in the interests of avoiding arbitrary constraints upon freedom of expression. There was a need, the Committee found, to educate the public in the operation of digital technologies, to provide them with knowledge about the use being made of their personal data, and to supply support for professional journalism of a

[6] Ibid., p. 6.
[7] Ibid., p. 7.
[8] Ibid.
[9] For the White Paper from April 2019, see Secretary of State for Digital, Culture, Media and Sport, *Online Harms White Paper*, CP 57 (HM Government, London, 2019). For its proposed definition of online harms, see pp. 31–2. For the outcome of the consultation on this White Paper from December 2020, see Department for Digital, Culture, Media and Sport and Home Office, *Online Harms White Paper* (HM Government, London, 2020).

high standard. The legal framework for elections, the Committee argued, required an overhaul to take into account internet-based practices.[10]

The idea of involving public institutions in decisions about online material was markedly sensitive, and raised matters that were of first-order importance to democracy. The Committee report contained a discussion that reflected this significance. On a reading of the sections that are most significant in this regard[11] it is possible to identify certain key considerations as follows. Freedom of expression is critical to democracy. The way in which this abstract concept is realised in practical reality is conditioned by various concerns. They include the need to reconcile this right with others (such as the right to physical security) and the particular mechanisms by which communications are transmitted. Just as earlier technologies such as printing and broadcasting had done, the Internet had altered the context in which these basic concepts were perceived and engaged with. Characteristics of the Internet that helped shape debate included the ease with which it allowed a wide range of participants – perhaps anonymously – to communicate, and with immense speed. The potential reach was extensive, yet there was also scope for specific targeting of recipients. These two latter features of the system were supported by algorithms facilitating automated decision-taking. The idea of machines rather than people making choices was itself a source of controversy. Some commentary tended to depict the retention of human control – for instance over who to circulate information to, or whether to supress online content – as more legitimate and a better means of avoiding bad outcomes. The Internet had – therefore – stimulated discussion, from a new perspective, of another perennial and fundamental subject: that of free will and the possibility of its being subordinated to non-human controls (albeit those that were of human genesis).

A further significant feature of the Internet from the point of view of freedom of expression was that the technology appeared simultaneously to be supportive of and a threat to the ability of people to disseminate content of their choice. It provided widespread opportunities to communicate. But it was dominated by a small number of players that could use the same technology that created the potential for participation to impose restrictions. Algorithms were significant in this context, since they could be used for the automated removal of material – potentially before anyone had accessed it – in ways that might appear arbitrary. Both aspects of the Internet – its capacity to facilitate communication and its susceptibility to sophisticated interference by the private interests that dominated it – could be motivations for those who advocated bespoke regulation by public authorities.

10 House of Lords Select Committee on Democracy and Digital Technologies, *Digital Technology and the Resurrection of Trust*, pp. 6–7, 125–80.

11 In particular, ibid., pp. 38–49.

Firm – but not universal – support for such intervetion had emerged by the time the Committee carried out its inquiry. While concerns were aired about the violation of freedom of expression, the report described receiving evidence emphasising the idea that – while this right was important – there was a need to limit it in certain ways. Arguments to this effect presented such approaches as supportive of, rather than detrimental to, democracy. They included the claim that it could protect vital public debate from contamination by manipulation and falsehood. A further point offered in support of regulation was that it could reduce the possibility of intimidation and abuse. Such activity on the Internet, those holding this position noted, had the effect of discouraging some potential participants from taking part in discussion. From this perspective, therefore, constraining freedom of expression for some would promote wider enjoyment of the same right. Proponents of public control might see it as a way of preventing actions that would be illegal were they perpetrated offline and therefore should be proscribed online as well (for instance, threats of or direct incitement to violence). But these advocates also potentially envisaged it as a means of prohibiting behaviour that might fall short of contravening existing law, yet – in their view – required suppression (such as disseminating misleading information, or communications aimed at particular groups intended to denigrate them or discourage them from taking part in discussions). Another aspect of the case for action related to the fact that content moderation already took place, carried out by individual platforms according to their own rules. When engaging in such action, it was noted, there was a tendency for them to do so in opaque and possibly unsatisfactory ways. A single, uniform framework provided by a public authority was in such accounts a means of imposing clarity, fairness, and consistency. It could, from this point of view, uphold freedom of expression against arbitrary interference, as well as protecting against inappropriate use of channels of communication.

Parliament was important to discourse around these subjects in a number of ways. As the inquiry and report demonstrated, it could provide a UK-level and even international public forum in which such discussion might take place. It could advocate courses of action and it might be provided with – and indeed seek – a role in any proposed new arrangements. Taking into account the debate it had facilitated, the Committee made its recommendation for a regulatory body that it described as 'an independent ombudsman for content moderation decisions to whom the public can appeal should they feel they have been let down by a platform's decisions. This ombudsman's decisions should be binding on the platform.'[12] Such appeals could presumably be made on a basis either of a platform taking down material; or refusing to do so when requested to. In this sense both negative and positive control over the dissemination of information was implied. While accepting the case for new forms of

[12] Ibid., p. 46.

regulation, the Committee noted the grounds for unease. It described how '[i]n Singapore, the Government has the ability to remove all online information that it deems to be incorrect and not in the public interest. This power vested in the Government inevitably led to the first uses of the law being to take down posts critical of the Government.' There was a 'need for independence from Government'. The committee presented this case in terms of the imperative of setting a good example for other countries and not providing a justification for bad practice elsewhere, rather than the specific protection of the UK from inappropriate regulation that violated free expression.[13]

The report envisaged a role for Parliament. A committee, without a majority for the government, drawing members from both Houses, would 'ensure transparency and accountability in the work of the regulator and the ombudsman'. It would set the budget of the ombudsman, and hold hearings with the candidate intended for the role of chief executive, whose appointment it could block.[14] While the purpose was to ensure that the regulator remained independent and not subordinated to the interests of the administration of the day, the idea of involving the legislature in such activities – even if motivated by the desire of preventing abuse – was constitutionally and historically delicate.

This report marked the continuation of a trend towards increasingly intense scrutiny of the Internet and its implications, carried out by an expanding range of parliamentary committees over the previous quarter of a century. The enveloping nature of the technology meant that manifestations of it came to the attention of a variety of these bodies in both the House of Commons and House of Lords (and joint committees of both Houses). Yet even as coverage became wider, it eventually tended towards convergence on a single cohesive account of the Internet. When a subject receives parliamentary attention, it is often of a critical nature, perhaps reflecting or encouraging emerging public concerns in a given area. In keeping with this pattern, while parliamentary scrutiny of the Internet noted positive potential, it was also prone to identifying and dwelling upon problems. By 2020, the raising of objections and proposing of solutions to supposed difficulties with the Internet had reached a new level of intensity, congealing around issues that involved the constitution and the democratic system. They involved matters such as human rights, public discourse, and political campaigning. This chapter tracks the development of this discernible parliamentary approach as expressed in reports by parliamentary committees over the timespan in question.

Parliamentary Perceptions of the Internet

During the period from 1996 onwards, as we have seen, there was impetus within Parliament towards the increased employment of the Internet as a

13 Ibid., p. 47.
14 Ibid., pp. 47–8.

means of improving its institutional efficacy. Uses to which it was put included the conduct of its day-to-day internal operations, and engagement with the outside world. In that the Westminster legislature was the principal instrument of representative democracy in the UK, such enhancements were by extension potentially (if they delivered what was hoped of them) beneficial to this overall system of government. Parliamentary investigations have also depicted the Internet as a tool that institutions other than itself might deploy for purposes of democratic improvement. In 2001, in a consideration of means of involving the public in democratic processes beyond simply voting in elections, the House of Commons Public Administration Select Committee (PASC) presented an optimistic but cautious account of the uses to which the Internet might be put. It remarked that '[t]he advent of e-government and the Internet represent important opportunities for extending public participation. Some wholly new forms of participation could open up by offering the possibility of responding to questions at the click of a mouse.'[15] It envisaged '[e]lectronic consultation' as 'much more than a replacement for paper questionnaires', and a means of conducting 'deliberative consultation'.[16] The report found, however, that there were difficulties in hosting meaningful online debates.[17] A gain it suggested might be had from 'electronic methods of participation' was that they could provide 'access to some of the groups who are hard to reach by, or do not respond to, traditional approaches',[18] Yet, the Committee recognised, 'IT is a useful tool for well-organised pressure groups, poised and eager to step into the vacuum left by the decline in traditional political activity. It could therefore actually intensify the exclusion of groups which do not have physical or psychological access to it.'[19]

The Committee concluded that 'new technologies, carefully used, are tools which offer the possibility of greatly improving the accessibility and use made by citizens of public participation opportunities'. Yet 'developing facilities exclusively for those with Internet access at home or work still carries an inherent risk of increasing social exclusion for those without access'. It therefore recommended that 'public agencies ... try and use money saved via e-governance developments to make an even more systematic outreach effort to give information to and solicit the views of groups without ready e-access, and other groups least present in such participation exercises'.[20] The Committee feared that government might fail to employ internet technologies in a way that maximised interaction with the public,

[15] House of Commons Public Administration Select Committee, *Innovations in Citizen Participation in Government*, Sixth Report of Session 2000–01, HC 373–I (Stationery Office, London, 2001), para. 55.
[16] Ibid., para. 62.
[17] Ibid., para. 63.
[18] Ibid., para. 59.
[19] Ibid., para. 60.
[20] Ibid., para. 67.

and it – to some extent – anticipated future issues that would later come to the fore, such as those involving privacy and controversial content.[21] But the main thrust of its findings were that the Internet offered advantages and that it was in the interests of democracy that access should be made as wide as possible to ensure that the benefits were fairly spread. This approach contrasts with attitudes that would subsequently gain currency. Later accounts were more likely to emphasise the idea of computer networks as a potential threat. Mass exposure was unavoidable and irreversible, creating a need for more effective protections. In the former narrative, large-scale take-up was required to achieve good outcomes; in the latter, it was, to some extent, a problem to be managed.

But though counter-narratives developed, such optimistic depictions of the democratic potential of the Internet were sustained into the following decade. In a 2013 publication, *Public Engagement in Policy-Making*, PASC held that 'digital technology has a significant role to play in opening up policy-making'. While '[t]he Government is making progress in its approach' it took the view 'that digital engagement for the purposes of policy-making could go further and embrace radical and innovative approaches which support the genuine and continuing involvement of citizens in policy'. The report concluded that the government should favour the employment of 'existing digital platforms' already in wide use such as Twitter 'to engage with citizens and to avoid "reinventing the wheel" or running costly parallel systems'.[22] The 'existing digital platforms' to which the Committee referred, the employment of which it advocated for the attainment of enhanced political participation, would soon acquire a more problematic reputation.

A regular focus for Parliament in its consideration of the Internet was on the business and economic opportunities it provided. From the late 1990s onwards, the House of Commons Trade and Industry Select Committee took a close interest this area. For instance, it engaged in detailed consideration of government plans to promote online business transactions.[23] In 2000 it reported on *The Post Office and the Future of the Network*. A section towards the end of the report was entitled 'E.commerce'. Considering evidence from Finland, it discussed the possibility that the Post Office (for which Tony Benn had once been responsible, taking an interest in the possible uses it might make of computer networks) could play a part in delivering 'e.purchases' to customers and 'dealing with returns'. Its outlets might provide 'a place to purchase goods over the internet'. The report noted that the latter service could be useful because of the problem of there being people 'unable or

21 Ibid., paras. 64–5.

22 House of Commons Public Administration Select Committee, *Public Engagement in Policy-Making*, Section Report of Session 2013–14, HC 75 (Stationery Office, London, 2013), pp. 24–5.

23 House of Commons Trade and Industry Select Committee, *'Building Confidence in Electronic Commerce': The Government's Proposals*, Seventh Report of Session 1998–99, HC 187 (Stationery Office, London, 1999).

unwilling to use credit cards to pay for internet purchases'.[24] This barrier to online commerce was subsequently to a large extent overcome.

The Committee identified other ways in which possible uses of the Internet might present complications for policymakers. Noting that an online purchasing trial was underway in the South West of England, it insisted that: '[t]he results must be candidly evaluated'. One concern was 'that arrangements between different parts of the Post Office should be seen not to be anti-competitive: the fulfilment of e.commerce transactions is of course a thriving private sector business'. The report concluded that '[w]hile we share the vision of post offices benefiting from the fulfilment of electronic ordering, the details of the commercial arrangements now being made between Post Office Counters, Parcelforce and electronic retailers, and their effect on other private sector fulfilment companies, deserve careful scrutiny by the regulator'.[25]

From the point of view of this Committee, the Internet was broadly an opportunity to be capitalised upon, in accordance with a defined set of regulatory priorities. In 2004, for example, it focused on the importance of making broadband connections to the Internet available throughout the UK, with competitive terms on offer to the public.[26] Central items of interest in this earlier period were how to enable people to use the Internet, and whether they would become willing to share personal information when doing so. Later, contrasting concerns would come to the fore. Once people were online, for instance, what might they do and what might they be exposed to? Would data be extracted from them on a basis they did not properly understand, and would it be put to inappropriate uses? Following its brief, the Committee was commerce-focused. Nonetheless, it also encouraged awareness of a wider context. As it stated in 2001, '[a]lmost any walk of life or aspect of Government, central or local, seems to have an e-aspect and to require an e-strategy. Many of the issues cross departmental boundaries.'[27] The Committee judged that a large portion of these matters fell outside of its remit, and proposed that other bodies give attention to them: a recognition of the need for wide-ranging attention to the Internet, that would in time come into being.

Parliamentary work on the subject of the Internet and business continued, as the use of the technology grew. A series of committee reports published in 2016 addressed the commercial aspects. The House of Commons Business, Innovation and Skills Committee presented '[t]he digital economy in the

[24] House of Commons Trade and Industry Select Committee, *The Post Office and the Future of the Network*, Thirteenth Report of Session 1999–2000, HC 724 (Stationery Office, London, 2000), para. 58.

[25] Ibid., para. 62.

[26] House of Commons Trade and Industry Committee, Second Report of Session 2003–04, HC 321–I, *UK Broadband Market*, vol. I (Stationery Office, London, 2004).

[27] House of Commons Trade and Industry Committee, *UK Online Reviewed: The First Annual Report of the e-Minister and e-Envoy Report*, Eighth Report of Session 2000–01 (Stationery Office, London, 2002), para. 3.

United Kingdom' as 'a success story'. It went on in celebratory tone to describe how 'the British economy has the highest percentage of gross domestic product attributed to the digital economy of all European nations; UK digital industries grew two and a half times as fast as the economy as a whole between 2003 and 2013; and the United Kingdom has the highest percentage of individual internet usage of any G7 economy'.[28] The same year, the House of Commons Culture, Media and Sport Committee, with similarly high regard for the economic benefits of the Internet, stressed the need to maximise access to it. The Committee described how: '[c]ompared to other countries the UK's digital economy has been extremely successful'. But it noted that 'over the last few years a key concern has been a growing digital divide between those who have good access to communication services and those who do not'. Once, the digital divide concept had referred to the cleavage between those who were and were not in possession of access. Now – reflecting the extent of permeation of the technology – it applied to the quality, not the possession or otherwise, of access. The Committee warned that '[a]ffordability and accessibility particularly affect low-income households and those living in areas of relative deprivation; over time these sections of society may be further marginalised'.[29] The Committee favoured measures to ensure that 'the full benefits of digital connectivity can be extended to all, regardless of location, across the UK.'[30]

Also in 2016, the House of Commons Science and Technology Committee advanced a further variant on the 'digital divide' concept, using it to denote proficiency of individuals in utilising the network. Emphasising the importance of '[d]igital skills' to the UK economy, the Committee regretted the existence of 'a digital divide where up to 12.6 million of the adult UK population lack basic digital skills'. The Committee also reminded the reader that the older conception of a digital divide – between users and non-users – retained relevance. It noted that '[a]n estimated 5.8 million people have never used the internet at all'. The Committee cautioned: '[t]his digital skills gap is costing the UK economy an estimated £63 billion a year in lost additional GDP'.[31]

In the same year, the Committee proclaimed that: '[w]e are living in the data age. Since Sir Tim Berners-Lee ... inadvertently launched the information revolution – the amount of data we share has exploded.' The Committee observed that '90% of the data currently in the world was created in the last two years'. Furthermore, '[t]he total amount of global data is predicted to grow

[28] House of Commons Business, Innovation and Skills Committee, *The Digital Economy*, Second Report of Session 2016–17, HC 87 (House of Commons, London, 2016), p. 3.

[29] House of Commons Culture, Media and Sport Committee, *Establishing World-Class Connectivity throughout the UK*, Second Report of Session 2016–17, HC 147 (House of Commons, London, 2016), p. 7.

[30] Ibid., p. 3.

[31] House of Commons Science and Technology Committee, *Digital Skills Crisis*, Second Report of Session 2016–17, HC 270 (House of Commons, London, 2016), p. 3.

40% year on year for the next decade'. If '[p]roperly exploited, this data should be transformative, increasing efficiency, unlocking new avenues in life-saving research and creating as yet unimagined opportunities for innovation'. But business was not yet making close to full use of this asset. As the Committee put it, '[t]he stakes for the UK economy are massive. Big data is already a UK success story but it has huge unrealised potential, both as a driver of productivity and as a way of offering better products and services to citizens.' The Committee recognised that, because of 'the scale and pace of data gathering', there were legitimate concerns about 'privacy and security'. However, it noted that '[p]-ersonal data is only a small proportion of big data, with huge potential from non-personal datasets for transport and weather forecasting, for example'.[32]

The House of Lords European Union Committee was another committee participating in the 2016 trend towards emphasising the commercial prospects of the Internet. In a report entitled *Online Platforms and the Digital Single Market*, it discussed the role of the '[o]nline platforms' of the title. Composed of 'a wide range of software-based technologies, from search engines and social networks to price comparison websites and collaborative economy platforms' they were 'drivers of growth, innovation and competition'. The Committee held that '[t]hey enable businesses and consumers to make the most of the opportunities created by the digital economy. Supported by the emergence of mobile devices and pervasive wireless connectivity, online platforms have transformed how we live, interact and transact.'[33] This passage read almost like paid-for promotional material (though the report went on to describe certain challenges to be faced). But events during the course of this year contributed to a deterioration in the standing of the technology it described. The European Union Committee report appeared on 20 April 2016. A little over two months later, the European Union (EU) referendum of 23 June 2016 produced a 'leave' result. This event cast doubt over future UK participation in the European Single Market which the Committee had assessed from the point of view of digital technology. Moreover, online campaigning activities in the lead-up to the vote themselves became a subject of controversy. Allegations about bad practice – emerging in part from parliamentary investigations – helped bring the Internet as a whole, and social media in particular, increasingly into disrepute.

Apprehensions

Concerns about possible downsides and misuse were already established. In 2008 (and again in 2012), the House of Lords Select Committee on

[32] House of Commons Science and Technology Committee, *The Big Data Dilemma*, Fourth Report of Session 2015–16, HC 468 (Stationery Office, London, 2016), pp. 3–4.

[33] House of Lords Select Committee on the European Union, *Online Platforms and the Digital Single Market*, Tenth Report of Session 2015–16, HL Paper 129 (House of Lords, London, 2016), p. 4.

Communications expressed concern about the impact of the Internet on the finances of news provision, leading to a reduction in the resources available for quality journalism. A decline of this type implied a diminution in the potential for scrutiny of those in positions of authority, a problem from the point of view of democracy. The Committee wrote that 'the traditional media are under very considerable competitive pressure. Newspapers, television and radio are losing advertising revenue to the internet, with the result that costs are being cut and economies are being made in traditional news gathering.'[34]

Another perceived problem involved the potential for intrusion into personal privacy. In an earlier era, digital data storage had generated concern of this type. By the end of the first decade of the twenty-first century, Parliament had shown revived interest in this area. In 2009 the House of Lords Select Committee on the Constitution published a report entitled *Surveillance: Citizens and the State*. It presented the Internet as one of a number of means by which people might be observed. Noting that 'Surveillance is an inescapable part of life in the UK', it went on to remark that '[e]very time we make a telephone call, send an email, browse the internet, or even walk down our local high street, our actions may be monitored and recorded'. The first source of such practices it identified was the public sector. The Committee described how '[t]o respond to crime, combat the threat of terrorism, and improve administrative efficiency, successive UK governments have gradually constructed one of the most extensive and technologically advanced surveillance systems in the world'. But it also noted that '[a]t the same time, similar developments in the private sector have contributed to a profound change in the character of life in this country'. The Committee depicted '[t]he development of electronic surveillance and the collection and processing of personal information' as having 'become pervasive, routine, and almost taken for granted'. It concluded that '[m]any of these surveillance practices are unknown to most people, and their potential consequences are not fully appreciated'.[35] The report detected cause for concern in these tendencies. In keeping with its constitutional brief, the Committee identified a 'a danger that the growing use of surveillance by government and private organisations in the UK could constitute a serious threat' to such principles as 'the freedom of the individual ... privacy and the principle of restraint in the use of surveillance and data collection powers'.[36]

Apprehension of this type persisted. The Intelligence and Security Committee of Parliament took a close interest in this area in the wake of the Edward Snowden revelations of 2013. Making the familiar observation about

[34] House of Lords Select Committee on Communications, *The Future of Investigative Journalism*, Third Report of Session 2010–12, HL Paper 256 (Stationery Office, London, 2012), p. 10.

[35] House of Lords Select Committee on the Constitution, *Surveillance: Citizens and the State*, vol. I: *Report*, Second Report of Session 2008–09, HL 18–I (Stationery Office, London, 2009), p. 5.

[36] Ibid., p. 9.

some kind of substantial transition having taken place, in a 2015 report, the Committee remarked that '[t]he way we all communicate has changed dramatically in the last 25 years'. Notably, 'the internet as a means of communication has had a significant impact on how we conduct our day-to-day lives'. A person could 'send an email while sitting on their train on the way to work, message friends on WhatsApp throughout the day and have a video chat in the evening with relatives who live hundreds of miles away'.[37] Intense debate had developed about what was an appropriate level of surveillance of such online activity for purposes of security and intelligence. The Committee discerned a conflict between two principles: on the one hand, 'the individual's right to privacy' and, on the other hand, 'our collective right to security'.[38] With these issues in mind, it undertook a broad overview of 'intrusive capabilities' and their use in the UK.[39]

A particular focus was on 'bulk interception'. The report found that 'the Agencies do not have the legal authority, the resources, the technical capability, or the desire to intercept every communication of British citizens, or of the internet as a whole'. It insisted that 'GCHQ are not reading the emails of everyone in the UK.' The Committee was also generally 'satisfied that the UK's intelligence and security Agencies do not seek to circumvent the law'. However, it took issue with the existing 'legal framework' on the grounds that it had 'developed piecemeal, and is unnecessarily complicated'. The Committee had 'serious concerns about the resulting lack of transparency, which is not in the public interest'. It therefore called for 'the current legal framework' to 'be replaced by a new Act of Parliament governing the intelligence and security Agencies'. It should 'clearly set out the intrusive powers available to the Agencies, the purposes for which they may use them, and the authorisation required before they may do so'.[40]

As well as involving public agencies, concerns about the violation of personal privacy had a commercial sector aspect. In 2014, the House of Commons Science and Technology Committee discussed social media as a source of 'big data' of which both government and private sector entities could make extensive use, analysing patterns of behaviour to inform their actions. While it saw immense potential benefits for society, the Committee drew attention to 'the tension that exists between the generation of data by individuals and the use of that data by organisations'. The Committee was 'not . . . convinced that the users of social media platforms are fully aware of how their data might be used and what redress they may, or may not have if they disagree with how an organisation exploits that data'. Moreover, 'terms and conditions contracts are

[37] Intelligence and Security Committee of Parliament, *Privacy and Security: A Modern and Transparent Legal Framework*, HC 1075 (House of Commons, London, 2015), p. 9.
[38] Ibid., p. 10.
[39] Ibid., p. 11.
[40] Ibid., p. 2.

simply too long and complex for any reasonable person to make any real sense of'. The Committee held that '[a]s a mechanism for showing that users have provided informed consent, so that organisations can process incredibly personal data, terms and conditions contracts are simply not fit for purpose'. The Committee detected willingness among the commercial entities involved to establish better practice. Nonetheless, this report represented the appearance of the tendency to identify a group of highly profitable corporations – in this instance, it named Facebook, Twitter, and LinkedIn – as collectively associated with undesirable outcomes. Parliament – and numerous commentators around the world – would increasingly come to cast such platforms in malign terms.[41]

The consent issue proved persistent. In 2019, the Joint Committee on Human Rights – in a report the title of which contained the phrase 'the Digital Revolution' – wrote that '[m]uch of what we are able to use on the internet is free because, from social media platforms to search engines, a business model has evolved in which companies make money from selling advertising opportunities to other companies rather than charging individuals to use the service'. Consequently 'having access to our data' was 'an extremely valuable commodity'. The Committee drew a distinction between 'advertising in a newspaper or on a bus stop' and 'internet content', which could 'be personalised (meaning different people using the same website can be shown different advertisements)'. Commercial entities therefore wanted 'as much information about us as possible, so that they can effectively target their advertising and maximise their revenue'. Largely, the 'legal basis' on which they obtained it was that of 'consent', when 'we click a box when we sign up for a service, to say we accept how our data will be used'. The Committee judged that 'the consent model is broken', and that often it was not being provided in a meaningful sense, because of the complexities involved. Children, it found, were particularly vulnerable. Therefore, the report argued, '[t]he bogus reliance on "consent" is in clear conflict with our right to privacy'.[42]

The idea that the Internet created potential threats to children was an already-established theme in parliamentary consideration. Such unease encouraged the assertion of a recurring attitude towards technology dating back over centuries: that it was both beneficial and a source of danger, and that public intervention was required to eliminate undesirable applications. In 2014 the House of Commons Culture, Media and Sport Committee captured this view. It held that '[t]he internet has revolutionised communications and

[41] House of Commons Science and Technology Committee, *Responsible Use of Data*, Fourth Report of Session 2014–15, HC 245 (Stationery Office, London, 2014), p. 3.

[42] House of Commons/House of Lords Joint Committee on Human Rights, *The Right to Privacy (Article 8) and the Digital Revolution*, Third Report of Session 2019, HC 122/HL Paper 14 (House of Commons and House of Lords, London, 2019), pp. 3–4.

information sharing'. This system had, the Committee held, provided 'an ever increasingly important platform for creativity and economic growth'. It allowed, via 'social media' for 'new ways of interacting and keeping in touch'. While these 'expressions of human behaviour' could be 'positive' they might also be 'negative' and in some cases 'downright criminal'. The Committee on this occasion focused on 'three disparate aspects of online content and behaviour, all of which are of widespread concern'. They were: 'illegal content, especially images of child abuse; harmful adult content being made freely available to children; bullying and harassment on social media'. It discussed various measures – including action by police, by the regulator, Ofcom, and by the platforms – that could help tackle these problems. The Committee was, however, 'anxious to avoid suggesting a significant extension of formal content regulation of the internet'. It cautioned that '[a]mong the unintended consequences this could have would be a stifling of the free flow of ideas that lies at the heart of internet communication'.[43] Later in the decade, such inhibitions appeared to weaken. Parliamentary opinion seemed to shift in the direction of more active intervention in the substance of online material – perhaps even involving public institutions, including Parliament itself – notwithstanding concerns about the impact upon freedom of expression.

Child protection stayed on the agenda. In 2017 the House of Lords Select Committee on Communications had discussed the 'well documented public concern about risks to children from the internet such as easy access to inappropriate content, loss of privacy, commercial exploitation and cyberbullying'. It made proposals 'for sustained leadership from the Government at the highest level, an ambitious programme of digital literacy, minimum standards for those providing internet services and content ... and a commitment to child-centred design'. The Committee argued 'that children must be treated online with the same rights, respect and care that has been established through regulation in offline settings such as television and gambling'.[44]

Further awareness of possible negatives associated with the Internet involved its use for deliberate law breaking. In 2013, the House of Commons Home Affairs Committee issued a report, *e-Crime*, on the subject. It proclaimed that '[w]e live in a world where terms like "Cyber crime" no longer belong in the realm of science fiction'. Technologies 'such as smart phones and tablets have brought the internet not only to our fingertips but to our bedsides, our pockets and to our children'. Notwithstanding the 'opportunities and benefits' associated with this development, it could 'put our businesses and our families at increasing risk of exploitation and internet-based crime (E-crime)'. The report listed a series of misdeeds: '[i]dentity theft, industrial

[43] House of Commons Culture, Media and Sport Committee, *Online Safety*, Sixth Report of Session 2013–14, HC 729 (Stationery Office, London, 2014), pp. 3–4.

[44] House of Lords Select Committee on Communications, *Growing Up with the Internet*, Second Report of Session 2016–17, HL Paper 130 (House of Lords, London, 2017), p. 3.

espionage, credit card fraud, phishing, child exploitation'. The perpetrators 'range from lone hackers, activist groups, Nation States sponsoring industrial espionage and organised criminal gangs'. On the receiving end '[v]ictims include individuals who fall prey to scams and password theft to multinational companies'.[45]

The following year, the House of Lords Select Committee on Communications published a report entitled *Social Media and Criminal Offences*. The Committee conveyed the speed with which the usage of 'social media', a 'new invention', had expanded. It noted that the leading players in the field – Facebook and Twitter – were formed respectively in 2004 and 2006. While they were 'new' they were also 'big', with 1.2 billion frequent users of Facebook worldwide, of whom 34 million were in the UK; '255 million regularly use Twitter, 15 million of them in the UK'. Various 'other social media forums, based all over the globe' operated, covering interests 'from flower arranging to sadomasochism'. Their shared objective was to facilitate 'social networking' or 'connectivity', making it possible for 'people to express themselves and interact using the internet'.[46]

The bulk of users of this form of communication, the report found, did so in a responsible way. However, a small group was 'spoiling it for everyone else'. The Committee identified a series of problematic activities, which were:

(a) cyber bullying – bullying conducted using the social media or other electronic means;
(b) revenge porn – usually following the breakup of a couple, the electronic publication or distribution of sexually explicit material (principally images) of one or both of the couple, the material having originally been provided consensually for private use;
(c) trolling – intentional disruption of an online forum, by causing offence or starting an argument; and
(d) virtual mobbing – whereby a number of individuals use social media or messaging to make comments to or about another individual, usually because they are opposed to that person's opinions.[47]

The Committee judged that alongside such 'apparently modern offences' it was possible to use 'social media' to commit more conventional 'offences … using words or images … for example threatening violence to the person'.[48] But while identifying novel technologically facilitated misdeeds, it judged that the existing legal framework was sufficient. The report found 'that the criminal law in this area, almost entirely enacted before the invention of social media, is generally appropriate for the prosecution of offences committed using the

[45] House of Commons Home Affairs Committee, *e-Crime*, Fifth Report of Session 2013–14, HC 70 (Stationery Office, London, 2013), p. 3.

[46] House of Lords Select Committee on Communication, *Social Media and Criminal Offences*, First Report of Session 2013–14, HL 37 (Stationery Office, London, 2014), p. 7.

[47] Ibid.

[48] Ibid.

social media'.[49] There might be a need for alteration to certain 'aspects of the current statute law' and the filling of particular 'gaps'. But the Committee rejected the idea 'that it is necessary to create a new set of offences specifically for acts committed using the social media and other information technology'.[50] The Committee stressed the importance of freedom of expression,[51] and insisted that 'what is not an offence off-line should not be an offence online'.[52] Again, these were attitudes that subsequent parliamentary outputs suggested a movement away from. While not necessarily advocating the creation of new offences, they did come to argue that legislative action was required to deal with various behaviours, some of which were not in contravention of the existing law.

Online crime of various forms continued to attract parliamentary interest. In 2016 the House of Commons Culture, Media and Sport Committee investigated the subject of data breaches, such as 'the TalkTalk cyber-attack in October 2015'.[53] Then in 2019 the House of Commons Committee of Public Accounts found that '[o]nline fraud is now the most prevalent crime in England and Wales, impacting victims not only financially but also causing untold distress to those affected'. It placed '[t]he cost of the crime' at around '£10 billion' over the previous year, involving about '2 million cyber-related fraud incidents'. Yet 'the true extent of the problem remains unknown'. Only around one-fifth of such 'fraud is actually reported to police, with the emotional impact of the crime leaving many victims reluctant to come forward'. Furthermore, the problem was 'growing rapidly and shows no signs of slowing down'. The Committee concluded there was a necessity for '[u]rgent action from government'. However, 'the Home Office's response has been too slow'. Moreover, 'the banks are unwilling to share information about the extent of fraud with customers'.[54]

A particularly problematic activity associated with the use of networked computers engaged the interest of law enforcement and security and intelligence agencies. In another 2016 output, the House of Commons Home Affairs Committee described '[t]he use of the internet to promote radicalisation and terrorism' as 'one of the greatest threats that countries including the UK face'. It proclaimed that '[w]e need to win the cyber-war with terrorist and extremist organisations'. To this end the Committee proposed that the Metropolitan Police Counter Terrorism Internet Referral Unit be 'upgraded into a high-tech,

[49] Ibid., p. 6.
[50] Ibid., p. 9.
[51] Ibid., p. 10.
[52] Ibid., p. 12.
[53] House of Commons Culture, Media and Sport Committee, *Cyber Security: Protection of Personal Data Online*, First Report of Session 2016–17, HC 148 (House of Commons, London, 2016), p. 3.
[54] House of Commons Committee of Public Accounts, *The Growing Threat of Online Fraud*, Sixth Report of Session 2017–19, HC 399 (House of Commons, London, 2017), p. 3.

state-of-the-art round-the-clock central Operational Hub which locates the perils early, moves quickly to block them and is able to instantly share the sensitive information with other security agencies'.[55] The Committee remarked that '[n]etworks like Facebook, Twitter and YouTube are the vehicle of choice in spreading propaganda and they have become the recruiting platforms for terrorism'. It found the response of these companies wanting. They were 'consciously failing to combat the use of their sites to promote terrorism and killings'. It insisted that '[t]hey ... accept that the hundreds of millions in revenues generated from billions of people using their products needs to be accompanied by a greater sense of responsibility and ownership for the impact that extremist material on their sites is having'. The principle it asserted was that 'what cannot appear legally in the print or broadcast media, namely inciting hatred and terrorism, should not be allowed to appear on social media'.[56] This report sought to exercise on behalf of Parliament the role of promoter of social obligation. Rather than changing regulations as such, it advocated those that existed being properly upheld, including by major financial interests. In this sense, the Committee engaged with the rule of law.

The following year, the Commons Home Affairs Committee reported on *Hate Crime: Abuse Hatred and Extremism Online*. In this publication, it is possible to detect a significant shift, beyond simply insisting that platforms uphold existing law. It proposed new legislation that would not only clarify the position, but that seemingly might also cover activities not previously specifically prohibited. While the early General Election of 2017 had cut short the inquiry, the Committee had gathered sufficient evidence to enable it to reach the conclusion that the government should 'review the entire legislative framework governing online hate speech, harassment and extremism and ensure that the law is up to date'. The report presented it as 'essential that the principles of free speech and open public debate in democracy are maintained'. However, it also held that 'protecting democracy ... means ensuring that some voices are not drowned out by harassment and persecution, by the promotion of violence against particular groups, or by terrorism and extremism'.[57] An online campaigning technique – the e-petition – helped draw attention in 2019 to a particular variety of appalling internet-based behaviour. Responding to a petition instigated by the celebrity, Katie Price (receiving nearly a quarter of a million signatories in a shorter-than-normal open period), the House of Commons Petitions Committee discussed 'the extreme level of abuse that disabled people receive online – not just on social media, but in online games, web forums, newspaper comments sections and

[55] House of Commons Home Affairs Committee, *Radicalisation: The Counter-Narrative and Identifying the Tipping Point*, Eighth Report of Session 2016–17, HC 135 (House of Commons, London, 2016), p. 11.

[56] Ibid., pp. 13–14.

[57] House of Commons Home Affairs Committee, *Hate Crime: Abuse Hatred and Extremism Online*, Fourth Report of Session 2016–17, HC 609 (House of Commons, London, 2017), p. 19.

elsewhere'. The Committee found it 'shameful that disabled people have had to leave social media whilst their abusers continue unchecked. Self-regulation of social media has failed disabled people.' It concurred 'with Katie Price's petition that the law on online abuse is not fit for purpose ... People should not have to avoid their town centre, local park or place of work to avoid sustained abuse, mockery and threats. Online spaces are just as important in the modern world and should be treated as such.'[58]

The growing reliance of society in the UK and internationally upon the Internet brought with it perceptions of vulnerability. The House of Lords European Union Committee published *Protecting Europe against Large-Scale Cyber-Attacks* in March 2010. It remarked that '[t]here is now scarcely any activity of our daily lives which does not rely on the Internet'. Uses included '[b]anking, travel and tax, trading, saving and dating'. As the Committee put it 'everything is increasingly performed online and so depends on the Internet'. It went on to remark that 'while any country can survive without online shopping, to be deprived for any length of time of online communication for government, energy or defence, to give only some examples, can rapidly bring a country to its knees'. It cited an occurrence in April and May 2007, when Estonia was a target for such disruption, the sources of which seemed to be Russian, but not necessarily the government of this state itself. The report also discussed the approach of the Chinese authorities in this regard.[59] Parliamentary interest in security-related aspects of the Internet continued.[60] In 2018 the House of Lords/House of Commons Joint Committee on the National Security Strategy registered concern 'that although the UK has one of the most vibrant digital economies in the world, there is not currently the cyber security skills base to match, with both the Government and private sector affected by the shortage in skills'.[61]

As already shown, reflecting the concerns of the agencies it oversaw, the Internet came to form a prominent part of the work of the Intelligence and Security Committee of Parliament. One context for its work was considering the possibility of an excess of action, amounting to inappropriate intrusion. But potential failure to act could also be an issue. In 2020, it published a report on the subject of Russia. Some of its content, discussed below, was uncomfortable from the point of view of the government, leading members of which were prominent within the 'leave' campaign in the 2016 European Union

[58] House of Commons Petitions Committee, *Online Abuse and the Experience of Disabled People*, First Report of Session 2017–19, HC 759 (House of Commons, London, 2019), p. 3.

[59] House of Lords European Union Committee, *Protecting Europe against Large-Scale Cyber-Attacks*, Fifth Report of Session 2009–10, HL 68 (Stationery Office, London, 2014), pp. 9–11.

[60] See e.g. House of Commons Defence Committee, *Re-Thinking Defence to Meet New Threats*, Tenth Report of Session 2014–15, HC 512 (Stationery Office, London, 2015), pp. 32–3.

[61] House of Lords/House of Commons Joint Committee on the National Security Strategy, *Cyber Security Skills and the UK's Critical National Security Infrastructure*, Second Report of Session 2017–19, HL Paper 172/HC 706 (House of Lords/House of Commons, London, 2018), p. 3.

referendum. The report was ready for publication in advance of the General Election of December 2019. But the administration appears to have contrived to stall its appearance until after the poll (which it won by a safe margin). Publication did not take place until July 2020. This delay was controversial and led to much criticism of the government, also stimulating further interest in the report itself.[62]

The Committee found that 'Russia seems to see foreign policy as a zero-sum game: any actions it can take which damage the West are fundamentally good for Russia.' The UK, it held, was a principal target for such action.[63] Use of the Internet, the report noted, was an important part of the Russian repertoire. It employed 'bots' and 'trolls' to promulgate messages 'on social media', and a 'hack and leak' approach, obtaining and then placing in the public domain inconvenient information at a time intended to influence voters in countries including the United States and France.[64] The UK, the Committee found, was subject to 'Russia's disinformation campaigns and political influence operations'.[65]

In particular, the report considered the 'widespread public allegations that Russia sought to influence the 2016 referendum on the UK's membership of the EU'. It did not seek to establish what difference such supposed interference might have made to the outcome of the vote. But it held that it was nonetheless 'important to establish whether a hostile state took deliberate action with the aim of influencing a UK democratic process, irrespective of whether it was successful or not'.[66] The methods it was alleged that Russia had employed included online messaging. The Committee therefore 'sought to establish whether there is secret intelligence which supported or built on' research that suggested such activity. The internal agency, MI5, 'initially provided just six lines of text'. The Committee judged that this 'brevity'[67] was 'indicative of the extreme caution amongst the intelligence and security Agencies at the thought that they might have any role in relation to the UK's democratic processes, and particularly one as contentious as the EU referendum'. Such an outlook was, the report concluded 'illogical; this is about the protection of the process and mechanism from hostile state interference, which should fall to our intelligence and security Agencies'.[68] The Committee had identified what it regarded as a gap in protective coverage in a critical area.

[62] BBC News, 'Russia Report: UK "Badly Underestimated" Threat, Says Committee', 21 July 2020, available at: www.bbc.co.uk/news/uk-politics-53484344, last accessed 12 September 2020.
[63] Intelligence and Security Committee of Parliament, *Russia*, HC 632 (House of Commons, London, 2020), p. 1.
[64] Ibid., p. 9.
[65] Ibid., p. 10.
[66] Ibid., p. 12.
[67] Ibid.
[68] Ibid., p. 13.

Gathering Criticism and Calls for Regulation

By this time, the raising of concern had become more frequent, involving a larger number of committees and wider range of issues. Furthermore, where there had once been a more discrete range of reservations, a single interlinked narrative of pathology had begun to emerge. In 2019, the Joint Committee on Human Rights captured the mood of entwined problems. It noted that '[m]ost of us use the internet every day. We use it for work, to learn, to shop, to socialise, to watch films and listen to music, and to access vital services like banking and welfare benefits'. The Committee recognised that this technology had 'the potential to enhance our human rights. It can support freedom of expression, the right to education, freedom of association and participation in elections.' But while there were 'benefits ... we are all too aware of the potential for harm'. They included 'threats and abuse directed at MPs on social media' and 'the danger posed by the graphic content relating to suicide and self-harm'. A further source of concern was 'the relatively easy access ... children have to online pornography'. Furthermore, '[o]nline misinformation campaigns aimed at influencing elections' had prompted 'inquiries across the globe'. The particular subjects the Committee was interested in on this occasion were 'the risk to our right to privacy, and the risk of discrimination, which arises from how companies collect and use our data online'.[69]

In a September 2019 report, the House of Commons Digital, Culture, Media and Sport Committee sought to emphasise that problems associated with the Internet extended beyond social media, that were attracting much attention at the time. It encouraged consideration of the impact of 'immersive technologies including games and virtual reality'. The Committee dealt with the familiar idea of a 'digital world'. The text suggested that people were able to 'immerse' themselves within it, through 'the power of everyday digital platforms, including games and social media'. This absorption took place 'sometimes at the expense of other priorities'. It could be connected to 'psychosocial and financial harms', and the World Health Organisation had designated the existence of 'gaming disorder'. This report suggested an approach to the Internet that treated it as a commercial enterprise in need of regulation for purposes of public welfare. In this sense it appeared in a similar light to longer-established activities such as gambling or the sale of alcohol. When presenting its findings, the Committee demonstrated once again the importance that speculative fiction could have upon the shaping of perceptions of technology and its implications. It recounted that:

> The film director Steven Spielberg made VR [virtual reality] a central feature of his 2018 film 'Ready Player One' [based on a 2011 novel of the same name by Ernest Cline], set in a dystopian future where people spend more time in a

[69] House of Commons/House of Lords Joint Committee on Human Rights, *The Right to Privacy (Article 8) and the Digital Revolution*, p. 3.

> virtual world than the real one. He said of this project, 'I think in the future VR is going to be the super drug. The message of the film is simply, it's your choice. Where do you want to spend the majority of your time? Do you want to spend it with real people in a real world, which is often harder than spending it in a virtual world where you can be the person you always wanted to be.'[70]

Optimism about internet-related technology remained possible, particularly among committees with a specifically scientific brief, rather than those more focused on constitutional, political, or cultural issues. In 2018, the House of Lords Select Committee on Artificial Intelligence, which noted the significant relationship between the technology on which it was focused and the Internet, presented the subject of its inquiry as creating immense opportunities to be grasped.[71] Artificial Intelligence and the science of automated decision-making on the basis of algorithms[72] were among a number of areas of scientific interest for Parliament, the operation of which was closely related to that of networked computing, which also included autonomous vehicles.[73] In July 2019, the House of Commons Science and Technology Committee considered the Government Digital Service, formed in 2011, and the strategy it pursued. The Committee found that past performance had been strong. But it detected signs of a loss of momentum, and urged the executive to renew its impetus and continue to innovate in this field. At a time of considerable concern about the use of such technologies, it held that 'the Government might be taking an overly-cautious approach' to the handling of data.[74]

But the overall tone had changed. In 2018, the House of Lords Select Committee on International Relations went as far as to depict the Internet as an underlying source of growing global instability. It wrote that 'the international scene is in a state of turmoil and upheaval'. Key aspects of this tendency were:

> new centres of world power and influence, increased populist and nationalist pressures, far-reaching networks of crime and terror, new and empowered networks of political dissent and assertions of identity, extreme polarisation of political viewpoints, the rise of non-state actors and movements, the disruption,

[70] House of Commons Digital, Culture, Media and Sport Committee, Fifteenth Report of Session 2017–19, HC 1846 (House of Commons, London, 2019), pp. 3–4. Other Spielberg work includes an adaptation of H. G. Wells, the 2005 film *War of the Worlds.*

[71] House of Lords Select Committee on Artificial Intelligence, *AI in the UK: Ready Willing and Able?*, Report of Session 2017–19, HL 100 (House of Lords, London, 2018). See also House of Commons Science and Technology Committee, *Robotics and Artificial Intelligence*, Fifth Report of Session 2016–17, HC 145 (House of Commons, London, 2016).

[72] House of Commons Science and Technology Committee, Fourth Report of Session 2017–19, HC 351 (House of Commons, London, 2018).

[73] House of Lords Science and Technology Committee, *Connected and Autonomous Vehicles: The Future?*, Second Report of Session 2016–17, HL 115 (House of Lords, London, 2017).

[74] House of Commons Science and Technology Committee, *Digital Government*, Eighteenth Report of Session 2017–19, HC 1455 (House of Commons, London, 2019), p. 29.

> and in some cases destruction of established industries, the distortion and corruption of news and views on a worldwide scale, and mass movements of migrants and refugees.

Discussing 'the root causes of this radical transformation', the Committee found that there were a variety of possible sources. Nonetheless it was 'clear that the influence of the ongoing digital revolution and the accompanying global connectivity on an unprecedented scale, affecting every sphere of modern existence, plays a central role in this turbulent scene'.[75]

A particular set of concerns involved the use of the Internet for political campaigning.[76] For example, in its April 2018 report, *The Politics of Polling*, the House of Lords Select Committee on Political Polling and Digital Media found that '[t]he evidence received' during its investigations 'on the use of social media to influence political debate adversely was deeply concerning'. It was particularly vexed about 'the spread of misinformation and the manipulation of political information on social media platforms'.[77] Suspicions and accusations about activities in the lead-up to the EU referendum (and claims connected to the Trump ascendancy[78]) – noted, for instance, in the Intelligence and Security Committee of Parliament report that finally appeared in 2020 – were an influential factor in this shift. Attitudes towards the technology were not solely determined by positions taken over the substantive issue of EU membership. But it is possible to discern the following pattern. An exercise in direct democracy – for which Parliament itself had legislated – had produced a result which a majority in each House, including the bulk of Conservative parliamentarians, had opposed. Not only was the policy objectionable to many MPs and Peers, but the way in which the decision was taken seemed to present a challenge to established conceptions of representative democracy, and the centrality of Parliament within it.[79] Doubts developed about online campaigning techniques used in 2016 – especially on the 'leave' side – and their properness. One subject of scrutiny involved the substance of issues raised – for instance, the focus by Leave.EU on inward migration.[80] Others included the acquisition and handling of data relating to personal

[75] House of Lords Select Committee on International Relations, *UK Foreign Policy in a Shifting World Order*, Fifth Report of Session 2017–19, HL Paper 250 (House of Lords, London, 2018), p. 5.

[76] House of Commons Public Administration and Constitutional Affairs Committee, *Electoral Law: The Urgent Need for Review*, First Report of Session 2019, HC 244 (House of Commons, London, 2019), pp. 14–15.

[77] House of Lords Select Committee on Political Polling and Digital Media, *The Politics of Polling*, Report of Session 2017–19, HL Paper 106 (House of Lords, London, 2018), pp. 82–3.

[78] Ibid., p. 9.

[79] See e.g. Andrew Blick, *Stretching the Constitution: The Brexit Shock in Historic Perspective* (Bloomsbury/Hart, Oxford, 2019).

[80] House of Commons Digital, Culture, Media and Sport Committee, *Disinformation and 'Fake News': Final Report*, Eighth Report of Session 2017–19, HC 1791 (House of Commons, London, 2019), p. 43.

details of voters by organisations connected to the 'leave' campaign.[81] For some – including people in Parliament across different parties – the Internet was connected to a problematic, divisive, and perhaps 'populist' tendency in politics and society, discussed in Chapter 1 and touched upon in various committee reports considered in this chapter. Parliament began to subject such online activities to close, critical scrutiny, in the process uncovering more evidence and stimulating further suspicion.

As concern grew within Parliament (and beyond) about the democratic implications of the Internet, the idea of regulation as a means of remedying perceived problems moved towards the forefront. The House of Lords Select Committee on Political Polling and Digital Media noted concerns about the negative impact of online campaigning in its April 2018 report. It stated: '[w]e appreciate the complexities of considering a regulatory solution to these issues. We are, however, acutely aware of the urgency of the situation, as many witnesses highlighted that governments, regulators and the platforms themselves are on the "back foot" on many of these issues.'[82]

Subsequent parliamentary inquiries were firmer in their advocacy of the 'regulatory solution'. In March 2019, for example, the House of Lords Select Committee on Communications published a report entitled *Regulating in a Digital World*. It acknowledged that '[t]he internet has brought huge opportunities, connecting the world as never before'. The part it played in 'all aspects of life' was 'ever-increasing'. But 'regulation of the digital world' had 'not kept pace with its role'. While this environment was 'not a lawless "Wild West"', nonetheless, it was the site of 'a large volume of activity . . . which would not normally be tolerated offline'. Such undesirable behaviours included '[m]isuse of personal data, abuse and hateful speech'. The Committee noted that the government had an 'Internet Safety Strategy' and intended to introduce legal measures to address 'online harms'. However, it argued that further issues required attention. One problem was that the 'digital world' had 'become dominated by a small number of very large companies'. They possessed 'a substantial advantage, operating with an unprecedented knowledge of users and other businesses'. Were appropriate steps not taken, 'the largest tech companies are likely to gain more control of technologies which disseminate media content, extract data from the home and individuals or make decisions affecting people's lives'.[83] While more than twelve regulatory entities had some kind of part to play in overseeing 'the digital world', an 'overall' body was lacking. There were problems of both 'overlaps and gaps'. In particular 'no specific content regulator' existed. The Internet needed both 'more regulation'

[81] Ibid., pp. 43, 50–3.

[82] House of Lords Select Committee on Political Polling and Digital Media, *The Politics of Polling*, pp. 82–3.

[83] House of Lords Select Committee on Communications, *Regulating in a Digital World*, Second Report of Session 2017–19, HL Paper 299 (House of Lords, London, 2019), p. 3.

and 'a different approach to regulation'. The Committee called for the formation of a 'Digital Authority' with a central function in maintaining standards, and set out '10 principles' to guide it.[84] The Authority would report to the Cabinet Office and to 'a joint committee of both Houses of Parliament ... established to consider matters related to the digital environment'.[85] In other words, the legislature (or, to be precise, one of its committees) was proposing an enhanced role for itself in addressing the problems it identified.

The parliamentarians comprising the Committee agreed there was a need for the development and application of a technology to be governed in accordance with ethical concerns, to the benefit of wider society,[86] and thought Parliament should play a part in achieving this change. Most notable – particularly taking into account the historic perspective of this book – were its proposals related to the regulation of 'content'. The Committee judged that '[s]elf-regulation by online platforms which host user-generated content, including social media platforms, is failing.' It found the 'moderation processes' they employed 'unacceptably opaque and slow'. The report therefore proposed that such services 'should be subject to a statutory duty of care'. Enforcement of this 'duty' would fall to Ofcom, the communications regulator, which would focus especially on 'children and the vulnerable in society'. The legal requirement would 'ensure that providers take account of safety in designing their services to prevent harm'. It would 'include providing appropriate moderation processes to handle complaints about content'.[87] Parliament was therefore advocating that it pass a law to promote supervision of material presented online, a complex proposition from the point of view of freedom of expression. Indeed, the Committee noted that '[m]any witnesses' from whom it took evidence 'were concerned that content regulation would be detrimental' to this right. It might lead to platforms becoming reluctant to allow themselves to be outlets for controversial content, reducing the diversity of views and stifling debate.[88]

However, the Committee defended its propositions on the grounds that they would strengthen, rather than weaken, freedom of expression, which it held was compromised by present arrangements upon which it sought to improve. One point it advanced was that online abuse, though it might be exercised in the name of free expression, intimidated other potential participants in discussion and deterred them from taking part. According to this argument, effective content moderation was needed to facilitate an open debate.[89] The Committee held that the consistent system of public regulation it recommended was preferable to existing forms of '[c]ontent moderation'.

[84] Ibid.
[85] Ibid., p. 63.
[86] E.g. ibid., p. 23.
[87] Ibid., p. 5.
[88] Ibid., p. 52.
[89] Ibid., p. 52.

The latter, carried out by individual platforms, were not only prone to being 'ineffective in removing content which is either illegal or breaks community standards'. There was a lack of 'clarity about the expected standard of behaviour' and of mechanisms 'for a user to seek to reverse a moderation decision against them'. This ambiguity meant that '[i]n cases where a user's content is blocked or removed this can impinge their right to freedom of expression'.[90] As we have seen, the House of Lords Select Committee on Democracy and Digital Technologies would adopt similar arguments in its report of the following year. The House of Lords Communications Committee report itself pursued themes developed in a previous inquiry, carried out by a Commons committee, the final output of which appeared in February 2019, the month prior to the Communications Committee report. The work of this Commons body in this field is the subject of the next section.

The 'Disinformation and "Fake News"' Inquiry and the Impact of Parliament

Of all the parliamentary inquiries considered in this chapter, that conducted by the House of Commons Digital, Culture, Media and Sport Committee into the subject of 'Disinformation and "Fake News"' achieved possibly the greatest impact. Initially launched in January 2017, it recommenced following the General Election of June that year. An interim publication appeared in July 2018;[91] and a final report followed in February 2019.[92] This prolonged work programme was ambitious in its scope and innovative in its methods. It addressed issues of fundamental concern and uncovered much. The interim output found that '[t]here are many potential threats to our democracy and our values'. Among them, '[o]ne such threat' came from 'what has been coined "fake news", created for profit or other gain, disseminated through state-sponsored programmes, or spread through the deliberate distortion of facts, by groups with a particular agenda, including the desire to affect political elections'. From this starting point, the Committee inquiry had found its way 'from understanding the phenomenon of "fake news", distributed largely through social media, to issues concerning the very future of democracy'. It considered the possibility that 'more invasive than obviously false information is the relentless targeting of hyper-partisan views, which play to the fears and prejudices of people, in order to influence their voting plans and their behaviour'. It discerned 'a crisis concerning the use of data, the manipulation of our data, and the targeting of pernicious views'.

90 Ibid., p. 59.

91 House of Commons Digital, Culture, Media and Sport Committee, *Disinformation and 'Fake News': Interim Report*. Fifth Report of Session 2017–19, HC 363 (House of Commons, London, 2018).

92 House of Commons Digital, Culture, Media and Sport Committee, *Disinformation and 'Fake News': Final Report.*

It had received 'evidence of Russian state-sponsored attempts to influence elections in the US and the UK through social media' and 'of the efforts of private companies to do the same, and of law-breaking by certain Leave campaign groups in the UK's EU Referendum in their use of social media'. Furthermore, '[i]n this rapidly changing digital world, our existing legal framework is no longer fit for purpose'.[93]

In raising these issues, the Committee built on the work of earlier parliamentary committees. One target for its scrutiny was social media platforms. The Committee stressed that '[t]he big tech companies must not be allowed to expand exponentially, without constraint or proper regulatory oversight'.[94] It was particularly critical of Facebook. Among those from whom it took evidence were Richard Allan, the former Liberal Democrat MP who we encountered in the previous chapter as an early enthusiast for parliamentary use of the Internet. By this point he was employed at Facebook as Vice President of Policy Solutions.[95] The Committee described how Facebook 'operates by monitoring both users and non-users, tracking their activity and retaining personal data'. It generated 'its money by selling access to users' data through its advertising tools. It further increases its value by entering into comprehensive reciprocal data-sharing arrangements with major app developers who run their businesses through the Facebook platform.' The Committee drew attention to the existence of 'malicious forces' utilising 'Facebook to threaten and harass others, to publish revenge porn, to disseminate hate speech and propaganda of all kinds, and to influence elections and democratic processes'. It regretted that 'Facebook, and other social media companies, are either unable or unwilling to prevent' such abuse.[96]

To address the problems it identified, the Committee called for 'a compulsory Code of Ethics', to be 'overseen by an independent regulator'. The Code would stipulate 'what constitutes harmful content', while '[t]he independent regulator would have statutory powers to monitor relevant tech companies'. These measures 'would create a regulatory system for online content that is as effective as that for offline content industries'.[97] Alongside calls for more effective public control, the Committee sought to alter the way in which its subject matter was conceptualised, and in this sense redefine the wider agenda. The interim report complained that '[t]he term "fake news" is bandied around with no clear idea of what it means, or agreed definition'. It had 'taken on a variety of meanings, including a description of any statement that is not liked or agreed with by the reader'. It proposed 'that

93 House of Commons Digital, Culture, Media and Sport Committee, *Disinformation and 'Fake News': Interim Report*, p. 3.

94 House of Commons Digital, Culture, Media and Sport Committee, *Disinformation and 'Fake News': Final Report*, p. 5.

95 Ibid., p. 13.

96 Ibid., p. 7.

97 Ibid., p. 16.

the Government rejects the term "fake news", and instead puts forward an agreed definition of the words "misinformation" and "disinformation"'. This 'shared definition', accompanied by 'clear guidelines for companies, organisations, and the Government to follow' would allow for 'consistency of meaning across the platforms, which can be used as the basis of regulation and enforcement'.[98] The Committee sought, through linguistic change, to alter perception and in turn shape behaviour.

The government accepted this proposal.[99] There was no guarantee that it would do so. Parliamentary committees lack hard powers. They report to the executive, which – by convention – is supposed to provide timely, substantive responses. But it is in no way compelled to act in accordance with the recommendations made. It may not address points made in a way the Committee finds satisfactory. Even where it appears to agree with a committee, it is difficult to discern whether it is doing so because the report has persuaded it, or if it has other motives; and the precise way in which it might implement an idea can alter the outcome significantly. The government might adopt some proposals, but not others, to the detriment of the whole package as envisaged from the parliamentary perspective.[100] Overall, the Committee was disappointed by the response to its interim output. It wrote in its final report that:

> We look forward to hearing the Government's response to these recommendations within two months. We hope that this will be much more comprehensive, practical, and constructive than their response to the Interim Report, published in October 2018. Several of our recommendations were not substantively answered and there is now an urgent need for the Government to respond to them.[101]

Around six months after the publication of its final report on 'fake news' the Committee issued a White Paper setting out policy regarding 'online harms'. Commenting on this output, the Committee recorded that: '[w]e were pleased to see that a large number of our recommendations were taken up in the White Paper'. The Committee noted that '[i]n particular, the establishment of an independent regulator for online harms, and the requirement for social media companies to a comply with a "duty of care", satisfied two of our most important proposals'. Yet 'a significant gap exists between our recommendations and the White Paper'. It detected 'scant focus on electoral interference

[98] House of Commons Digital, Culture, Media and Sport Committee, *Disinformation and 'Fake News': Interim Report*, p. 8.

[99] House of Commons Digital, Culture, Media and Sport Committee, *Disinformation and 'Fake News': Final Report*, p. 10.

[100] For analysis of the impact of select committees, see Meg Russell and Meghan Benton, *Selective Influence: The Policy Impact of House of Commons Select Committees* (Constitution Unit, London, 2011).

[101] House of Commons Digital, Culture, Media and Sport Committee, *Disinformation and 'Fake News': Final Report*, p. 7.

and online political advertising, both of which we highlighted as requiring urgent action'.[102]

The picture was complicated – some signs of influence, though difficult to quantify with precision, as well as clear areas of frustration. But the inquiry made an impact in other ways. It helped draw immense international attention to the alleged activities of certain previously obscure professional campaigning organisations that utilised social media and the data they gathered. It wrote of 'SCL Elections – and other SCL associates, including Cambridge Analytica – set up by the businessman Alexander Nix'. They had a 'role in manipulating foreign elections', from which they gained 'financial benefits'.[103] The inquiry became an event in its own right.[104] Perhaps more than the reports themselves, its quest for evidence, and the material it uncovered, generated publicity around the world. Sessions – such as that held with 'Christopher Wylie, a whistle-blower and ex-SCL employee' – were a focus for attention. Also generating publicity were the difficulties the Committee experienced in securing the attendance of some of those it wished to question. It was 'forced to summon two witnesses: Alexander Nix, former CEO of Cambridge Analytica; and Dominic Cummings, Campaign Director of Vote Leave, the designated Leave campaign group in the EU Referendum'. Nix eventually relented, but the 'contemptuous' (as the Committee described his actions) Cummings did not.[105]

The Committee employed convening power, identifying, capitalising upon, and nurturing a growing international movement to subject a global issue to a parallel form of representative democratic accountability. Working closely with equivalent bodies abroad, it 'invited democratically-elected representatives from eight countries' to take part in 'an "International Grand Committee"'. Held on 27 November 2018, this initiative was 'the first of its kind'. The purpose was 'to promote further cross-border co-operation in tackling the spread of disinformation, and its pernicious ability to distort, to disrupt, and to destabilise'.[106] Between them, those in attendance represented 'a total of 447 million people'. These participants took evidence from witnesses and 'signed a set of International Principles at that meeting'. They continued to meet as the 'International Grand Committee' subsequently in different world locations.[107] Someone else was notable for his absence from

[102] House of Commons Digital, Culture, Media and Sport Committee, *The Online Harms White Paper*, Twelfth Report of Session 2017–19, HC 2431 (House of Commons, London, 2018), p. 3.

[103] House of Commons Digital, Culture, Media and Sport Committee, *Disinformation and 'Fake News': Interim Report*, p. 5.

[104] See Peter Pomerantsev, *This Is Not Propaganda: Adventures in the War against Reality* (Faber & Faber, London, 2019), Pt 6.

[105] House of Commons Digital, Culture, Media and Sport Committee, *Disinformation and 'Fake News': Interim Report*, p. 5.

[106] House of Commons Digital, Culture, Media and Sport Committee, *Disinformation and 'Fake News': Final Report*, p. 5.

[107] Ibid., p. 4.

rather than presence at the Westminster session, however. Mark Zuckerberg, CEO of Facebook, was invited to attend and give evidence but he declined three times.[108] Further action the Committee took to amplify and sustain its impact was the formation, in March 2019, of a 'Sub-Committee on Disinformation', on the grounds that 'there is a public interest in continuing our examination of the continuing threat posed by disinformation to democracies'.[109] The impact of a committee, then, in this area as in others, is not determined solely by the extent to which a government does or does not indicate agreement with the recommendations made in given reports. We must look behind and beyond such formal responses, considering the wider political, public, and even international environment and the potential for ongoing pressure to yield results.

In summarising its concerns, the Committee reiterated views about the potential good and bad of the Internet, and the need for concerted public action to maximise the former and exclude the latter. It held that '[i]n a democracy, we need to experience a plurality of voices and, critically, to have the skills, experience and knowledge to gauge the veracity of those voices'. The Committee recognised that 'the Internet has brought many freedoms across the world and an unprecedented ability to communicate'. But 'it also carries the insidious ability to distort, to mislead and to produce hatred and instability'. Moreover, this network 'functions on a scale and at a speed that is unprecedented in human history'. The Committee insisted that '[w]e must use technology . . . to free our minds and use regulation to restore democratic accountability. We must make sure that people stay in charge of the machines.'[110]

As I have suggested, the sustained, growing body of parliamentary scrutiny related to wider controversy regarding the Internet. By the time of the 2019 General Election, this technology and related matters had attained pronounced salience. The ubiquity that the Internet had attained by this point, and controversies connected to it, found numerous expressions in party manifestos. For example, Labour, among other pledges in this general area, echoed its 1983 programme discussed in Chapter 6 by stating that it would 'deliver free full-fibre broadband to all by 2030'. The party pledged to 'establish British Broadband, with two arms: British Digital Infrastructure (BDI) and the British Broadband Service (BBS). We will bring the broadband-relevant parts of BT into public ownership, with a jobs guarantee for all workers in existing broadband infrastructure and retail broadband work.' Furthermore, the party would 'enforce a legal duty of care to protect our children online, impose fines on companies that fail on online abuse and empower the public with a Charter of Digital Rights'. It would also 'consult media-sector workers and trade unions to establish an inquiry into the "fake news" undermining trust in

[108] Ibid., p. 9.
[109] Ibid., p. 3.
[110] Ibid., p. 6.

media, democracy and public debate, and on a legal right of public interest defence for journalists'.[111]

The Conservative Party, for its part, pledged to 'legislate to make the UK the safest place in the world to be online'. It would protect 'children from online abuse and harms, protecting the most vulnerable from accessing harmful content, and ensuring there is no safe space for terrorists to hide online'. It would 'at the same time' defend 'freedom of expression', especially 'recognising and defending the invaluable role of a free press'. Furthermore, it would address problems with regulating internet gambling, 'tackling issues around loot boxes and credit card misuse'.[112] The party referred to intended 'measures to prevent any foreign interference in elections'. It pledged to 'ensure that no one is put off from engaging in politics or standing in an election by threats, harassment or abuse, whether in person or online'. The Conservatives would 'improve the use of data, data science and evidence in the process of government'.[113] Calling for '[m]ajor multinational companies' to 'pay their fair share of tax', it would 'implement the Digital Services Tax'.[114]

Some might see irony in the Conservative reference to 'foreign interference in elections'. The Conservative government had denied the voting public the opportunity to read the *Russia* report by the Intelligence and Security Committee of Parliament in advance of the 2019 General Election. This publication contained an account of efforts by the Committee to inquire into the official response (or lack thereof) to possible efforts to influence the result of the EU referendum. More generally, Cummings – a subject of interest for the parliamentary 'fake news' inquiry who had refused to co-operate with it – had been, since mid-2019, the most senior special adviser to the Prime Minister, Boris Johnson, since he was installed at No. 10, and was a central figure in the Conservative campaign (the departure of Cummings was announced in November 2020). The idea that a government in which he – and others associated with the 'leave' campaign, including Johnson himself – was so prominent might fully address concerns about problematic aspects of the Internet was always unlikely to command wide acceptance. During the 2019 campaign itself, both Conservatives and Labour were linked to controversial uses of the Internet. Nonetheless, regardless of possible transgressions on their part, it was significant that they included the material they did in their manifestos. The policies the two parties advocated differed in emphasis. Labour, for instance, stressed public ownership and provision. But both parties addressed similar issues, such as threats to democracy and to children, and proposed more regulation. This attitude suggested the existence of a widely

111 Labour Party, *It's Time for Real Change: The Labour Party Manifesto 2019* (Labour Party, London, 2019), pp. 54–5.

112 Conservative Party, *Our Plan: Conservative Party Manifesto 2019* (Conservative Party, London, 2019), p. 20.

113 Ibid., p. 48.

114 Ibid., p. 35.

perceived threat. It is reasonable to conclude that parliamentary activity – including but not confined to the work of the House of Commons Digital, Culture, Media and Sport Committee – had made a contribution to this outcome. After the election, Parliament continued to press this agenda, for instance through the continued activities of this Committee (including its work on the 'infodemic' during the coronavirus emergency[115]), the appearance of the *Russia* report, and the work of the House of Lords Select Committee on Democracy and Digital Technologies.

Public concern and political controversy surrounding the Internet had, by the beginning of the third decade of the twenty-first century, reached a new high. Approaches taken from within Parliament matched this pattern. Parliamentary activity over the period from the late 1990s had reflected the growing importance of this technology and developing social attitudes toward it, as well as influencing those same perceptions. The Internet fell outside neat policy categories, and no one committee could monopolise investigation of it. In the Commons, the Culture, Media and Sport Committee adopted the word 'Digital' at the front of its name, replicating the equivalent change in the name (in July 2017) of the Whitehall department the brief of which it monitored, the Department for Digital, Culture, Media and Sport. This rebranding took place not because the Department had been given a new portfolio, but because the execution of its existing responsibilities had drawn it further into online and related activities. As the Secretary of State, Karen Bradley, put it at the time: 'The department has taken on significant new responsibilities in recent years, so that half of its policy and delivery work now covers the digital sectors – telecommunications, data protection, internet safety, cyber skills and parts of media and the creative industries.'[116] But neither the department nor the Commons select committee holding it to account could realistically expect exclusively and effectively to oversee all matters pertaining to the Internet. Other committees continued to investigate. The idea of 'a joint committee of both Houses of Parliament . . . established to consider matters related to the digital environment' proposed by the House of Lords Communications Committee in 2019 suggested a desire to establish a consistent central focus for this work. But such a body, though it might contribute to cohesion, would not be able to encompass the whole of the subject matter.

This realisation emphasises how great a spread of significance the Internet had attained. When considering the many manifestations of this device, Parliament (through its committees) engaged with some of the most fundamental human needs, sometimes understood as rights. They involved matters

[115] House of Commons Digital, Culture, Media and Sport Committee, *Misinformation in the COVID-19 Infodemic*, Second Report of Session 2019–21, HC 234 (House of Commons, London, 2020).

[116] 'Change of Name for DCMS', 3 July 2017, available at: www.gov.uk/government/news/change-of-name-for-dcms, last accessed 13 September 2020.

such as privacy; personal security; free expression; preventing discrimination; access to information; associating with others; safeguarding children; protecting other groups; maintaining social rules, such as laws; commerce and the pursuit of material wellbeing; and the protection against malicious activity, perhaps perpetrated by hostile groups from within or without the UK. Another recurring theme was the ability of individuals to assert some kind of control over their destinies and to hold those in positions of authority to account, through the democratic system. Practices associated with the Internet forced parliamentarians to reconsider how they understood these different imperatives, the way in which they might come into conflict or be mutually supportive, and means of maintaining them. Initially, parliamentary attention tended to focus on the relationship with existing structures and rules. Subsequently, it came to emphasise the role of entities that had come into being because of the Internet, such as social media platforms and search engines. Eventually, committees grew more likely to promote the idea of new regulatory systems, tailored for the purpose of harnessing the Internet to the goal of social benefit rather than harm. They also showed a willingness to innovate in their own methods, most notably through the efforts of the House of Commons Digital, Culture, Media and Sport Committee in establishing a mechanism – the 'International Grand Committee' – by which a supranational power base such as Facebook might be made subject to democratic control. The implications of this initiative were substantial. Might it point to more collaboration between parliaments to address a range of challenges of a global nature? Such possibilities lie in the future. But it was fair to conclude that the relationship between Parliament and communications technology remained, as it had been in the seventeenth century, capable of generating dynamic force, raising difficult questions, and leading to radical courses of action.

Conclusions

By 2020, Parliament had fully incorporated the Internet into its work. It was at ease with the technology as part of its day-to-day routine. Employing networked computers for its basic functions, they helped Parliament to fulfil its constitutional role as a representative of the public and supreme law-making entity, providing a basis for governments, and holding them to account. It used the Internet to help it to continue functioning during the coronavirus emergency. Yet, at the same time, parliamentarians had become increasingly disturbed about the wider social consequences of the technology. It was now a major theme in their various deliberations. Among MPs and Peers there was a deepening concern that this communications system might even be associated with threats to the very democratic system to which Parliament was central. Such was the gravity of these concerns that parliamentarians began to reassess the way in which they might realise their commitment to fundamental values, such as the right to freedom of expression. The apprehensions and the reactions they stimulated connected with and formed a part of prominent global debates about the Internet and its implications. A significant portion of humanity had – in a relatively short period of time – become, in significant ways, dependent upon the technology; but doubts about the desirability of this arrangement were intensifying. An assessment of the parliamentary approach to the Internet was, therefore, important to an understanding of the particular institution and wider issues.

The matters under consideration were of historic significance. They should be analysed as such. With this consideration in mind, this book has provided such a perspective on the Internet and Parliament in two senses. First, it has shown how the relationship between the technology and the institution are best understood as part of a long-term continuum. Ideas, inventions, and developments that precede the rise of the Internet – in some cases by centuries – need to be taken into account in a contemplation of this interaction. Secondly, it has shown how parliamentary engagement specifically with the Internet and associated technology has been dynamic in nature, developing over time, and presenting a variety of possibilities at various points. By combining these approaches, it is possible to offer a series of conclusions.

A recurring set of ideas have influenced the way in which observers and practitioners have sought to utilise and have interpreted the impact of successive technologies. In some instances, those presenting these accounts have consciously adopted aspects of or reacted against earlier works. In others they seem to have arrived at their positions more independently. However they reached their views, they can be seen as part of a pattern. At least as far back as the eighteenth century, there has been a tendency – discernible among contributors based in the British Isles as well as mainland Europe and North America – to regard science and invention as in some way connected or conducive to radical transformation or even revolution. Such ideas inspired participants in and admirers of the American and French revolutions and those of socialist, communist, or anarchist persuasion from the nineteenth centuries onwards. The idea that electrical communications might allow for two-way interactions between governors and governed gained ground. By the 1930s, the proposition began to germinate that technology could facilitate mass decision-making through referendums, in which voters could participate remotely from their own homes. Large-scale, rapid, communications devices, in some accounts, could be a force for international unity. Exponents of the idea of technological transformation might depict it as a means of bringing about major changes in the physical surroundings.

Three broad schools are identifiable regarding the desirability of such perceived impacts – though it is not always possible cleanly to attach all the exponents discussed in this book to any one alone. Some of the most influential versions of such outlooks are found in works of fiction, that could take on a special authority in public debate as emblematic of certain tendencies. They had the power of myth. Discussion could relate to actual inventions, or those that – it was speculated – might come about in future. The first school entailed a view of scientific advance as potentially underpinning an idealised, egalitarian society. The second was the perception of technology as dangerous and a crushing tool of oppression. The third was the view of invention as both source or instrument of, and potential solution to, problems. Accounts of the final variety might perceive technology as connected to negative social dynamics, but – if made subject to carefully devised principles – able to serve rather than compromise the interests of humanity. It might play a part in the restoration of that which it helped erode. While enabling the undoing of damage, it would also facilitate the realisation of benefits that would not have been attainable without it. In some instances, such scenarios could perceive a new invention supplanting an earlier. In others, the same technology was both detrimental and beneficial. This third school could apply to the Internet, as shown by the findings of the House of Lords Select Committee on Democracy and Digital Technologies published in 2020.

Alongside these three general perspectives on technology, it is possible to identify patterns in attitudes towards particular devices, including those employed for communications, such as radio and television. They might be greeted early on as supportive of democracy, facilitating education and more inclusive political processes. Then disillusion can develop, with claims being made that they are – for instance – sources of distraction and manipulation. Eventually, a new technology – or different deployment of the offending invention – might come to be regarded as a means of salvation. So, the cycle continues. While these different accounts can manifest themselves in parallel, often one particular variant is more prominent at a given time. There was much similarity between such discourse in earlier eras and that which surrounded the Internet. Indeed, there was some direct continuity. Sustained discussion of the use of telecommunications devices for democratic purposes from the 1960s onwards (sometimes using the term 'teledemocracy') focused on devices such as cable television (though with some reference to computers also). Yet this debate segued with thematic ease into internet discourse by the early 1990s.

This theoretical and cultural background provides a framework within which we can assess the Internet and its relationship with the UK Parliament. A motive for those involved in the conception and development of this communications system was an idealistic desire to empower and enhance humanity as a whole (though practical impetus came from sources such as military research funding). Crucial steps in the development of what became the Internet occurred around the same time as the emergence of a broad movement known as the counterculture. Indeed, some of the key scientific research took place in academic institutions and in a geographic locale, on the West Coast of the United States, which was also a centre for this disruptive social and political tendency. The counterculture contained within it the potential for hostility towards computing, in as far as it might be perceived as a vehicle for dehumanising social control, the promotion of corporate, commercial values, and the pursuit of military goals. But a subset of the movement became interested in online networks as a means of overcoming such tendencies and attaining a wider dispersal of power within society. Such conceptions found expression in views of the Internet as a force for the strengthening of democracy, variously in its representative and direct forms. By the 1990s, these ideas had achieved mainstream status, in the United States and elsewhere. Advocacy came from across the political spectrum, with shared themes but also characteristically divergent emphases. The Internet could, moreover, appear as a cause in its own right. It was often perceived as a revolutionary force and even as facilitating the existence of a parallel world of some kind.

There were clear countercultural strands in these perceptions of the technology. In a UK context, ideas that existed in the 1970s and eventually found their way – via activists of the late 1990s – into Parliament derived influence from countercultural sources and traditions. But though this movement was undoubtedly of historic importance, the view it promoted of science as a source of problems, but also – if properly utilised – a means of solution and transformation, long predated it. Moreover, it was part of an intellectual tradition some of the roots of which lay beyond the United States, and can be traced in part to the UK (indeed the counterculture itself, exhibiting international manifestations, was more than solely a US phenomenon). The role of the Internet became subject to increasingly intense criticisms similar to those levelled at the uses of previous technologies; for instance, that they were vehicles for propaganda, oppression, and exploitation.

In a 2004 interview, Paul Baran, one of the early scientific pioneers of what became the Internet, dating from his work at the RAND Corporation on communications networks in the late 1950s and early 1960s, spoke to the historian Morten Bay. During the course of the interview, he expressed the hope that the advance to which he contributed would 'be used for universal education. That it be used to reduce the disparity between the rich and the backward countries. You won't have peace unless you do.' But in practice he anticipated that 'one day, we're going to view the Internet as being the most horrible thing ever done. I think so. No good deed ever goes unpunished. It's going to be so distorted, it'll cause so much damage, people will be cursing it and wish it never existed.'[1] These comments suggested an awareness on the part of Baran of the repeating pattern of attitudes towards inventions. (In fact, even by the time he spoke, some key concerns about the nature of the Internet had already been raised. They would become more forceful, with certain features coming to the fore.) The framework for this debate, including both more and less favourable perceptions, had been sketched out long before, predating the Internet – as the continual references to Orwell and *Nineteen Eighty-Four* demonstrate.

The UK Parliament – and its arguable direct English precursor – has, over the centuries, encountered a series of developments in communications technology. As an institution, even in pre-democratic times, it has always performed a representative function, supposedly acting in some sense on behalf of the people as a whole in disposing, for instance, of its legislative and financial functions and in its dealings with other constitutional bodies, in particular the executive. Consequently, inventions that impacted upon the nature of public transmission of information mattered to it. Parliamentary approaches towards them could be cautious, but also motivated by a sense that they needed to be engaged with, and that there were benefits to be obtained from doing so. Changes in communications technology and practices were connected to alterations in the way in which people perceived Parliament and how they interacted with it. Parliament could potentially utilise the new dynamics created for its own purposes.

[1] Morten Bay, 'Conversations with a Pioneer: Paul Baran in His Own Words', *Internet Histories* 1(3) (2017): 273–82, 281.

The response to one invention could pave the way for another. Printing helped bring Parliament as an entity into public sight in a sense it had not previously been. Radio and television provided for extensions of this process, of which the Internet was a continuation. In each case, there was resistance, but it was eventually overcome. The time-lag between dissemination of the technology and its full acceptance by Parliament grew successively shorter. For printing, it was centuries; for broadcasting, about half a century; for the Internet – partly depending on how one measures it – less still. From the early 1960s, interest began building in Parliament in the use that might be made of computers. Particular early impetus came from officials, including in the House of Commons Library. That these devices might be involved in the remote transfer of information – rather than simply its storage and processing – was envisaged from an early stage. A number of commentators and experts were speculating from the 1960s about mass usage electronic networks, possibly involving computers, that might be employed for a range of purposes, including of a political nature. But – in as far as they were aware of this discussion – parliamentarians and officials at Westminster could not predict precisely how such tendencies, if they manifested themselves at all as anticipated, would play out precisely. The embryonic ARPANET form of the specific internet technology was brought to the attention of Parliament (or more precisely the House of Commons Select Committee on Science and Technology) by 1970, the year after it first became operational. But the future pre-eminence for this particular application was markedly difficult to predict at this point. Even when it had become established as a prominent form of communication during the 1990s, the exact ways in which it and associated technology would develop were hard to discern.

It is fair to say that the UK Parliament lagged behind some equivalent institutions internationally in the move both to computing and the Internet – though by periods of time that do not seem immense from the vantage point of a few decades later. Factors inhibiting adoption that had to be surmounted included fear of public failure and cultural barriers. They were overcome partly as a consequence of observation of international practice, new cohorts entering Parliament that were more familiar with the technology, and greater take-up of the Internet across UK society. Financial cost often appeared as a blockage. In fact, the presence of this constraint was an indicator of wider priorities. As a proportion of the entirety of public expenditure, any system, however lavish, would have been slight in cost. It was the idea of allocating new amounts to Parliament, and within it a digital experiment, that was the problem.

Some of the same considerations (for instance over allocation of resources) continued to apply once proper incorporation of the Internet had commenced from about 1996. Fears existed about possible misuse of services offered to the public. There was concern about the encouragement of unrealistic public expectations, and of visible failure leading to disenchantment and criticism. Objections might be raised to specific applications of internet technology. The use of mobile devices came up against existing rules of conduct, and e-tabling seems to have prompted a controversial surge in questions for written answer. Parliament is, for constitutional reasons, often to some extent dependent upon cooperation from the executive. This principle has applied to its adoption and use of computers and the Internet. If the government lacked enthusiasm for a particular initiative, its chances of success could reduce significantly. The prolonged nature of the process of introducing parliamentary e-petitioning demonstrates the existence of this limitation.

Against these hindrances, a number of important forces drove enhanced utilisation of the medium. Rising public usage prompted a response in kind from Parliament. Indeed, the increase in uptake from the late 1990s onwards was not only a reason for efforts to employ the technology, but was a prerequisite to their being a successful means of connecting with the population. The sense that the Internet was a coming international phenomenon, employed increasingly by legislatures around the world, with special qualities that Parliament would benefit from using, was another motivator. A view existed within (and beyond) Parliament that, as an institution, its public standing was in a condition of deterioration. Advocacy of internet usage could present the claim that to do so was a means of improving the position of the legislature. It might also hold that to fail to engage properly with the technology was to risk appearing increasingly irrelevant. As trends in internet-based activity shifted – for instance, with the advent of what was known as Web 2.0 – pressure was felt within Parliament to adapt in response. The coronavirus emergency of 2020 onwards created a powerful imperative to overcome – in the short-term at least – procedural, practical, and principled barriers to participation in proceedings by those who were not physically present.

Another feature of Parliament, to be taken into account when considering the use it made of computers and the Internet, is its diverse nature. For instance, it has no single point of leadership as such, and is divided into various units and two distinct Chambers. At various points efforts were made towards a more concerted, consistent approach in – for instance – the provision of equipment and the provision of online services. However, some of the initial early progress towards the adoption of computers was achieved by discrete entities, such as the House of Commons Library. A more uniform system might have halted some individual advances. When considering the role of the two Chambers, while there is a temptation to concentrate on the Commons as the primary body, it is important to note that the House of Lords was capable of taking a lead, as it did in the late 1970s with the use of computers.

The website was subject to continual criticisms and – in response – revisions and relaunches. At first, the relative amount of focus on straightforward information provision was greater than it would later become. Subsequently, there were attempts at utilising the Internet for purposes of two-way communication. The most important early experiments in this area – in the late 1990s and early 2000s – involved the operation of online forums. This model was groundbreaking. It involved Parliament creating its own mechanisms into which outside participants were incorporated, making qualitative contributions. The emphasis of interactive activity would later shift. The petitioning system that developed during the 2010s could involve millions of people, but they were simply indicating assent to a pre-existing proposition. It was the revival of a long-established practice more than a new departure. There was also a move towards utilisation of social media from the late 2000s onwards, on the grounds that Parliament might benefit from their popularity. Taking the latter course involved collaborating with platforms that would become increasingly controversial, and – ironically – be a subject of criticism from within the legislature. Those who wished to partake of new services created by Parliament seemingly had to expose themselves to entities some of the practices of which parliamentarians condemned as detrimental to the rights of users and of the democratic system itself.

Parliamentary engagement with social media involved fitting in with an external template, rather than one that was designed to serve the specific purposes of the legislature. It represented a willingness to relinquish control, at least over the format within which Parliament operated. Various communications technologies over time have forced Parliament to tackle issues of this type. Printing, as previously discussed, led to questions about the public representation of parliamentary activities. Later, there were concerns that the broadcasting of proceedings might lead to unwanted distortions. Placing Hansard online raised licensing issues. Ultimately, parliamentary engagement with the Internet has created potential for the use and reuse of its materials at a speed, on a scale and in ways more extensive than could previously have been contemplated. Early examples of creative activity of this type include The Public Whip and TheyWorkForYou from the early 2000s onwards. Discussion of the use of online forums and petitioning partly turned on the question of whether the public might use it in ways that were unwanted and could lead to reputational damage, and what effective means – if any – there might be of avoiding such problems. The Internet has led Parliament to become more flexible about its content and the way it is represented.

When making decisions about use of this technology, then, concern that it might expose Parliament to malicious behaviour could be a deterrent to some forms of activity. A sense of the gains on offer could help overcome such misgivings – as in the case of e-petitioning. Over time, the institution developed increasing apprehension about online activity extending beyond interactions with it, and across society as a whole – and indeed across the world. In doing so it engaged with the many debates and concerns regarding the Internet that had become of such salience by the outset of the 2020s. At their core were doubts about the continued viability of democracy itself. Another technological cycle from optimism to despondency had taken place.

What lessons might be derived from this historic study for those faced with such contemporary concerns, in Parliament and elsewhere, and responsible for formulating responses to them? First, at least from the point of view of the legislature and its supporters, there is an optimistic aspect. Despite predictions from some quarters (echoing claims made on behalf of earlier technologies), the Internet has not (or not yet) presaged a decisive shift towards direct democracy. Such a development, if it occurred, would presumably threaten the position of Parliament. Yet as an institution, rather than be rendered irrelevant by the Internet, it has incorporated it. At times, such initiatives may have been slower to take place than perhaps seemed optimal and have been less than perfect in their execution. But Parliament – as well as using related technology for internal operations – has successfully developed a new way of communicating with those its Members represent. The techniques established have helped it perform key roles – such as providing a focus for public debate and holding the executive to account – more effectively.

By the mid-2000s, as the distinguished political journalist Peter Riddell informed the House of Commons Select Committee on Modernisation of the House of Commons, the Internet had become 'the principal means by which Parliament as an institution' communicated 'with voters'.[2] Millions came to access content in ways they could not have done before, to communicate instantly with parliamentarians and various offices in Westminster, and to input into actual parliamentary proceedings, in particular via the e-petitions process (considerably accelerating a revival in this practice that began in the 1980s following a long period of decline). In this sense, a *direct* relationship was established in the context of the *representative* system; the two concepts need not be mutually exclusive, and can form what Stephen Coleman has termed 'direct representation'.[3] To characterise Parliament straightforwardly as a conservative or slow-reacting institution, remote from those it is supposed to serve, would – on this evidence – be misleading. It showed that it could change to reflect patterns in wider society – that is, the shift towards internet usage and various developments within it – in such a way that deepened its connections with the public. That it achieved this outcome should infuse in parliamentarians a greater confidence and willingness to assert themselves on the part of their institution. They can do so, for instance, through innovating both in the use of the Internet and in their investigations into practices connected to this technology, as the House of Commons Digital, Communications, Media and Sport Committee has done with respect to dis- and misinformation.

At the same time, Parliament is correct to proceed on the basis that, however pervasive and innovative the Internet has become, it has not rendered all other

2 House of Commons Select Committee on Modernisation of the House of Commons, *Connecting Parliament with the Public*, First Report of Session 2003–04, HC 368 (London, Stationery Office, 2004), p. 16.

3 Stephen Coleman, *Direct Representation: Towards a Conversational Democracy* (ippr, London, 2005).

forms of communication obsolete, though it has to some extent absorbed them within itself. For instance, television remains the main source of news for the public. Radio and newspapers, though respectively in third and fourth places behind the Internet, retain considerable significance. Older means of human interaction, notably face-to-face meetings, persist (pandemic notwithstanding). Not everyone is a confident user of the Internet, or employs it for political purposes, or indeed accesses it at all. But Parliament should be able to represent them regardless. Furthermore, it is conceivable that, at some point in the future, a new technology will arise to challenge the Internet. It might not be possible now to comprehend the form such a medium will take. But it could be that developments which, retrospectively, will seem to have led to it are already underway, but not fully recognised. Parliament would need to adapt to such a transition, if it occurs, while balancing it with various other considerations.

Collective self-doubt is a sustained theme in the history of parliamentary engagement with communications technology. A key argument in favour of the broadcasting of proceedings was that it might help address a perceived decline in the public standing of the legislature. Such claims of deterioration were not new and would continue to be made. They were used in favour of the employment of the Internet. An alert sounding continuously in this way could, conceivably, be correct at any given time – but it would seem reasonable at least to question its reliability. There does not seem to have been sufficient scrutiny of this type in the debates of the 2000s surrounding the possibilities for parliamentary use of the Internet. They tended to accept as given both the decline and the potential of the Internet to halt or even reverse it. It is possible that decisions were taken on a false premise. Closer attention to history might at least have made those involved aware of this possibility. How they might have proceeded had they been so is a matter of speculation. They might have done less, the same, or more. They might have followed other paths or placed different emphases on their approaches – pursuing some options more rigorously and others less so. Few would now question that Parliament needed to make use of the Internet, and do so extensively. But a better informed, more aware basis for action is surely in principle preferable.

Earlier in the present century, there was a significant level of agreement that a parliamentary and democratic malaise existed and that the Internet could help solve it. In 2021 there is a similarly widely held view that the same technology is in some way the source of a problem requiring correction, including through legal intervention of some kind. It is beyond doubt that, in connection to this technology, a whole range of unacceptable behaviours, problematic business practices, intrusive activities, and other difficulties have manifested themselves. However, historical consideration suggests that a wider appreciation is needed fully to appreciate the problem and ways of engaging with it. The introduction of the printing press to Western Europe, for instance, cannot be understood in isolation. It interacted with pre-existing cultural and political tendencies in the region. Centuries later, the adoption and use of computers and the Internet by the legislature took place within a setting of wider parliamentary and constitutional change. The same point about context might be made with respect to more recent debates regarding the consequences of the Internet, including of a democratic nature. We can illustrate this point by considering the specific case of the 2016 EU referendum. Online campaigning techniques – possibly of a dubious nature – might have contributed to the 'leave' result (though certainty on this point is difficult to establish). But they do not explain why such a vote was held at the time it was, in the way it was – and why indeed Parliament legislated for such an exercise. Nor do internet-related activities wholly explain the political instability that followed, or why Parliament – despite containing within it majorities in both Houses that had opposed departure from the EU – felt unable decisively to reject the result during this time (whatever view one might take on whether it would have been correct to do so).

Resentment regarding the 'leave' campaign and its supposedly objectionable methods seemed to make a significant contribution to growing disquiet among parliamentarians (and others) regarding the Internet. They have responded with various proposals that will not necessarily deal with wider aspects pertaining to the problem they perceive, and could in isolation lead to new problems. One issue is that any efforts made from within Parliament are subject to its particular relationship with the executive. The government, for instance, is under no firm obligation to implement the recommendations of select committees, or to do so in a way that fully meets with their approval. Parliamentary inquiries can generate pressure through public attention but there are no guarantees that they will achieve their objectives. Lately, opinion within the legislature has turned significantly in favour of a system of content moderation involving a regulatory body applying some kind of code, with a statutory underpinning. In doing so, it has engaged with issues of deep historical sensitivity, impinging upon concerns raised by John Milton in his (nuanced) opposition to a parliamentary regime of pre-publication censorship (though the system envisaged today differs from that to which Milton objected). Parliamentary proposals show awareness of the gravity of the matter, and have safety mechanisms built into them, including an effort to make the legislature itself a safeguard against, rather than source of, political abuse. The implementation of any such measures is dependent upon the executive. As of 2021, the group that holds power in the UK government found its way into this position as a consequence of the very chain of events that helped create a climate of suspicion around the Internet. One possible outcome is that it will not implement the called-for legislation. Another is that it will do so in a way that is flawed.

Difficulties involving the Internet, and the means of resolving them, must be considered as part of a wider picture. This observation might lead to the conclusion that solutions are more difficult to arrive at than was previously imagined; but it is preferable for reality – however unpalatable – to be revealed than for it to remain obscured. Digital networks – though often depicted as somehow comprising their own world – are in fact significant because they are part of the reality we inhabit. To acknowledge this point is to help avoid technological determinism in its many variants, each of which is fallacious. Inventions are created and operate within our universe. They are neither brought into being externally nor do they impact upon it from the outside. In as far as they are associated with radical transformations or revolutions, they are events that occur within this plane, involving the many interactions that take place within it. To make such an observation, however, is not to deny the importance of such devices. They form a part of – and, in this sense, contribute to – change in the environment that surrounds them. As Manuel Castells has put it:

> technology does not determine society. Nor does society script the course of technological change . . . the dilemma of technological determinism is probably a false problem, since technology *is* society, and society cannot be understood or represented without its technological tools.[4]

The way in which we perceive and seek to utilise technology is shaped partly by the myths we attach to it, but also by its practical qualities and the way they have effect within their environment. Means of realisation of freedom of expression, for instance, differ across varied media such as printing and broadcasting, according to their particular modes of functioning. Perhaps increasing disjuncture between the myth and the emergent reality contributes to disillusion in previously heralded technologies of the sort we have witnessed recently. History suggests that such cycles will persist; but it is not possible to predict the precise form in which they will do so. If we take, respectively, ARPANET and the invention associated with Johannes Gutenberg as starting points, the Internet is roughly the same age that printing in Europe was in 1500. This digital network might be at only a formative stage of its history; or perhaps it has reached a stable level of maturity. But the characteristics of the Internet and possible future media, whatever path they take, will play out alongside many other tendencies. It is on this basis that Parliament and other policymakers will need to interact with them.

[4] Manuel Castells, The Information Age: Economy, Society and *Culture*, vol. I: *The Rise of the Network Society* (Wiley-Blackwell, London, 2010), p. 5.

Further Reading

The following is a selective list of twenty items for those interested in reading more about this subject. Some are easier to find than others. For sources used in this book, see footnote references. A discussion of literature in the fields involved is provided in the Introduction.

James W. Carey, *Communication as Culture: Essays on Media and Society* (Routledge, London, 1992).

Hillary Rodham Clinton, United States Secretary of State, 'Remarks', The Newseum, Washington DC, 21 January 2010, available at: https://2009-2017.state.gov/secretary/20092013clinton/rm/2010/01/135519.htm, last accessed 4 February 2020.

Stephen Coleman, John Taylor, and Wim van de Donk (eds.), *Parliament in the Age of the Internet* (Oxford, Oxford University Press, 1999).

Digital Democracy Commission, *Open Up! Report of the Speaker's Commission on Digital Democracy* (Speaker's Commission on Digital Democracy, London, 2015).

Katie Hafner and Matthew Lyon, *Where Wizards Stay Up Late: The Origins of the Internet* (Simon and Schuster, New York, 2006).

Starr Roxanne Hiltz and Murray Turoff, *The Network Nation: Human Communication via Computer* (MIT Press, Cambridge, 1993).

House of Commons Information Committee, *Digital Technology: Working for Parliament and the Public*, First Report of Session 2001–02, HC 1065 (Stationery Office, London, 2002).

House of Lords Select Committee on Democracy and Digital Technologies, *Digital Technology and the Resurrection of Trust*, Report of Session 2019–21, HL 77 (House of Lords, London, 2020).

Internet Histories journal, in particular: Leopoldina Fortunati, 'For a Dynamic and Post-Digital History of the Internet: A Research Agenda', *Internet Histories* 1(1–2) (2017): 180–7.

Julianne Kerr Morrison, Ravi Naik, and Stephanie Hankey, *Data and Democracy in the Digital Age* (Constitution Society, London, 2018).

Brenda Maddox, *Beyond Babel: New Directions in Communications* (Andre Deutsch, London, 1972).

A Manifesto for Local Online Communities (c.1999, maintained online), available at: http://partnerships.org.uk/cyber/index.htm.

Vincent Mosco, *The Digital Sublime: Myths, Power, and Cyberspace* (MIT Press, Cambridge, 2004).

Parliamentary Informal Joint Committee on Computers, *Report of the Informal Joint Committee on Computers to the Leaders of both Houses*, January 1977.

Jason Peacey, *Print and Public Politics in the English Revolution* (Cambridge University Press, Cambridge, 2013).

Sadie Plant, 'Babes in the Net', *New Statesman and Society*, 27 January 1995, p. 28.

Rana Roroohar, *Don't Be Evil: The Case Against Big Tech* (Penguin, London, 2019).

Fred Turner, *From Counterculture to Cyberculture: Stewart Brand, the Whole Earth Network, and the Rise of Digital Utopianism* (Chicago and London, University of Chicago Press, 2006).

Wayback Machine, The Internet Archive, available at: https://archive.org/web/.

Shoshana Zuboff, *The Age of Surveillance Capitalism* (Profile, London, 2019).

Index

Other Books in the Series (continued from page iv)

Likosky: *Transnational Legal Processes: Globalisation and Power Disparities*
Lixinski: Legalized Identities
Loughnan: *Self, Others and the State: Relations of Criminal Responsibility*
Lunney: *A History of Australian Tort Law 1901–1945: England's Obedient Servant?*
Maughan & Webb: *Lawyering Skills and the Legal Process, 2nd Edition*
McGlynn: *Families and the European Union: Law, Politics and Pluralism*
Mertens: *A Philosophical Introduction to Human Rights*
Moffat: *Trusts Law: Text and Materials*
Monti: *EC Competition Law*
Morgan: *Contract Law Minimalism: A Formalist Restatement of Commercial Contract Law*
Morgan & Yeung: *An Introduction to Law and Regulation: Text and Materials*
Nicola & Davies: *EU Law Stories: Contextual and Critical Histories of European Jurisprudence*
Norrie: *Crime, Reason and History: A Critical Introduction to Criminal Law, 3rd Edition*
O'Dair: *Legal Ethics: Text and Materials*
Oliver: *Common Values and the Public–Private Divide*
Oliver & Drewry: *The Law and Parliament*
Palmer & Roberts: *Dispute Processes: ADR and the Primary Forms of Decision-Making, 1st Edition*
Palmer & Roberts: *Dispute Processes: ADR and the Primary Forms of Decision-Making, 3rd Edition*
Picciotto: *International Business Taxation*
Probert: *The Changing Legal Regulation of Cohabitation, 1600–2010: From Fornicators to Family, 1600–2010*
Radi: *Rules and Practices of International Investment Law and Arbitration*
Reed: *Internet Law: Text and Materials*
Richardson: *Law, Process and Custody*
Roberts & Palmer: *Dispute Processes: ADR and the Primary Forms of Decision-Making, 2nd Edition*
Rowbottom: *Democracy Distorted: Wealth, Influence and Democratic Politics*
Sauter: *Public Services in EU Law*
Scott & Black: *Cranston's Consumers and the Law*
Seneviratne: *Ombudsmen: Public Services and Administrative Justice*
Seppänen: *Ideological Conflict and the Rule of Law in Contemporary China: Useful Paradoxes*
Siems: *Comparative Law, 2nd Edition*
Stapleton: *Product Liability*
Stewart: *Gender, Law and Justice in a Global Market*
Tamanaha: *Law as a Means to an End: Threat to the Rule of Law*
Turpin & Tomkins: *British Government and the Constitution: Text and Materials, 7th Edition*
Twining: *General Jurisprudence: Understanding Law from a Global Perspective*
Twining: *Globalisation and Legal Theory*

Twining: *Human Rights, Southern Voices: Francis Deng, Abdullahi An-Na'im, Yash Ghai and Upendra Baxi*
Twining: *Jurist in Context: A Memoir*
Twining: *Karl Llewellyn and the Realist Movement, 2nd Edition*
Twining: *Rethinking Evidence: Exploratory Essays, 2nd Edition*
Twining & Miers: *How to Do Things with Rules, 5th Edition*
Wan: *Film and Constitutional Controversy*
Ward: *A Critical Introduction to European Law, 3rd Edition*
Ward: *Law, Text, Terror*
Ward: *Shakespeare and Legal Imagination*
Wells & Quick: *Lacey, Wells and Quick: Reconstructing Criminal Law: Text and Materials, 4th Edition*
Zander: *Cases and Materials on the English Legal System, 10th Edition*
Zander: *The Law-Making Process, 6th Edition*

International Journal of Law in Context:
A Global Forum for Interdisciplinary Legal Studies

The *International Journal of Law in Context* is the companion journal to the Law in Context book series and provides a forum for interdisciplinary legal studies and offers intellectual space for groundbreaking critical research. It publishes contextual work about law and its relationship with other disciplines including but not limited to science, literature, humanities, philosophy, sociology, psychology, ethics, history and geography. More information about the journal and how to submit an article can be found at http://journals.cambridge.org/ijc

For EU product safety concerns, contact us at Calle de José Abascal, 56–1°, 28003 Madrid, Spain or eugpsr@cambridge.org.

www.ingramcontent.com/pod-product-compliance
Lightning Source LLC
LaVergne TN
LVHW062206200926
848484LV00006B/1327